FERGIE'S FLEDGLINGS

The Story of Manchester United's Youth System under Sir Alex Ferguson

Wayne Barton

Vertical Editions
www.verticaleditions.com

Copyright © Wayne Barton 2014

The right of Wayne Barton to be identified as the author of this work has been asserted in accordance with the Copyright, Designs and Patents Act, 1988

All rights reserved. The reproduction and utilisation of this book in any form or by any electrical, mechanical or other means, now known or hereafter invented, including photocopying and recording, and in any information storage and retrieval system, is forbidden without the written permission of the publisher

First published in the United Kingdom in 2014 by Vertical Editions, Unit 4a, Snaygill Industrial Estate, Skipton, North Yorkshire BD23 2QR

www.verticaleditions.com

ISBN 978-1-904091-79-0

A CIP catalogue record for this book is available from the British Library

Cover design by HBA, York

Printed and bound by Jellyfish Print

Contents

Introduction 5
Prologue: Dave Ryan 8
1　Tony Gill 11
2　Deiniol Graham 20
3　Alan Tonge 34
4　Mike Pollitt 44
5　Russell Beardsmore 50
6　Giuliano Maiorana 57
7　Chris Casper 67
8　Kevin Pilkington 84
9　Ben Thornley 102
10　John Curtis 105
11　Alex Notman 113
12　Danny Higginbotham 123
13　Nick Culkin 131
14　Bojan Djordjic 139
15　Lee Lawrence 155
16　Adam Eckersley 163
17　Phil Marsh 174
18　Markus Neumayr 186
19　Sam Hewson 193
20　Ben Amos 202
Appendix 1: Reserves and FA Youth Cup Statistics under Sir Alex Ferguson ... 207
Appendix 2: First Team Appearances by "Fergie's Fledglings" under Sir Alex Ferguson 262
Appendix 3: Trivia 268

Dedicated to the enduring memory of Frederick Ward

Introduction

When I began work on this book in October of 2012, it was originally intended to be a chronological look through the evolution of Sir Alex Ferguson's youth system at Manchester United by marrying it with the autobiographical accounts of some of the more noteworthy "Fledglings" who didn't quite make the big time at Old Trafford. Work on the book was more than halfway complete in May 2013 when the legendary manager announced his retirement from the game. While not quite forcing a complete re-write, I was obliged to now revisit the stories I had already written and look at things from a different angle. What was designed to be a celebration of the continuous and continuing work done in the role with an open end had now become an account of something that had reached completion in at least one sense. The project was always a labour of love but now it seemed more important to ensure that I did justice to the entire story, the 26 and a half years that Sir Alex was in the role.

However hard it is to come up with your own vision and then implement it and succeed to the extent that Sir Matt Busby did, it is equally hard to replicate that and in some eyes, even surpass it. The top five appearance makers for Manchester United came from the youth system – Gary Neville on 602 appearances, Bill Foulkes on 688, Paul Scholes on 718, Sir Bobby Charlton on 758, and Ryan Giggs on 943. In the history of Manchester United and Newton Heath, 863 players had played for the club's first team by the time Sir Alex Ferguson retired. 100 of those were Fledglings under Ferguson. I'll do the maths for you – 11.6% of all players to have played for the club, in whatever form, were young players given a chance by Sir Alex.

There are a number of statistics associated with Sir Alex's contribution to the first team from the youth system at the back of this book with them all dependent on the actual definition of what constitutes a Fledgling. There is no right or wrong answer, and having debated this with a number of fellow historians and statisticians for the club, I originally defined that the official number of Fergie's Fledglings who made an official competitive first team appearance (i.e. not including recognised friendly games) was 98. Under the same logic applied for the inclusion of Jules Maiorana (who was most certainly in that original wave who were labelled by the press) I felt it appropriate to add Erik Nevland and Rodrigo Possebon, thereby rounding up the number to a magic 100. I wanted to ensure it was authentic and not contrived so as to make it a round number, but after much revision it would have been contradictory to the nature of the project not to include them.

In this book there are fascinating stories about the psychology of the club in the early days of Sir Alex's reign. How the personalities of coaches from Eric Harrison through to Rene Meulensteen contributed to the success of the youth system, tales of lost mercurial talents, stories of tragedy and near tragedy, as well as personal battles which resonate with the very core and identity of the club. I hope you enjoy reading them as much as I enjoy sharing them.

*****

I wish to thank all of the players involved for their time and co-operation with the project. Kevin Pilkington and Markus Neumayr are two that have long shared their stories with me and provided the original inspiration for putting this record together. Deiniol Graham was charming and funny, and managed to convince Jules Maiorana to get in touch with me. Jules was someone who was surrounded by mystery so I didn't know what to expect. I half expected to encounter someone embittered by the way things turned out for him at United, but he was so friendly that it turned out my persistence to include him in the book was one of the most rewarding things I'd done. Likewise, one hears things about certain characters and I couldn't have been more delighted to learn that Bojan Djordjic is nothing like the difficult person he is reported to be. Far from it, he is tremendously self aware and that made for one of the most refreshing accounts I was able to record. Nick Culkin was wonderful value if only for the brilliance of his pride at the record he holds for the club – I won't spoil it for you. I could spend all day, and another book. singling out each and every one of the number of players who were only too willing to help out with this project, but lastly on the playing side I wanted to reserve a special mention for Phil Marsh, whose battle back from near tragedy to achieve what he did deserves far more credit than perhaps it received.

There are a number of people, beyond the players, I want to acknowledge for their help, motivation and inspiration. Dan Burdett for his continued and thorough assistance and research, a constant sounding board at any time, and whose help has been so invaluable throughout the years. Thanks for keeping me sane, Dan – and you as well, Kim! Profound thanks to Eifion Evans who contributed and helped with the thorough statistical records at the back of this book which helped to transform it from a story to a comprehensive and complete statistical reference. Mikiel and Phil Gatt for their help throughout. Thanks to Tony Park who assisted with some last minute verification. Barney Chilton at *Red News* who supported the project from the early days. My close friends Elfyn and Hayley Roberts who were there every step of the way. Thanks to Karl Waddicor and all at Vertical Editions for constantly working with me every step of the way to make this the most thorough record it could be.

And of course, my family. First of all my grandfather to whom this book is dedicated. My love of writing and football was inspired by you and I hope that finally getting here makes you proud. To my nana who I love and adore so much, and to my mother who has gone to ridiculous lengths at times to help make dreams like this, to have a book of mine published, come true. My beautiful wife who inspired and encouraged me, as she always does, to make the most of the opportunity to make this book better than it was. My brother who shared my excitement about this project. Taggy, who has been all a best friend could have been and more when helping.

I won't be allowed to let this opportunity go by without thanking the in-laws, thankfully I'm blessed with fantastic extended family that I love dearly so it's not a chore. Thanks to Andy for his genuine pride which means more than words, and Sara, Pat and Teide too. Thanks to Lisa and Paul for their constant support and encouragement and Macy and Maddy for helping me with my "homework" and reading lines from the manuscript in such a peculiar accent that it made the entire experience worthwhile. Thanks to Nell for always giving me a makeshift office at a moment's notice, and a genuine thank you to anyone who I've absentmindedly left off of this list, including those that always ask for an update and always asked about how the book was going. Now you know! Simple words cannot articulate how amazing it is to have a family that is so supportive to dreams that, at times, appeared unrealistic.

Thanks to you too, for reading.

Prologue: Dave Ryan

I first started training at the club when I was 14 in 1971, and I signed as an apprentice in the 1973/74 season. Frank O'Farrell was the manager when I arrived at Manchester United though it wasn't long before Tommy Docherty came and shook everything up. I left in 1979, played for other clubs and after I retired as a player, in 1992 I got a phone call from Brian Kidd to tell me the club were setting up a football development community scheme and wanted me to be involved. I've been back at the club ever since. Tommy was one of those who tried, with some success, to re-establish the youth system, and then of course many years later Sir Alex Ferguson came to the club to do the same. On a personality level they were all different, but what they shared with Sir Matt Busby, aside from their nationality, was their commitment to making Manchester United the best club.

The club has changed almost beyond all recognition since the days I was there. The Cliff has retained all of its charm and character and most of its original features from when I first joined, though there have been some additions and modifications, but the first team obviously now use the first class facilities at Carrington. The club became a massive commercial entity. I think when I first started there were only about 90 full time employees and now there's over 600 permanent staff and so many casuals too, so that the operation is incredibly massive. There's the football side and the business side and I think the club have always tried to keep a healthy balance. It's something that the Gaffer did with remarkable success while never abandoning the basics.

In particular, Sir Alex was very vocal about it following Sir Matt's blueprint which brought so much success in the 1950s and 1960s. After his tenure, it's something that I feel will always be there and something that I'm sure that managers in the future such as David Moyes will follow the standards set by Sir Alex, Sir Matt and even Tommy Docherty too. Sir Alex would also be very active in ensuring the players were aware of the boots they were stepping into and the shirt on their chest. He would come into the dressing room regularly in Youth Cup games and remind the players of just who they were playing for. He didn't pull any punches, that's for sure, those kids would get exactly the same kind of treatment as the first team players.

My return to the club coincided with the increased recruitment of players from an age that just got younger and younger. It wasn't just a United thing, clubs around the nation set up skills centres from six years of age, and now local boys have to compete against youngsters from all around the world. I think Brian Kidd was very much instrumental in that, developing an infrastructure for scouting around Greater Manchester and the same model was used to discover players internationally.

With United being trailblazers and trendsetters, it's a huge testament to the foresight of Sir Alex that the vision he had and system he created with his staff turned out to be so wonderfully successful. The main emphasis in the infant years is essentially enjoying the game and skill development, Rene Meulensteen was very much a big part of that, and it creates a fantastic environment to prepare players for the academy team. Coaching has become specialised for specific age brackets and maybe that's a step in the right direction. Rene was a one-off and could work with any age. I've always been a big fan of Rene. His personality and knowledge was outstanding and his ability to relate to players of all ages was so important.

In this book you will read stories about Eric Harrison, Sir Alex and the other coaches and how tough they were. United have always been a strong club at helping develop you as a person and not just a player. That goes back to when I was at the club and was something that was very prevalent under Sir Alex. It was important to teach qualities like punctuality, life skills. Now they educate the players in media training and try to prepare them for everything they have to deal with. In the earlier days, younger players cleaned boots and the changing rooms, it was a great grounding – they have kit men to do that now though. Of course, he practised what he preached and he really would remember every single name as that was something he felt was a very important mark of respect.

Everybody will obviously point to the class of 1992, as well they should, but there are so many others that broke through into the Manchester United first team under Sir Alex, he was just as consistent in giving them chances in his later years as he was in those first years. It's not only the United first team that benefits from the club's youth system. I was coaching the Youth Cup winners of 2003 alongside Brian McClair and so many members of the academy at that time including Chris Eagles, Kieran Richardson, Phil Bardsley, Alan Tate, Luke Steele and more, went on to have very good league careers. Sir Alex was fantastic at making sure youngsters who didn't make it at United found another club. You'll read about some players who unfortunately had to quit through injury. Sir Alex helped so many in those kind of circumstances by using his vast network of contacts that he's built up through the years. A reference from Sir Alex is worth its weight in gold.

There are so many things that the Gaffer can take credit for, and there are so many things said and written about him. So many players earning a career in the Premier League, Football League or overseas. So many who had to go into other careers. One thing they all have in common is that they take the experience from United as something to carry into everyday life. I can attest to that, too – things I learned at United which Sir Alex has upheld and maintained – good manners, respect, good time keeping, basics for any young player. These things are perhaps hidden in the background compared to all the other glorious things he achieved, but perhaps that is the greatest compliment or accomplishment of all, and it might take a long time until that is properly appreciated.

1

Tony Gill

There's no better place to start. In 1987, Tony Gill became the first outfield Fledgling to be given a debut by Alex Ferguson. In 1988/89, when the term "Fergie's Fledglings" was first adopted by the media, he was part of that group and as Gary Walsh at the time was injured, Gill could almost lay claim to being the first of them all.

Such a claim would be disingenuous. The Bradford-born former utility man actually signed at Old Trafford in the early weeks of Ron Atkinson's tenure. Of the stories in this book, some players fell into obscurity, with Tony Gill being one of them.

"You're lucky to get hold of me, actually," he admits. "It's not something I talk about very often." Fortunately for me and this book, when Tony does speak he speaks very candidly.

"I was a Leeds United fan as a kid and actually trained with them quite often. In those days before academies, you would get spotted playing for your town team against either the best boys in the town or some of the best from across the region," Tony explains. "I was offered terms by Leeds when I turned thirteen. The chief scout was a guy I'd grown up knowing as he was heavily involved in my Sunday League boys club and then went on to become Leeds' chief scout. I'd go as far as saying he was a family friend.

"They offered me a contract which was far better than the one I'd get at United. There was a guarantee of a two year apprenticeship after my schoolboy days at Old Trafford, but at Leeds they offered the guarantee of a two year professional contract after my schoolboy deal.

"My dad gave me some great advice and told me that I should sign for the club where I enjoyed it most, as that would be where I'd play my best football. Based on that advice I chose to sign for Manchester United, though I suppose it helped that Leeds were struggling at the time as that was their relegation year."

Ron Atkinson would later be accused of a dereliction of duty with the youth system but it's worth remembering that while Tony was learning his trade as a schoolboy, the likes of Clayton Blackmore, Mark Hughes and Norman Whiteside were all getting first team opportunities. In 1986, United even got to the FA Youth Cup Final against local rivals Manchester City. It had been twenty two years since the Reds had last tasted success in the competition but they had been beaten finalists in 1982. Both senior and younger players were under pressure to replicate the success of those who had played before them yet Tony feels it was easier for the youngsters to deal with.

"Because it's something that you grow up with, it's almost second nature to handle that weight of expectation," he says. "The kids can be comfortable with it as it is all they've known. You're not really conscious of it at the time, in fact I only became truly aware of it when I became a football coach outside the club. So getting to the Youth Cup yeah it was exciting, and it was heightened by the fact it was against City with a group of players we knew quite well, but there was nothing that we felt that was extraordinary in terms of pressure.

"Because we knew the City boys personally, I think that's what made that rivalry a bit more intense. We went to college with them on a Monday, your David White's and Paul Lake's. It just wasn't seen as any big deal to us and we were quite comfortable with it."

Comfortable they may well have been but that didn't prevent a second loss at the final hurdle in just five years. City achieved the bragging rights with a 3-1 aggregate success and there was every reason to believe that they were on the cusp of a golden generation themselves, certainly much more so than United. It's not an observation made by Gill himself, but it's interesting to consider that there was no particular pressure to win. Such an outlook is fine for the development of youngsters as it's all about the path of preparing a player for professional life at United.

When it's all you've known, you can consider it to be the best environment simply because of its reputation. When something happens to come in and shake everything up, your expectations of what is exceptional can be redefined.

"At the back end of Ron's time at the club, one or two of the coaches had talked about me making the move into the first team, so someone had identified I was ready," says Tony. "But as soon as Alex Ferguson came in, there was an instant difference in that you felt that you were being watched.

"The first match at United after he came was a reserve game and he was there – I scored in a win. The big difference was that he was there to see it. He would be in the dressing room before games, and we had never seen that with Ron. Alex Ferguson would watch the reserves training away from the first team and that never happened under Ron either. That was understandable in a way because Ron had to be interested in the first team, but there was a huge shift in focus when Alex arrived."

The game which Tony refers to is a 3-1 win over Middlesbrough on the 11th of November 1986, which was actually three days after Ferguson's first game, the infamous defeat at Oxford. However, the Middlesbrough reserve game was the first that Ferguson had an opportunity to watch, which illustrates how keen he was in the early days to digest as much football as he could at his new club.

Gill was an Old Trafford veteran by comparison and though he would be seen as a youngster cutting his teeth under the new manager, his first team debut for the club came a full five and a half years after he'd first signed schoolboy terms.

"I can remember it vividly, going down to Southampton to stay in the Crest Hotel", Tony recalls of the game at the Dell on Saturday, 3rd January 1987. "I remember the manager taking the piss out of me because at the meal the night before, I'd eaten about eight chocolate profiteroles. We were in a posh restaurant and I was a kid making hay while the sun shone.

"I roomed with another young lad named Martin Russell and my thought process regarding the game was that John Sivebæk was touch and go. Having played most of my reserve team football at full back I felt that it depended on John's fitness whether I'd play or not. I also felt that was why I was in the squad. The next day – it's very clear – we were at the team meeting in the hotel with the manager announcing the team. He starts out with Chris Turner in the net, and at right back Mick Duxbury. I've got to say at that time, I switched off. It was a big surprise when he got to central midfield and said it was me and Liam O'Brien. I'd never played for United as a central midfielder until that day."

Despite the increase in interest and obvious attention to Gill's development, the new manager gave nothing in the way of encouragement to the player who was about to make history in terms of what Ferguson would achieve over the next quarter of a century. "There was nothing at all really," Tony remembers. Wearing the number seven shirt, Tony and his team-mates were only too aware that he was standing in for the injured Bryan Robson – Gill was literally stepping into his shoes. "It could not be more apt," he laughs. "A lot of the lads had New Balance boots, because Bryan wore them and had brought in a load of free boots as freebies from the sponsor. A lot of the senior lads were taking the piss out of me as I put on my number seven shirt with my New Balance boots. 'You're not Bryan you know, who the fuck do you think you are'. I was certainly given an introduction there!"

If such an approach was to put the new kid at ease, he was given a stern test just moments into his debut. Liam O'Brien was making only his fourth appearance and was given one of the quickest red cards in league history. "I think they said after the game that it was the quickest red card in about sixty years and it just so happened to be my debut," says Tony. "I didn't think about it too much – the manager moved Frank Stapleton back into midfield and Terry Gibson was up front on his own. It was all hands to the pump as the Dell could be a difficult place to go.

"My perception of my performance was that I'd done very well and that was what the manager said as he brought me off with about ten minutes to go for Peter Davenport. I was very positive about my contribution and it was good to have that vindicated by the manager and Archie Knox. To do myself justice in such a game and such conditions in a position I'd never played, was something I was very happy with. I said the word before but it remains true, I was comfortable when I was in the first team, and I think the same could be said for any young player who gets in to the United team. Because they've grown up with it, and the size of the club, it's easier for them to handle the pressure than it is for perhaps someone coming from the outside, a club that's not so big. We're used to watching full houses for United against Liverpool, that's our environment, so you know what's expected of you. I don't want to sound blasé about it but it was the norm, if there was any weight of expectation then that came from the manager and the dressing room, not the fifty odd thousand sat outside."

United drew 1-1 at Southampton but as well as Tony had done, for the rest of the season he continued his progress in the reserves though he was kept in the squad for the FA Cup win over Manchester City the week after his debut. The following campaign, he suffered an achilles injury that would keep him out for almost a full season.

"In the pre-season, I picked up the injury which more or less did me for the year. I had two operations and remained on the sidelines. I was just getting somewhere near, had a chance of fulfilling my dreams, and there was nothing more frustrating than suffering such a serious injury. I had a number of setbacks along the way by trying to resolve it without surgery, then I had to have it. When I finally got back to fitness it was difficult to get back into the swing of it."

To look casually at Gill's career statistics you would draw the conclusion that he served a purpose for a short while when United were struggling, and was then released. That couldn't be further from the truth. Following his year out, Gill found himself a regular in the reserves alongside a number of players who would go on to be regarded as the first wave of Fledglings. Mark Robins was scoring goals for fun and Russell Beardsmore and Deiniol Graham featured often in a team that was arguably more entertaining than the first team in the first few weeks of the 1988/89 season.

He was called up to the squad to face Southampton, ironically enough, in November 1988. He maintained his place in the squad, making another five league appearances before the FA Cup clashes with Queens Park Rangers which were the trigger for the media to pay close attention to what Ferguson was doing. Gill had plenty of confidence and assurance about his own ability but feels that the sheer volume of youngsters used, particularly in the first replay at Loftus Road, was not necessarily of the manager's choosing.

"His hand was forced, we had so many injuries," he admits. "He needed us to be able to step up and to be fair he must have had confidence in us to do that. Mark Robins didn't play in that game but he was an incredible finisher who was getting his chance along with David Wilson, Deiniol and Russell. We were a good reserve side and enjoyed our football, so playing in the first team with the others who were making that step up with you made everything a lot better. Throw Lee Martin and Lee Sharpe in – for six of us to be in that game was a huge gamble by the manager."

Gill made a huge impression. "The manager had told me to make movements from the right wing infield. I made one such run, received the ball, my first touch was good and I smashed it with my left foot. Though I played from the right, I did quite often play on the left as well and was comfortable on either side. I was delighted to see it fly in."

Deiniol Graham's equaliser made it 2-2, leaving the press and those in the game purring about the impact of these kids who had seemingly come out from nowhere. A little strange then for Gill, who had by now been at the club for almost eight years and had a complete journey and recovery back from a long term serious injury, to be named alongside a group who had "burst on to the scene."

"It wasn't odd, it was just comfortable at that point, like it was all natural and fun", insists Tony. "I was loving every minute of it – it was the reward for what we'd worked hard for that entire time. I guess it was strange that Gary Walsh and I had broken through a long time before and without those injuries maybe I'd have been more established, but in real terms, it's easy to understand why I was viewed the same way as the others. It was a second coming but the perception was that it was the first time we'd been seen."

With that being the case and the attention that followed, Gill's reaction was perhaps a little predictable. Fergie's Fledglings is very much an alliterative nod to the Busby Babes but inside the club the players did their best to keep their feet on the ground. It's important, then, at this point, to acknowledge that this was as much an education for Ferguson as it was for the youngsters. Later on, he would be famously protective of the class of 1992.

Though it could not be said that in the main, the exposure to the media harmed the development of the youngsters, perhaps one case stood out – Lee Sharpe. Sharpe enjoyed a party lifestyle and it was no surprise that this was cited as a reason why Ferguson eventually sold him to Leeds in 1996. It was clear that the manager wanted to maintain total control, and looking at the pattern of events it is clear to see that he used his experience from this early attention to control the situation later on. For Gill, however, it was just another thing that came with being a United player.

"I don't want to sound dismissive of it – we knew of the attention, people wanted to know who we were and where we came from, but it wasn't as if we were having a collective discussion about how daunting it was. We just carried on as we were, hoping to impress in training and get that chance at the weekend," Tony says. "People who aren't involved in it and haven't experienced it don't understand how I could be so at ease with it, but that was just life for us."

That could fairly explain the attitude of most of the group but not for a player who would make his debut in the game following the QPR draw. United welcomed Millwall and Gill scored again in a comfortable 3-0 win that featured Lee Martin, Lee Sharpe, Russell Beardsmore and Tony from the start. David Wilson came on as a substitute, as did Jules Maiorana, a young player who had been plucked from non-league football just two months previous. If heads were turned by the ease at which these youngsters were performing to a high standard for England's biggest club, then a few eyebrows were raised at the precocious talents of Maiorana. His story will be told later but it's not a spoiler to refer to him as one of the great mysteries – a player of untold potential.

"I would have to go along with that," says Tony. "Playing right back in training I'd come up against Jules a lot in practice matches and exercises and I remember having a few ding-dongs with him. I was very quick, but he was as quick if not a bit quicker, and he was very strong and had bags of technical ability. I played right back against many players while I was there, Jesper Olsen, Peter Barnes, Arnie Muhren. Honestly, if you asked me who I'd prefer playing against, then I'd pick any of those in front of Jules. He was a bloody good player." Maiorana's career would be cut short before it had any opportunity to develop and sadly, the same was about to happen to Tony.

He played in the win at West Ham and was a used substitute in the cup wins over Oxford and Bournemouth. With twelve games under his belt so far, it's a suitable conclusion to draw that Tony was well on his way to becoming an established first team squad member at United. On Monday, 27th March, 1989, in an away game against Nottingham Forest, Tony's career was about to meet a devastating conclusion a million miles away from what everyone thought it was destined to be.

"We were 2-0 down and not playing well so with twenty minutes to go, the manager brought Lee Martin and myself on to play left back and left midfield. Archie Knox said 'Make sure you get plenty of tackles in' and that was at the forefront of my mind as I went on to the pitch. Neil Webb, who was playing for Forest, went to make a square pass to Brian Laws, the full back. If it had been a better pass I'd have had no chance of getting there but it wasn't, and it was an opportunity for me to go and win it in a fifty-fifty.

"With Archie's instructions ringing in my head I went in. Perhaps if I'd been on the pitch a little longer I might not have gone for it but I was so eager and my legs were full of running. I wanted to make a difference to the result and so I went into the tackle with Brian. I've never seen it since so I don't know if I got the ball, if I got there late, if Brian did, the only thing I know is the outcome of the tackle. I knew instantly it wasn't normal. The pain was different. I remember Bryan Robson holding my hand, Jim McGregor asking me questions, and me not answering him as I was so out of it. Perhaps I was in shock. There were waves of pain which went over me. I'd feel okay for a few minutes then I'd feel excruciating pain. Jim took me into the medical room and then the chairman, Martin Edwards, came down to see me which was a fantastic gesture.

"I was in the ambulance while the match was still on. From a pain point of view I felt okay once I was in the hospital. I remember the manager and Archie literally running into the room, as they'd been around the hospital looking for me." It was there that Tony received the terrible news. "Jim McGregor got the X-rays and at first he didn't think it was broken, but then he found where it was," he says. "There was half a second where I felt I was okay, where I thought I'd be alright, but then Jim showed me where the break was. I was taken to the Queens Medical Centre for an operation that night."

Tony had suffered extensive damage to his leg and his ankle but battled, almost in deliberate ignorance, to try and save his career. "I think I tried to consciously ignore the extent of the injury. I didn't want to face up to it because ... well, I just didn't want that worry," confesses Tony. "I felt that negative attitude wouldn't help my recovery, so I think that there was also a conscious effort from others to not let me know the true extent. After the operation and my return to Manchester, there were a lot of discussions involving the management about me.

"On my recovery from injury, I was with Bryan Robson and one or two others and we were running around the pitch at the Cliff. Bryan turned to me and asked what my thoughts were if I didn't recover. It really sticks in my memory because until he said that I'd never given it a thought. That was my first realisation – was it because he'd been involved in those discussions and that was their way of breaking it to me?

"Until that moment it had sincerely not entered my head that I wouldn't recover. I prided myself on my athleticism and I'm sure anyone who played with me would vouch for that and what a good runner I was and I really struggled to deal with the fact I couldn't run like I did before. I had a final operation the following year as my leg wasn't aligned properly. A wedge of bone was taken from my ankle to try and make it better and I remember Jim McGregor saying 'this is the last one'. It was last chance saloon. It made things better for my leg but there was no way I could be the same athlete I was before."

Tony faced the fact that he would have to retire. "I've got to say that the manager was fantastic with me. He was so re-assuring saying the club would look after me and I would be okay, and they were very sympathetic and empathetic. They did all they could to make it easier for me," says Tony. Whilst Gill holds no grudge against Laws for the tackle, there are a few questions that he has been unable to answer. "He did a newspaper interview where he said he was able to sleep at night, that kind of thing. I always thought that if the shoe had been on the other foot, I'd have gone and visited the guy in hospital. I did kind of expect him to visit me. If it was an accident then fine, but if I'd played a part in hurting someone in that way I'd still have made sure I'd gone to see if I could help. It wouldn't have taken much for him to do that," he says. "That's from a human perspective but in terms of the incident, who knows."

"Brian was experienced, so should he have read that whole situation better. Did he think he had to cut me down to size? I just came on and wanted to change the game while he wanted to knock me down a bit. Only Brian Laws will ever know what was running through his mind at that time. That said, I don't blame him, but I was just disappointed he didn't visit or even call."

Gill's reaction to suddenly having to retire was much worse – having come to terms with retiring, just a few days later he was in another world. "The manager had sown the seed of coaching. While I was getting my coaching badges, Bryan Robson had helped me out with a job. He was involved with a birthday greeting cards company and got me sorted there. On the Friday I was a Manchester United footballer, and on the Monday I was in a van delivering greeting cards around the country.

"It's a character builder to say the least. I was stunned for quite a while and I felt lost. It was a tough spell," confides Tony. "The first bit of luck in a long time was when I got my advanced coaching qualification at Lilleshall and literally twenty minutes after I'd got the qualification, I was offered a coaching role at Bristol Rovers. While I was still out there doing my last sessions on the Lilleshall pitch, there was a phone call for me. I thought they were taking the piss but I took the call and it was Martin Dobson, who was then the manager. He was in reception, so I went to see him and he offered me the job of youth team manager there and then."

Tony had a successful spell in Bristol. "I was there for six years but Martin got sacked after six weeks, and that was the start of a bit of a rollercoaster," he says. "His assistant Dennis Roach was made caretaker manager but at the start of the following season, Malcolm Allison was brought in to help him. Dennis didn't like that so he left. John Ward was appointed in 1993 and funnily enough he has just recently taken over the club as manager again, nearly twenty years later.

"At the time I think I was the youngest professional coach in the country. I spent three years working with John and Dennis Booth and those three years were the happiest years of my working life. It was like going to management school and what we achieved at Bristol was incredible. To say we punched above our weight was an understatement. Marcus Stewart was just one great player we brought through and there were so many youth team players who got chances. The management skills that I learned from John, I still use today."

In 1996, change at the club meant that Tony was soon to depart. "John left and Ian Holloway came in. Let's just say that having worked under John who was fantastic, I found it difficult working under Ian," he says. "I was friends with Steve Millard who was manager at Bath City. He asked if I would help out there and I actually played two or three games, basically on one leg. It was never really a comeback as such, I was just helping Steve out but sadly, on Christmas Eve in 1999, Steve passed away of a heart attack."

Tony had departed Bath after just a few months and has not been involved with football at all since 1997. Since then he makes no excuses about the fact that he has deliberately shunned the limelight. Where others have remained involved in the game in some capacity, and as we will discuss later on, many represent the post-retirement "Legends" teams that play local football, Tony moved out of the game and found a new career entirely.

"It was a conscious effort to sort of move away from it all," Gill admits. "I didn't keep in touch with many people, the only one I did was David Wilson who was my best friend, and I've since lost touch with him, though I'd like to see him again. After leaving Bath I got a job based in Bristol selling office supplies. Initially that was working alongside my commitment at Bath, but then it became full time. I did receive a job offer to go back into the game but I'd been involved in my new career for about ten months and so decided to turn it down. For me at that point, football was gone, it was over, and I wanted to concentrate on my new career."

Despite his best efforts, Tony does still get recognised. "Of course it happens and my colleagues have known about it. It's not something you can keep secret, really," he says. "It's not something I shout about in the work that I do. I want to be recognised for what I do now, not what I did twenty five years ago."

At the age of forty five at the time of our discussion, Tony is still relatively young in coaching terms should he wish to get back into the game. However there appears to be no chance of that. "None whatsoever," Gill confirms. "I don't really take any interest in football these days. My son is a Man Utd fan and I'll watch games with him, but I don't make it an issue to do so. We watched United play Arsenal at the weekend and of course, if you ask me who do I want to win the league, I want United to. But if you ask me firstly if I am a United fan, then no I'm not, and secondly if I'm a football fan, then no I'm not again. I've got a really good job and made a different career my own. My plate is well and truly full and I have little time for anything beyond my job and my family. I have no connection with football anymore and even if I had the odd feeling of wanting to play again, my injury forbids me from doing hardly anything on an exercise point of view."

It's a huge shame considering Gill's potential. He openly confesses that he was not quite a Giggs or a Scholes, but suggests, "With the way I was playing, I think I was at the level of a Nicky Butt or Gary Neville. Would I have been a United legend, probably not, but could I have made a very good career, well I'm confident enough in my own ability to say that I would have. It's difficult to be objective when assessing yourself. I wouldn't dare say I was as talented as David Beckham, but I'm certain I would have played many more times for United and I might even have played for England, especially considering that caps were given away like confetti."

Ferguson himself appears to share that opinion. In his first autobiography published in 1999, *Managing My Life*, Gill is described as a player "establishing himself at the top level" and his retirement was "a sad loss". Tony sees those words as vindication of his own personal belief. "It's nice to hear, isn't it", he says. "It's difficult when you're saying things about yourself because you sound arrogant and I'm certainly not. I'm sure I could have had a long and successful football career but one tackle on the 27th of March 1989 put paid to that."

2

Deiniol Graham

"It is quite surreal, in a way," responds Deiniol Graham, when asked what it means to still be referred to as "former Manchester United player". "I don't have an ego in that way at all. I look at it as I left school and went to Manchester United to do a job. Possibly if I'd had a bit more of an ego and a bit more about me in that sense, I might have done a bit more. I didn't have the pushiness or boastfulness about myself to see it any other way than a job. Looking back and speaking to my family and friends who are and were all envious, perhaps I might have looked at it a different way had I thought about it, but I honestly just saw it as an every day thing.

"Manchester United were still the biggest club in the world," explains Deiniol on his decision to sign for the club ahead of a number of suitors in the summer of 1986. "I was sought after by many clubs but there were a few reasons why I chose United. Being from North Wales originally, I'd been to Manchester a few times, loved the set up, and knew it was only a couple of hours on the train which made it much easier than going to the London clubs that were interested."

Moves had been made to sign Graham a year before in an aggressive manner many would associate more with United manager Ron Atkinson's successor. "It's funny, because my Dad only told me the story a couple of years ago", laughs Deiniol, almost hesitant to share the tale.

"United were playing a midweek match some time late in the 1984/85 season. We were invited to a game there while I was still undecided about where I was going to sign, my choices being Watford, Cardiff, Leeds or United. Mick Brown and Ron were there and they followed my dad into the toilet!

"They were offering sweeteners but hints, not in the form of cash, asking about our car and mortgage. Yet Dad resisted their pressure and left it up to me. When I asked him why, he said he wanted to leave it up to me. I was gutted. I said he could have kept the money for me!"

United's reputation as a club appealed not only due to their size but their reputation for bringing through youngsters that had survived since the days of Sir Matt Busby. "The background of the way that United worked in bringing through their players was something that was talked about when I was being signed. They reeled off names of players that were coming through and getting chances and I thought 'Yeah, that could be me in a few years.'"

In the last league game of the 1985/86 season, United had more than their fair share of youth players in their squad at Vicarage Road in a 1-1 draw with Watford. Billy Garton and Clayton Blackmore were just starting out on their careers while Arthur Albiston, Mike Duxbury, Norman Whiteside and Mark Hughes had accumulated over 1,000 games between them after breaking through as youngsters in the United set up. Six players through the academy in a senior line up would be a fine achievement for any Football League club yet Ron Atkinson's tenure, while successful, had been undermined by the perception that he had done less to encourage youth players than his predecessors Sir Matt Busby, Wilf McGuinness and Tommy Docherty. Perhaps the figures mentioned before show that Atkinson is sometimes unfairly given such a perception. In the months before Graham arrived at the club, United had even reached the final of the FA Youth Cup, losing 3-1 on aggregate. That success meant that for a player without a bulging sense of self confidence, Deiniol found it a little difficult to settle in those early days, particularly given the uncertainty of the manager's future.

"We had a bunch of players in front of me that had done so well. I thought a few of those might have possibly broken in, a few more than actually did," says Deiniol. There was little time for Atkinson to take such a gamble. With pressure mounting, his concentration was purely on the present. "I only really had the spell of June to November in 1986 with Ron and in that time he had the first team to one side, and everybody else had to deal with themselves. When Ron was in charge we never really got to mix with the first team as much. It was a difficult time and not just because the club were struggling a little. Being a young lad, it was hard to understand what was really going on, and what the expectations were for the manager at the time.

"Looking back, the results weren't good and it's a results game, so it was inevitable that he was going to go. He was still making big signings and spending money, so everyone was looking for the club to be challenging Liverpool in the league. The expectations at United would always be massive due to the size of the club and the support. We were still the best supported club even when we weren't doing well. It wasn't just expectation from the manager and supporters, it was there from the board and players as well."

There's an understanding of Atkinson's dilemma and also a support for the charismatic former boss from Deiniol regarding his track record with young players. "Being signed by Ron, and understanding United's tradition and policy, I felt I would get a chance under him. There were a few players under Ron who came through such as Mark Hughes and Norman Whiteside. Players who ended up becoming proper legends at the club. Obviously Ron didn't bring through players in the same way that Sir Alex has in his conveyor belt fashion."

Aside from the personal intervention Atkinson took in attempting to bring Graham to the club, he recalls only one fleeting moment of interaction with the manager afterwards. "It was on the first day of pre-season up at Heaton Park," smiles Deiniol. "I was probably the fittest one at the club at the time so was ahead in the running and I was praised for it. Other than that there was only one time we really spoke, and that was when the entire squad were sat down at the Cliff when he told us he was going in the November."

In Graham's opinion, Atkinson's reticence to field the youngsters was replaced by Ferguson's caution to the wind approach upon his arrival. "There was a real change in impetus in the approach of the new manager. In the early stages, maybe he just thought he had nothing to lose by throwing kids in. He was on a hiding to nothing with a big clear out, so if the kids did it for him he'd be a hero and if not he had a ready made excuse. It was a brave move." Though previously in support of Ron's policy, Graham acknowledges that Ferguson's substantially more prolific use of youth players gave him a far greater chance of getting his opportunity. "He gave me a chance that I possibly might not have had under Ron. He had brought one or two real legends through but I'm grateful to Sir Alex for giving me an opportunity I might not have had otherwise."

Ferguson's immediate attention to rebuilding the youth system, or revamping it at least, was clear. While change on such a fundamental scale is most often gradual, Deiniol felt the waves were moving immediately. Perhaps, not surprisingly given Atkinson's attention was elsewhere, the first thing Deiniol recalls is the presence. "Straight away, you knew he was always there. You knew that about every game. A youth game, a reserve game, a training session even. He'd sometimes leave the first team to come and watch us and step in and have his say. He'd have a go at us or praise us, he'd make sure that everyone was together training at Littleton Road, and often he'd take some of the younger lads to go and train with the first team, which was a great experience and a great lift."

Ferguson was assisted by some renowned characters. "There were some great staff in the early days, and a few not so good. He brought Archie Knox with him, a hard but fair man who was someone you didn't mess with, and we already had Eric Harrison. He was phenomenal, what a man. I went on to manage in my later years and some of the words I would come out with were words and phrases that originally came out of Eric's mouth. He had a massive impact on me."

Also drafted in were names associated with the club's illustrious past. "I remember Kiddo (Brian Kidd) coming in. He was working with schools at the time and helping with the link up between schools and the club, and he sort of progressed. The gaffer took him on, and he was a great character. He was different – not as right in your face as Archie was, he was a joker who you could have a laugh with. To have a man right there who had come through, a local lad who scored in a European Cup Final for the club and now was back helping us come through the same way he did, made for a massive incentive for some of us. He lived dreams and was somebody who we all looked up to."

During Deiniol's time through the academy and then reserve sides, Ferguson kept up a healthy dialogue. "He always kept track of my progress. He'd tell me what I was doing right or wrong, and there were plenty of times he would tell me what I was doing wrong," laughs Graham. "Leaving Holyhead at 16 years of age and moving to a big city, I took time to settle in and probably didn't settle until around Christmas time. I lived in digs by myself near the Cliff – after I left, David Beckham went in the same place – but when I first moved in, Graeme Hogg was there with me. He left and Joe Hanrahan, who I'm still good mates with, moved in for a short while. All the lads just sort of naturally mixed anyway. We'd socialise together and go down to the snooker hall. It was there that I met what turned out to be my best mate, who is out of football, and we've been close for almost 30 years."

This helped Deiniol to settle and he found his rhythm on the pitch. "After Christmas, I had my bearings and my game just took off. I was flying past other lads that were ahead of me at the time and I broke in really quick. I was scoring goals for fun, the confidence was there and the gaffer could see that. I had only played a handful of reserve games before I was being considered for the first team. By this time, big Frank Stapleton had left and his departure meant there was a space for a young lad to come in and get an opportunity, and at that time the one in the best position was me."

Days after his eighteenth birthday in October 1987, Graham got his opportunity in the first team. Readers might be accustomed to Ferguson's deployment of youngsters in League Cup ties but back in 1987 Deiniol became the first ever Manchester United youngster to be given his debut by Sir Alex in the competition. A strong side had taken apart Hull City at Old Trafford in the first leg of the second round with a comprehensive 5-0 scoreline, rendering the return little more than a formality. Still, a strong side including Robson, Strachan, Whiteside and McClair were all in the starting line up at Boothferry Park.

Graham recalls discovering that he would be part of the travelling squad. "At the Cliff, they'd put a team sheet up on a little board at the bottom of the steps next to the changing rooms," he says. "I remember looking at it and seeing my name on it and thinking 'well no-one's called me yet!' I was supposed to be cleaning boots, or cleaning something in the dressing room anyway, and one of the lads said, 'you're in' and that's what made me look at the board. The next thing, I was called up to the gaffer's office by Eric and he told me 'You've been performing, so you're going to be included in the squad. This is the type of thing that's going to happen, if you're performing, he's going to bring you in.'

"I was like, 'great, okay', but gobsmacked by it all really." Not that he was overawed by it. "I had been doing well, and I'd been there long enough to not let it get on top of me. I'd had such a rapid rise. I'd arrived and was doing well in the B team so got into the A team over Christmas in 1986, and then the reserves where I just kept banging the goals in. When you're in the reserves, you're training with the first team and working with them so much anyway that even though I wasn't exactly expecting my opportunity to come so soon, it didn't phase me that it did."

Deiniol remembers much of the events of the day he made his first team debut for United. "It was a really cold day and night at Hull. We'd gone in the afternoon to settle down in the hotel and then go through all the pre-match stuff. I think I came on for Micky Duxbury in the game with ten or fifteen minutes left and I had a chance to score. Their goalkeeper was a fellow Welshman called Tony Norman and I'd been played in by Liam O'Brien. I turned and hit a weak shot at the goalkeeper which he got down to save, but I probably should have scored."

Ferguson was keen to keep Graham's feet on the ground and, as he has become renowned for since, didn't heap huge congratulations on the teenager who had just made his debut for the biggest club in the world. "He just said 'Well done, you've done quite well there'. He didn't want me to get too ahead of myself or above my station so he wouldn't build you up massively to your face, however much he might have championed you to others. That was a key thing about what he did, he didn't want you to be out of your stride, and didn't want to hype you up. Even being treated the same way as seasoned first teamers made an impression, though."

In not finding out about his inclusion in the squad until the day before, Graham had less time to get nervous or over confident before the game. His ascent in squad status was clear by the time he was next to get some game time. "For my full debut against Wimbledon I was given a few days notice," explains Deiniol. "I remember Archie shouting me over in the Cliff car park on the Thursday to ask me how I was feeling. I said I was fine, he asked if I was fit and ready. When I said yeah, he said, 'right, you're playing on Saturday', and it gave me a few days to get to terms with it."

There to help him was a fellow Welshman, Clayton Blackmore, who himself had come through the ranks. "He was the one I'd tend to go to for advice, as was Gary Walsh," says Graham. Not that an overzealous approach to motivating was taking place. "I'm not sure about encouragement, it was more about taking the piss out of you to keep you level, if anything. Never an arm around a shoulder from your team-mates, more words and having a laugh to try and relax you and settle you that way instead."

At Plough Lane against Wimbledon on Saturday 21st November 1987, as he made his first Manchester United start, the relaxed approach might not have helped the team to a win but it certainly made Deiniol feel more at ease with playing in the side. "My dad was gutted as he was working in Anglesey and couldn't get time off, but the game was live on Irish television with Johnny Giles commentating. Where my dad lived, he could get signal for it, so he videotaped it for me and watched it, even though I've never seen it back."

Deiniol's father reminds him of how he played even to this day. "'There were some great little things you did, there was a chance you should have scored, but that wasn't your fault, it was Brian McClair. He should have passed and you'd have had a tap in.' He was probably right, the gaffer had a go at Brian for that afterwards. I don't remember that much about the game, I'm sure I was nervous, but as soon as it starts you just get on with it and forget the crowd around you."

United lost 2-1, Blackmore the goalscorer, and although it would be some time until Deiniol played for the first team again, he continued to figure in Sir Alex's plans. With just two substitutes permitted, there wasn't the ease in which substitutes could be used that you can sometimes see in today's game. A substitute would be used in case of an injury or a tactical shift but a significant change in emphasis has been put on the role of a substitute in recent years. The increase in two to three permitted and the growth in the size of a substitutes bench has led to many ramifications as it's not uncommon to see players brought on with seconds or minutes remaining with the sole intention of wasting time in a game.

In the late 1980s, a player in the Manchester United squad on a match day was a player that Alex Ferguson thought could make a positive contribution in the match, someone he had figured in his plans for that particular game. Though Graham wouldn't play for the first team for another thirteen months he would consistently make the squad. "I was in the squad quite often without really getting a sniff. But this was the time when Fergie was really beginning to bring in players for the future, and a few other youngsters were starting to get chances as well. He was trying to share it around, giving different players opportunities, so much so that I didn't actually realise it was so long in between my appearances."

Ferguson had truly begun to stamp his mark on the club but with mixed results on the pitch, though Deiniol did his best to remain upbeat. "There was one time when Sparky (Mark Hughes) came back from Barcelona and Bayern Munich that I thought my chances would be limited. It's only natural when a player comes in who plays in your position that you worry about slipping down the pecking order but, then again, it never really crossed my mind that I wouldn't get another opportunity. Everyone was getting a chance, a fair chance too. If you were doing well in the reserves for a few games, you'd get a chance in the first team. Mark Robins was one who did just that. David Wilson, Tony Gill, Lee Martin, myself, sometimes it felt like a rota system who would make it into the squad."

In fact, Gill, Martin, and Wilson were all in the squad the next time Graham saw first team action, as were young Lee Sharpe who had signed from Torquay, and Russell Beardsmore, who was making his tenth appearance when United travelled to Queens Park Rangers for an FA Cup third round replay at Loftus Road on Wednesday, 11th January 1989.

In a distinct progression and an indication of future intent from Ferguson in that cup tie from his very first in which Graham featured, only one of the starting eleven had played for United more than 100 times and that was Mark Hughes. who had played that many in his first spell at Old Trafford under Atkinson. Martin, Sharpe, Gill, Beardsmore, Graham and Wilson's combined total of appearances before the QPR game was just 46.

Graham's inclusion came about as a bit of an odd series of events. "We'd drawn against them in the cup with a 0-0 at home. On that morning I'd gone with the reserves or the A team to play against Preston and something had happened at the club. This was in the days before mobile phones, so there was no way of getting hold of us. We won 2-0 and I scored both goals but as soon as we got back after the match and I arrived at my digs, Brian Kidd was waiting for me. I said, 'I'm just going to have some beans on toast,' and he said, 'No, come on, you're playing, you're the fittest lad at this club!' We got in Kiddo's car and he rushed me down to Old Trafford where the gaffer had already got half way through his team talk and I was to be on the bench with Paul Ince and Lee Martin. After the manager had done his team talk, I wanted to know what was going on, and then it was said that Paul McGrath was not fit to play."

With that, Ferguson had frantically searched for an available player and despite having already played a full game earlier in the day, Deiniol was relied upon as an emergency substitute. Thankfully for his legs he wasn't needed, but the youngster was rewarded for his commitment to the cause with a place in the squad for the replay.

"They'd only just had the grass refitted at Loftus Road and it was a horrible, rainy Wednesday night", recalls Graham when talking of the replay. "The re-laid pitch hadn't taken very well and it was boggy as anything. I was on the bench, Tony Gill started and scored a great goal. It was nip and tuck and probably quite a good game for the neutral. I came on in extra time for Lee Sharpe and put us ahead. David Wilson ran down the left skinning Paul Parker who we signed not long after, knocked the ball across and I just ran and tapped it in. That put us 2-1 ahead and in the second half of extra time I almost set Sparky up. Lee Martin and myself were involved in a lovely little move. I nutmegged a lad called Mark Dennis who had the record amount of sendings off in the League at the time, then I pulled it back for Sparky but he lashed it over the bar. It would have made it 3-1, but they equalised and the game went to another replay. It was the proudest moment, scoring my first goal and doing really well in the match. The lads all had a dig at me afterwards on the bus for 'megging' Mark Dennis, saying he was going to get me next time!" He might well have because Dennis was actually dubbed "Psycho" in the media before they gave the nickname to Stuart Pearce. But a young player showing such confidence and demonstrating that he didn't care for reputations was the kind of young player that Ferguson wanted to see in his team. "I think that's when it began to turn around for the Gaffer, especially considering the number of kids who were in the team that night," muses Deiniol.

Six, to be precise. Deiniol says, "The injury crisis we were going through over the QPR tie was something that was forced upon Sir Alex. It was make or break, even though we were all performing well, we all had to make sure that we took that chance. I think we all did. Me for a small part, some of the others for longer parts, we seized the opportunity at the time. I believe it saved the gaffer's job – they could see what he was trying to do, and we were doing it for him. I think after that spell he looked at it and believed that he could keep the youngsters in but that he had to bring in a nucleus of experience to help them. From then on, it's the sort of model that he has worked from consistently and successfully." Ferguson was showing he wasn't afraid to spend big to replace players he didn't think were up to the standard, but also that he was equally confident in complementing the new recruits with youngsters from the reserves.

Deiniol's theory is interesting as there were two waves of Fledglings, but the group that most refer to when using the tag given by the media is the 1992 Youth Team. When people refer to how well youngsters flourished and how much they achieved, the 1995/96 season is put forward as Exhibit A, but it's worthwhile to note that in the early successes of Ferguson's reign, the intervention and contribution of the young players who were drafted in was critical.

"I think the fact that we were able to make a contribution afforded him some extra time. There are a lot of little circumstances that went in the manager's favour regarding the youngsters in those early years, including that QPR tie with us scoring, obviously a year later with Mark Robins' goal at Nottingham Forest and then Lee Martin winning the cup. But that's what makes the club, isn't it? I know more people will look to the team in 1992 but what you tend to get with young lads coming through is that there's generally more passion to achieve for the club. Bringing in players from abroad with a price tag on their head, they've probably never been United fans, they have an expectation and a pressure to achieve. With the younger lads, they didn't have a price tag or pressure, they're playing through passion and I feel that's a difference. I think that's probably something that Sir Alex identified and saw as a big thing, and why he stuck with it."

There seems little doubt that Ferguson would have stuck with Graham too, if only to use as a squad player in the future. Having done so well when given an opportunity, he had once again forced his way into the reckoning. Shortly after, fate struck a cruel blow, though not according to Deiniol himself. "I'm never bitter towards my career, I don't believe in fate or destiny or things like that, and there are a few things that maybe I could have done better myself. But I can remember the day I got injured well. It was a massive turning point in my career at United. We were playing in the fifth round of the cup against Bournemouth. The gaffer said I was unlikely to make the bench but I was welcome to travel with the squad. He also said that we had a reserve game arranged at the Cliff against Bury. I hadn't had a full ninety minutes for five weeks as I'd been on the bench and involved with the first team squad so we agreed that in order to keep my fitness up I'd play for the reserves. I was on fire, too. I think we were winning two nil and I'd scored both goals. Giggsy was also in the team and I think he even played the ball to me when it happened. Sods law. The ball was pinged into me, I went to glance it out wide for someone to run on to, and as I did, the defender came in and kicked my legs. With the momentum, my legs were still going forward, I put my hands out and my arm just snapped. It was a big disappointment, I was so buzzing at the time, in form and having just scored my first senior goal."

The advances in medical science and physiotherapy have worked wonders for injuries to players. What would have been seen as career threatening in 1990 can be a six month lay-off in the modern game. Deiniol's broken arm was going to keep him out for a long time. "I was out for the rest of the season, and wasn't allowed to take part in the pre-season training either because of the plate in my arm. I was fit, but I wasn't match fit. I was on the bench and got on for a game against Derby County early in the season. When I finally started to get a run of games in the reserves, my confidence was gone and I just wasn't the same player."

Mark Robins and Lee Martin had their headline moments, playing their part in the FA Cup triumph in 1990, Ferguson's first trophy. The domestic trophy success earned United a spot in the now defunct European Cup Winners' Cup tournament, and Deiniol managed to find himself around the squad. "I finally got a bit of form going but it took me about six or seven months. I was in the squad for a number of the European games that season. I was on the bench for the game against Wrexham but I didn't get on. Still, after my arm injury, I just didn't feel the same."

Returning to the point about the evolution of physiotherapy, it seems odd that an arm injury would have such a profound impact, though in Deiniol's case it appears to be the effect of the length of the time out as much as the injury itself that was the issue, though it was far from a straight forward broken arm injury. "To be fair, I had complications with my injury," he says. "It was a clean but nasty break, I needed an operation on my elbow to slice some of the bone off so it could be grafted on. There was no way of just putting it back to place. The plate had to stay in and there was always the concern that should I ever knock it again then I might be in serious trouble. I had to strengthen the arm, give it eight months to heal, and it wasn't strong enough for a long while to be able to get the plate removed. I remember having that operation in 1990, as I was in plaster at Wembley for the 3-3 against Crystal Palace."

By the time Deiniol was both physically and mentally ready to figure for the first team, Mark Hughes and Brian McClair were being challenged for a striker position by Mark Robins, whose successful contribution in 1989/90 had essentially leapfrogged him into first choice reserve striker. "I didn't want to be sat there as a reserve player at the age of twenty one," says Deiniol. "I'd had a few games, I needed to have more and I hadn't gone out on loan. Maybe I should have done that to get some more experience, but then I had a fall out with the manager. Having been in the squad for three of the games in the Cup Winners' Cup run, I was left out of the final squad when we played Barcelona and I was quite disappointed, even though we were all flown over there.

I reacted, and had a few drinks with Derek Brazil on the trip. I had been offered a contract – another year on it, with twenty or thirty quid more. I thought it was nothing as I wasn't on much money so I was thinking about leaving and perhaps getting some more money, so I'd said no to the offer. After we'd got home from

Rotterdam, he found out about me drinking on the trip so called up and we had an argument. He said 'you can find your own fucking club', and I said 'does that mean you're giving me a free transfer then gaffer?' He said 'am I bollocks, you better make sure you're back here for training'. He left me out of the pre-season tour to Norway and I ended up going with the ressies and youth team to Cornwall so I knew my time was spent and I'd sort of blown it with him. He's the gaffer and what he says goes."

Still, Deiniol has a philosophy of no regrets and believes in it regardless of the way he fell out of favour at United. "No regrets. I'm often asked, why did you say that, why didn't you stay, why didn't you sign the contract?" says Deiniol. "I look back at the players who stayed an extra year, David Wilson and Derek Brazil, and they were released anyway. The club sold me and got money, I got what I wanted out of it and even having had the spat with the gaffer I left the club on good terms. He was the last one that I spoke to when leaving the club and we have never had a problem since. I've met him a few times and everything has been great." It would be understandable if, given the injury, Graham harboured resentment for the youngsters who came in and did so well in 1990, a position he could arguably have been in. Not so, indeed, Graham speaks enthusiastically about them. "No, these were great mates of mine. Lee Martin is still a good friend to this day. Each to their own, every career goes its own way. Mark Robins and I came through the same year, I was ahead of him at one time, but he was a natural goalscorer where I was more of a workhorse. I always knew he'd bang in goals when he got on the pitch. I'd never say anything bad about any of my team-mates, you get out of the game what you put into it, and Mark and Lee were two very dedicated lads. Far from being frustrated, I was absolutely delighted to see them score such vital goals for the first team. It was brilliant to see and I was made up for them and not only that, I was made up to see the next bunch of lads coming through as well. I was part of that and it was amazing."

That "next bunch" would go on to dominate the domestic game and achieve what most would beforehand have dismissed as impossible. As impossible, say, as replicating such a youth team. "Seeing the 1992 team with the likes of Beckham and Scholes in, I don't think you'll ever see something like that happen again, that number of lads with such ability," states Graham.

Graham's own memory of that team are limited. "I can remember Becks coming up as a schoolboy and he used to come along to the snooker club with us, he was a nice quiet lad. But we didn't get a chance to see them much as they were often off by themselves. By the time I was with them on the tour to Cornwall, I was in negotiations to leave, so I didn't get to see them a great deal on the pitch. Obviously, I'd played with Giggsy quite often, and I can remember one time being beaten in a game before he joined the club. Eric Harrison sat us all down and was effing and blinding. He said 'listen lads, I am telling you now, no threats, you better start bucking your ideas up because there is one lad who is coming here next year. He is going to romp past you all and be in the first team within a year. He is absolutely exceptional and there will be more of him to come, and more like him to come.'

Graham is predictably gushing over his compatriot. "He was amazing to play with, and you just knew how special he was. The ball was glued to his feet, he was beautiful on the ball. The only concern was whether he would have the physical presence for the first team but it turned out he didn't need it. He had natural balance, would beat players for fun, and look at him today, still doing it. Brilliant." Giggs would go on to break and set records for the club, becoming its most decorated servant and, some would argue, its finest player. "It's amazing to say I've graced the same field as Giggsy. You won't find many people to say they've played as often as I did with someone who isn't just a legend of Manchester United, a legend of the game. I've got something to tell my kids when they grow up."

The record of players leaving Manchester United is mixed. With the size of the club, it's only natural that in most cases, the only way is "down", yet even so, the number of players who go on to have successful football league careers is remarkable. Deiniol didn't quite go on to achieve that but is expectedly frank about it. "I spent three years at Barnsley after Mel Machin signed me. I expected to go there as a centre forward but he obviously didn't see me as that. He wanted me to play in the hole and work hard, or on the right wing, but I wasn't quick enough. I was sharp, but not a quick dribbler. I was in and out of the team and I wasn't happy, so I went on loan to Preston where Sam Allardyce was the caretaker manager." The temporary move to Deepdale presented a false dawn. "I did really well there, scoring goals, and Sam wanted to sign me. I wanted to go, as a move to Preston meant that I could move back to Manchester. Unfortunately, Sam didn't get the job on a permanent basis, John Beck did, and he preferred to play long ball and didn't like fanny merchants like me. It didn't work out and I went back to Barnsley, but because I'd done so well on loan, I ended up getting straight back in the team for a while. I made some really nice friends there but things didn't work out for me."

One of those friends took Deiniol on a short loan at Carlisle, before his career took a few twists and turns. "It was strange how that came about. Mick Wadsworth had been a coach at Barnsley and we'd had a few fall outs and I didn't think I was his type of player. But he asked for me on loan, got me and to my surprise I absolutely loved the second spell I had with him. Maybe it was because I was a little bit older. Sadly that was cut short by injury. I was released by Barnsley and was interested in going back to Carlisle but Mick wasn't quick enough to get the deal done and Stockport were straight on the phone. Because it was just down the road it was the easy move. I enjoyed it and thought I played quite well. We went to Plymouth for a midweek match, won 2-1 or 2-0, and I scored in the first minute. On the Saturday we travelled to Shrewsbury, but in between games, the manager, Danny Bergara, had a meeting with the chairman and they came to blows. Danny got the sack straight away and Dave Jones came in and took over, keeping the same team for the Shrewsbury game. I scored early on again but we drew the match.

"I felt I was on a roll, my confidence was high yet for the next game, another away match at Bradford, I was put on the bench. Starting in front of me was Peter Davenport – just like he used to at United! I came off the bench and set Dav up to score the winner, but for the next game I wasn't even in the squad. I went to see Dave and asked him what was wrong as I'd done well and not even complained when I was dropped, but he was one of those type of characters that never tell you the truth. He did the same to Dav, too. He would try and feed you lies instead of the truth, he kept saying they were trying new things until a new manager came in, which I knew was a lie. I lost all heart and thought bollocks to this, I'm going to play non-league and get a job. I did have a little change of heart and went to Scunthorpe scoring on my debut, but they started messing me around about a contract so it just reinforced my desire to drop out of the professional game."

Deiniol was able to find a local side he could play for while he tried to forge a new career for himself. "I played for Emley in Yorkshire for about a year and half. We did really well in the League, got through to the third round proper in the FA Cup in 1998 to play West Ham at Upton Park. It made loads of money for the club. During my time there I was scoring so often I was up for the non league Golden Boot, but then I got an achilles injury and was out for a couple of months. I still came back and managed to score about thirty goals overall – the manager said that he'd had calls from Macclesfield where the former United winger Sammy McIlroy was in charge and Peter Davenport was his assistant, and they wanted to sign me. They agreed a fee but I turned them down because I just had no desire to go back into it. I was earning decent money in non-league and didn't think that Macclesfield had anything to offer me in regards the security of a three year contract. Lincoln City and Dumbarton made offers but I just rejected them as it didn't interest me. I was working with Nike as Director of football camps around the United Kingdom, and also outside of football in a concrete works."

Eventually, Deiniol decided to move back home to Wales, where he found himself in demand once more by the local clubs, but his taste of the non-playing side of the game had whetted his appetite. "I found a club right away without a problem but I also applied for a job at the Welsh FA. Where we were in the County of Conwy in Llandudno didn't have a football development officer so I did some of my badges and applied. With my experience and CV I got the job but it was possibly the worst thing I ever did though, because I hated it. It was office based and that's not me. I didn't mind working with kids in schools but it became monotonous, so I resigned and decided to get a trade." Over a year, Graham worked with his wife's father to learn how to become a plasterer. "I've been doing that ever since", he says.

The lure of the game proved too much for Graham to stay away for good, and on entering his mid-thirties, he found himself with management opportunities. "I enjoyed managing Llandudno, and I've had a decent history with the club. We built the team from nothing, worked on the players to make them better and it was very satisfying. In my first year, the club won its first trophy in 13 years, the North Wales Coast Challenge Cup, which is a replica of the FA Cup. I believe it was made around the same time. It was quite prestigious."

Life away from football was beginning to eat into Deiniol's time, starting a family with his wife took precedence. "We had our first child and I carried on. We were alright, but as soon as we were expecting our second we had to make a decision. My wife runs her own business, so I made the decision to drop out of football, and I was out of it for three years." Though leaving his managerial role, he was a familiar face at the club. "I'd still go and watch matches as they were all close friends.

In October 2011, with the kids having grown up a little, I decided to go back into the role at Llandudno as they were getting rid of the manager. The players were good enough but just needed a lift. We were brilliant, the form side and I was expecting really good things for the following season. However we couldn't bring in the players I wanted to, and we lost our key players and suffered injuries. I decided it wasn't for me but that I would help bring someone in who knew how to scout for players better, the people there were great with that. With my three young girls and the commitments I had, I just didn't have the time to go and watch games too. It's sad but a weight was lifted off. The girls are six, four and three, and I love spending time with them."

Deiniol may have decided to move away from a regular involvement in the sport, yet Manchester United remains with him. "I've been playing for a Legends side for about four years now", says Deiniol. "We've been everywhere, brilliant trips to Ireland, Dubai, Gibraltar and loads in the UK. We get four or five a year, usually we do pretty well but when we come up against teams that have players under the age of thirty five it can take a bit out of us.

We do have a decent mix of players such as David May, Ben Thornley who's probably the youngest, who weren't there at the club when I left but I've become really good mates with. Andy Ritchie and Sammy Mac were there before me but I've got to know them well too. Apart from that most of them are lads that I knew from my time at the club, and it's always great to catch up."

When remembering players who didn't quite make it from the first wave of Fergie's Fledglings, Deiniol is one of the names most often referred to, and is still remembered at the club. "One of my mates sent me a text message the other night. He'd been to the club megastore and there's a picture of George Best which was made out of names of all the players who had played for United. My name was on his neck," he laughs. "I haven't seen it myself, but I'm told my name is in the museum too. I was there for five-and-a-bit years. It doesn't matter that I only played a handful of games, I'm massively proud to have played for the biggest club in the world."

3

Alan Tonge

It's an awkward joke that the studious Alan Tonge decides to kick off with. "I often say I was born two years too early. I blame my mum and dad", he laughs. Alan, a hard working full back capable of working both sides, spent five years at Manchester United shortly after the arrival of Alex Ferguson from Aberdeen. Indeed, while the internationally recognised Viv Anderson would become Ferguson's first senior signing at Old Trafford, Alan claims to be the very first player that the manager signed as a schoolboy, some time before Anderson arrived.

Tonge had already been scouted by United long before Ferguson's arrival. A boyhood Red, once he was aware of their interest there was only one team he wanted to join. "I was playing in the junior leagues as there was no under 8s or under 9s, just a school of excellence which, if I remember rightly, you could go in from about twelve years of age. I was playing in Sunday teams and representative teams you don't hear of nowadays. Bolton Schoolboys, which was the best of our area, was one and I was also selected to play for Greater Manchester County which encompassed all the different boroughs. Joe Brown came to a game at Macclesfield Town's ground where we were playing Cheshire. He approached my mum and dad and said 'It's very rare we see a boy who can play at full back and cross the well as well as Alan does.'

"Joe invited me to train on Monday and Thursday nights, where the likes of Deiniol Graham, Mark Robins and Russell Beardsmore would be giving us a bit of coaching as part of their own apprenticeships. Eric Harrison was there watching over us and them, and then Sir Alex took over and Kiddo came along too." It was shortly after Ferguson's arrival that Alan's move to United gathered pace. "I was invited to a trial over the New Year, funnily enough. I stayed at the Halls of Residence at Manchester University. There we trained and had a couple of practice games on the astro pitch and the grass pitch at the Cliff and I played really well. Joe was the one who approached me and said United wanted me to sign schoolboy forms. Bolton were sniffing about and I'd had a trial at City, but my family and I wanted the security of signing schoolboy terms and then having a guaranteed two year apprenticeship.

"Early January we got a call up to see the great man, who said that the club would give me a two year YTS. I was made up. My dad was a big Red, he'd seen Bestie's debut, watched Denis Law, he always speaks of the great imagery of United playing at Old Trafford, with the green and white nets, and that was something that was passed on to me, so it was quite surreal."

Tonge joined an already competitive youth set up and it wasn't long before he witnessed the more unfortunate side of being a trainee at United. "I think I was a year younger than most of the lads who were training regularly there. There was a lad called Ashley Ward (who would go on to play Premier League football for Norwich City, Derby County, Barnsley, Blackburn Rovers and Bradford City) among a bunch who all thought they were going to get apprenticeships. I just remember one evening at the Cliff, all the parents seeming to be very, very disappointed, so that must have been down to Sir Alex saying they weren't going to be taking any of them on. There were some good players in there too. I'm not sure if that had anything to do with Sir Alex putting his foot down and saying 'This is my system, not Ron Atkinson's'. I just remember there were quite a few tears that evening."

The opinion maybe carries a little weight for though Ferguson had demonstrated a commitment to those already with terms at the club, it is reasonable to conclude that the manager's first steps into the thorough overhauling of the system that he was so intent on doing would begin at the very roots. He has gone on record as saying to the scouts, "We're not interested in the best boys on the street, we want the best boy in the town or the area." Perhaps referring back to that stay with the team that Alan remembers, Ferguson continued, "Right away Archie Knox and I were in the gymnasium every night with the young players, assessing the quality. What we did is sign four local boys who we knew weren't of the quality we were looking for, but what we had to do was show an intent, that we'd arrived and we were going to do something about it." It's fair to assume that Alan was one of those, with his fine record of representing local sides. "It is a little bit harsh to say we weren't of the best standard, but it was part of what he had to do to re-invigorate the youth teams. The quote of 'best boy in the area' was doing the rounds in the press. It sounds crazy but I sometimes wonder if our team or the team straight after us were sacrificial lambs in order for him to get it right."

When observing a managerial change at a club in the modern day it's probably fair to say the most commonplace chain of events is that a manager will bring a number of familiar, trusted staff with him from his previous employers. Ever a man to buck the trend, Ferguson brought only Archie Knox, who had been his assistant at Aberdeen. "He kept Eric Harrison and Brian Whitehouse, Nobby Stiles and Brian Kidd came in … It was like a growth thing rather than a new slate. When the manager arrived I think he was disappointed with the number of scouts that covered the North West, so he wanted to grow that." Consequently, it was difficult to predict what kind of plans the new manager was putting in place, particularly for a group of fifteen year-olds.

Alan's own transition hadn't exactly been smooth, or helped by his school. "When I was just training at United, before I'd signed schoolboy terms, I was with them on Mondays and Thursdays and playing games on Saturdays. However, the school I was at had an ethos that you represent your school first, even though you might have as fantastic an opportunity as I had. The school would give me every second Saturday off to go and play with United's B team, and the other I'd have to play with the school. You have to look back and wonder what was that teacher thinking. There were other lads, Mickey Pollitt, a Bolton lad who was goalkeeper, another Bolton lad, Paul Sixsmith, a lad called Jason Lydiate who was a centre half from Salford, all local lads who had no problems in playing for the B team, they all got released from their schools. It was a bit disappointing and my parents had to go and see the head-teachers."

Alan could feel aggrieved with some justification. After all, such restrictions from the school were hampering his chances of settling in seamlessly and making a spot his own. It was around two to three years in to his reign, and Ferguson was beginning to have strong faith in putting youngsters in the first team. "It possibly had an effect, though the lads who got chances were a lot older than me so I wasn't expecting to get in," says Alan. "By the time they were getting opportunities, I was at the club full time. The gaffer was looking to give them a go, a run, and some of them did quite well. When I was training, before I'd signed terms, I was at the club Monday, Thursday, the second Saturday, then Tuesdays I was training with the school, Wednesday extra training with the lads' team. Friday was the only night I got off, because I was playing Saturday and then Sunday morning I'd be playing for Bolton Lads club. With all that training I had to do my GCSE's too!"

In between all that, Alan still had to find time to be a United fan. Perhaps softly hinting at his hopes, his father used to take him to the Youth team games too. "In the early 80s I can remember watching Norman Whiteside, Clayton Blackmore, and Mark Hughes, and there was a game in 1982 where we played Spurs at Old Trafford. Terry Gibson was the captain of the Spurs youth team. I was only about ten at the time but I remember it well. To play in FA Youth Cup games after that was magic, as you would expect. I can recall that I often was quite nervous," says Alan.

When looking back at a professional footballer's career it isn't often that one would be asked to focus so vividly on games they were playing in the Youth team in their mid-teen's. However, most professionals haven't played for Manchester United, and most haven't played in those early days of Sir Alex Ferguson. With the continued success of the manager and the continued emphasis on the youth system, there comes a natural curiosity about the evolution of it over time. Of course, since Alan joined Manchester United in 1987, the world has changed. The role that technological advances have played in how you can instantly communicate with someone on the other side of the globe has in turn had a pointed impact on the way that football supporters can easily communicate with former players.

With the multi-millionaire footballers kept at a distance, supporters are left turning to social networking sites to converse with those who are infinitely more accessible than the well protected mega-stars. Alan began using social networking websites in 2010 and found himself a popular person for United supporters due to his honesty and openness. He confesses, though, that it is only through using social media that he has spoken about his time at Old Trafford. "I'd never really thought about it before. It was part of my life that I went through for a short time, things happened and life moved on. Since using these networks I've done blogs, interviews for newspapers, and you sort of realise the millions of fans that we do have across the world, that some of them have a bit of an interest in what you have to say. It's great. Having said that, it's difficult then to remember exactly what was going through your mind in specific games as a fifteen or sixteen year old.

"I can remember my first game in the Youth Cup, at Darlington. The pitch didn't have much grass on it, it was very tight, and you worry a bit because when you're playing for Man Utd against Darlington you think they're going to want to rough you up a bit. I was nervous, trying to deal with the emotions and the pressure of the expectation to win and you didn't want to cross Eric. We started alright and went two nil up, but they came back and equalised before we pulled away and got another three to win 5-2. Wayne Bullimore scored a free kick and Lee Sharpe played well too.

"Looking at it, our youth team was pretty good. In my first year as an apprentice we reached the quarter final and then in the second year we got to the semis. It was like we were getting there but not quite taking off – like Sir Alex had sown the seeds but it hadn't yet developed. Giggsy (then, of course, Ryan Wilson) arrived in our team a couple of years later and then after that came the team where about seven of them went on to get in the first side. So it is something that I guess you could say, with being born two years earlier, being in that side with that exposure then you never know but you could have got a couple of first team games. You see a lot of great players who perhaps don't make it, then you see some who do make it who perhaps don't necessarily have the talent but have the right attitude. Maybe it is even good fortune."

It wasn't as if Harrison was always so forthcoming in his praise. Most of the time the youngsters lived in fear of him. "Eric had been an uncompromising centre half as a player but hadn't played for top sides. He was a tough customer who would praise you but you'd really have to earn it. He'd like the battles on the pitch, the tackles and he'd really encourage it."

Harrison's methods of motivation have become the stuff of legend, and Alan's recollection of Ferguson's involvement is familiar too, when considering Deiniol's tales. "If United were playing at home especially, you'd notice that Sir Alex or Archie had turned up to watch. They'd go and watch the A team at the Cliff for about twenty or twenty five minutes and then come and watch some of our game at Littleton Road. Even then you could see what a profound interest he had.

"You'd just want to perform well. Even in those days he had a presence due to his achievements, so even though some times I'd be nervous, I learned to concentrate on my own game. You'd still notice if they were around though, because they wouldn't hold back if they saw you do something wrong."

Despite being a regular in the lower teams, Alan feels that he was always going to struggle to get an opportunity in the first team, even with Ferguson's famed faith in youth players. "You don't want to be too critical of yourself and beat yourself up about it, but maybe I just lacked what was needed. I could play in the A and B team, held my own in the Youth team, and got a run or two in the ressies but the transition from reserve football to the first team is a bloody huge jump. I fell a bit short of having what was needed to make the jump from playing in front of a few hundred people to what would always be a sell out when United were playing."

Though that senior appearance ultimately eluded him, playing in the other United sides still gave Tonge plenty of opportunities to play alongside legends of the club. It also presented the chance to play against famous names, though in one of the most memorable A team encounters of his time, Alan was missing with a knee injury. "I'd been out for a couple of weeks by the time we welcomed Liverpool to the Cliff. Our A team gave theirs a murdering, I think we were 4-0 up and Alan Hansen scored an own goal on purpose. The corner came in, he just turned round and banged a header in his own net – he was that furious with losing."

Such determination could be found in United's own ranks, notably Bryan Robson when he was on one of his injury comebacks. "Robson was one of my heroes as a young lad. There's something in psychology called the unspoken word, about people who just have a presence without having to say anything. Eric Cantona has it, so does Bryan. He was the number one in the club at the time, he'd always pull us out of the shit quite a lot. If there were tight games, he'd be the one coming up with a late header or something. It largely depended on Robbo playing whether we had a chance or not. He was fantastic to play alongside too, he had a good head, was great to talk to and could run all game. He was a supreme player who had everything."

After Alan's two year apprenticeship was up, he was given a one year contract. "Through the 1990/91 season, I was still in the reserves or A team, but I wasn't really knocking on the door. We must have had a bad winter, because in the last three weeks of the season we had to play something like six games. In the last week alone, we had four games. We drew with Burnley, then on Tuesday night we won at Morecambe. We won our next game too, and the last game was against Manchester City who were battling with us at the top of the table. It was an end of season decider on Platt Lane and a Manchester derby to boot. Ryan was playing too, and Fergie came to watch. I played at full back and had a good game against a lad called Jason Beckford who was on their left wing and went on to play for Oldham. I kept him quiet, he barely got a kick and we got the result we needed. Afterwards, Fergie came into the dressing room and was full of praise, saying 'Absolutely magnificent lads, and Tongey, absolutely brilliant son'. I was thinking 'hey, that's not bad is it?'"

It proved to be a red herring. "On Monday when I went in for training, I was told he wanted to see me. He said, 'We're not renewing your contract, son.' You look at some of the stories about players being built up before a let down and you wonder if that was what was done with me," Alan laughs. Sincere as he is about whether he was good enough to have made the grade at United, it's hard not to empathise or feel compassion, particularly with the cruel twist that was to follow later for Alan. Away from that, though, there is perhaps more than just a bit of truth in the suggestion that being associated with the better players in the 1992 Youth Cup team gave those with not quite as much natural ability an opportunity due to the spotlight being upon them. "You can't be bitter about timing," says Alan. "You look at that side and see how it gave so many young players the opportunity to play, and that continues today. You can see six or seven youngsters in the first team and they might not have had that opportunity if not for some of the better players in 1992.

"Look at the exposure in today's game. There's even live television coverage of academy league games on the club's television channel, so someone performing well gets attention and mentioned a lot more, possibly fast-tracking them into a chance they might not have got twenty years ago. The everyday life of an apprentice has changed considerably too. I watched a documentary where the journalist Henry Winter went to Chelsea's new training ground and the groundsman had been asked to make car park spaces bigger for the kids as they had 4x4s! Things change, so it's not that I'm bitter about it – it's just an observation. Personally, I look back at what I had to do as an apprentice, the small jobs we had, and I look at those as valuable things I learned for later in life."

The most natural train of thought leads to the case of a young player who is gifted but doesn't make the most of his talent. The 2011 FA Youth Cup winning side was lit up by the sensational performances of Ravel Morrison, yet within a year, after repeated reported incidents of problems in his personal life, he was let go from the club becoming a "what if". Yet in the 2013/14 season his sparkling performances for West Ham lead to speculation that he could be part of the England squad for the 2014 World Cup. "Ravel had such a huge reputation. Just as Giggsy was billed the next Best, he was labelled as the next Giggsy. It's difficult to know exactly what went on. Maybe his background had an impact or perhaps he didn't like the discipline that comes with representing United. It's sad because of what might have been, but people mature and get there at different rates. For arguments sake, Gary Neville might have been a very mature eighteen year-old, and the difference that kind of thing can make cannot be underestimated. You can have all the talent in the world but if you have the wrong attitude you won't last long under Sir Alex".

Even the right attitude, it turned out, wasn't enough to save Alan's career at United and in the summer of 1991 his search for a new club took a bit of an unexpected twist. "It was an interesting one. Exeter's quite a long way, isn't it, but the move becomes a little more logical when exploring the background. When I was an apprentice in the B team, I'd been having a good season and Sir Alex told me he'd put me forward for a Football League representative side in Moscow. The managers of the side were Alan Ball and Lawrie McMenemy – they named me captain of a decent team that included Andy Marriott in goal, Paul Kitson and Carl Griffiths. We won 2-1 and it was a great experience and a great trip. My mum laughs about the trip because they got a phone call from Archie Knox to tell me to pack loads of toilet rolls in my suitcase and my own mug. I don't know if they were winding her up, but the food was horrendous. The first night we had something that looked like an egg swimming in dishwater. The hotel was very basic and I think we might have needed that toilet paper in the end!"

The performance had left an impression with Ball, who by 1991 was the manager of Exeter City. "He remembered me at least so I must have done all right", recalls Alan. He quickly discovered that even though he hadn't made the first team at Old Trafford, being a former Manchester United player carried its own lofty expectations. "Wherever you go, even if you don't want it as a tag, it sticks. It'll always raise an eyebrow, but it wasn't so bad at Exeter as there were a lot of older professionals there including former Arsenal player Steve Williams and Steve Moran, who was an experienced striker. In fact, I can remember Alan feeling that Moran had lost his way, that he could have been a good striker for England."

Not only was Alan making a bold move to leave his family and go to the other end of the country, it was also a significant change in expectations. He was going from playing with other reserves at United and not really expecting a chance, to being a first team former Manchester United player in a team of seasoned pros. "It was magic to start getting games and a proud moment making my league debut", says Alan, "But living down South did take a little getting used to. I stayed in digs with about seven other players and we still had to wash our own kit, spending Sunday nights inspecting bubbles down at the Launderette."

Alan went on to make nineteen appearances for Exeter over the following two seasons, and scored a fine goal from the edge of the area against Stockport County along the way. However, after settling into life in Devon as a squad player in a football league team, disaster struck. "It was strange, something that just came on. I was getting pins and needles down the side of one of my legs and I told the physio I was feeling uncomfortable. It's unbelievable, but we had a match at Swansea and I'd been in the team so I was trying to keep my place. I was in a bad way but felt I had to play against the pain or I might not get my contract renewed. Before the game against Swansea I rubbed that much deep heat on my lower back that I must have looked like the Ready Brek man."

It was a decision that backfired. After the game, in so much agony, Alan sought the advice of a specialist and had an MRI scan. "It was only when it was being explained to me that I wondered what was I doing. My disc had slipped and I was told that one sharp, hard bang would have severed my spinal cord. I'd been generally fit, in fact my game had sort of changed – it's a funny thing, football. Sir Alex had told me he thought I lacked a yard of pace to play in the first team in the top league, yet Alan Ball said I was quite quick. Maybe it was just an excuse to move me on."

Alan underwent rehabilitation in order to save his career. "I had an operation at Frenchay Hospital in Bristol to try and cure it and was in bed for ten days. After I recovered it took six months until I could start light training again but as soon as I did I felt the tingles and had to have another operation. More surgery, and the surgeon told me he recommended that I call it a day as he didn't think I'd ever be right again."

Alan stayed in Exeter until late 1996. He met the lady who would become his wife and give birth to their daughter Lauren there before deciding to move back up North to Bolton and then Scunthorpe, where his wife was originally from. After a relationship split, he moved back to Bolton where he had a son, Sam. He decided to move into education – not necessarily the predicted career path of most former footballers. "When careers end, a lot of players struggle with the transition", admits Alan. "You love the game and it suddenly goes, some can go into the media, but some suffer terribly and can't handle the change. They turn to vices to replace the buzz, but having all my time off with the injury, I began to look at the more psychological aspects of it. I did a degree in sports science, and towards the end of it I looked at how people thought and behaved. From that, it's grown. I picked up a masters degree in philosophy and I've started a PhD on the subject too.

"I'm interested in looking at how players deal with critical moments on a daily basis and if I can get into some writing on that it's very much something I believe in. I think it's a big part of United's success even though I think generally speaking, it's something that in England we're not as great on as you might see elsewhere. There's so much pressure from different sources that it suppresses rather than motivates and there's pressure on what people want you to become. Anyone can remember playing and pretending to be their hero as a kid. My parents always said that they couldn't get me inside when I was eight or nine because I was out playing football. It was a love of the game that I feel gets killed these days, and it's a responsibility of the coaches in today's game to keep that flame burning."

Unsurprisingly, given how passionate Alan is about the impact of psychology in the game, he feels that it will represent the next significant move in the development of quality young players.

"From the mid-nineties to the present game, there's no denying that the alteration of diets and training methods to physically prepare players has been the most fundamental change in the game. "I absolutely believe that dealing with the psychological aspect will be next. You look at clubs today setting up development centres for six to eight year olds. I envisage that clubs will employ coaches with an emphasis on dealing with the mental and psychological aspects, under whatever title or guise that may be. Different levels of ages present different challenges for the players and their bodies. An infant is different to a teenager, a fourteen year-old is different to a sixteen year- old. There are so many different transitional points without even taking into account the external factors of the finance, the cars and the big houses, that it proves very difficult to keep somebody grounded. The earlier you expose people to it, the more you risk changing them as people."

As a self confessed United fan, it's perhaps not surprising at all to learn that Alan feels the club have long benefitted from the master of the art of psychology. "Over the years, Fergie has been the master of keeping that unity. Like the time when he walked round the dressing room and said, 'Look at the person next to you and be glad he's in your team. If you can do that with everyone, then you've got a side'. He's a clever man, a trendsetter of this kind of thing. What Fergie did, you won't find in psychology textbooks or any research that's carried out. He worked fear, normally a bad thing, but used it to its advantage. Manchester United is bigger than anyone, bigger than Sir Alex Ferguson, but he can even use that, and the fact that nobody wants to leave the club, to his advantage.

"He's a master of preparing teams, and there's no-one over the time that he was in charge at United that could rival it." The man who credits Sir Alex as a genius also heaps praise on the impact he has had on other areas of his life. "I carry this into my personal life and my teaching too. You get the core right then you get the discipline right. Fergie got the timekeeping right, the canteen girls serving porridge for breakfast ... if you get the core right, the right level of discipline, it can have a profound impact on all walks of your life. The humility, the mental toughness, that's the thing that I learned most from people like Eric and Sir Alex Ferguson. Not necessarily playing in the first team, but in the right grounding."

With such a fresh, modern outlook on the game, Alan harbours hope that he could one day be back at United explaining his thoughts and predictably, the matter of psychology is something that the club are exploring as they continue to stay ahead of the rest when it comes to the development of young players as people. He had spoken to staff at the club around the time they were waiting to discover which Category Status they had been awarded under the new Premier League system for youth development. "United were ultimately granted the highest status, Category One, and plan to recruit analysts for the junior teams," says Alan. "I hope, as part of my PhD, to work with some of the junior players in this field. I would hope that my experience of the environment at United, my knowledge of the culture of a professional footballer that perhaps your traditional sports psychologist might not have, will help me communicate with players. Players are sceptical about academic types so maybe people like me can make a breakthrough. After all at the end of the day, you've had that experience. You might have only had it for a short period of time, but you've rubbed shoulders with big hitters, you've been in the goldfish bowl, so hopefully the things you say and do can make a difference. Though being United daft, I'm not quite sure I'd be as enthusiastic to do the same developing Liverpool or City youngsters."

4

Mike Pollitt

The remarkable fact that two members of the class of 1992 were still registered to play professionally in English football at the time of the 2013/14 season will be discussed later, yet Mike Pollitt, a member of a youth team prior to that most famous one was still registered with FA Cup winners Wigan Athletic as they began life in the Championship following an eight year stay in the Premier League.

Pollitt's football career could almost be described as like the "Benjamin Button story" in terms of how it's gone about. Where most footballers either stay at one or two clubs and then later in their career add a few more to their CV in short stays here and there, Pollitt's early footballing life was relatively nomadic until he reached the age of 29. That was when he signed for Rotherham United. Up until that point, in a career that included permanent transfers to Bury, Lincoln City Darlington, Notts County and Sunderland, and loan spells at Oldham Athletic (twice), Macclesfield, Lincoln (again), Altrincham, Gillingham, and Brentford, (so, just the eleven clubs then), Pollitt's longest spell at a club was the three years he was at Manchester United after he was brought to Old Trafford as an apprentice in 1988.

"I was at Bolton Boys Club and was scouted by a man called George Knight who sadly passed away in 2011," says Mike. "I went down for a week's trial at Salford and it went from there. At the end of that week, Alex Ferguson and the youth development officer Joe Brown offered me schoolboy terms. I turned it down as I was going on a trial to Everton the week after, but when I told them that they came back to me more or less straight away and offered me a YTS so I signed as with the schoolboy deal, there would be no guarantee of a YTS.

"As a kid you always want to go to the best teams. United were still up there and still had the reputation even in those days, and my team Bolton were in the old Fourth Division. I had been training with them and wanted to play for them, so I think I was seen as something of a traitor to go and sign for United. I really was Bolton crazy, I'd go and watch them home and away and to be honest I'd be one of those chanting against United.

"It was quite funny at the time, but I didn't want to miss out and once I got to the club it sort of changed my mind, changed my alliances and even to this day I still want them to win the league." The size of the club would never be questioned, but the condition of the facilities in those early days was more or less down to opinion, with some feeling it was basic, and others who were used to lower level facilities more appreciative of the Cliff. "Obviously compared to these days it looks very basic but at the time they were very good," Mike says. "Nobody had the kind of things they have these days so I'd say United had some of the better facilities."

Another story that differs depending on any individual that you speak to is the approach to youth development of Eric Harrison and Sir Alex Ferguson in the early years of the Scot's reign. "I got on well with Eric. I was a bit of cheeky chappie as a youngster so I think he, Brian Kidd and Nobby Stiles kind of took to me because of that," Pollitt suggests. "Eric was an old fashioned centre half and was a tough disciplinarian but I think it stood me in good stead. Youngsters today get away with far too much and at United we would always know if we stepped out of line. He was always a fair guy with me. Yeah, there'd be days when Fergie and Archie Knox would make us stay behind all afternoon and clean the sauna and the boots. I actually used to clean the manager's boots. He wanted them nice and shiny. I also did Mike Duxbury's boots, he was a really nice fella, and Paul McGrath too.

"We'd have to clean the changing rooms but it was just a test for the youngsters to see the other side of it. Archie would put his finger on the top of the door and if there was dust on it he'd be like 'Right, let's start again!' We'd be there all day. At the time it annoys you but when you look back it was a good grounding for us all. People go to United and have the world at their feet so it was a really good process to bring us back down to earth."

Mike feels that the routines put in place by the staff were character building. "I'd say that is the case. There was one time when the season was over and they had us at Littleton Road helping the ground staff. We'd wonder what they were playing at but looking back you realise they were helping you," he admits. "You look at the youngsters today, their lack of responsibility and wonder if it has had an effect on their personalities. I'm old school, though, aren't I? But I do try and pass on my experience and things that I learned at Old Trafford."

Jim Leighton, and later Les Sealey, were the senior goalkeepers during Mike's time at the club, with Gary Walsh out injured. "They were very different characters. Jim signed in my first year and he was a very lovely fella, always willing to help. When Les came in he was completely different, a typical Cockney, always screaming and ranting and raving," laughs Mike. "It was no different to how he was on the pitch and you definitely knew when Les was there. I really got on well with Gary, I do to this day, we spent time at Wigan together. At the time, Mark Bosnich was at United as well so we had a fair few good keepers."

The quality in front of him meant Pollitt was forced to look elsewhere for first team football early on. In October 1990, shortly after signing professional terms, Mike went on loan to Oldham Athletic. "Eric Harrison spoke to me and said Joe Royle wanted to take me as cover. I was playing for the reserves on a plastic pitch and wasn't really happy about diving about on a car park so I went there. It had only been a few months since we'd been playing against them at Maine Road in that FA Cup semi final, too. I was only with Oldham for a short time but then came back."

Another short loan at Macclesfield Town followed where Pollitt made his senior debut against Boston United in the Conference, but at the end of the 1990/91 season, with Ferguson about to bring in Peter Schmeichel, the decision was taken to release Mike. "The amount of keepers who were in front of me was just too much," he said. "I signed professional hoping that I'd at least get in the reserves, but then I was in the A team, then the B team, and then I had a spell where I wasn't playing at all and after the loan spells I knew the writing was on the wall," Mike admits. "The manager was fantastic with me though, and said he'd try and get me another club. He was good to his word and got me a trial at Bury where Wilf McGuinness and his son Paul were, and then I signed a contract there. Unfortunately the highly rated Irish keeper Gary Kelly was there in the first team but it was still a decent step up for me in that I could at least play reserve team football, which I wasn't doing at United.

"I was part of the first team squad without really being selected, and at the start of the 1992/93 season I went on loan to Altrincham for a few months and played a few games. Then I went on loan to Lincoln almost straight after and they took over my contract when I started becoming their first choice goalkeeper." It was at Lincoln where Mike made his Football League debut at the tender age of 20 but after a two year spell where he played 57 games, he moved to Darlington for a year where he played more than fifty games.

In November 1995, he was signed by Notts County, who were managed by Steve Thompson, the man who had managed Mike for a while at Lincoln. "It didn't really work out. Darren Ward was in goal, he was difficult to dislodge, and life as a goalkeeper can be difficult," he said. "I signed in 1995 but didn't play my first game for County until 1997. Sam Allardyce came in as manager and I had a crazy season in 1997/98 when I was on loan at four different clubs, Oldham, Gillingham, Brentford and then I finished at Sunderland," says Mike. "I just wanted to play, I ended up playing more than thirty games that season but it was difficult living away from home and not being there for Christmas. At the end of the day I was getting games and that's what I wanted. I was hoping at the end of the season I'd get a move where I could settle, and fortunately that's what happened."

After much movement in the seven years that had passed since he was at United, Mike finally settled down in South Yorkshire when Rotherham United signed him. "That was obviously one of the best times of my career, it's where I played the most games and we had some good times," he admits. "We played in the Championship which was a tremendous achievement for a club of that size. The stadium wasn't massive, we were just a bunch of lads who rolled our sleeves up and did everything together. It was a really good journey and I had six good years at Millmoor. It shows what a close bunch of players we were that we still keep in touch all this time later."

Pollitt played 269 league games for Rotherham from 1998 to 2005 (with only one punctuation – a year at Chesterfield in the 2000/01 season where he played every league game) and is regarded as the best goalkeeper in the Millers history. "Obviously I'm very proud of that achievement and that recognition and it's a club that I will always look out for."

Following a record 77 clean sheets at Rotherham, and at the age of 33, Pollitt's commitment to getting an established career despite his problems of getting a run were rewarded by a move back into the big time. Wigan Athletic had just been promoted to the Premier League in 2005 when they swooped for Mike as back-up to their goalkeeper John Filan. It was an opportunity he couldn't turn down.

"I'd had four seasons in the Championship but Rotherham were in big financial trouble and had just been relegated, plus I was a Bolton lad and travelling to Rotherham every day wasn't easy so when Wigan came in it felt like a great move and my last opportunity to play in the Premier League. I'd done the rounds a little bit so you could say it was payback time. I would say that I'd been a sales rep for ten years and finally got an office job," he confesses. "I signed thinking I'd be number two but then John got injured and I was there, playing their first ever game in the top flight. It was a bit surreal playing Chelsea who were the Champions, and we were a bit gutted to have lost in the last minute."

Thankfully that wasn't to be a sign of things to come as the Latics were a real success story that season. "It was a bit of a fairytale, to be honest," says Mike. "We went on a long unbeaten run and then were in the top five for quite a long time, even second at one point, it was an unbelievable start, and of course there was also the Carling Cup run. We got to the semi final and were drawn against Arsenal. I think we all thought we were going to get knocked out, but we won the first leg 1-0 and managed to go through on the away goals at their place. They had their full team out, including some top players like Thierry Henry and Dennis Bergkamp. It was one of the best games of my life."

Pollitt was in inspired form, saving a penalty from Jose Antonio Reyes in the first half and stopping a multitude of attempts with every piece of his body from the Gunners before finally being beaten in the 65th minute by Henry. Wigan held on to take the game into extra time and future United hero Robin van Persie looked to have put Arsenal through with a stunning free kick that Mike had no chance with, but then in the last minutes of the second period of extra time, Jason Roberts pounced to strike a crucial away goal.

Wigan had done the unthinkable and qualified for the League Cup Final where, as fate would have it, they would face Manchester United. Pollitt had been in goal for the first ever league clash between the two in December 2005 when United won comprehensively at Old Trafford, but to repeat that in a major final was to be a special day for the goalkeeper who had departed the club some fifteen years previous. However, the occasion at the magnificent Millennium Stadium in Cardiff was to end in disaster for Pollitt. "I've never been injured in my life, it was unbelievable. The only time it happens is in the first few minutes of a major Cup Final against Manchester United", Mike exclaims. "I wish I had a pound for everyone who told me how sorry they were for me as everyone was saying to me for ages. I was disappointed, gutted, but there's not a lot you can do when your hamstring snaps in half."

With less than quarter of an hour on the clock, Pollitt was replaced by Filan. Just as Mike had done in Manchester, Filan conceded four goals to the Reds, with a second half spell of three goals in six minutes in a blistering attack that they just had no response to. Sadly for Pollitt, the injury had a significant impact on his first team career at the JJB/DW Stadium. Chris Kirkland, once capped by England, came in as first choice and ever since then Pollitt has more or less moved into a coaching role as Kirkland and more recently, Ali Al-Habsi, were number one goalkeepers at Wigan.

In the immediate aftermath of the 2006 Carling Cup Final, Pollitt's woes were exacerbated with the speculation that he may even have made England's World Cup squad, such was his great form. "England had a few injuries at that time so it was encouraging to see my name mentioned", he says. "There weren't loads of English keepers in the Premier League, so people were saying I might have had a chance, but I was injured and Scott Carson, who was playing for Sheffield Wednesday in the Championship went instead. You never know, I might have gone, but it's not something to really dwell upon, and funnily enough, Scott just joined Wigan and I was sharing a room with him in pre-season in America, so we were talking about it."

It may not make up for the disappointment in 2006, but Mike proved he was still capable when called upon as he participated in the historic FA Cup success for Wigan in the 2012/13 season, playing against Bournemouth in the third round. "To get to the Carling Cup Final was a great achievement but to win the FA Cup with Wigan, is an achievement that you compare with Wimbledon beating Liverpool back in 1988", says Mike. "With all the millions spent by Manchester City, it might even have been bigger. It was a surreal day, Ben Watson coming on after being out so long injured with a broken leg, and then getting the winner in the last minute. I think every neutral in the country, or everyone who wasn't a City fan, wanted us to win. I said to Gary Caldwell on the bench when Ben was coming on that it would be amazing if he got the winner for us, and he did. It was just a really incredible day."

It wouldn't be too far fetched to consider that Pollitt may have kept his place in the cup run, especially considering Joel Robles, who featured in the final, was signed following another ill-timed injury to Pollitt. "I'd ruptured my thigh against Bournemouth so that did me for the rest of the season," he says. "I was able to take part in the warm up and sit on the bench for the final so I was kept involved and to at least have played a little part is nice."

Twenty two years after signing professional terms at Manchester United, Mike has no intention of retiring as a player just yet. "I'm going into my ninth season at the club and I've enjoyed it, I might well get a testimonial", he laughs. "It's now the longest I've spent at a club and I've seen so many players come and go, I'm actually the longest serving player at Wigan having signed when I was 33! Even at 42, I'm fighting fit ... everyone keeps asking me that but I want to keep going. We've got a day off today, I woke up this morning at about 4am and found myself running for about an hour and half. You're a long time retired, so I want to keep at that as long as I can until I move into coaching."

As Mike moved more into the coaching side of the game, the most United supporters would see of him was when he and Ryan Giggs would often be seen talking on the pitch before and after games. The pair played together back in 1990. "It's amazing to think what he's gone on to achieve. He's one of the best ever players and you can't imagine anyone will ever have the same success as he has had at one club," says Mike. "I remember being in that Italian tournament when he changed his name from Wilson to Giggs – the coaches had our passports and shouted out 'Giggs', none of us knew who it was, we thought it was a new signing! He's come a long way since then and it's always good to have a chat. And it's the same with the manager as he never forgot me, it's fantastic. I'm still a staunch Bolton fan but if you spend any length of time at United you sort of get converted. I learned things there I wouldn't have learned anywhere else. Knowing the Manchester United way of behaving and conducting myself has stood me in good stead."

5

Russell Beardsmore

One of the first Fledglings to make a really successful mark on the Manchester United first team scene was Russell Beardsmore. The Wigan-born midfielder had been brought to the club under Ron Atkinson but echoes the thoughts of Deiniol Graham when explaining why he wasn't given a chance under the charismatic personality. "There's no disrespect intended to Ron but at the time he really didn't seem to be that focussed with the youth or reserve teams," says Russell. "He had the first team squad and that was it, he wouldn't look outside that fourteen or fifteen. As soon as Sir Alex came in he made it his business to know about every single individual at the club. It was something he'd go on to do forever, but it was a huge change when he first came in.

"He'd always be asking how players were getting on. He'd call Eric Harrison when we were on the coach going to a game, asking how such and such had got on. It was a completely different mentality to what we were used to." Such an approach inevitably had an invigorating effect on all of the players. "Speaking for myself, I was only a year into my apprenticeship so I was a bit nervous," he admits. "But the good thing is that when a new manager comes in, it can be a new clean slate for everybody. So even those who weren't in Ron's plans could start afresh. It was clear that the manager was going to give everyone a chance and for me I just felt I could at least get my head down and concentrate on my apprenticeship.

"I was staying in digs around the corner from the Cliff – it was literally overlooking the pitch. I stayed with Iris and Bill, and Drew McBride and Paul Harvey were there. I apologise to Iris and Bill as I can't remember their second name. Mark Hughes lived on the corner of the street, so it was strange being that close to it and having it around you all of the time."

It would be a misconception to attribute the early wave of young players breaking into the first team picture under the new manager simply to an injury crisis. In the pre-season of the 1988/89 season, Russell was taken alongside Lee Martin and Jonny Rodlund on the pre-season tour of Scandinavia. "I was called up after Micky Duxbury was injured, and played in games against Valerengens, Karlstad and Trollhattans," says Russell. "I think the manager's approach to us as younger players was that we should be good enough so he was going to give us that chance and we could sink or swim. We were getting tasters – a couple of days later, I played against Hamburg at Old Trafford and it was just starting to happen all of a sudden."

Just five games into the season, and Beardsmore was named as a substitute against West Ham at Old Trafford. "I was nervous, but we were winning so that calmed me down a bit," says Russell. "I came on in the second half and the atmosphere was brutal. I tried to shout something to Lee Martin who was only about five yards from me but he couldn't hear me. The stadiums were all standing then, and when the Stretford End was full you just had no chance of communicating on the pitch.

"West Ham had Paul Ince in their midfield and I was directly up against him. A lot was being made of him at the time, as to how good he was. I remember things like that but not much from the game itself." Beardsmore made another substitute appearance four days later, on his twentieth birthday, in the League Cup win at Rotherham and a fortnight after that was given his first start against the same opponents at Old Trafford. Substitute appearances at Wimbledon and Arsenal followed before he was given the perfect Christmas present, his first league start, at Old Trafford on Boxing Day against Nottingham Forest.

"Because I'd been around the squad for a time I knew that I might get an opportunity but I was still surprised to get the chance," he says. "It was such a tough game. In the last quarter of an hour I was exhausted from playing against England players like Steve Hodge and Neil Webb. Steve Hodge was such a great runner, always going forward, and it meant that I was trying to play my own game but watch him too. It drained me."

Russell had clearly done enough to retain his place for the visit of Liverpool five days later. It was to prove a pivotal moment in his career and that of the media interpretation of Sir Alex's plans at Manchester United. The game on New Year's Day was televised and a strong Liverpool team took the lead on 70 minutes after a fiercely contested game. United responded immediately and it was a mesmerising dribble from Beardsmore that created the equaliser for Brian McClair. Russell was involved in the next goal for Mark Hughes before grabbing a goal of his own, a wonderfully controlled volley in front of the Stretford End. "A lot of my mates were scousers and I knew they'd all be watching," recalls Russell. "We were a decent side but that was a good Liverpool side, I don't think they've had a better one since. I can't remember much of the goal going in but I can remember that we had a spell of about twenty minutes, a real purple patch, where everything went well. Then of course I can remember Lee Sharpe crossing the ball for me to volley in. The only bad thing about it was that we had to play Middlesbrough away the very next day! I couldn't move, the pitch was hardly fantastic, and after about an hour we were drained. It was ridiculous, the high of beating Liverpool to the low of losing to Middlesbrough the day after." Injuries did play a part in the following couple of weeks including the QPR FA Cup tie in which a number of the youngsters were called into the squad.

For Russell, he was delighted that his friends were all coming through at the same time. "It was fantastic to have trained with all these guys and then they all started playing in the team with you," he says. "We'd all been together for about three years. We weren't all pally-pally but most of us were mates off the pitch and it was a big thing for us. It was also a big thing for Eric Harrison, a huge feather in his cap. He would never take the plaudits but he deserved a lot of credit for the work he'd done. We weren't just breaking through as one-hit wonders so to speak, but we were getting in on a regular basis, and that was a big reward for how hard Eric had worked."

Russell shares the view that Harrison was hard but fair. "I think he was harder with certain players because they had so much potential. He knew they weren't a million miles away but they might just be drifting. Yeah, he could definitely shout at you but it was because he cared and wanted you to make the best you could of yourself," says Russell. "Eric would always be there to give advice, I'd always find him approachable. He was down to earth and I knew he wanted the best for me. I found him great, definitely hard but definitely fair too."

Russell was also benefitting from the guidance of experienced professionals such as Mike Duxbury and Bryan Robson. "They were all amazing, but for me personally, I'd have to say Bryan Robson if only because I played directly alongside him in midfield. He was absolutely fantastic with all the players and the kids," Russell enthuses. "He'd take you to one side in training or at half time to give you little bits of advice. When you're losing a game at Old Trafford and the crowd are restless, having Bryan saying 'Don't worry, play your game' is absolutely valuable. He was definitely the biggest influence and it meant a lot having encouragement instead of criticism if I gave the ball away, for example. The other players did the same, spoke to you and gave you advice, but I have to say Bryan stands out for me."

Such interaction and guidance was to prove vital. In the early months of 1989, and particularly following the televised game with Arsenal in which Jules Maiorana became the latest youngster to shine, the press attention and description of the Fledglings really began to intensify. "The club were good in keeping us grounded. Eric wouldn't let it go to our head," he laughs. "I thought it was a bit over the top comparing us to the Busby Babes, you could see where they were coming from but it was a lot to ask from a bunch of kids who had played half a dozen games. I think if anyone was to take the pressure from that, it was the manager and not us players."

Ferguson attempted to alleviate that pressure by making a number of big money signings in the summer of 1989. "I remember being on holiday and reading the paper, Mick Phelan, Danny Wallace and Paul Ince coming in. All midfielders," Russell laughs. In the short term, he needn't have worried, he was riding the crest of a wave and even with a new flurry of arrivals, could still consider himself to be a first teamer. As the 1988/89 season drew on, Russell was selected for the England under-21 side on five occasions, including being in the squad for the

Toulon tournament.

"It was like a blur as that season went on," he says. "You just have to keep your feet on the ground, and concentrate. You can't afford to have one or two bad games at United because they are such a big club, the expectations are huge." Indeed they are, and that was certainly true of the first weeks of the 1989/90 campaign. United were to suffer one of their darkest days in September with a crushing 5-1 defeat at Maine Road. The supporters were unhappy and staged a pitch invasion, and following Russell's substitution after he'd been one of the better players, they chanted for him to be brought back on.

"I remember the pitch invasion and a few of the lads looked terrified. We just never got going, even after Hughesies goal which I set up," says Beardsmore. "I don't know the stats, but it seemed like they only had five attacks and scored every time. Everything went in. I have to be honest, it's the worst I ever felt after a game in my career. I lost big at Bournemouth, but nothing came close to that feeling. I was local, living in Salford, and it bothered me that much I didn't go out for about six or eight weeks. I was gobsmacked."

Thus followed a period of intense pressure on the manager, to the point where his very future at the club was up for debate. If he was feeling any pressure though, it did not translate to the players. "He is unbelievable at keeping some emotions in check, at not putting some of it on to the players. As time goes by people say he got more mellow on match days with United winning, but in those early days you do sense a natural tension following the result. But on the Monday, it'd all be forgotten, he'd be sat whistling in his office and preparing for the next game. He wouldn't show if he was feeling it."

Protests on the terraces were becoming more prominent and there was a growing feeling, as the FA Cup game against Nottingham Forest came closer, that defeat would mean the end of Ferguson's spell as manager. Entering 1990, United were in 15th position and just two points above the relegation zone. Going into the Forest tie, Beardsmore and his fellow players understood how difficult the game was going to be. "We were underdogs going in, massive underdogs. Nobody expected us to win," he says. "It wasn't a great game, but the goal from Mark was. I got a whack from Gary Charles and needed stitches but it was brilliant, I didn't mind. In the dressing room afterwards, there was relief, but also an excitement in the air. It started a feeling that we were moving in the right direction."

From that point, everything changed at United. An epic cup run masked league disappointment (with United finishing in 13th and still only five points away from relegation) and there was a poignancy in another Fledgling, Lee Martin, scoring the goal that won Sir Alex his first trophy as United manager. Beardsmore is immensely proud of being part of that group. "It was a difficult time at the club but we played a part in the cup run, we all did, and that was the one that got the ball rolling. Obviously it's a different task to win the league but at the time, that first trophy was vital," he says.

Sadly for Russell, United's own development was in direct contrast to his own. First team opportunities became rarer as Ferguson sought to build on that initial success. "It doesn't matter who you speak to from any time at United, they'll all say they should have perhaps played more games, and I'm no different. I'd have loved to have played a hundred more times, and played alongside the likes of Roy Keane. It would have been wonderful but it wasn't to be – it's still great to have played your part in a great history," says Beardsmore.

His contribution wasn't done just yet. Of the games he did get, they more often than not came on European nights, with United embarking on a landmark season in the European Cup Winners' Cup during 1990/91. "I was excited to play my part in the earlier rounds and maybe I was unlucky as when it got to the later rounds, more senior players came in and kept their place," he says. "If they had the same rules then for substitutes, and bigger benches, then I may well have got winners medals for those games but it was just one of those things. Two subs in the FA Cup – how harsh is that on players who played in earlier rounds as they deserve a medal too,"

He was to get a medal, as a substitute who didn't get on to the pitch, for United's win over Red Star Belgrade in the European Super Cup. "I'm not one for collecting but I'm obviously very happy to have got it, and maybe I did deserve it for just missing out on the other occasions. My mum and dad have it alongside my Charity Shield medal for the time we shared it. They're proud of it, and one day in the future they'll probably go to my son."

An unsuccessful loan period at Blackburn Rovers did not help Beardsmore's chances of first team football and, with hindsight, he is disappointed for a few reasons. "It's not just the success which followed, although that is a part of it," he says. "But it would have been great to have played with some of those brilliant players who came along. I think how I could have played alongside them, what I could have achieved. In practice games I'd play against the likes of Cantona and Keane, but it wasn't the same as it would have been playing with them."

In 1993, at the age of 24, Russell made the difficult decision to leave. "It was said to me by Brian Whitehouse that I probably left a year too late but I had an injury, and to tell the truth, the manager did actually offer me another year on my contract," he says. "He was honest and said I was a good lad but that he didn't really see me as part of his first team plans but he would give me that chance. It was a wrench. When you're at United you're dangling, thinking, if there's an injury or something I could be right back in. And what would happen if I'd left and then that opportunity came up? It was never going to happen. Maybe it was naïve but if there's that small half of a percent chance, you hang on. I decided to leave after the manager's offer, and he wished me the best."

Contact had been made with Russell by Swiss club Grasshoppers and Birmingham, but no firm offers were on the table. "Because I'd been out injured, they wanted me to come and train and not have a contract. But I couldn't really train at that point," says Russell. "It was difficult to commit to anything and with pre-season dragging on, it was frustrating without a wage coming in. But then I met Tony Pulis, the Bournemouth manager, at the Hilton Hotel at Manchester Airport. He said not to worry about my fitness, it was okay for me to miss a couple of months, and offered me a good three year deal. They also signed Joe Parkinson who was a friend of mine, and the plans they had at the club seemed good. It was a wrench as Bournemouth is a world away from Manchester United in terms of the size of the club and obviously being so far away from home."

Little did he know at the time, particularly after a difficult start, but Beardsmore was on the first steps to a relationship with his new club that exists to this day. "Even though Tony brought me to the club, it wasn't until he left and Mel Machin came in that I really began to enjoy myself," he says. "That's not meant as anything against Tony, but his style of football is obviously very different. Mel played me in midfield, and I really enjoyed it. We got better and better and had two seasons where we probably should have been promoted twice. It was tough with seasoned professionals playing aggressively but once I was settled I had some really good times."

Having played over 170 times for the Cherries and really enjoying his career, disaster was to strike when Russell was forced to retire with a back injury, prompting an unwelcome comparison between his situation and that of Alan Tonge who had endured similar heartache. "I took it really badly, I admit," he says. "I had the operation on my back and it didn't get any better. I was out of contract and didn't know where I was going. You get lost and don't know who you are, the phone doesn't ring anymore. Football can be such an isolated game if you find yourself out of it. I went up to Bolton to work there as a Community Officer but that didn't work out, even though it was good for me being back in the game. My marriage fell apart and I got divorced and my daughter, who had left all her friends in the South, was alone up North. Within two years I'd done a full circle and went back to Bournemouth in a similar role, and I've been there ever since. It's a rewarding job, very varied, where I'm coaching all sorts of people in all sorts of environments. I'm as proud of the work I've done with Bournemouth as I am for what I did at United."

As with some other former players, Russell has been selected for the Masters football tournaments in recent years representing Manchester United and that has led to a re-birth of sorts in his relationship with the club. "After I played in one of the tournaments, Viv Anderson told me to call him and he'd put me in touch with someone at the club," says Beardsmore. "I go up and do match-day hospitality. I love Bournemouth and don't mean any disrespect to them but when I'm back from United I'm on a high for two or three days. I admit it's difficult to go back to normal work after, as to be remembered after twenty years means so much to me. Everyone always looks back and picks that 'one game', and mine obviously is the Liverpool match. To have played 73 times for United is something I'm very proud of. It's not a matter of being big-headed but for people to remember you and acknowledge you as part of the history of the club is something that is very special."

6

Giuliano Maiorana

No record of this nature would be complete without the story of Giuliano "Jules" Maiorana. In fact, Maiorana would sit somewhere near the top of most people's "Where are they now?" lists when looking back at brief but notable first team careers at Old Trafford. Perhaps the fall into relative obscurity hasn't been helped by the man himself. "I would get people recognising me and asking if I was the guy who used to play for Manchester United," he says. "I would deny it as I didn't really want a fuss. I didn't want people to just come up and talk to me because of a novelty factor, I want to be liked and known for who I am as a person." Such a black and white view is typical of Maiorana's pragmatic overlook on life. It was from obscurity, of course, that he was plucked and thrust into the limelight back in 1988.

Perhaps one of the reasons why Maiorana's name sticks in the memory is because of the exotic sound – his Italian grandparents were Prisoners of War in World War II, captured by Americans. They were transferred to Cornwall where they were treated well by locals, so well that they were invited to return to work in the late 1940s, and moved to Cambridgeshire. "Both of my parents are from a small village in Italy called Cassino Irpino, in the province of Avellino. Over time most of my grandfather's family moved over here, including my father who was married to my mother", says Jules. "I was born in 1969 and from the age of four or five I had a football under my arm, I was football mad."

There are a number of different accounts as to how Maiorana was discovered and how the transfer to Manchester United came about out of the blue. One thing consistent in all stories is that he was playing at a level that would be kindly described as semi-professional. Jules had trials with Cambridge United but was never signed. However, in November 1988, he was able to enjoy a rapid rise to prominence. "The Cambridge thing was odd – they said I was too small. We had a practice match with the triallists and they asked me to run the line as linesman. After about ten minutes I thought 'I'm not having this' so I just chucked the flag down and went. I was only playing Sunday football until I was about 18, and the dream of becoming a professional footballer had faded. I was playing a five-a-side competition with my brother, and the manager of Histon watched it. He invited us to go to training there and in about six months I was in the first team," he says.

"I played about twenty or thirty games there until one Wednesday night I was told after a game that Manchester United wanted me. I thought it was a load of bull, that I was being wound up, but when I went in to see the club on the Thursday they confirmed it was real and that United wanted to give me a trial. I was nervous as hell so was hoping it would be in two or three weeks but it turned out to be straight away. United are United aren't they, you don't turn that down. On Sunday I was told I had to go on the Monday for a week." Maiorana's head was spinning, as anyone's would be, yet the craziness had barely begun.

"I went up with Alan Doyle, who was the Histon manager, and we were late. Thank God we were as I was so nervous and knackered too. We got up at five and drove up to Manchester, getting there for about ten. I got to training which hadn't even started as they were waiting for me and Brian Kidd shouted, 'What's your name?' I told him and he asked what they call me for short. I said 'Ju', but he said, 'Alright Jules.' I was going to say something but then I thought I'm only going to be here for a week so I'll let them call me what they want. I never thought I was going to be there any longer. Six weeks later I was in the first team."

United had acted fast to sign him. Sir Alex Ferguson wrote in his New Straits Times column on December 11, 1988, that Tottenham Hotspur and Chelsea were among the admirers who wanted to sign the young winger. "I knew of Spurs but Chelsea was news to me. I had heard something that Spurs were interested, or rumours to that end – it was just so surreal that I'm driving up to Manchester on a Monday and the day after I'm playing for them." Before that, Jules played in a practice match. "I was actually hoping, with being late, I'd missed training but when I got up there they said they'd waited for me. I thought 'You're having a laugh', but we had a practice game and I remember how tough it was. I was taking players on but they were sticking to me like glue. I was quick and I could get past players but these guys I was up against at United – I was 19, and they were 17 or 18 but I couldn't shake them off. I wasn't used to it."

Jules had done enough to convince Ferguson to give him a chance the following day in a testimonial that had been arranged for Ian Handysides, the Birmingham City player who had suffered an injury in pre-season and had to retire from the game with immediate effect. Maiorana was starstruck. "It was weird. I remember looking up at some point in the game and there was Trevor Francis in the opposition. I'd only seen these guys on television. It might have been alright if I'd actually been at Cambridge and had some kind of exposure or experience of playing with these professionals but it all felt a little strange. I'd only been with them one day training, but I went down on the coach and there was police around. I didn't know what was going on, but we were late and were being given a police escort to the ground. I was used to going to games in a minibus if not a car. It really was a strange time, especially coming from where I had," admits Maiorana.

If he was suffering from nerves, his performance didn't show it. In front of 22,000 spectators at St. Andrews, the youngster gave a fearless display in what Sir Alex would describe in that Times column as "one of the best displays I have ever seen from a triallist" – it shouldn't come as a surprise then, that they reacted immediately to secure the signing of the young prodigy. "I was brought off at half time and they offered me a four year contract there and then," says Jules. "Within six days I had gone from learning that United wanted to see me on trial to signing a contract. People use the term 'it's like a rollercoaster' but it really was, it was ridiculous."

Gradually, Maiorana became acclimatised to his surroundings. "After a few weeks of training I got quicker myself, so I was able to play more naturally. In January 1989 I was on the bench against Millwall at Old Trafford and went on. I was running down the wing and it was a strange experience, it kept feeling like my ears were blocking and then unblocking through breathing heavily after running down the wing. I just heard the crowd chanting 'United, United' fading in and out of my ears. I remember then looking around the whole of the ground, it was a surreal moment seeing all of those supporters, there were 40,000 people there, as I was used to playing in front of fifty people."

At the time, it didn't really come as much of a surprise that Jules had got an opportunity, even if the way he had been brought to the club in the first place was a big surprise. After all, Ferguson was giving chances to the kids – David Wilson, Tony Gill, Russell Beardsmore, Lee Martin and Lee Sharpe had all played fewer than twenty games and all featured in that Millwall game, with Deiniol Graham, as we've already discussed in this anthology, a player who had also featured as well as Mark Robins. Still, it is understandable that it would take some getting used to. It's difficult enough to imagine the pressure on a bunch of young players getting opportunities all of a sudden even if they've been at the club for a couple of years, but to be thrown into such an arena with only weeks of preparation is something else entirely.

Maiorana's next appearance came two months later, again as a substitute, against Luton Town, before being given the ultimate exposure the following week in a start against Arsenal at Old Trafford. It's fairly difficult to comprehend the enormity of the occasion – one of the biggest games in English football, given a television slot too, without even taking into account the conditions of the pitch that day. "If it had been in today's era, I think they would have called it off," says Jules. It didn't faze him. "After the game I had to do a presentation in one of the suites at Old Trafford and there were still loads of fans there. They were saying 'Do you realise you've just taken the piss out of the England full back? The thing is with football, it's like anything else, when things are going well people are quick to pat you on the back, but as soon as things aren't going well they can act like you don't exist," he explains.

Jules' words give a hint about the troubles he was about to face. Though Ferguson had spoken with glowing praise about him in the media, behind the scenes they struggled to get along, which probably goes some way to explaining the fact that after three more first team outings, as sub in the return against

Millwall, a start in the home game against Derby County and then coming on as a substitute in the win over Wimbledon at Old Trafford in early May of 1989, Maiorana would struggle to get back into the first team.

"I have to admit, I didn't really see eye to eye with Ferguson. My idols were Italian, and I had some of that character in me naturally, but Ferguson would always be on at me to cut my hair. It wasn't as if I had hair like Karel Poborsky either" Jules says. "I wouldn't even say I was a rebel, I was just my own person, but perhaps the fact that I didn't bow down to him or do everything he said meant things weren't great between us."

It provides an interesting contrast to the stories of Ferguson and/or the coaches breaking the confidence of the younger players through their strict disciplinary methods. Though not necessarily rebellious or a natural contrarian, the fact that the strong-willed Maiorana stood toe to toe with a man equally recognised for not giving an inch, may have stood him in bad stead when looking at his long term future at United. The contrast, however, lies in the fact that Maiorana was not disheartened by the hard way United trained their youngsters at the time. In fact, it was quite the opposite, with Jules receiving some lofty praise. "Some people need the 'hairdryer' as it's known, and some people need an arm around the shoulder. It was great at first, I really got on with everyone. Perhaps that's the most hurtful thing, I got on very well with everyone apart from the man who counted. One time when I was out injured, I was watching one of the games and Brian Kidd came up to me and said 'It must be sickening for you to watch that lot, if I was the manager, you'd be one of the first on the team sheet.'

"There was another tournament in the Isle of Man where Lawrie McMenemy took a load of young players from North West clubs, Liverpool, Everton, United. We played a couple of games and Lawrie got all the group together and said, 'What would you all do if you had this kid's talent?' pointing at me. I did an interview for ITV where they said, 'Look what they've said in the papers about your skill'. Looking back, I almost wish I hadn't had skill, that I'd been average. If I hadn't been good enough and United released me then I could have probably taken it a lot easier, and got on with my life instead of having a few years of torment and struggle. But I'd get labelled the next George Best, and people would say to me 'You'll play for Italy one day'. There's nothing better in life than being praised, especially for doing something you love," admits Jules. "There are certain things in life you can't teach, and you have to be lucky to be born with them, and I was lucky. We came off at half time against someone and Robbo said to me, 'You're playing like a mix of Eusebio and Maradona.' I thought that was a massive exaggeration as Maradona was untouchable for me until Messi came along. Still, even if someone says that to you in a Sunday league game it gives you a boost but for it to come from the captain of England at the time, it just means everything."

After a whirlwind first season, United travelled to Histon for a friendly game that was arranged as part of the transfer. Jules enjoyed returning to his old stomping ground. "It was great to go back and see some of the old faces, and I couldn't believe what a great reception I got. The only downside was that at half time, me and Lee Martin had to have a shower and get changed and go back up North to play in a reserve game", says Jules. "I felt that was a bit odd, considering it was a game to recognise me and Histon. I'd have liked to have spent a little more time with my old team mates, but that never happened".

Playing in the reserves, Maiorana set about proving right those with faith in him and getting back into the first team. In the relative obscurity of a reserve match against Aston Villa, Jules' shining star was about to be shattered. "Being the player I was, I was never one to do things like a normal player", he admits. "I tried to be different, I would try and express myself on the pitch. I found five yard passes boring, I always wanted to try a new trick, or an overhead kick or something. In this game the ball bounced just outside our area. I should have headed it, but the worst mistake I ever made, I chested it and tried to volley it as hard as I could. Being me, it wasn't even a regular volley, it was a scissors volley! Then Dwight Yorke came across to tackle me, I kicked his hamstring or his calf and the momentum pushed the bottom of my leg away and that's how I did all my ligaments in."

Jules doesn't hold any grudges or ill will against the man who would go on to win League titles and a European Cup at United. "I heard that Dwight was fined by Villa but to be fair I don't know if any of that was true, I did see him a couple of years after the incident and he said 'I done your leg in didn't I'. I told him yes and he said he was sorry, he didn't mean it and he wasn't that type of player. I said, 'Listen Dwight, if I'd have thought you did it on purpose you'd have heard from me before now.' Shit happens and unfortunately it happened for me. It was just one of those things and I'm sure he didn't mean for it to happen."

For many of the Fledglings, their United career begins in the League Cup with the odd League appearance to follow. In Jules' case, he was thrust in to the limelight of the First Division and, unbeknown to him at the time, his last appearance would come in a League Cup defeat at Tottenham. He came on as a substitute at White Hart Lane four days after his last league appearance, a 4-1 win at Highfield Road against Coventry, also as a sub. Jules' injury at the hands of Yorke was to follow soon after.

"With the benefit of hindsight I could say I wish I'd soaked it up more but obviously I didn't know that would be my last appearance at the time," admits Maiorana. "But hindsight is all you're left with. Of the eight games I played for United, I only started two, against Derby and Arsenal. My dad came up for a game and wanted to buy the Derby game on VHS from Old Trafford. He said to me in front of a few players I was in digs with, like Shaun Goater, and my response was 'Get out of it!' ... I didn't want them to think I was a big time Charlie and my dad, God bless him, never bought it.

That's one of my biggest regrets now, because I don't have that game on tape. I didn't play too badly. If I'd have known about it all shortly coming to an end, I'd have bought the tapes, but then, I'd have also headed the ball out of danger before Dwight got near me." Jules' single-minded approach to success is highlighted in an interesting comment. "For me, I just took one day to the next. I had confidence in my own ability, so like I said, I'd try things differently", he says. "I was being told about Ryan Giggs being someone who would challenge for my position but honestly, I didn't really care who was behind me, because I was that confident in my own ability. I believed in what I could do."

For Maiorana, the most frustrating thing would be that the subsequent events would be out of his control because of the injury. Giggs did break through, and after a tussle with Lee Sharpe for the left wing position (and for the purpose of clarity, it's worth pointing out that Sharpe had been forced to play left back when Jules had been selected, indicating a preference there), the Welshman of course became synonymous with the left wing and United's number 11 shirt. Injured at the turn of the decade, Maiorana stayed at Old Trafford until 1994, by which time so many of that class of 1992 had begun to take their baby steps into the first team and he was becoming something of a forgotten man already. It was a difficult rehabilitation for him.

"I was there until 1994 so on the record I suppose it does look like I was kept around by the club to try and regain fitness and get back to playing at the level we all knew I was capable of," explains Maiorana. "After my first operation, it was the end of the season and I went to Heathrow to pick my cousin up from Italy. When I got back to my parents house in Cambridge, they told me that Ferguson had called and that he wasn't renewing my contract. He didn't even tell me – he left a message with my dad. I tried to get hold of the manager and I got a meeting with him set up for the week after at Old Trafford. In the meantime, I received a letter from the club thanking me for my service but telling me that I was free to approach another club about playing there. I went up to Manchester anyway to see Ferguson on the Friday and went into his office on my crutches. I gave him the letter and said 'Would you give me a job if I walked into your office like this?' He didn't respond, but after a while he said 'Why don't you take the insurance?' This was back in the days before Bosman free transfers – the club had your registration and if they wanted to keep that they could." The problem, Jules reveals, went back further. "There had been a bit of a breakdown in the relationship with the manager due to us not seeing eye-to-eye and I had wanted a transfer before I did my knee in", he admits. "At that time, he said to me that they had seen Peter Beardsley and David Platt leave and go on to big things and the club had been left with egg on their faces so they weren't going to let it happen again."

With Maiorana's contract finally due to expire at the end of the 93-94 season, he began to seek advice from other players in a similar position. "I would ask them if they'd had a new contract offer and if they said no, they would say that they'd been told by Ferguson three months before the end of the season they'd be 'put in the shop window' to give them a chance of finding another club," says Jules. "With me, it got to about three weeks from the end of the season, I had to knock on the manager's door and ask if I was getting a new contract. When he confirmed I wasn't, I just asked why he didn't get me in like all the other lads. He just started talking about my knee being screwed up and I knew it was just an excuse."

The breakdown in communication with player and manager had led to some resentment as the club began their first steps on the way to the unprecedented success in the newly formed Premier League. "Even though I could have been a part of it I didn't begrudge the players their success but if I'm being honest then I probably did a little bit with the manager", he admits. "I'm not one to get jealous of others, I'd get on with them all – there was just one I didn't."

In all honesty, Maiorana's relationship with Sir Alex had been difficult since before the player had even had that starring role against Arsenal. "We went up to Scotland for a game to commemorate the Lockerbie disaster where we played Queen of the South in Dumfries", Jules recalls. "I came on in the game and we won, and we stayed up there overnight, due to fly home the day after. We were in the hotel and I think it was about 7:30pm. I said to some of the lads, 'Let's go down to the bar'. They were saying, 'Don't be crazy, the manager will go mad'. I didn't even drink and wasn't wanting to – I said 'What are you talking about, we're 19-20, we can go and get a drink'.

"They agreed and we went down to the bar. I can't remember if it was Archie Knox or Jim McGregor, but one of them came up to me and said 'Jules what are you doing down here? Make sure the gaffer doesn't see you'. I said I was only getting an orange juice – and he said alright, but as I turned around, the three or four lads who came down with me had disappeared. I was there on my tod. I got my orange juice and was walking away when I heard 'Hey, Maiorana' from the manager. I turned around and said 'Yeah, boss?' He was sat down with about twelve of his mates and said to me loudly in front of them all, 'Get to fucking bed. Does your mum know you're up at this time?' He repeated it several times. I said to him, 'You know what boss, the last person to tell me to go to bed was my mum when I was thirteen.' All of his mates were laughing – it was very belittling, and I didn't know them from Adam. I wonder if he would have appreciated it if someone had treated his son Darren the same way."

Jules' recollection goes slightly further than the stories of tough love told by other players who were at the club in the early days, but doesn't stray so far that it seems unrealistic, and indeed fits in with the atmosphere of sometimes harsh behaviour with the apparent desire to build character. With some of the individuals, depending on their personality, they responded negatively and took the criticism personally. In the collation of the different stories and accounts from various people, one wonders if this was in fact a deliberate ploy to separate the men from the boys. The difference being with Jules, that his strength of character remains to this day and his sense of wrong or right was determined by the way he was personally treated. It may be possible that over time it was agreed that a more soft approach was needed, as we'll come to discuss and learn through the approach of Rene Meulensteen after the turn of the century. Another theory is that success softened Ferguson, and once the first trophies were in the bag, he could begin to consider altering his approach. It's unclear to determine which is accurate, when you consider the formidable character of both Maiorana, and later in this anthology, Chris Casper, both of whom reacted to what would arguably be similar approaches in completely different ways.

Jules goes further and believes that maybe the era of football being a "real man's" game (enter your own definition for that one) determined the attitude and approach towards coaching youngsters. "Maybe you could just get away with it more back then", he considers. "Maybe because of not having won anything at the club when I was there early on, he was bitter and driven by that. I have since spoken to Luke Chadwick fairly regularly who was there in the late Nineties and early 'Noughties' and he says that the manager has calmed down a lot since I've been there. Maybe that's because he started winning things, then maybe it was a learning curve for us all. After a while you get to the stage where people know you're being singled out, belittled, bullied even, then it's not nice.

"There are many accounts of what people think and feel about Fergie, that he's clever, shrewd, and they're right. In my opinion though he's also a bully. I'm not the only person to say that too." Maiorana also had another bad experience with Ferguson. "Before I ruptured my ligaments, Ferguson wanted a meeting with me and my parents because I had agents knocking on my door and he kept saying that we shouldn't get one because all they do is take money. He hated agents. The last thing he said to my parents was 'Don't you worry Mr and Mrs Maiorana, he doesn't need an agent, I'll look after him, I promise you that.' My biggest downfall was not getting an agent. I thought it was brilliant ten or fifteen years later when I found out that his son Jason was an agent. Let's just say I found that a bit strange."

Following the expiration of his deal at United, Jules moved to Sweden with his former team-mate David Wilson to play for Ljungskile SK, but the move was to be short and ill-fated. "Willo got me over there, we had a phone call and he invited me over", he says. "My knee was just about right at this point, I had a medical done at Gothenburg by the same guy who actually did my second operation and was cleared, so stayed in Sweden for about three months. I started to get other injuries and niggles and it just didn't work out. I tried it but it just wasn't working. I was coming to the realisation that I would have to retire and it was the hardest thing I ever had to do.

"It was so difficult for me to give up the game, especially when you've got the words of people like Lawrie McMenemy, Bryan Robson and everyone ringing in your ears. It really does feel like you've had that ball under your arm and been playing for all your life, but to get injured at 21 and then be forced to retire at the age of 24, it feels like someone's just come up to you and snatched the ball away. You go to bed sleeping and dreaming about the game, thinking about mad things to do with a ball, and your brain's conditioned that way. You don't want to think about it when you retire but it's all that's there. It's not like a nine to five thing, this is something you've been doing since you were a kid. At that time, football was really taking off publicity-wise and I couldn't turn left or right without being reminded of the game. It seemed like every time you went past a field someone was playing football, but you couldn't even pick up a paper or turn on the news without it being about the game. I couldn't get away from it."

It was a tough time for Jules, who really hit a low point. "In all honesty, after I retired, I think it was about six or seven years until I actually got around to watching a game. I've been glad to see former players like Clarke Carlisle come out and speak about the effects of depression in football. Fair play to him for doing something now but they should have been doing it twenty or thirty years ago, because once you get injured and released, you're on your own. Luckily for me I had a great family who were able to get me back on my feet."

It was in those early days of post-retirement that Jules would deny being the person he is to try and avoid the attention. "Some would just accept it but others would tell me that it was me, that I was a lying so and so," he laughs. "I would admit it and their response would always be 'Well why are you saying you're not then?' I'd say, like I said earlier, that I wanted people to talk to me because they liked me as a person, not just because I played for United. Some people lap it up but I just didn't like that kind of attention."

To a casual observer unaware of Jules' story, the contrast of him playing first team football for Manchester United and his next career move is often considered one of the most remarkable falls from grace in modern times however, upon realising certain aspects of his personality and his grounding, it comes as no surprise whatsoever. "My family were so important for me, as they always have been. I come from a really close Italian family and after you've been through something like I did, that kind of support is so valuable", he confesses. "It's helped me to reflect on the good things that happened to me in Manchester. My wife is from Salford and I now have a teenage son and a teenage daughter. My football didn't work out there but my life did. I've no end of Northern mates and I feel like I'm a converted Northerner myself now."

Maiorana joined the family upholstery business where he still works to this day and admits it took a while to get used to it. "I hated it at first. At sixteen I was doing it and I hated it then. I tried other things and it didn't work out, then I went to United. They say life's a vicious circle and they couldn't be more right, as I was back working with my dad," he laughs. "Now, to be honest, I don't mind it at all. You learn to appreciate the simple things and what you do have, as long as you can put dinner on the table and pay the bills, and you and your family and friends have good health, you can be happy, and I'm happy."

Maiorana's connection with the game – and United for that matter – is not quite done just yet. As well as being one of the most frequently enquired about youngsters from the early years of Ferguson's reign, he has in recent years been meeting up with some of his old team-mates to participate in the Legends tournaments that the ex-pros take part in.

"After I retired I basically washed my hands, if that's the right term, of every player I'd played with", he admits. "I didn't see or speak to anyone for about seventeen years. I got a call to play in the Masters team and it was absolutely brilliant to go there and see my old mates, it meant more to me to actually go back and see the faces than it did to play live on Sky Sports. I speak to Sharpey every now and again, Deiniol, Wayne Bullimore, and although he wasn't there when I was, I've become pretty good mates with David May too. I hadn't seen the players like Neil Webb or Deiniol since they left the club and it was brilliant. The only thing that wasn't right was me playing in the team because I'm no legend, that's for sure."

In a story of contrasts, it is then a little sad to learn that someone who had so much confidence and paved the way for millions of kids playing on the school playground to believe in pipe dreams, is so depreciative of his own time at the club. Though it certainly isn't out of character in terms of the matter of fact way with which the opinion is delivered.

Despite his mixed relationship with Manchester United, he has a lot of positives to take. "For football reasons maybe I should have signed for Tottenham," he laughs. "But it was the right thing in that I got such a brilliant family from my time there. People say to me that I played for United and that should be great but to be honest it really doesn't matter that much to me. The fans will look at my name, 98% of people don't remember me, 1% of people remember that I did play there, and probably only about 1% of people actually watched me play and are able to say whether I was any good or not. I don't get a great buzz out of someone telling me that I played for United anymore, but maybe that's just because of everything that went on while I was there."

Perhaps the reluctance to celebrate what he did achieve is simply because of the potential he had to achieve so much more. Aside from him being mentioned in trivia references, it stands to reason that the path he walked is unlikely to be followed. "The scout who first recognised me – who's sadly since passed away – said that what happened to me will never happen to anyone again, to sign from a division that was about five lower than the football league and be in the Manchester United first team within a month and a half," says Jules. "Maybe he has a point, and that at least is something to be proud of."

7

Chris Casper

"The earliest recollections of your life tend to go back to when you were five or six. Mine are of kicking a ball around the park with my Dad, so it probably went before that too," says Chris Casper of his father Frank, who was a professional footballer himself for Rotherham United and Burnley. "The first game I went to was at Burnley against Barnsley in 1980, when I was four or five. I remember the atmosphere and the crowd – it was great."

Frank had been at Turf Moor since 1967 as a player and by 1980 was involved behind the scenes. "I just remember him always being at Burnley, be it coaching or managing. There was a culture and environment in our house at home that Saturday was match day. I was lucky as I can remember that when I was on my school holidays, and dad was coaching at Bury, I used to go in and watch the first team train. When I was about 13 I was joining in with the apprentices who might have been four or five years older than me. Then when Dad got the first team manager's job at Burnley, I began training with the first team and it was a fantastic experience. Training with seasoned professionals was a real learning curve. There's a thing, the Ericsson ten thousand hours deliberate practice, but for me that was a massive part of my development. Players who were fighting for their career, and then some fourteen year old comes along. Make no mistake, I had to make sure I could look after myself. If I looked like an idiot, I wouldn't get invited again, I'd be back to kicking a ball about by myself."

With such a heavy involvement in the club, not to mention that Chris himself had, naturally, been a Burnley fan, the logical step to most would be to start his career with the club. Given the toughness of his assimilation, his choice was perhaps not out of character even if it was a little surprising.

"I'd been at the centre of excellence in Burnley, and those centres were new around the time. When it came to picking a team to choose when signing schoolboy terms, Dad was the manager of Burnley, and I didn't really like the idea of compromising him or myself, or put either of us in that kind of position. It was nothing to do with his ability as a manager."

That one of his potential suitors was Manchester United sweetened the deal. "With all due respect to Burnley – and I'm a Burnley fan myself – if Manchester United offer you to come along, most people would be daft to turn it down. I was given the chance to go to Nottingham Forest, Aston Villa, Tottenham Hotspur and other clubs, but I never went, I just wanted to go to United. Though I was a die-hard Burnley fan, after the 1983 FA Cup I'd developed a bit of a soft spot for United."

It was a bold move. Had Chris gone to Burnley, or indeed another club, his route into the first team may have been quicker, though on the other hand failure at a smaller club may have left him with little choice. Failing to make the grade at Manchester United doesn't necessarily mean the end of your career, as there are still plenty of clubs who are willing to take a chance on someone from such a big club. However with Chris, that hadn't even crossed his mind. "I'd trained with physical first team players so I knew I could handle it, but I wasn't arrogant enough to think I would walk straight in. And I wasn't thinking that if it doesn't happen at Man United, it could happen somewhere else. When you commit to something, you commit to it and give it your best. It might be that way further on, but certainly not when you sign."

Casper signed schoolboy terms with Manchester United in 1989 and as an apprentice in July 1991. "I'd been around the club for a couple of years so I wasn't daunted by it. When I signed terms, it was essentially a six year contract I got – two years schoolboy, a two year apprenticeship and a two year pro contract. Again, if United offer you that, who in their right mind would turn it down. It wasn't about money, but an opportunity to think 'I've got five or six years to plan my career here'. I'd go over to stay in Salford University Halls of Residence in my school holidays, and Keith Gillespie and Robbie Savage would be there. There were some other good players there too. Jamie Forrester and Kevin Sharp both ended up at Leeds but they were there, as they hadn't signed yet. They came down from Blackpool. As far as the youth team was concerned, and the age group, these were some of the high flyers, so you knew the club was attracting good players. Nicky (Butt) was there, Scholesy was there though I can't remember him much from those days. There was Karl Brown, who was one of the better players too."

Part of United's wooing technique involved the first team. "I remember going to see an evening game against Aston Villa where Mark Robins scored twice," says Casper of the fixture on Tuesday 17th April 1990. "They took us to the game, but on the morning of the match, we all trained with the first team. We didn't do much, but there we were as 14 year olds, training with the likes of Bryan Robson, Mark Hughes, Steve Bruce, Paul Ince – it was incredible.

"Whether that was a tactic from the manager to get the young players involved and see what they could be among, I don't know. At that point, he'd still not won the FA Cup in 1990, so it was clear that his long term vision was to include the young players." Ferguson's blueprint for scouting the best local players was discussed in Alan Tonge's recollections, but Chris reveals that others were just as hands on. "I know Eric Harrison, who's still a good friend, was tasked with bringing through that next generation and when the manager shared his plans, Eric said he wanted his scouting network trebling. If you're going to put that kind of commitment in, then you can see how they managed to build the kind of foundations that they did. And when you get introduced to world class players as we were, and get the opportunity to train with them, then you're not going to turn it down."

Casper's belief that he would get an opportunity at United with their revitalised impetus and focus on bringing through young players was not only strengthened by what he was seeing around him. The FA Cup tie at Loftus Road the previous season against Queens Park Rangers, in which six young players were in the squad alongside academy graduates and long time professionals Clayton Blackmore and Mark Hughes, when David Wilson and Deiniol Graham scored, was proof positive that the manager would put his money where his mouth was. "You only had to look at the contribution of players like Mark Robins and Lee Martin. Lee was an outstanding player. Lee Sharpe was coming through, Ryan was around the first team so you could see the philosophy of the club and the direction it was taking."

If that philosophy of the club was grand and of legend, then the facilities that were provided to facilitate the development of the young players was, by comparison, rather primitive. The accounts of other academy players of the time, indeed, going back to the days of Matt Busby, paint the Cliff as a very basic training base. Chris doesn't necessarily agree with that perception. "At the time, the facilities were alright," he says. "You had the Cliff, but we trained at Littleton Road, and the pitches were in good nick there. The Cliff was basically a base but it was alright. The dressing rooms were fine, there was a canteen and a gym. There was nothing I'd describe as ground breaking but still, I don't think there were many better about. As the club grew they obviously had different visions and developed Carrington, but at the time I'd say it was okay. It's important that you have the right facilities for the things that you need, whether it's equipment, indoor areas, sports science, medical facilities – but it's not facilities that make a player. If United moved back to the Cliff today they'd still develop players. Sometimes you have to put up with things, sometimes you need to be able to show resilience. It's part of your development and character, jobs like tidying the dressing room and sweeping the showers out might take you ten or fifteen minutes, but it was important to see the other side of things. It's part of learning."

Of the provisions given by the club, if the actual physical facilities were of secondary importance, then the guidance and involvement of the coaches and other important figures at United was crucial. "One of my first memories from the first year of being at United was playing in the B team before Christmas at Marine against their A team. It was a dreadful day, but on the sidelines were Nobby Stiles and Bobby Charlton. Nobby was picking the side but Bobby was there involved too, so you had World Cup winners, European Cup winners, League winners stood watching a B team game. If anything is going to personify Manchester United, that's it, that's what it's all about. Nobby was a great inspiration, Eric Harrison was, Brian Kidd was, you would run through brick walls for them. They treated you like men – it wasn't a matter of giving a softly, softly approach, they just spoke like they would to any man. 'How are you? Ready to train? Good lad.' They'd tell you what you did well but they'd tell you what you needed to work on and most importantly they told you straight. I appreciated that, and I'm sure the other lads did too. Sometimes when kids come out of school and into the football environment, people say that you can't say this or that to them. It's a matter of treating kids with responsibility and giving it to them.

"Eric is one of the best people to speak about football as he absolutely loves the game. Some say he was hard, and he was, but what was he supposed to be? Because once you go past him and you go up to the next level, you've got somebody who's a million times as hard! It's not hard as in bullying, they're demanding that you perform."

Chris feels that it goes further than the coaches, once again referring to the entity. "It's the pressure that comes from needing to perform for Manchester United, absolutely. The difference is something you even see in the tournaments at youth level. With all respect to the other clubs, they don't have Manchester United's tradition, and that's the difference. The culture is great, but the tradition is something else. Go back to the 1940s when Old Trafford was bombed. There's the resilience. Building an unbelievable team with Roger Byrne, Duncan Edwards, Tommy Taylor … and that getting obliterated and torn apart. It was so sad and provokes one of the great conversations, such as who would have been in that 1968 team without the disaster. It's fascinating to think about and discuss and that's all to do with the tradition of the club."

Chris speaks with the enthusiasm of any die hard United supporter. Yet having come through the same youth system for the same club as some of those that perished in Munich, it's only natural to wonder if, after speaking with such passion about what once was, the tradition carries a burden for those representing the club. "You don't think about it. When you think of clubs like Barcelona, Bayern Munich, AC Milan, top football clubs in their countries, they might go out and have an expectation on them to win. When you play for Manchester United, you have to win, and you not only have to win, you have to win playing a certain way. You're immersed in it. You don't go on to a field thinking about the tradition, it's already been built into you, and when it gets to a game, you're just thinking that you have got to perform." Naturally, that has a flip side. "You also have to think that the opposition are going to do anything they can to defeat you because you are Manchester United. I imagine some teams will go onto a pitch and think, 'we'll see how this goes, we'll try and get a foothold in the game'. You're not allowed to think like that for United, you simply can't think like that."

The "must win" mentality is something ingrained into United under Sir Alex Ferguson and can be seen in the numerous late comebacks and winners that have won games and trophies. As with Harrison, Casper's memories of the manager are fond. "The one thing that strikes you is his photographic memory, he remembers unbelievable things. But as a young boy, a schoolboy, for the Manchester United manager to walk past and he knows your name – it makes you feel wanted." The desire to perform well for a man who takes the time to make it his business to know everyone at the club is clear in his recollections about the familiar tales of Ferguson taking time to watch the other sides play and train after he has finished the first team session. "He has a great presence. If we were playing for the A team at home and the first team was at home and he was watching us, we'd know. Not by him barking or anything, just his presence. You can't let him down – if he's got a massive game with the first team in the afternoon, and you have to remember this is a time when he hadn't yet won the league, and he's taking the time to come and watch you play in the A or B team, you don't want to let him down. For him to take such an interest in your development spoke volumes and meant so much."

After being in charge for five or six years, though Ferguson maintained an interest in watching the sides play, his level of personal involvement remained scarce. "We'd have a talk about what representing Manchester United meant, but aside from that, it was generally Eric that carried the message. What people might not know about the culture we were brought up in was that not only were we expected to play at a certain level, but train to that same level too. We'd talk about the elite players who were playing in our positions at that time. I was fortunate that United had two unbelievable centre backs in Steve Bruce and Gary Pallister to look up to. You were expected to look and monitor their performances, and those of others. If Arsenal came to play, you'd be watching Tony Adams or Steve Bould. We'd have conversations leading up to games, we'd be told to watch Alan Shearer and how Pally handled him, or how Brucey did against Les Ferdinand. Players who we expected problems from and Eric Cantona was another, we were told to watch how Pally would handle them. It's always said about how United have all the money, and for all we're talking about with facilities, it goes a lot deeper than that.

"The reviews would generally come on a Monday, there was no point doing it after a game because your head is all over the place. Eric would sit down with us on the Monday, after we'd had a weekend to think about the performance, and we were expected to have a conversation about it – and rightly so as well. You can't just play a game and move on, you might as well take the bits out of it that you need to analyse, and this was before the days of video technology. Because of all this extra work, we hardly got any days off. In between going for pre-season in June and signing in July I think I got three days off, including Christmas too. It makes me laugh to hear kids complaining about being tired these days as they've got all the recovery sessions, ice baths, sports scientists coming out of their ears. For the two years as an apprentice you have to give it absolutely everything."

Chris speaks with the fierce determination one would naturally associate with the character, the "DNA" of the class of 1992. The stories of extravagantly talented players that never quite made it stretch right back from the Busby Babes up to the present day, and the most significant difference one can reasonably suggest is simply application. It's fair to say that the 1991/92 academy side (if we're to include Ryan Giggs simply by his occasional involvement despite the fact he had already played plenty of senior football, and Paul Scholes despite the fact he didn't feature in the 1992 FA Youth Cup run) had more than its fair share of players with natural ability, though the importance that sheer determination had on the eventual accomplishments of the individual players and the club cannot be understated. "The talk about clocking hours up and deliberate practice," explains Chris. "Eric would come out and chat to you and set little things up. Gary and me would work on one v one's, and then get a couple of the younger lads over to help us with our defending crosses and heading too.

"We'd train with six versus eight overloads so there'd be six defenders or four defenders against eight forwards These would be things we'd be putting on ourselves because we were thinking about our own performance. There's so much talk about developing elite players and I don't know what the other lads thought of it at the time but that's what United were doing. We were being given responsibility and taking it, being put in a position where we needed to demonstrate independent decision making, it wasn't simply down to technical coaching."

Between his arrival in 1986 and 1991, Ferguson was busy trying to change the overall culture at the club. He had made a stand against the alcohol culture that was prominent in football, not just at United, and made important strides to ensure that United were at the forefront when it came to advances in the evolution of the sport. "As a young player, or as a player in general, we never had a drink. Well, only at the right times but let's get it right, we weren't a bunch of angels," says Chris. "But we were professionals from an early age. And our time there coincided with the different people the manager was beginning to bring in. Steve Lyons, the podiatrist, Trevor Lea, the dietician who joined in 1993 and was there every single day. Now, these kind of people are expected at clubs, you'd find them, with all respect, at Championship or League One clubs but it just wasn't known at that time at English clubs. There was no full time dietician, I can guarantee. Trevor was brilliant. He wasn't saying that you need to watch your diet, you need to put weight on, you need to focus on this or that, he was just there if you needed him. You could go and speak to him regularly and it helped to really get to know your body, to know what you are actually filling it with. The food at the Cliff changed too.

"When I first started in 1991/92, Friday lunchtime was sausage and chips and it was great. I could burn it off, to be fair, but then again the culture was changed and it'd be pasta, fish and chicken. Little things like that which were important things." Looking after the body and feet better seem like logical, natural advances in order to better prepare players. Ferguson's attitude towards healthier players was clear, yet if these were steps that every club in the country would follow, the

United manager was intent at proving the theory that Chris clearly subscribes to – that the facilities available extend to using every resource to gain every conceivable advantage.

"Gail Stephenson was an eye specialist who came in to help us work on our vision and perception. I don't know if any other club had anything quite like it. Your eyes are the most important part of the game and they can be trained too," Chris suggests. "That's what United do, the kind of thing they were doing for years."

Another thing the club had a tradition of doing over a period of time was winning the FA Youth Cup. In the first five seasons after it was introduced in 1952, Manchester United won each time, yet after a victory in the competition in 1964 United had not tasted victory. Regardless of all the help the club were giving all of their players and the incredible foresight of Ferguson, there was still a responsibility on the players to perform. If the young men at the club had provided the sweat from the famous "inspiration/perspiration" quote, they still had to prove just how talented they were.

There had been a succession of successful young players coming through the ranks post-Matt Busby, notably under Tommy Docherty, while under Ron Atkinson United reached two finals in 1982 and 1986, but lost each time. Ferguson then, faced something of a similar task with the academy side as he did with the senior crop. Teams capable of producing good players, but not the ultimate success which they craved and saw as their rightful achievement.

Breaking the barren run wasn't going to be easy – any team would have expected a struggle against some of the teams and players they would come up against in the 1991/92 FA Youth Cup run. Sunderland fielded Michael Gray (himself a former United trainee) and Craig Russell, Manchester City had Steve Lomas and Richard Edghill, Tottenham Hotspur could boast Sol Campbell, Darren Caskey and Nicky Barmby, all outstanding prospects of the time. "We had one ace up our sleeves, didn't we?" says Chris, referring to Ryan Giggs, at that point a professional being labelled as the next George Best.

"Yet Ryan didn't play until the later rounds. He didn't play against Sunderland, against City, against Tranmere, but played in one leg against Spurs and against Palace. We had a good squad. Eric kept saying of each tie, 'If you win this game, you'll win the cup.' City had big Adie Mike who was a real handful up front, but we didn't know that much about our opponents. Today, thanks to websites and the media, you know far more about who you'll be facing and can do your research. We knew Tottenham had a decent team and I knew Sol Campbell from Lilleshall but I didn't know much about the others. We didn't even have a video of them, it was just a matter of going out and playing.

"But the big game for me was that home game against Tottenham. We were three-nil up in about fifteen minutes, with Ryan and Ben Thornley in our side, Keith Gillespie too, in an unbelievable performance. Nick Barmby was sent off, so we kept possession which wasn't easy as the Old Trafford pitch wasn't great. They sat back thinking they could try and get us in the return but we weren't going to lose 3-0 down there, and we ended up winning 2-1 at their place."

Defeating Tottenham may have been removing the greatest obstacle between United's youngsters and the Holy Grail but the final, with the first leg away at Crystal Palace, was far from a formality. "Maybe the Tottenham tie was the one which won it for us but the first leg of the final was a very big game. We knew their goalkeeper, Jimmy Glass, could boom the ball down the end of the pitch, so every set piece and goal kick they had we were defending in our own box. They had some big physical players like George Ndah and it was a terrible night down there. But we stuck in. At 2-1 to us, Kevin Pilkington saved a shot with the back of his leg when he spun around – I'll never forget it, I don't know how he did it. Then Becks smashed one in the top corner to make it three."

Having won the first leg with such a convincing score, the side were simply required to keep their concentration. However, that is easier said than done when the ties were thirty days apart, and perhaps that goes some way to explaining what happened early in the return. "The first leg was the 15th April and the second was 15th May. We had a month to prepare. We knew their strengths would be from being physical and at set pieces but they came to Old Trafford with us 3-1 up and that should have been it.

"Within three minutes we were one-nil down as they scored from a corner, and we'd done so much practice on them it was untrue. We were under a bit of pressure then but Ben Thornley scored a great goal and that relieved us a bit. We always knew we had goals in us, but at half time Eric had a right go at us." United went on to win with goals from Simon Davies and Colin McKee sandwiching another from Palace in the second half, ending a twenty eight year run without the trophy.

"It was only after that it sunk in. When you're immersed in it and thinking about what a great accomplishment it is – but then, it was the end of my first year, and we'd gone and won it, so it didn't seem like it was anything out of the ordinary," says Chris. "Looking back you're proud of your achievements and successes, and it was the way that we won it as well which was pleasing. Kevin Pilkington was still at school, me, John, Gary, Ben, Nicky, Becks and Keith were all first year apprentices too. It's difficult to see something like that happening again." In the 1992/93 Youth Cup run, one name making the team was Paul Scholes but though he was part of the squad the previous year, he wasn't making the team. "It says something about how strong the side was that he couldn't get in it. He had a few problems with injuries, though."

Scholes was a graduate of the Boundary Park side that included Gary Neville and Nicky Butt, and like the 1992 side, Chris feels it will be difficult to replicate. "There was Karl Brown too, who was one of the best midfielders in the country. In the first couple of months of his apprenticeship he broke his ankle badly, otherwise he could have had a real opportunity. A technically able, aggressive player brought up with that Boundary Park culture. It's difficult to put your finger on what it was about the team, it'd probably take a week trying to figure out just how it all came together. Look at Ryan, still an exceptional player today. I can't see it happening again."

Though some of the 1992 side never quite got an established run, the accumulated first team appearances from the combined squad clocks in at well over two thousand, 2,395 under Ferguson in fact. Besides the man who had made nearly a thousand by himself, at the time Chris didn't feel as if there was anything to suggest what would happen in the next ten years would immediately follow after the success in 1992. "There was only one who we knew for sure would go on and have a great career and that was Ryan. The rest, for the first three years ... well, having won the Youth Cup in 1992, we were expected to win it again the next season. The A team that we were in would play on a Saturday against maybe Rochdale reserves, but there were no professionals in that team. In the past there would have been, but the A team from that season was filled with second year apprentices. We were still, with all respect, killing teams and when we played at the Cliff there might be three or four hundred there. They might say that they could see what was happening with the players coming through but we never did, we just played and played our best because that was the expectancy. It seemed like a natural progression, sign for the club, win the Youth Cup, and win games for fun in the A team. I played in the reserves when I was still sixteen. I wouldn't say we took it for granted but it was just one of things where we took it all in our stride. There were players like Keith Gillespie who had a fantastic career, Robbie Savage who played more than six hundred games, before you even got to the likes of Beckham, Butty and Scholes."

The grounding and footballing education that the players had benefitted from ensured that they were never allowed to get too arrogant around their team mates. "If anyone did get above their station they soon got knocked down. Becks is a London lad, things are obviously different down South to up North, but he too was immersed in the culture of the club. We all had our own characters, but if anyone did get ideas above their station they'd be reminded that they're part of a team." Looking at the sheer size of some of the personalities that came from that one team, and knowing now what so many of them have gone on to achieve in the game, it's perhaps a surprise to hear there wasn't often conflict, particularly considering, as Chris explains, that they were just as large as life back then. "Robbie and Keith could be quite funny together to be fair, I thought they were great. Nicky and Gary were strong characters, probably I was as well. We had John O'Kane, Scholesy was a quiet lad but in the dressing room was very influential. We'd got a great core, and you had to be able to handle yourself. It was competitive. If you stepped out of line you'd be punished.

"It was funny in the early months at lunchtime when the older lads came in and tried to force us to do stuff. The younger lads had taken a few hits – not physically, obviously – but the older ones thought they could take a few liberties with us. They'd put the mop in the corner and you'd have to pretend you were in a nightclub and go up to it to chat it up. But that was what it was like for everyone, and if you didn't do it, you weren't part of the group. You had to show you had a bit about you, but it never went too far." Neither did Chris. It's no surprise, with his upbringing and attitude, that he was a dedicated professional, or that the most memorable tellings off from Ferguson and Harrison were associated with defeats rather than misbehaviour. "When we were defeated by Leeds in the Youth Cup that still hurts, and it hurt Eric", recalls Chris. "They were better than us. Stronger than us over the two legs. They'd got five or six who had already broken into the first team, Rob Bowman, Forrester, Tinkler, Noel Whelan, Mark Ford, whereas we hadn't yet. We were taking our time, I suppose. But after the first game, the manager had a go at me and Gary because we didn't do well against Forrester and Whelan and to be fair he was right."

The young players might have been feeling the weight of expectancy to repeat their Youth Cup success yet there was no pressure from the manager or staff for the players to suddenly be able to perform in the first team. Ryan had been running up and down the left flank for the senior side since March 1991 but, fleeting appearances aside, it was to be quite some time before anyone else from the 1992 FA Youth Cup side got anything like an established run in the first team. "After winning the cup in 1992 and getting to the final again, I was part of the England under-18 side that won the European Championships in 1993. I was playing for the reserve side on a regular basis and I was keeping older professionals out, too. It was that steady progression that we'd been used to," says Chris.

Following on from success in the inaugural Premier League season in 1992/93, United followed that up with their first League and FA Cup double in 1994. In the final league game of the 1993/94 season, Gary Neville and Colin McKee made their first team debuts at home to Coventry. Considering the fondness with which Ferguson has referred to that 1994 side over time, and the physical presence of the powerful men which filled it, it serves as a stark contrast to know that the manager was slowly preparing for the next generation. Even with two years of development since their Youth Cup success of 1992, the likes of Neville, Beckham and Gillespie all physically resembled boys more than men. In the pre-season of 1994/95, Casper recalls the first flush of serious involvement the class of 1992 started to get around the senior side. "I played at Wolves and Rangers in friendlies, and went on tour with the first team," he says. "Then I was hit by a bad ankle injury and struggled with it for a couple of months, and this was when the lads were starting to break through."

Chris recovered in time to participate in a tie that would become famous despite it's relatively low key status. A League Cup tie with Port Vale had caused outrage due to United's decision to field what was dubbed a second string side. "I missed the first game of the tie due to the injury," he says. "I wanted to play and I knew I was going to get the opportunity, but I was injured the day before in a reserve team game prior to the first leg. Some of the lads went in and played that first game at Port Vale and did really well. You don't always sit there and think 'what if' but that was a tough time. I played in the return leg at Old Trafford where I made my debut. It was great that the manager saw enough of us to include us. I hardly covered myself in glory but I did alright, and Pally and David May were excellent in helping us settle. We were lucky as we had so many strong characters around the squad and the work ethic they had. The likes of Eric Cantona too, really had an effect on us."

Cantona's arrival from Leeds in November 1992 is widely acknowledged as a turning point in Manchester United's history. His on-field contribution speaks for itself when acknowledging the number of trophies won during his spell at Old Trafford but, as Chris says, his influence ran far deeper. "There were huge reactions from Eric arriving. One was his influence on the first team in a side who were struggling and had endured a really difficult run. We should have won the league the previous season but had struggled to score goals from the turn of the year and had exactly the same problem at the start of the new season. The first team took a real influence from him, observing his quality and technique. We had some great characters but he really turbo-charged things. We were putting in the training and working hard but not to the intensity that he was. He'd got the ultimate respect of everyone. A few weeks before we signed him, we had played Leeds at Old Trafford, and he was outstanding. Pally and Brucey didn't give compliments lightly but they said he was unplayable and maybe that put something in the manager's mind.

"Even so, it wasn't a logical signing for him to make. He'd had problems in France, been kicked out of Sheffield Wednesday, he'd won the league at Leeds but wasn't wanted. It wasn't a logical signing like Roy Keane, Rio Ferdinand and Wayne Rooney were. But he was the catalyst, he put a bomb under the place. The manager took the decision because he had to win the league. If there was one thing about the signing, it was that he'd just won the league and had experienced it. Pressure didn't affect Eric, it was just like he arrived and said 'I'll win you the league'.

"In the game against Norwich away in 1993, he just ran the show, and calmed the entire team down. The team were outstanding but they needed that extra something which Eric brought." That subtle change – the intensity of preparation – had a profound impact on the club and attitude of all the players there. After their success in 1992, the youngsters now had an extra source of inspiration, a new benchmark of performance to aspire to, and by and large they were responding to the task.

Ferguson's pre-season decision to include some of the young players around the first team squad was also due, in no small part, to the rules in European competition. "The foreigner rule for European football was still in effect so even Welsh lads like Giggsy and Mark Hughes and Scottish lads, were counted as foreign, which meant only five of them could be included in the matchday squad of sixteen", says Chris. "To fill the squad, we were all being brought in and training with the first team. We'd be travelling to Gothenburg, or the Nou Camp – even Galatasaray. I wasn't involved in the game but what an experience, arriving at the airport as a 17 or 18 year-old with maniacs screaming. It was so aggressive, and it was something I'd never experienced. After we'd arrived in Turkey, we put the television on in the early afternoon and the ground was already full. The game itself, what an atmosphere, Eric gets in trouble and Robbo needs stitches ... even seeing it and witnessing it is all part of your education. Whether the lads coming through today are experiencing that kind of stuff, I don't know, but it was forced on us because of the regulations. Still, it was great that he saw enough in us to include us." The restriction on what team United could actually field hugely contributed to their early elimination from the tournament. With an exit a virtual guarantee, Ferguson opted to play some of the youngsters in the last group game, and both Simon Davies and David Beckham repaid the faith with goals in a 4-0 win over Galatasaray.

United's fortunes dipped in the second half of the 1994/95 season as Cantona's suspension for a "kung fu" kick at Crystal Palace provided a huge dent in their chances. Andy Cole was brought in with a record transfer fee but couldn't provide the goals or inspiration under the weight of expectation and United finished the league in second place, as well as losing in the FA Cup Final. By this time, Neville, Beckham, Butt and Scholes were all regulars around the first team squad but it was still a bombshell in the summer of 1995 when Ferguson decided to sell Paul Ince and didn't act to replace the departing Mark Hughes. When Andrei Kanchelskis forced a move to Everton, moves to sign Darren Anderton from Tottenham, and even a tentative enquiry to bring back Keith Gillespie, who had moved to Newcastle as part of the Cole transfer, were rebuffed.

Despite the problems, United's youngsters flourished and became an integral part of the side that won the double again in 1996. Notable by his absence was Casper, whose own chances of breaking into the first team were restricted by the form of Pallister and David May, who had emerged as first choice in front of Steve Bruce towards the end of the season. Chris managed to get some first team action on loan at Bournemouth. "I played about 16 games and it was great, it really toughened me up mentally wise as there's a huge difference between preparing for reserve games and first team games," Chris explains.

In the summer of 1996, Casper's chances were given something of a bittersweet twist. Now a prominent member of the reserve squad, often captain, his route into the first team may have been a little clearer following Bruce's decision to move to Birmingham City. However, changes in regulations meant that the foreigner rule in European competition had been abolished, and United brought in the experienced Ronny Johnsen who could play both centre half and holding midfield. "It was a challenge, but one I accepted", says Chris. "I went on to make my league debut and play in Europe. It didn't happen perhaps as quickly as the other lads but I was there. I was thinking I was only 21-22, so as a central defender I might have to bide my time and wait for the opportunity."

Between October 1996 and January 1997, Chris enjoyed his most successful time at United. League Cup appearances against Swindon and Leicester were followed by a European debut, from the bench, in Vienna. After Christmas, Chris made two substitute appearances in the league, at Tottenham and then Coventry the following week, before being selected from the start against Wimbledon in the FA Cup. Wimbledon were a physically strong team with the luck of the cup on their side. They took the game to a replay, where Chris was on the bench, before knocking out United. Chris featured as a regular in the squad, even getting on the bench in the Champions League semi final in Dortmund, but did not feature for the Red Devils again.

"We finished the season strongly and won the league, and throughout the summer I just had thoughts of working hard and getting in. But two days into the pre-season, I did my hernia and needed an operation," Chris says. "I'm pretty sure I did it towards the end of the last season and masked it, hoping it was a twinge, but as soon as I'd increased the workload I did it in and was out for six or seven weeks. We'd just signed Henning Berg, too, so I was concerned about my chances. I went on loan to Swindon who were top of the First Division and that was the first time I began to really think about my long term chances. I left Swindon after about two and a half months. They put an offer in but United didn't accept the fee."

The taste of first team action had whetted Chris' appetite, who, after seeing his former youth team mates play and feature in sides that were winning trophies, wanted to start to make serious strides in his own professional career. "I might have played the odd game but not enough for a four or five hundred game career which is what I wanted. I thought I'd got a move to Barnsley, who had just been promoted to the Premier League, but that fell through. There was some interest from Reading, managed by Tommy Burns who was a fantastic coach. They had a new ground and the backing of John Madejski, and after a short loan spell there where everything was going really well, the two clubs agreed a deal for me. I felt I could play at a higher level but thought for the rest of the season or eighteen months, the intention of Reading was to get in the Premier League, and I could be part of that. It was such a good club that I couldn't turn it down, and I accepted that in order to get where I wanted to be I might have to sacrifice part of my career in a division I didn't really want to be in."

At the age of 23, Chris was finally blossoming as a centre half, albeit in the third tier of English football. In a Boxing Day fixture against Cardiff City in 1999, fate was to cruelly strike. "I dealt with it badly. You try and put into words that at 12pm on a Sunday morning you've got your whole career ahead of you and at twenty past twelve it's all over. I knew as soon as I was lying in the ambulance that I could never play again. The leg was a mess, the state of the injury was terrible, and psychologically, to be taken out like that, I just knew I wouldn't be the same."

Cardiff's Richard Carpenter was the man whose tackle broke his leg in two places and also caused ligament and serious ankle damage. He attempted to come back, but to no avail. "It came to me one day. I was out for fifteen months, my tibia healed but my fibula just wouldn't. If I was to block a shot and it hit my fibula it hurt, I couldn't even lay on a bed, it was that painful. I worked so hard, I even had a bone graft on my leg, but because of the damage done, even after two and a half years of trying to get back it wasn't the same. My confidence had gone, and one Friday morning I just felt that I needed to move on. My daughter had just been born, I went through a lot of soul searching, and I came to the decision that I was going to retire."

Fortunately for Chris, he was able to move into coaching almost straight away. Part of his rehabilitation had taken place at Bath University, and he monitored some of their training sessions. Articulate and intelligent, Chris had finished school with plenty of qualifications, but with his whole life revolving around football, he wasn't ready to give up on the game completely.

"It was all I've ever known", admits Chris. "I knew I had to stay involved in it and I had a great time at Bath. I was coaching the University team, the A team and B team, and Team Bath all within a week, it was a fantastic experience. On the back of it we got together a half decent team of young students, we put them into a decent shape, we were organised, and we got into the first round of the FA Cup in the 2002/03 season. We ended up winning more games than Arsenal, who won it. It was a fantastic achievement. We ended losing against Mansfield 4-2, but it was a respectable score, and there were 5,000 at the University."

Chris left Bath and went to coach at Bury before an unexpected turn of events. "I'd done two or three years working with the youth team and reserves. One Monday morning early in the 2005/06 season the manager knocked on the door and said he'd been sacked, and that the directors wanted to see me. Two things ran through my head, either I'd be gone too or they might want me to look after the first team as a caretaker. When they said they wanted me to look after the team for Saturday, my initial response was great, but I don't want the job full time ... I don't know why I said that, I spoke to my dad, and he asked me why. I said that I didn't feel ready for it, but he reminded me that if I didn't try I'd never know. And also that if someone else came in, I might be out of a job too! After a couple of weeks, we'd been doing well, I told the directors I was enjoying it." Chris got the position on a permanent basis and received some encouraging words from his old manager. "Sir Alex wished me all the best and told me if I needed any help I knew where he was."

Faced with the obstacles that present themselves to many league clubs – having to sell their best player, and not being given the funds to reinvest in players – Chris concentrated on developing younger players. "We had to show resilience in order to stabilise the club. I thought we were going in the right direction but then they brought in a Director of Football in May 2007."

The Director of Football chosen by the Bury board was the late Keith Alexander. Chris explains that though the relationship between the two was fine, they had very different footballing ideas. "The lads were wondering what was going on, and I had to explain that I was still the manager and was picking the team. Personally Keith and I got on great but our philosophies were quite different. It was quite a public demonstration from the club as well to say I was an inexperienced manager. It would have better if we'd all have been involved in that decision."

Bury's fortunes on the pitch were not so bad. Having drawn against Championship club Norwich City in the FA Cup in January, Chris was preparing his side for the replay. "We should have won the first game with the last kick of the game, but we drew, and the following Saturday we lost against Darlington. In the build up to the Norwich game I lost my job, halfway up the league." Chris returned to a youth team coaching role at Bradford City before cutbacks following a failed play-off attempt meant that the staff needed to be restructured. As Chris didn't have a contract he once again found himself looking for a position in the game. "That's life in the lower divisions. With all due respect, sometimes it's not about who's the best person for the job, it's the person you can afford," Chris reflects. After a period as assistant manager at Grimsby Town, he was headhunted for an important role as part of the Elite Player Performance Plan that was proposed by the Premier League, a strategy with the long term focus on increasing the number, and quality, of footballers in the domestic game.

"My role involves, amongst many things, working with and supporting clubs on the new EPPP. It's a new system at the moment and everything is changing but it's an exciting role and will hopefully lead to an increase in home grown players through the academies", explains Chris. Unsurprisingly, he will be calling on his experiences at United. "Personally, the most successful part of my career was that young part of it. I didn't quite break through but I played some games. I captained England at Under-18 level, so putting that kind of experience back into the system is something that interests me. My experience working on the managerial side and knowing what goes on will hold me in good stead, too. I've been at Bradford when we turned up for training and the Dog and Duck had played on our pitch the day before. You go into academies today and the pitches are perfect, unbelievable. Everything is done for them. I'm sure most of them appreciate it but having seen the other side of it from when I was younger, you think 'Wow'. St. George's Park is the prime example. You have a tournament there and the kids stay over in luxury hotels. You wonder if they're getting too much, but if you don't give it them you'll never find out.

"Somewhere down the line there needs to be a benchmark to look at how many players we're bringing through, and part of that is looking at other sports and seeing what they're doing to bring through their next generation. British cycling, for example, their elite cyclists ride into work. When they go on a training camp, it's literally a camp, they take their bag and kit, and record their own diaries for performance. That's something that goes right back to United twenty years ago."

In the two decades plus that have passed since Chris was in the Manchester United youth team, much debate has centred around the lack of achievement from the English national team. Talented stars like Paul Gascoigne and Alan Shearer preceded a so-called "Golden Generation" of players, and their own failures at tournaments – or, indeed, to even qualify – has subsequently led to much discussion about whether or not England have the right facilities to develop world class players in the long term. Chris is in no doubt that the new systems are a huge step in the right direction. "The systems are there so they will be challenging clubs, measuring their progress and making them accountable," says Chris. "For the 2011/12 season in the Premier League, I think the statistics showed that around 33% of players were home grown. In Spain, it was almost 80%, and in Germany it's over 50%. We're underachieving on a huge scale so something needs to change, we need to start producing more young players and better young players. There are players there to prove it can be done, nobody can say that the likes of Giggsy, Scholesy and Becks haven't been elite, world class players. Even the England team with Ashley Cole, Wayne Rooney, Frank Lampard and Steven Gerrard, they're all quality players. England have underachieved, there's no question about it. The players have been produced, we just need to produce more."

He's been involved in so many different roles in the game, there's no denying the path to where Chris is now has been an intriguing one. "Coaching gives you control over a session, managing gives you control over the game and who is going to play in it. With the step up comes different pressures. As a coach it's like you're preparing players for a game, whereas the manager is always preparing the team to go out and win. You're responsible for transfers, team shape, formation. The other side of having those extra responsibilities is that if you don't get the results then it's your head on the block. There are different responsibilities, but I loved coaching, especially the younger lads. At Bury, Richie Baker, Nicky Adams, Colin Kazim-Richards are players who have gone on to have good careers. It's a huge credit to Bury who with all due respect are operating under the shadow of all the big clubs in the North West, and to be part of helping with their day to day development was a great feeling. I don't look at it really as a preference as I enjoyed both, I enjoyed my time at Grimsby."

It is without doubt that Grimsby appreciated Chris' services, too. The manager at the time, Neil Woods, went on record to voice his disappointment at losing Chris in June 2010, but then said it was a job prospect he couldn't turn down.

It's certainly an interesting view to take. The fact that Chris was exposed to a managerial role so early in his career suggests that he has been on a journey trying to find a role in the game where he can give as much back as possible. He is enjoying the challenge compared to his days as a manager. "It's different, though I suppose it's still a managerial role with the processes you use. You obviously don't deal with the day-to-day running of a football club but the end product of winning a game of football on a Saturday and long term player development remains the same.

"The thing at Bury was that at such a young age, and with such a young family, it was a tough time. The pressure financially on the club was tight, but in the two and a half years I was manager I think I gave something like thirteen young players their debut which is not a bad ratio." The importance of developing young players, which resonates so clearly in his post-playing career, undoubtedly stems from his time at Old Trafford. He speaks enthusiastically about the influence the club has had and continues to have on his life. "The club doesn't stand still, it can't, it has to stay at the front in everything it does. It continues to grow. If there's one influence the club has on you, it's that. You have to continue to grow and develop, you can't stand still. If you do, you'll get walked over. You have to give your best the entire time, and even then, you might not perform, your best might still not be good enough. I gave everything. I can remember a video where the manager said I was the best professional he ever worked with, but I probably still wasn't quite good enough. That's life. But I got a grounding to know whatever I do in life, whether it's my job or even raising my family, that I have to give my best. It's such a huge club, but such a close-knit friendly club, that you can go back and still feel part of it. There are people there that have stayed there for over twenty years, people who have performed in their roles to the standard expected, from Albert Morgan the kitman to players in the first team."

Having been part of one of the most famous youth teams ever to win the FA Youth Cup, Chris' current role feels unsurprisingly like he's come full circle in his career. "I'm very privileged to have played for such a massive club. I've also played in the league for other clubs and met lots of great managers and coaches, so I feel there's a chance to impart some of that knowledge and experience to the kids I work with now. Having been involved with United from schoolboy age for 9 or 10 years, I suppose not to would be a bit of a loss really."

8

Kevin Pilkington

At the time of writing, only two members from the class of 1992 were still playing professionally. David Beckham had retired after a swansong at Paris St. Germain, while the evergreen Ryan Giggs was still making a significant contribution at Old Trafford, now as a coach as well as a player having spent his entire career with Manchester United. The second member still playing was the goalkeeper, Kevin Pilkington. After signing for the club in 1991, Pilkington spent a number of years as understudy to Peter Schmeichel, before a combination of frustration at not getting an opportunity, the acquisition of other goalkeepers and, of course, the Dane's unsurpassable presence as United's first choice, meant that he was forced to look elsewhere for a first team career.

That career lasted over 350 league games before Pilkington moved into a coaching role at Notts County. But without a senior back-up goalkeeper he was not able to hang up the gloves just yet, as he was registered to play for the 2012/13 season, more than twenty years after that famous success alongside "Becks" and "Giggsy". As late as February 2014, he put in a man of the match performance for Notts County against Preston.

Kevin's path to Old Trafford was similar to Chris Casper, in that both had experienced life with senior professionals much older than themselves before being introduced to the idea of signing for the most famous club in the world.

"I was playing non-league football at the age of seventeen", recalls Kevin. "I was spotted by Ray Medwell, one of the scouts at United, who came to watch a couple of the games I was in, and in one I did really well. Afterwards, he came up and introduced himself – my parents knew that he was coming but I didn't know anything about it – and invited me to go up on trial at United for three weeks." The trial didn't exactly go to plan. "My first game was against Preston on an artificial pitch. In the first half I had a bit of a stinker. In the second half I played okay, and was picked for the next two games.

"Thankfully I did enough for the club to say they'd take me on and they offered me schoolboy forms as I was still at sixth form. I wasn't there full time. I'd travel and train on a Friday, play on a Saturday, and occasionally I'd stay there and train on the Monday as well because Alan Hodgkinson, who was the goalkeeping coach, only used to work on a Monday."

Like all of the young players who weren't local, Kevin shared digs. "I was with Keith Gillespie, Robbie Savage and Pat McGibbon in Lower Broughton. Richard

Irving and David Johnson were there too. Lots of different characters, they were proper wind up merchants." The identity of the more prominent culprits aren't a surprise. "Sometimes it would get annoying as we'd get back from training and the lads would be up to their games. Pat and I were good friends and we were a bit older, so when Keith and Robbie got together we'd be like 'oh no, not again!'

"They were loud more than anything, especially Sav. He was so loud you could hear his laugh a mile away." Beyond that camaraderie there was an undeniable, inherent spirit and determination to do well. "You're there to win games and do well, it's something you know as soon as you go through the door. There's the sense that you are there to achieve. Our digs were so close to the training facilities that we were always there, either training or in the gym kicking a ball around. You'd always see Chris and Gary with Eric trying to work on their defending and heading, and there was a big wall at the Cliff I'd practice my kicking against. We'd always be together, we'd always have a football and everyone wanted to improve."

Kevin's arrival saw him join a team tipped for big things, but a team under the considerable weight of expectation. While the first team were striving to win their first league title in over a generation, the same could be said for the youngsters in the FA Youth Cup. Near misses in finals against Watford in 1982 and Manchester City in 1986 were the closest the club had come to success in the competition since their last taste of success in 1964. The club's proud history came with a guarantee that no matter what position someone played in, they would feel the pressure to succeed.

Pilkington feels that the timing of his arrival, relatively late to proceedings compared to the others, was to his benefit. "The other lads had been there since they were fourteen or fifteen so had lived with the weight and the story of everything in the club's history, where I was sort of just chucked into it at the age of seventeen. It was a massive opportunity, I was like 'wow, I'm at Man Utd', but perhaps because I was more emotionally mature I was able to cope with it fairly easily. Don't get me wrong, there was pressure and the club had some great names in their goalkeeping past but also some great 'keepers there at the time, with Schmeichel, Les Sealey, Jim Leighton and Gary Walsh.

"My first training session was with all of them and it was great, a dream come true, which every young boy wants to be doing. I was training hard but loved every single minute of it. You have to enjoy it, those opportunities just don't come often enough." Nonetheless, the pressure to win was still prevalent. Kevin might have been thrown straight into a club with a history of success in a competition that recent sides representing it had failed to live up to, but the expectation was there from within. "Right from the start, Eric Harrison was telling us that we had to win it. But that was great, the run was great, playing against Sunderland and Manchester City, Crystal Palace, all these big grounds. Sometimes I would think how did I ever get to this point, but then you realise you're representing United and there's that desire and expectancy to win. It's drilled into you from minute one, so you can't forget it."

Playing against teams that had fairly high reputations themselves, it would have been easy and to some extent forgivable for the United players to have not understood just how good they were. Kevin was in no doubt and, as the goalkeeper, was in the perfect position to admire the ability of his team-mates. "You could see how special all of the players were. Giggsy, obviously, was the stand out who was already playing in the first team, but there was Becks, Neville, Chris Casper. Even Colin McKee, Simon Davies, George Switzer … they were all fantastic footballers and you could see it straight away.

"In one of my trial games Scholesy played, and my dad said then that he was going to be some player. He couldn't even get in that Youth team! You could see just how good they could be. Becks could put it on a sixpence even at that age, his passing was incredible. Gary was so mature defensively wise, his desire to succeed was so influential. Nicky Butt was head and shoulders above most of the players who he played against, a box to box player just like Bryan Robson. Keith Gillespie was one of the best, with his pace, power and ability to dribble. His delivery was that good he must have made so many goals up at Newcastle when he finally went there. When we played against other teams, you could see just how good we were."

That maturity in Neville also exuded from Casper, which was understandable given his own background before he arrived at United. With Pilkington's age and experience, the three were able to form a mature defensive core simply unimaginable for some so young. The benefit of playing behind players of that ability was clear. "Their organisational skills were outstanding, they knew how to get defenders in the right position," says Kevin. "I was lucky that I was playing men's football from fourteen and fifteen with my dad's mates in a Saturday league, and that did me a world of good and I'm sure that was the same with Chris. They would talk and say what you needed to hear, not talk for the sake of talking, it'd be the right information."

The footballing education enjoyed by Chris and Kevin is one factor behind what made the 1992 team so special. In this anthology there are tales of players who perhaps saw Eric Harrison as harsh, people who, as young men, felt that the aggression displayed at times was unnecessary. The recollections of Casper and Pilkington present an alternative theory – that such pressure was necessary in order for the players to achieve what was expected of them and what was expected of Manchester United when they were at the club. The grounding that the pair had in dealing with men, some senior professionals at the lower levels of the game, where mollycoddling of younger players was essentially non-existent, prepared them for tougher, sterner words. The maturity that came from their ability to not only cope but thrive under the words of Eric Harrison is something that could influence their team-mates to respond in the same manner. Furthermore, it stands to reason that with age-specific academies and the ever growing focus on youth development, such a footballing education will be extremely rare in the future, rendering the team of youngsters representing Manchester United at that period in time even more unique.

"You listen to Eric and respect what he had to say. Some might think he was having a go, but we were able to acknowledge that there was a purpose and a reason for what he was saying to you, and that purpose was so that you would develop into a better player," says Kevin. "In football, I've never taken anything personally as the shared goal is to go out and win. Eric was hard, but fair. He'd have a go during a game, after a game, or even at half time as he did to me in the second leg of the final." Palace had scored early on from a corner, which palpably aggrieved the team and the staff. "Eric said to me at half time 'Is there any danger of you starting to come out for some crosses?' He said that with aggression but I deserved it, because I wasn't. For some reason I was stuck on my line, but in the second half I dealt with it more confidently. There was no agenda with it, or nothing he wouldn't say at any other time. He would say something and it would be dealt with, he didn't harbour any grudges. Like I said, everything he said was done for a purpose, which was our development. I've got so much time for Eric, he's a great man."

Kevin's improvement in the second half helped stabilise United, yet his contribution in the first leg that was more significant to the Reds' victory cause is something that doesn't spring naturally to mind. Chris Casper is able to recall the instinctive save from Kevin with his legs yet the man himself struggles. "I really can't remember," admits Kevin. "The club recorded special clips of us all to commemorate twenty years since the win and gave me a DVD of the tie, but I've still not watched it. All I can remember from the tie is Nicky doing an overhead kick and me getting hammered for not coming for crosses."

Kevin's memory of what winning the Youth Cup meant is clearer. "Afterwards, you sort of realise just how big it was, and how long it was since we'd won it. We were aware of how special it was, to achieve something that the Busby Babes did, and then for the first team to go and win the league the following year was a really special time for the club." The good times kept coming for Pilkington. Shortly after the FA Youth Cup win, he was rewarded with his first professional contract at the club. "I was made up, it was unbelievable. To be asked to play for United in the first place was one thing but to be offered a contract at the biggest club in the world was incredible, a dream. It would have been a privilege to have only had a year there but to go on and stay as long as I did was a delight."

The years that Pilkington spent at Old Trafford coincided with the "boom" in the game. 1991/92 saw a seismic change in British football. BSkyB's acquisition of television rights for the newly formed Premier League, due to commence in time for the 1992/93 season, was to have a profound effect on the financial destiny of English football, with Manchester United inevitably the pioneering club in that regard too. Away from the money and the superficial changes, an alteration in the rules had an impact on the game itself. The 1990 World Cup had been dogged by perceived time wasting and a flaunting of the rules whereby defenders and goalkeepers would pass the ball between themselves. In the latest in a line of attempts to speed up the game and make it more entertaining, the "back-pass" rule had been enforced, forbidding goalkeepers from handling deliberate passes from their team-mates, subsequently meaning that goalkeepers had to be pretty good footballers as well as shot stoppers. It was something that was to have significant consequences to the strategy of many successful teams but, as ever, Manchester United had long since being playing a different ball game.

Back in the days of Sir Matt Busby, the club had developed a reputation for using the goalkeeper as an eleventh man, as someone responsible for starting attacks and being the eyes in the back of the head of his defenders. Harry Gregg started the trend and when Alex Stepney was signed in 1966, his ability as a ball player was prominent in the foresight of Busby. Peter Schmeichel had almost redefined the position of goalkeeper already. Coming with a history of playing handball, the high standard of his reaction and distribution set him apart. As pro-active as United had already been in the area, they still modified training in order to keep ahead of the game. "The changes weren't necessarily profound, more subtle," explains Kevin. "For example, we'd join in more of the possession training, and more of the outfield training. To be honest, after the first couple of weeks of getting used to it, it was okay, the change didn't really affect me that much. I was quite good with my feet anyway as I'd played outfield at school."

Pilkington's form and ascent was noted when he was named as substitute for the UEFA Cup ties against Torpedo Moscow early in the 1992/93 season. The "foreigner rule", which dictated Alex Ferguson's selection to an extent, meant that as an Englishman, Kevin could occupy the seldom used reserve goalkeeper spot on the bench and free up a spot for another non-English player. If his squad selection seemed like faint praise for the first leg at Old Trafford, then Ferguson's decision to take Kevin along to Russia for the return was more reflective of the reward for his good form at the lower levels.

Fellow former trainee Gary Walsh had started between the sticks in the home leg. As a Dane, Peter Schmeichel was rested in a calculated risk by Ferguson to allow him to field Andrei Kanchelskis but it didn't pay off. Walsh kept a clean sheet but Kanchelskis was unable to inspire or help his colleagues to a goal of their own, and Schmeichel was recalled for the slightly more intimidating prospect of a game in Russia. Schmeichel continued his run as United's secure first choice goalkeeper, but the return of the charismatic Les Sealey moved Pilkington to fourth choice, behind three senior and experienced goalkeepers.

Ferguson's decision to bring back Sealey might not have been too much of a surprise given that he had recently signed Fraser Digby (himself a former United keeper) on a short term loan as back-up for Schmeichel. Understandably, with just three substitutes named, Ferguson wanted to ensure that he had a senior back up for Schmeichel ready. After all, it was only as recently as the 1991 League Cup Final where Sealey had to play for a period of the game with a deep gash on his leg. Such occurrences, an injured or sent-off goalkeeper, may well be extremely rare but when they do occur they can change an entire game.

Pilkington didn't see first team action for almost two years after his experiences in the squad for the UEFA Cup games as Ferguson's decision to rely on experience proved invaluable towards the end of the 1993/94 season. Schmeichel was sent off in an FA Cup tie with Charlton which meant he was suspended for the League Cup Final and Sealey wore the gloves in a 3-1 Wembley defeat to Aston Villa. When Schmeichel was injured in May, putting his place in the FA Cup Final in doubt, Ferguson selected Gary Walsh who performed so capably with a string of fine saves in a home game against Southampton that he was awarded a new contract.

Schmeichel would recover to take his place for the double-winning final, but Pilkington might well have been justified in being slightly aggrieved at missing the final league game of the season, that being a home dead rubber against Coventry City where fellow Youth Cup winners Gary Neville and Colin McKee made their full league debuts. Walsh's first team selection did at least mean that Pilkington was given his first taste of reserve team football towards the end of the 1993/94 season. In the summer of 1994 Sealey was released, thereby promoting Pilkington back to third choice. The promotion motivated Kevin to perform so well he was named the Reserve Player of the Year in 1994/95 as he became a regular, playing almost thirty times for the second string, in a year that Schmeichel was underlining his status as the best goalkeeper in the world.

Pilkington would have to wait until 1995/96 to get some League Cup action for the Reds, but was in the squad for the famous Port Vale tie which attracted political attention. Port Vale supporters lobbied complaints with the media and even the House of Commons where an MP questioned the integrity of United's decision to field a team of younger players. According to Ferguson, the Vale manager at the time, John Rudge, told him that his own wife was one of those to complain. The first tie on September 21st, 1994 at Vale Park saw the likes of Neville joined by Keith Gillespie, Nicky Butt and Paul Scholes. It almost seems laughable, looking back at Scholes' career, that his potential presence was deemed so insulting by the host club. Also in the team that day were David Beckham and Simon Davies. Both would go on to score goals in the Champions League before Christmas, though that did not prevent the row from rumbling on about the decision to select youngsters instead of fit, senior professionals.

With the foreigner rule still in play in European competition, Ferguson made a couple of bold choices for a crunch Champions League game with Barcelona on Wednesday, November 2nd 1994. In order to take the game to the Spaniards, Ferguson went with Andrei Kanchelskis, Roy Keane, Mark Hughes and Ryan

Giggs, while Schmeichel was replaced by Walsh. The attempt to take the game to Barca was ultimately suicidal. Hristo Stoichkov and Romario ran rings around the experienced, but by comparison, leaden-footed, defence of Steve Bruce and Gary Pallister to register a shell-shocking 4-0 win. Pilkington watched from the bench as the Catalans ran riot in one of the first signs that such a fantastic side would need to evolve in order to compete in Europe.

"To even be involved at Barcelona was surreal. As a ten year-old we'd gone there on a family holiday and my mum decided to take us to the Nou Camp," Kevin remembers. "Seeing all the trophies and pictures and observing the history was unbelievable. Then to be told those years later I'd be travelling with the squad and training on the pitch, yet again it was a dream come true. Watching Stoichkov and Romario play and do what they did – it's the worst I've ever seen United get battered, they were on a different level. It was a learning curve to watch those players and try and think what you would do differently, though having said that, I don't think Gary Walsh could have done anything with the goals." Walsh's experience and form the previous season's end meant Kevin couldn't really grumble with the selection. "Gary had terrible luck with injuries but was unbelievable when he was younger according to everyone who knew. He was a great goalkeeper in his own right, although I naturally hoped I would be selected. He was – and it was for the right reasons."

Pilkington may not have benefitted from Ferguson's decision to rotate, or indeed the foreigner rule, but he was still called upon to make his first team debut that November, albeit in unexpected circumstances. "I didn't really have time to think about it. I was sat on the bench for the home game against Crystal Palace thinking I could just sit and enjoy a win. After about eight minutes, Peter pulled up with an injury to his back and I was sent on," he recalls. Palace came with an experienced side. John Salako and Chris Armstrong were quick, highly rated young forward players while Chris Coleman and Gareth Southgate represented danger from set pieces.

"I did okay to keep a clean sheet," says Kevin. "There was a moment when I smothered a ball at the edge of the area and Palace wanted to get me sent off. The day went in a bit of a blur, too quickly to take in. I wish I had as it was such an amazing experience. I was a bit lucky as we scored through Denis Irwin almost as soon as I came on which relaxed us – well it did me".

Having performed capably on his debut, Kevin discovered the dangers of getting ahead of himself. "There was a European game the following week in Gothenburg. After the Palace game, the manager said that everyone who played should come in and have a bath and a massage. The next morning I got to Old Trafford as that's where we were training that day. I was on the table getting a massage from Jimmy Curran when the boss walked in. He said, 'what are you doing?' I replied that I was only doing what was said, and he replied, 'you've only played one game, get off'. I don't think I've had a massage since! I don't think he meant it nasty, it was just because I was so young."

The Palace game was something of a milestone. On the bench alongside Kevin that day were Gillespie and Scholes who would both come on and make their 9th and 10th appearances respectively, while Gary Neville and Simon Davies had started the game, making it a reunion of sorts for the class of 1992. "It's a credit to Eric that five of us were in there together at the age of 18 and 19, though personally I have to thank Alan Hodgkinson as he was my main coach," says Kevin. "To go home the day after to see my family and friends and having them all say well done was fantastic."

Hodgkinson's training had stayed consistent as Pilkington ascended from the youth team to first team deputy. Training was tailored to the requirements of Schmeichel, though given the Dane was now widely regarded as the best in the world, Kevin continued to regard it as vital experience. "Peter would want things done a certain way and to be honest, that benefitted me too," admits Kevin. "I was working with the best in the world. Even if I wasn't training I'd just watch him, and I was fortunate to do that and to be training to the same pattern. Mondays were the best days as we used to spend two and a half hours diving about. I loved it, and still do. Peter was a great man too, it was a privilege to work with him as he's the best ever."

For Schmeichel you could almost read Cantona. The account of most, if not all, who trained alongside Eric vouch for his intensity. Casper regarded it as a defining characteristic that made a subtle yet profound difference to United's success. Kevin concurs when thinking of Schmeichel. "His mentality was what made him so special. He would just say he wouldn't be beaten, and sometimes in training he wouldn't. You could watch his technique, the way he spread himself and the way he did things, the way he contributed to United's play. He could throw a ball further than most goalkeepers could kick it which, to players as quick as Ryan or Andrei Kanchelskis, meant he could put players in on goal. It was the best possible education I could have had, to have trained with the best in the world."

In January 1995 one of the most controversial incidents in Manchester United history occurred in the return fixture with Palace at Selhurst Park. A fairly low key 1-1 draw was overshadowed by Eric Cantona jumping in the crowd to kung-fu kick Palace fan Matthew Simmons. Cantona's influence on the development of the class of 1992 is still referred to today. The knock-on effect that influence has continued to have on the modern day United side is still sometimes fairly plain to see for all. On the evening of the incident, Kevin was with some of the squad who hadn't travelled at Littleton Road. "There were a few of us stayed back playing pool and they had the news on the big screen there," remembers Kevin. "We thought, 'oh no' it was one of those moments where you always remember where you were."

With a number of youngsters now beginning to find their feet in and around the first team, and Ferguson essentially using the 1994/95 season to monitor who was capable of handling the step up, Cantona's actions threatened to set the worst possible example. Ferguson was left with one of the most tricky decisions of his reign – how to discipline his star player, a player who seemingly was untouchable and could do what he wanted, without upsetting him to the point where he would want to leave the club. There was no room for leniency. No matter how highly regarded Cantona was within United, the club had to be seen to be sending out a stern message. Half the battle had already been won by Cantona's earlier influence on his colleagues. He was held in such high esteem that they wouldn't hold a grudge against him for his actions, nor the fact that they consequently would have a crippling effect on the club's ability to win the Championship for the third consecutive year. "Everyone looked up to him because of his ability. He was a joy to watch, and some of things he would do in training you'd never see anyone able to replicate. But when you saw what he did at Selhurst you realised he would be gone for a while," says Kevin.

Far from the squad harbouring an undercurrent of resentment for Cantona, Pilkington feels there was a sense of empathy. United were suffering the consequences of being a successful team, specifically dealing with jealousy from supporters of rival clubs which manifested itself in particularly ugly behaviour at times. "I'll say it. I think every footballer has had that kind of thought in their head due to the abuse they get from behind the advertising boards," admits Kevin. "Some of the things they come out with are unbelievable, but you can't say anything back or you'll get in trouble. It's alright for them to say what they want to you. They'll be calling you from a cat to a dog but as soon as you turn around and say something back, they'll probably just run to the police. I say good on Eric – it was obviously just down to jealousy. Palace fans were watching one of the best teams in the world and that's what they wanted for their team, unfortunately they weren't, and it got taken out on Eric. It's just that Eric wasn't having any of it." The strength of the ban laid out by United – five months, ruling him out of the rest of the season – rammed the message home to the rest of the players that a repeat incident would not be tolerated. Kevin says, "There was definitely a message there, if Eric can't do it, then the rest of us definitely can't. It was the right thing to do by the club, they acted before the FA".

Kevin's good form for the reserve side continued throughout 1994/95 yet shared the pain of his team-mates as they suffered heartbreak on the final day of the league season. "I was happy with my own form but just as devastated as the other lads after that West Ham game. We had so many chances, and then for Liverpool to beat Blackburn as well was very disappointing," says Kevin. Further disappointment was to come as Everton defeated United in the FA Cup Final yet amid the doom and gloom around the club, there was reason enough for Pilkington to feel optimistic approaching the new campaign. Gary Walsh turned 27 in the March of 1995 and, approaching his peak, sought a move away. Bryan Robson, who had moved to Middlesbrough as player-manager in 1994, signed his former team-mate. Pilkington was now deputy. "With my improved form, I was happy with how I saw my chances, though I never really expected to challenge Peter for the number one spot," concedes Kevin. "To be there on the bench regularly in case anything happened was a big step up. I was just told to keep doing what I was doing and working hard."

1995/96 would begin with mixed fortunes for Pilkington. After a pre-season where he featured quite regularly, he was on the bench for the opening day battering at Aston Villa where an under-strength team were 3-0 down before a late Beckham consolation. Paul Ince had left for Inter Milan, Andrei Kanchelskis was closing in on a move to Everton and Mark Hughes had departed to sign for Chelsea. The core of the United side still had plenty of experience but the class of 1992 were now forming a strong section of the squad. Roy Keane, Lee Sharpe and Ryan Giggs were just 23, 23 and 21 respectively and were now relied upon as elder statesmen of the United midfield. Nicky Butt made a fourth member of the midfield while Paul Scholes position was still undetermined. Cantona's suspension and the unsure form of record signing Cole saw Scholes move between a midfield and forward position at various times through the season.

In the local press pressure grew for different reasons. The decision of Ferguson not to sign anyone following the departure of Hughes and Ince was criticised by some. It was even suggested that with the club redeveloping the North Stand, the manager's hands were tied. Chairman Martin Edwards attempted to placate supporters by insisting that "the manager of Manchester United decides on the squad he wants". Newspaper polls indicated that a growing number of supporters were losing faith in the manager who had brought the glory days back to the club. The reaction to that opening day defeat was damning from all corners of the press. Former Liverpool defender Alan Hansen stated on the BBC programme *Match Of The Day* following that United "would win nothing with kids."

Despite perceptions, the ship was decidedly steady. "We were all delighted that we were getting opportunities", insists Kevin. "You had Alan Hansen saying that but he'll never say it again. The club knew what they were doing and everyone inside the club knew how good we were. Comments like that didn't affect us in the slightest." Criticism is almost as good a motivator as fear when a professional footballer gets his pride stung, though Ferguson remained consistent to the long term development of his players rather than trying to instigate a short term reaction. "The gaffer never put any pressure on the lads, he never said 'such and such is saying this so you need to go and prove yourself.' He knew how to handle us. Although the big stars had left, he knew that the young players that were there were good enough." Despite Ferguson's level headed approach, the comments by Hansen did provoke a reaction from the younger players. "Yeah, there was an element of we'll show him," says Kevin. "I'm sure plenty of the other lads were thinking it too. Especially him being an ex-Liverpool player."

With Cantona due to return from suspension, the club organised some behind closed doors friendlies for the Frenchman to gain some match fitness, but the FA caught wind and insisted that the forward would be ineligible for any organised game. There could be no mistaking Ferguson's intentions in the games that did occur, though. "The gaffer would tell us before the games to just give the ball to Eric," laughs Kevin. "I can remember one of the games when a couple of the lads didn't pass to him in a good position. We went in at half time and the manager absolutely ripped into them, saying it wasn't about them, it was about Eric."

Without their talisman, United recovered to do just fine in the league. A youthful team travelled to Ewood Park to take on the new Champions in their first away game since Villa Park, and despite having nine members of their squad aged 23 or younger, they managed to exude enough maturity to achieve a win with an accomplished performance. Another fine result at Everton was followed by a 3-0 win against Bolton Wanderers in which United went younger still, handing 17 year old Phil Neville his fifth start and giving a debut to 18 year-old Terry Cooke who ran riot down the right wing. Just as things were looking up, a League Cup tie on Wednesday 20th September where Pilkington would make his first start for the club, brought everything crashing down. "I don't know what went wrong but everything seemed to," says Kevin of the stunning 3-0 defeat at Old Trafford to York City.

"The first goal was one I got the blame for from the gaffer but to be fair it got a nick off Pally before it went in the corner. The second was a penalty after Pat McGibbon was sent off. After that you're out of your comfort zone, trying things you wouldn't normally do and taking risks you shouldn't. I came for a cross that I shouldn't have, the lad got in front of me and scored. It's just one of those things that happens. It's happened before and it will happen again to United and in recent years there were defeats to Coventry and Southend. I've had grief every year since, everyone remembers the York game. It's a learning curve."

In order to repair some of the damage, United fielded a much stronger side in the return leg but were unable to overturn the 3-0 first leg deficit, suffering a humiliating exit. Pilkington's position as deputy was not under threat, however, and following an injury to Schmeichel he found himself making his first Premier League start against Chelsea at Old Trafford on Saturday, December 2nd 1995. "I can remember before the game, the gaffer told me 'You're a man now, you need to stand up and forget about the York game. This is what you're doing now.' That always stood out to me. The game finished 1-1 but there was nothing I could do about the goal. I thought I did well, and obviously I enjoyed it," says Kevin.

Pilkington kept his place against Sheffield Wednesday in a 2-2 draw at Old Trafford. "I felt I did okay again. Nothing outstanding, nothing really bad, but it was good to get the York game out of my system", he says. Schmeichel returned to fitness but was unable to prevent United from defeats at Liverpool and Leeds. A victory over Newcastle managed to temporarily halt the Magpies charge as they were storming to a commanding lead at the top of the table, before United endured another nightmare result. The New Year's Day fixture of 1996 where Ferguson's team went down 4-1 to Tottenham Hotspur is best remembered for the hapless performance of triallist William Prunier. Kevin came on at half time for Schmeichel, who was injured. "I spoke to Peter Schmeichel a couple of years ago when his son Kasper was at Notts County and we talked about the Spurs game. He said he should never have started as his calf was in a bad way. I came on at 2-1 down and it was frustrating, though obviously I enjoyed playing for United," remembers Kevin, "We should have had an equaliser because Coley scored an overhead kick but it was disallowed for a high foot even though no-one was near him. It should have stood but they ended up winning the game as comfortably as they did." And what of the Prunier experience? "Difficult", laughs Kevin. "It was difficult for him as well though to be fair. There was a fair bit expected of him but that was a game nobody will look back on with fondness. We didn't see much of him afterwards."

Kevin kept his place for the FA Cup game which followed, a favourable home tie against Sunderland. United made heavy work against the First Division highflyers, needing a late equaliser from Cantona, who else in this season, to salvage a 2-2 draw. It was the last action Pilkington saw that year, though not necessarily due to the form of the youngster. Schmeichel's unreliable fitness had become such a concern that Ferguson simply could not afford to be without a senior back up any longer. As it turned out, the signing of Tony Coton for around half a million pounds from Manchester City turned out to be a typically inspired piece of business. Schmeichel, coincidentally or otherwise, didn't miss another game that season and turned in some of his most memorable displays in a United shirt. Of Coton's signing, Kevin says, "No-one said anything to me, it was just the way it was. The gaffer thought he needed experienced cover. I was disappointed, but I was only 19 so I couldn't complain."

The latter half of the 1995/96 season also saw what was undoubtedly Schmeichel's best performance for the club in the game at Newcastle. The Reds triumphed 1-0 in a victory that underlined the significance of the contribution of both Schmeichel and Cantona at opposing ends of the United line-up. Pilkington could only admire the Dane's masterclass that Monday night in the North East. "I was there and saw how outstanding he was. He saved everything. You could see how frustrated Les Ferdinand was, and seeing Eric score the goal, it was the game that showed how much it was down to the two main men."

Cantona's match winner was the first in a run of four league games where he scored United's only goal, earning them three wins and a draw at a critical part of the season. The Reds were now closing in on their third league title in four years, and an increasing sense of inevitability about the destination of the Premier League came after Liverpool won a thrilling game with Newcastle at Anfield.

United's "Fledglings" were due to come head to head with Liverpool's "Spice Boys" at Wembley in the FA Cup Final. First things first, Kevin Keegan's live on-air meltdown gave a clear insight into the lack of mental stability the passionate manager was able to instil into the Toon Army. "We all found it funny more than anything, just like everyone else. No disrespect to Kevin Keegan who was a great player and is a great person, but we as youngsters just found it hilarious that he did it. The gaffer definitely knew how to wind him up," says Kevin. In a telling recollection, Pilkington insists that neither the experienced players or the manager used this to galvanise the younger members of the squad. "More than anything, there was an added concentration to ensure we won our own games and that we didn't blow it. We wanted to go out and perform," says Kevin.

Whether it was down to United's mental strength or just the probability that they were the better team, the last day triumph in the league was barely as difficult as it looked on paper. There was no question that Bryan Robson's Middlesbrough would lay down for United, in fact they almost led twice before David May scored, but by this time the Reds were so full of confidence that they were always likely to win at a canter, as they did. Pilkington missed out on a medal but played his part by stepping in when required. "I was so proud to be part of the team. I know I didn't play in many games but I was on the bench for a lot. The frustrating thing is that you don't get a medal for being on the bench," says Kevin. "As second-choice goalkeeper to play the ten games required is always difficult. But to look back at it and to be able to say I played a part in Manchester United winning the Premier League is fantastic."

Newcastle's role as challengers for honours saw them as United's major rivals in the mid-Nineties, as Liverpool had struggled to continue their dominance of the late Seventies and Eighties. Still, that didn't stop both Press and Liverpool supporters getting over-excited about their own crop of youngsters. In David James, Rob Jones, Jason McAteer, Steve McManaman, Jamie Redknapp and Robbie Fowler, Liverpool had their own answer to the Fledglings – unflatteringly labelled "the Spice Boys" (a reference to the popular music group at the time, the Spice Girls). The young players were complemented by the experience of the likes of Mark Wright, John Barnes and Ian Rush. Fowler had already scored four goals against United and Ferguson's decision to sign Andy Cole instead of Stan Collymore was derided by some on Merseyside. Liverpool's acquisition of Collymore for £8.5 million was seen as the smarter move, with Cole struggling for fitness, goals, and even a place in the United side with Paul Scholes in goalscoring form.

Arriving at Wembley, the Spice Boys appeared to be believing in their own hype, turning up in ridiculously coloured cream suits. "That's just the difference in the way that Sir Alex handled his players", suggests Kevin. "We weren't allowed suits that weren't grey or black. To see their suits, we were like, 'wow they're a bit lairy!' To be fair, they were great players, but the suits were definitely a bad choice" Liverpool's "Indian sign" run of form and trump card in Fowler was seen as a potential deciding factor. But just as Chelsea and Gavin Peacock discovered two years earlier, Eric Cantona was the ultimate man for the big stage and overturned the form book, scoring with minutes remaining to seal a second double in three years.

Having dealt with the disappointment of not getting a league title medal despite being the only other goalkeeper to feature for the club that season, Pilkington had to endure some unexpected Cup Final heartache. "I was actually called into the squad on the Thursday because Tony Coton had got an injury in training. I was measured up for my suit and travelled with the team. I was thinking how great it would be just to sit on the bench and get a winners medal if we won, which would have made up for not winning a league one", says Kevin. "Before the game, we arrived at the stadium and got into the changing rooms. I took my blazer and tie off, before I got a tap on the shoulder from the gaffer saying, 'sorry son, but I'm not having a goalkeeper on the bench today'. It was really hot and he'd decided to put an extra outfield player on the bench. To console myself I thought that I could at least be able to sample the atmosphere and warm up on the pitch before the game but Peter told me 'TC's going to warm me up'. Tony's injury was just to his wrist, so he could help with the other training. I didn't even get to do that, and was gutted to miss out on a medal."

The 1996/97 season was not going to get any better. During the pre-season, the club made five senior signings and conducted a high profile transfer battle with Newcastle United for Alan Shearer of Blackburn Rovers. "Despite the final and missing out on a medal, I went on holiday to Spain thinking I was doing okay at the club. I'd been on the bench a fair amount, and I was getting to the point where I wanted to be. During the holiday I met a few United fans who would chat to me every day around the pool. One day they came up to me and said, 'we've signed someone'. I thought, 'oh great, Shearer, brilliant', but then they said it was a goalkeeper called Raimond van der Gouw. That was about five days into my holiday. Then I began to feel that I'd have to leave the club to get some first team football."

Like many others in a similar position, Kevin felt he would have to go on loan in order to get games. "I went to Rochdale for a few games and didn't enjoy it to be honest," Kevin confesses. "I went to Rotherham for a few months, and played seventeen or eighteen games. Yet I missed the training at United as it was difficult going to work and not getting the training that I needed. It was frustrating." Kevin wasn't alone. Though he would return to United in time to feature in the game that sealed the reserve title for the club, a 0-0 draw with Blackburn Rovers, he did so alongside the likes of John O'Kane and Chris Casper. Five years after the Youth Cup win of 1992, they were beginning to accept that their futures lay elsewhere. Terry Cooke, who had shown such promise on his debut, was nowhere near the first team, while Alex Notman, Jonathan Macken and David Healy were scoring goals by the bucketload in the A and B team but were not getting a sniff of an opportunity.

Those that had made it from the class of 1992 were now established league stars well on their way to becoming world class footballers, but the squad was being rounded out with experienced European players now that the foreigner rule had been abolished, and Ferguson was almost hell bent on achieving success in the Champions League. It was no surprise that Kevin felt he would have to move in order to have the career he wanted. "As soon as Raimond arrived, I felt the writing was on the wall," admits Kevin. "There were so many players who were quality but third or fourth choice. That wasn't in my nature, I wanted to play football. I didn't want to leave United, I absolutely loved it and still do, I still speak to the coaches and when I go back now I'm still treated like a member of the family."

Kevin would leave the club on a permanent basis in 1998, but not before a couple of interesting twists. First of all, in the pre-season of the 1997/98 campaign, United faced Inter Milan at Old Trafford in a friendly. Kevin had played no part in pre-season but found himself called into action in bizarre circumstances as an outfield player! After Ole Gunnar Solskjaer went off injured, United had no more outfield players on the bench and so Kevin came on as a makeshift striker. With the match poised at 1-1, he threw himself into a sensational overhead kick that only narrowly missed the target!

He was recalled to the team – in his usual position this time – by surprise over the Christmas period of that season for a game with Everton at Old Trafford. "It was a bit of a shock. I'd spent Christmas with my wife's aunt and uncle," says Kevin. "They didn't really get the football side of it so they were encouraging me to have a drink and relax but even though I wasn't playing I was still preparing. I had a small plate of food and went to bed at about 9:30pm with the family thinking I'm really boring. I got to Old Trafford the next morning and went into the changing rooms. I was looking for Pete but couldn't find him, so assumed he was getting a massage. The gaffer came in at around 1:30pm and read out the team, saying, 'right, there's Pilks in goal', I was stunned, like, 'Really? Nobody's told me!' The next thing I thought was that Duncan Ferguson played for Everton so I was worried that I was going to get smashed. Unfortunately, or maybe even fortunately, he didn't play so I got away with that, and I managed to keep a clean sheet too so it was a good memory to leave Old Trafford with."

A few days later Kevin was in the team again for a game at Coventry City where the Reds conceded a lead late on to lose 3-2 in what turned out to be Pilkington's final game for the club. Though he only played eight times for United, no goalkeeper coming through the academy has made more appearances for United under Sir Alex Ferguson as of March 2014, if we are to discount Gary Walsh who arrived at the club before Ferguson did and Mark Bosnich, who had established himself elsewhere.

If Pilkington had accepted that his time was up as the 1998 season drew to a close, where he would spend the final weeks of it came as a total surprise even to him. "Celtic enquired about taking me on loan so I went there for a few weeks," says Kevin. "Even though Celtic Park was being redeveloped the atmosphere was still tremendous. This was the year when Celtic stopped Rangers from winning ten league titles in a row, so it was an incredible time to be there. In those days there were only three substitutes permitted in Scotland, and they often didn't select a goalkeeper. Jon Gould was the number one, but his understudy Stewart Kerr was injured so they needed someone there as back up. The first game I was there for was a cup semi final against Rangers and I was at Celtic Park in the directors box right next to the Rangers fans. I've never heard such language in my life. But the atmosphere was just so intense it was ridiculous. I think I've only been in an atmosphere like that once before and that was at Galatasaray when I travelled with the squad in the 1994/95 season. We had a walk around two hours before the game and it was already full, the stands would chant at each other and then the whole place went in uproar. But the Celtic and Rangers game was right up there. Beating St. Johnstone on the last day to win the league was incredible. So on my CV I'm lucky enough to say that I've been at two of the biggest clubs in the world. United are the biggest of course, but Celtic are very close."

In June 1998, Pilkington was granted a free transfer and moved to Port Vale. He endured a difficult time as he was unable to get a run going in the first team. When Vale replaced John Rudge as manager with Brian Horton, Kevin got a few first team games but was released at the end of the 1999/2000 season. Short stays at Aberystwyth Town and Wigan Athletic were followed by a move to Mansfield Town where Kevin finally got an opportunity to establish himself as a number one goalkeeper.

"My time at Mansfield was fantastic and I had a brilliant five years there," says Kevin. "We had a great team and great team spirit and were lucky enough to get promoted. We suffered relegation, but then got into the play-off final. It was an eventful five years. I met some great people there and some great managers too, including my current gaffer Keith Curle."

If eventful was a good word to sum up Kevin's spell at Field Mill then super eventful might be fitting for his next move. A transfer to Notts County followed in 2005 where Kevin was once again first choice until he suffered a terrible injury in 2008. "The season before, I'd had a bit of a rough spell but I'd worked hard and come back. I was in great form, doing really well and was hoping I'd get a new contract or a good move somewhere," Kevin remembers. "I don't normally do shooting practice on a Friday but one day I was the only goalkeeper available so agreed to do it; One of the shots I faced was swerving in the air and I tried to shift my weight back to get it but my ankle stayed where it was. I fractured my tibia and was out for the rest of the season. My form had been so good that even though my season ended in February I won all three player of the season awards for the club. They brought Russell Hoult in but I did sign a new contract. After that, Kasper Schmeichel was signed and he did fantastic – but behind a Schmeichel again! He was a nice lad, and it was good to bump into Peter every now and again. I always got on with him, even if some people had concerns about his attitude, but he was always fantastic to me and my development. I couldn't have wished to have learned from anyone better."

The summer of 2009 was quite an eventful one at County, with uncertainty facing every player after a takeover. Former England manager Sven Goran Eriksson joined the club as a Director of Football, while Sol Campbell made a controversial move from the Premier League to sign for County. "It was absolutely crazy. Everyone thought we'd be the next Manchester City, that all this money would be poured in, and we'd get all the best facilities," says Kevin. "It went horribly wrong, they had no money whatsoever. Peter Trembling, who was the face of it at least to us, came in for a meeting once. We asked where the money was and he said all he had was £50,000 and that was a loan. I don't know what happened to the fit and proper persons test, but we were worried about administration and getting paid. Fortunately for the club, Ray Trew came in and spent a lot of his own money to save the club. The lads got promoted after he got Steve Cotterill in too."

Kevin moved to Luton afterwards and then had a short spell on loan at former club Mansfield in 2011. In the 2011/12 season, having played a few games for Luton, he found himself second choice again. When an offer from new Notts County boss Keith Curle arrived, Kevin found himself contemplating retirement from the game. "I had a great time at Luton who were a fantastic football club. A club in the Conference getting up to seven thousand a week shows how well the club is loved," says Kevin. "I'd had a great run, seven clean sheets in 12 games and we were unbeaten. I got dropped suddenly after Christmas and spent a couple of games on the bench when I got a call from Keith who had just got the job at County. He said he needed a goalkeeping coach and asked me if I fancied it. It was a tough decision because I knew I wouldn't be playing. I've always looked after myself and loved playing and I'm always in the gym or on a bike. Then I realised it was moving on to the next step in my career, so I just thought I'd go for it."

In 2012 Kevin rejoined County as a coach, but was registered as a player just in case of emergency. In the 2013/14 season he was still registered just in case. "I've really enjoyed it and I've even been on the bench a couple of times – and of course got some minutes as well," says Kevin. "I've also managed to get in a couple of reserve games and enjoy training. I like being able to put the experience from the likes of Peter, Eric, Alan, and Dmitri Kharine, who was at Luton, back into the game. I did my coaching badges with Eric Steele and I listen to what he has to say because he was at the best club in the world. The benchmark is to get one of my 'keepers to the standard of Peter because he is the best I've seen. I hope that I'm able to put all that experience from others, but also a lot of myself, into it too. I hope my work ethic can rub off on the others."

Pilkington also keeps busy by representing the United "legends" teams that play in various smaller side tournaments. "It's great to be asked – Andy Cole rang me a couple years ago to play in a tournament in Barbados and it meant so much that he thought of me," says Kevin. "And it was great to meet up with the lads like Maysie (David May), Lee Martin, Ronny Johnsen, and Michael Clegg who I knew of course. To still be involved with United at any level is an absolute privilege. I've been so lucky to have played for the best club in the world – I'll never take anything for granted because I've already had a dream come true."

9

Ben Thornley

There have been numerous players labelled "the next Ryan Giggs". Those outside of the club – Damien Duff springs to mind – suffered with the tag, a player whose peak came and went while the first Giggs was still doing the business at the very top of the game. But it was just as difficult for those inside the club. Bojan Djordjic is one who will be discussed later, Luke Chadwick another, yet for Ben Thornley, he had to endure that pressure despite playing in the very same team as the man who would go on to play for Manchester United more times than any other player.

Thornley was, of course, part of the class of 1992 and had immense potential in his own right. He remains philosophical about the comparison. "Ryan Giggs is a phenomenal talent and he was, in my eyes, just in a little class above so just to be on the same pitch as him to watch him work and to help me develop my game was an absolute honour," he says. "I never compared myself to Ryan, only to aspire to reach the already high standards he had set for himself, even at that time." He may have been in awe of the ability his team-mate had, but Ben was very much a part of the tight-knit group that learned their game together. "I spent most of my time with Gary Neville, Becks, Chris Casper and Mark Rawlinson but to be honest, we all got on really well and you could just as easily include Robbie Savage and Keith Gillespie amongst players who spent time together away from the club. Training was always a pleasure, everyone worked hard and listened and you always felt, each Friday, that you had learned something which you could use to add to your game and become, hopefully, a better player."

The class of 1992 will always be remembered – those who went on to break and set club records, those who were around the squad for a few years such as Ben (Chris Casper and Kevin Pilkington, too), and even those who didn't get that far, names such as Colin McKee and George Switzer are fairly memorable by their involvement. Ben is understandably proud of that time. "They were very exciting times. We had such a vast array of talented lads all arriving at the club simultaneously and to be considered an integral part of our youth team and what we, as players, managed to achieve is something I will never forget and gave us all the platform to build a wide variety of footballing pathways", he says.

It may surprise some to learn that Thornley played as many as fourteen times for the club. After making his debut against West Ham in the 1993/94 season he was injured in a reserve game against Blackburn Rovers. Ben suffered knee ligament damage at a time when he almost certainly would have been selected in the squad in the run-in to the end of the season. Thankfully, the club stood by him. "The club were superb, so supportive," admits Ben. "Sir Alex Ferguson and, in particular on the rehabilitation side David Fevre, our physiotherapist that the manager brought in from Wigan RL in the summer of 1994, were incredibly helpful in giving me the best possible treatment.

"It was a long road back to full fitness, twelve months if not slightly more. To suffer such a career threatening injury at such an early stage was very disheartening but I was determined that, should the injury halt my progress at Manchester United, I wasn't going to let it stop me from staying in football and carving out a career elsewhere, albeit at a lower level. The support of both Sir Alex Ferguson and Man United, and my family and friends definitely helped me to do that."

There can be no denying that the injury and the subsequent problems that it caused, prohibited Ben from fulfilling his potential. He showed great determination to return to the United first team and after spending the 1994/95 season on the sidelines, he was brought on as a substitute (again against West Ham) early in the 1995/96 season after featuring in the pre-season tour to Kuala Lumpur and most of the friendlies that preceded the campaign. A loan spell at Stockport County saw Thornley get a run of first team games and in the 1996/97 season build-up, he was again involved in United's pre-season, this time featuring in the defeat to Inter Milan at the famous San Siro. Ben was involved with United's first team, making his first start for the club in the League Cup win over Swindon Town, and a month later making his first league start at Middlesbrough. After appearing as a sub in the win over Sunderland (famous for that Eric Cantona chipped goal), Ben went on loan to Huddersfield, beginning a fairly long relationship with the Terriers. He would eventually move there permanently but not before he enjoyed his best season in terms of appearances for United. In the 1997/98 campaign, with Ryan Giggs suffering from hamstring injuries, Ben was called into action on eight occasions, the last of which was a substitute appearance on Good Friday against Liverpool at Old Trafford. The 1-1 result put a huge dent in United's title aspirations. It may have represented a premature end for their Premier League hunt, but it most certainly did represent something of a premature end for Ben's Manchester United career.

Having impressed at Huddersfield on loan, Ben moved there on a free transfer after his contract expired at United. "I enjoyed playing at Huddersfield Town and I'm really pleased to see them fighting for a place in the Premier League these days," says Ben. He was to share his time in Yorkshire with a couple of familiar faces. "Steve Bruce took over at a time when a new consortium had come in and ploughed a lot of capital into improving both the club and its playing staff. I was in and out of the team under Steve Bruce and, unfortunately, after a bad run of results in his second season in charge, he was sacked. Shortly after, the money men upped sticks and the club was left in financial difficulty with not much money but hefty wages to find too. Lou Macari took over and we quickly had to get used to a more fitness-orientated training schedule.

"However, the club's crisis was worsening financially and they were desperate to offload players after suffering the first of two consecutive relegations. Although I was a permanent fixture in Lou's starting eleven, I knew that being out of contract and the club not being in a position to offer an extension, then my time at Huddersfield was over." After three years at the McAlpine Stadium (which would later be renamed so many times that it's barely worth writing its current name here just in case it's out of date once printed) Ben was signed by Aberdeen. He spent a year in the Scottish Premier League, scoring three times, before returning to England and the North West with Blackpool. Short spells at Bury and Halifax Town followed before he dropped out of League football in 2005 to play for a number of teams on a semi-professional level. Though an impressive career to carve out taking into account the injury he suffered, it was not the path that many felt Ben was destined to walk, however, he does not hold any bitterness. "I would never blame anyone but myself for my own career. Let's just say that it would have been interesting to see the path it may have taken had the injury not occurred," he says.

To this day those fourteen appearances and the fact that he played for the class of 1992 mean that despite playing over a hundred times for Huddersfield, when people mention Ben Thornley's name, they always use Manchester United as the reference, something that satisfies the man himself. "I could not be more proud of my time at Manchester United. Pulling on that red shirt, for whatever team I was playing in, was an incredible privilege and achievement and something that can never be taken away from me," he says. "It was an honour to play with some wonderful players, and to face some too, and as recently as the summer of 2013 I was able to share the same pitch as the great Zinedine Zidane and a Real Madrid team that played at Old Trafford in a return leg charity match in front of 65,000 spectators. "I would never have been involved if it wasn't for the fact that I'd once been a Manchester United player."

Ben is one of a list that probably goes well into treble figures of people that feel implored to credit Sir Alex Ferguson with much of their own development. "I can't thank Sir Alex Ferguson enough, both for what he did for me and my career and what he has done in the last twenty six years to turn the club I have supported from a boy into one of the forces in European football. He is a terrific person and the greatest manager to ever grace our fantastic game. I will be eternally grateful to him for giving me the opportunity to fulfil a boyhood dream by playing in the first team at Manchester United – something that will live on in my heart until the day I die."

10

John Curtis

The 1992 FA Youth Cup winning team is widely and accurately regarded as the most prolific youth team that Sir Alex Ferguson put together in terms of players who broke into the first team. The United side that won the Youth Cup in 1995 would be lauded as just as prolific had it been at any other club. This would not be the only problem with succeeding such a side, but for any single Youth Team to provide six first team players was still a hugely commendable achievement.

One of the major problems with following the class of 1992 was not only trying to replicate their success but doing it while they were still around. One of the most highly regarded players from that 1995 team, John Curtis, responds in a way that we've come to expect of those schooled with the United mentality. "The players in 1992 had their own obstacles, with senior professionals in the side that they had to compete with, so our challenge was nothing new", he says.

In the interest of clarity and complete accuracy it ought to be put on record that the very identity of the class of 1992 has descended into ambiguity as time has wore on. Paul Scholes played no part in the final against Crystal Palace yet is put among that group while Phil Neville, who is always included in any reference was in actual fact, part of the class of 1995. In the early weeks of the 1995/96 season, Terry Cooke, another from that the Youth Cup team of 1995, looked as if he would have an opportunity to prove himself worthy of a space on United's right hand side. Due to the fact he never did, Cooke is often cruelly cut out of some of the photo shoots when he was included with Phil Neville and the likes of Beckham and Giggs.

It still represents a huge challenge for those unable to cement a first team position at United to go on and achieve a long and fruitful league career, as many of the stories in this anthology go to show. Cooke's own story is something of a stencil for so many who leave Old Trafford as a youngster. A handful of under-21 caps, a succession of ultimately unsuccessful loan moves before a move down the ladder to have a league career either in the lower divisions or abroad. Cooke enjoyed the majority of his career in North America and coincidentally (not contrived in the slightest, I promise) that leads us to the subject of this chapter, John Curtis. Following retirement, John has moved into coaching and after seeing much of the world, is currently based in Connecticut, in a youth programme run by Everton. "It's a very different world, it's the same game but there are so many differences", he says. "The whole set up of youth development in soccer, with scholarships and college and so on, is so different to what we're used to in Europe. That said, I'm calling it soccer now, so maybe I'm getting the hang of it".

John's own path to United was effectively conventional. "The United scout who first noticed me, Jeff Watson, comes from Nuneaton, like me", he says. "He remained there for a long time under Sir Alex. It's strange, I had to ring up a few a months ago to get some help for my visa over here and it was still the same people at the club who were there twenty years ago. That's an amazing thing, and goes to show what effect continuity can have on success."

United have a principle of continuity through success and John, as a schoolboy, was able to taste that not long after being at the club in 1995. "It was fantastic to be drafted in," he admits. "I was in the FA national school at the time, training every day, so it wasn't as alien as it may appear looking at the statistics because I wasn't your regular schoolboy. It was great to play with the older players. My first game was against Charlton in one of the later rounds and it was such a superb experience to be involved." United faced Tottenham Hotspur in the final with Curtis appearing as a substitute in the first leg. Having waited so long to win the Youth Cup, United now had a recent run of success with that 1992 win and 1993 final appearance.

Whereas earlier accounts of time under Ron Atkinson suggest that the usual expectation of success was clear to see, under Sir Alex it had been transformed into a demand for success that was in part inspired simply by the level of attention and detail paid to the youth system. "In those first months at United it was clear to see that it was a club that had a culture of success and we as players knew what was expected. There was no doubt that he had spent such a long time and invested resources developing those young players. He was building a club, not a team, and we as kids definitely felt a huge part of it."

The 1995 final was won on penalties at Old Trafford, and while not seen as a seminal success at the side of the earlier one, it was another huge feather in the cap of the work done by Eric Harrison and Sir Alex. It could be fairly said that fear was used as a motivational tool in the earlier days but with the growing success of the club at all levels, Ferguson and his staff were having to find new ways of evolving to ensure continued chances of victory. Ferguson, for one, had learned that the "hairdryer" was one that should be tactically deployed at the right time when it came to the betterment of his players development. "I remember a game at Leeds, it was a first team game and I think it must have been one of Wes Brown's first games," shares John. "I was watching from the side as I wasn't in the squad and I think Wes made a mistake. Anyway, the Gaffer nailed him. It wasn't as extreme as you'd expect from the hairdryer but it was enough to describe it as a proper nailing. He turned around to walk back to the coaching staff on the bench and started smiling right away.

"What he'd done was to get a reaction because he knew that would get Wes going. He was a master at reading each individual person and how to get the best out of them and that's exactly what Eric did too. It would be naive of us as players to think they were just on and off with their anger and that they didn't know what they were doing. They were very, very clever. Eric was superb from a psychology aspect, a master. He instilled the winning mentality into his players. I suppose that comes from the manager but Eric was so good at it. It was a very special environment for us to grow up in. They used the club and the stature at the appropriate times though I don't think anyone needed to be reminded of that."

It certainly helped that with the recent success of the club, Ferguson and Harrison were now able to confidently refer to their own achievements to prove that they knew best. It wasn't just Manchester United with a fine tradition and historical track record that had to be lived up to, it was the here and now. The likes of Chris Casper and Gary Neville had shown a willingness and a response to being treated like young men and that was now the expectancy of others.

"That was definitely the case," agrees John. "We were able to play at Old Trafford, we were being treated like we were part of the first team so we knew that playing for United was a big event. If there was pressure, we weren't really feeling it. It felt like it was a big family, with everyone around you if you needed any help whatsoever. That went through to the players ourselves who knew what we had to do amongst each other. It could be tough at times – I remember the court cases that we used to have in the changing room. It could be brutal – people would be painted with boot polish and told to run around the Cliff in their undies in the freezing cold. I had loads myself. I don't know a player who wasn't, if you didn't do your job properly, a court case. Hadn't cleaned the first team's boots properly – a court case. My job was to clean the gym and there'd be sweat everywhere. If I didn't do it, I'd be up for a court case. You'd sit on the physios' bench with a towel over your head and two people whacking balls at you wrapped in a towel. It almost knocked me out! Have a disagreement on the training ground, then afterwards it'd be in the changing room, forty lads surrounding you, the two who fought in the middle, they'd have a boxing match to sort it out. It wouldn't be allowed now. Eric would be sacked within a week. He didn't promote it, but it was part of that system and environment, and it was character building. People might say it was bullying, but there was no singling out.

"As soon as you walked through the door in a morning, looking back, you were walking into a pressurised environment where everything had to be done right and that's the best kind of insight you can give about the United youth system. If you didn't do it right, you'd be punished, and it was that kind of pressure which made people get better. It was a collective and environmental thing. The only place you were really safe was in the kids changing room but even there you'd hear someone going 'the Gaffer's coming!'"

There was plenty of reward on show for anyone able to handle that pressure. Phil Neville had already seen first team football by the time of the Youth Cup win and in the early autumn of '95, Terry Cooke enjoyed that period where he looked a future first team starter. United hadn't replaced Andrei Kanchelskis and Cooke was seen as a more natural stand-in than the eventual successor, David Beckham. "Terry was a super player, arguably the best crosser of a ball you'd like to see," says John. "But those chances in the first team for that second Youth Cup winning team were limited by the fact that the first Youth Cup winning side were in there. There's only one jersey for each position so it's very difficult. In an ideal world you could have a great youth team every 10 years that comes in and refreshes the senior side. In a way we were victims of our own success but like I said earlier, it can't be just as simple as that. Those guys in 1992 had to come through as well and to say they had an easy path into the first team does the players they replaced an injustice, remember, they'd won the title in 1993. If they had a benefit or advantage on us, it was probably only that the guys they were replacing were older."

United had plenty of cover in defence and so John's footballing education would continue via the reserves. After appearing for the first team in the late season testimonial against Celtic for Brian McClair in April 1997, it seemed only a matter of time until Curtis would receive his first team debut, particularly as at the end of the season he was named the Jimmy Murphy Young Player of the Year. "It was a massive honour when you look at the people who won the award around that time and who's won it since. Everything about being attached to the club has so much prestige. Okay, I didn't play so many games, but I was at the club for a fairly long time and the kind of doors and opportunities it opens for you is extraordinary. Getting back on track, I didn't take it for granted but it wasn't a surprise when I got my debut," he admits. "I played against Ipswich in the League Cup and the Gaffer had always got a lot of stick for playing youngsters in that competition so I half expected to get a chance. It was much more of a surprise to get my league call up."

The Ipswich game had come in mid-October in 1997 and John had to wait less than two weeks before he was back in senior action again. "It was absolutely brilliant," he says of the games against Barnsley and Sheffield Wednesday where United hit seven and then six goals respectively. "It was great, but then you're bombed straight back into the reserves when people are fit so you're on terra firma very quickly. Still, when you're playing alongside those kind of players and they're playing football like that, what an experience, and Gary Pallister was so helpful to me on my league debut. He was immense."

A whirlwind year for Curtis was capped off when he was included in the artist Michael Browne's famous painting that depicted Eric Cantona as Jesus Christ, with Curtis placing a crown on Alex Ferguson's head. "That came about as I had played for the England Under-21 side. The message was that aside from Eric and the Gaffer, all the players had to be English, so I think that more than anything was the reason that I was chosen. It was a surprise but an honour as it's such an iconic image isn't it. We all got a copy but mine's back at home at the minute."

Curtis was kept around the squad, making a handful of substitute appearances following the hammering of Sheffield Wednesday, before he was back in the first team for a decisive game against Arsenal at Old Trafford. United were decimated by injury and forced to make a number of big changes. "I was pretty nervous, coming up against the likes of Bergkamp and Vieira," confesses John. "It was a tough game. I was marking Overmars who was lightning quick and gave me problems. I enjoyed it, but then with an injury I was moved to left midfield and then substituted. After that, Overmars scored and we couldn't get a goal back so it was very disappointing." Curtis feels that it is futile to get concerned with the butterfly effect, whether he'd have been able to do better than Gary Neville did in the race with Overmars for the winner. "Who knows? It was a bouncing ball, you can't be too critical of Gary and who are we to criticise the Gaffer for making the change he did," he laughs.

Curtis played in the dead rubber match at Barnsley on the final day. Amid tough competition for the centre back spots in the 1998/99 season, he found himself as an almost ever present for the reserves. He did manage to play a big enough role in the treble season to feel he contributed, with seven appearances and four of those being from the start. His most memorable outing came against Nottingham Forest at the City Ground in the February. "I came on at the same time as Ole and he gets all the credit, but it was me who made the difference," laughs John. "It's all in the positioning, I'm sure if I'd have been up front I'd have got those four goals. In all seriousness, Forest were in real trouble, they were like lambs to the slaughter and Ole punished them."

John is pragmatic about his own contribution. "I was always on the periphery, a bit part, but I was proud of what I did achieve while I was there. In hindsight, maybe it would have been a bit better if I'd have left a year earlier. I still went on to play in the Premier League for four different teams. I don't regret my time there, joining or leaving, and it stood me in good stead," he insists. After a couple of appearances at the start of the 1999/2000 season, including featuring in the European Super Cup loss to Lazio, Curtis went on loan to Barnsley. "I thought that if I wasn't playing regularly by the age of 21 then I needed to go out and get some football and so I went to the gaffer. A week later I'm playing at Maine Road against Manchester City. I scored against them later in the season which is always nice as a United player," he says. "Going from United to Barnsley was like stepping out of a pressure cooker, almost like a breath of fresh air. For a time it was a welcome change."

Curtis' good form at Barnsley did enough to convince Blackburn Rovers to pay £1.5m for him in the summer of 2000. "The idea was to establish myself there and that's what happened in the first year. Everything went great and we were promoted back to the Premier League. Then early in my second year there I got injured and that really set me back. I was never going to get an England place if I couldn't get a run in the Blackburn team," admits John. He was an unused sub in the 2002 League Cup Final victory but knew that he would have to seek pastures new for regular football. "That's life in the game, you have to become very pragmatic very quickly or you'll end up a manic depressive. It's just the way it is, it's ruthless, nothing personal."

What followed was a mixed couple of years for John. A loan at Sheffield United preceded a move to Leicester. From there he was signed by Portsmouth, and then he went on loan to Preston. "It was a difficult time, moving around a lot, though I'd say my best football came while I was on my loan spells. My time at Sheffield United was fantastic, playing in the semi final of the FA Cup against Arsenal was brilliant and that was at Old Trafford. I played a lot better than I did against them the first time. At Leicester we were always up against it but I didn't really enjoy working with Micky Adams. I jumped at the chance to work with Harry Redknapp but that didn't work either."

After impressing on loan at Preston, Nottingham Forest signed Curtis where he would enjoy a healthy, two year first team run. "I'd say the best spell of my career was probably the year at Barnsley and the first year at Blackburn but I did enjoy being at Forest. It was great until we were relegated," he says. "It's a super football club, so professional, so much history and identity. They've got a heritage and a style. I think that's a good thing but I suppose it can be very difficult for a manager coming in."

Without a club, Curtis signed for Queens Park Rangers but when John Gregory was sacked early in the season, the defender found his chances limited again and the club terminated his contract just after Christmas. "I shouldn't have left before I found myself another club because I spent about two or three months doing nothing," he says. "I was having a few trials but nothing came of it. I was all set to sign for Tranmere in the pre-season, but then the chairwoman said they wanted me to prove my fitness as I hadn't played for six months. I then suffered a groin injury and spent ages trying to get over that. My old coach at Forest, Ian McFarland, let me do some rehab at Notts County but they didn't have a reserve side so I couldn't play. Richard Dryden, who's a mate of mine, was manager of Worcester City and so I played for a few games there. That news made the non league paper and was noticed by Dean Saunders, who was manager of Wrexham. He rung me and offered me a deal until the end of the season – after that, I was signed by Northampton. I enjoyed it there and would have liked to have stayed longer, but then Stuart Gray was sacked and change is never good. I was looking for my next move, and was actually hoping to go to America, but then a move to Australia popped up."

A testing time had now seen John enter his thirties and so, nearing the end of his career, he now had to make a choice that would be a good one in terms of his chances of playing. "I'd been fortunate enough to have made money in my earlier career so finance wasn't the motivating factor. I wanted to have a different experience, see a different side of the game, and felt that it would be another feather in my cap moving forwards. I went over to Australia and after I landed I was sick as a dog with terrible food poisoning. Nonetheless, I went and had a trial at Gold Coast United, and after training they offered a deal there and then, so I spent a full season there and it was fantastic. They finished third in the league – it was a good standard of football and far more appealing than, with all respect, playing at Accrington Stanley on a Tuesday night in February," laughs Curtis.

The year in Australia can certainly be detected in John's multi-regional accent. "People tell me that all the time. I think it's just because I've moved around so much", he says. "I'm from the Midlands, spent most of my time in the North West, I'm married to a girl from London, had a year in Australia and now I'm in the States." That move came about via another stop, this time in Italy. "Gold Coast was folding anyway and not renewing contracts," John says. "With no hope of getting a new deal and only a slim chance of getting another club, my options were either play at a low level in England or concentrate on coaching. I'd been coaching on and off since I'd been at Forest and as playing became less important, coaching took over. I took a job for six months in Italy at a coaching school working with Australian, Canadian and American kids who would play against the Serie A teams. It really was a fantastic experience and a chance to really observe the Italian culture. I then heard of an opportunity working for Everton over in America and that's what led me to where I am now."

John played more than 300 professional games, a total he is satisfied with. "If things had worked out differently it could have been a lot better but then it could have been a lot worse, too," he says. "I don't look back with regrets, I gave my all, I was always professional and never went off the rails. I thoroughly enjoyed being a footballer, it was a great lifestyle and it gave me an awful lot. I was and am very privileged. It's massive and only now that I realise the power of my history with United. You observe how others operate and understand it's not done with the same class and style that you were used to, so now that's drilled into you, that's the standard you have to try and set. Only when people experience it can you realise the benefits of it. I'd be a fool not to take my experiences and put them into what I do now but then, those experiences moulded who I am anyway. So I couldn't do things differently anyway. The standards I have will always be Manchester United standards and that can only be a positive thing. The path for me now is to try and be the best I can possibly be the other side of that white line. I've been blessed with such an insight on the development of young players that I hope I can put that to use back in the game."

It's no surprise then, that John is not hesitant in calling upon his former mentor for help. It's enlightening to know that even after retiring, Sir Alex keeps an open ear and a sage word of consultation for his former charges. "Funnily enough, I spoke to him a couple of weeks back. Since retiring he's done a few things at Harvard. I wanted to know if I could possibly get in and listen to how he does his work," says John. "I rung Les Kershaw and he passed on a message and the

Gaffer rung me up to give me some advice. That's a measure of the club and the man. It's only now that I truly appreciate what an honour it was to have worked with him and I'm going to continue to try and do what I can to be a successful coach. I have had the best possible background, after all."

11

Alex Notman

There was a running joke in the early years of Darren Fletcher's Manchester United career before his contribution was really appreciated, that he was Sir Alex Ferguson's son and that was why he was in the first team. Perhaps that's connected to the fact that Ferguson's son Darren actually did play in the team in the early 1990s. If there was one player from United's youth system over Ferguson's reign that was likely to curry favour, then Alex Notman's name would be right near the top. He was a diminutive striker with a real eye for goal, and a boyhood Rangers supporter with a good, working class Scottish background. "I was born just outside Edinburgh in a place called Mayfield," says Alex. "My earliest memories of playing football was for Easthouses Boys Club, although I'm told that as soon as I started walking I never had a ball out of my hands. Growing up Ally McCoist was my idol. I loved to score goals and that's what he did, so that's how I became a Rangers fan really."

It would be unfair to say that Notman was brought to the attention of Ferguson merely because of the general similarities between the pair as youngsters. Far from it. Notman had proven ability and was making waves as an infant, so much so that the major clubs in Scotland were keen on him right away.

"My dad was a Hearts supporter and they were the first professional club that I went to train with," Alex says. From Hearts, he was soon noticed by his dream club. "When I was ten, I got invited to train with Rangers on a Friday night locally, which developed with me travelling through to Ibrox on a Monday night to train on the astroturf there." As well as Rangers, Notman would continue to turn out for local clubs and with his connections, it would come as no surprise that United would hear of him soon enough. Coincidentally, it was the scout Andy Perry, who was responsible for alerting United to Fletcher years later, who spotted Alex. "I remember I was playing for Tynecastle Boys Club at the time and training with Rangers on a regular basis. After a training session with Tynecastle my dad told me that the Man Utd scout was coming along to my game on the Saturday to watch me," says Alex. "I think I was around 13 years-old at that point. After the game Andy spoke to my dad and said he wanted to get me down to Manchester for some trials. It then progressed from there to going down in school holidays. I remember when I was about 14-15 they used to bring lads from all over the country in the school holidays to have trial games at Littleton Road, with all the scouts and the Gaffer around the pitch with their pen and paper."

To get Notman and his family to put pen to paper, the manager made a special effort. "I remember this so well, but then I suppose it's not something you can ever forget", admits Alex. "I had learned from Andy that they wanted me to sign, so they got all of my family down to the Castlefield Hotel in Manchester for the weekend. Then we were told the gaffer was coming along to have a meal with us on the Friday night. During that meal he said that he wanted me to sign and this would be the best club for me in my development as a player. For him to take the time to come along and say in person he wanted me definitely helped to sway my decision to sign, not that it took much swaying".

In the mid-90s, Rangers were at the peak of their powers. There was genuine debate about whether the Scottish Champions were better than United, so it says much about their appeal that Alex was persuaded to leave his boyhood club and home surroundings so readily. "To be honest, the decision to leave wasn't that difficult," he insists. "After going to Manchester and training during my school holidays, there was only one place I wanted to be. United is a real family club and I loved every minute of being there. The hardest part was moving away from my family at 15, but they were down all the time and went everywhere to watch me play."

Alex signed terms in the summer of 1995. Rangers, with Paul Gascoigne pulling all the strings, would go on to win the Scottish League and Cup double, but Manchester United would do exactly the same in England. There was no pressure for Alex, then 16, to get into the first team right away but his progression in that first year was rapid. Alex was to start playing in a number of different teams as soon as he arrived, scoring 21 goals in 26 games for the B team, and three in seven for the A team in his first season.

Going into the 1996/97 campaign, he was to enjoy a great year. "There was an expectation, when you play for United you are expected to be successful at any level, so I suppose that brings a bit of pressure, but that is something that I never really felt," Alex says. "When you are a youngster the Youth Cup is the one that everyone wants to win and I was disappointed that we never managed it."

Nonetheless, Notman would make his own impression on the tournament in his first two outings. On his FA Youth Cup debut, United faced Wrexham and destroyed them 7-0, with Notman becoming the first player since Ryan Giggs to hit four in a single game. Not a bad way to introduce yourself. "That was amazing. My family had come down from Edinburgh for the match so to get four goals was an amazing feeling," he says.

In the next round, United were drawn to face Liverpool at Anfield. In the build up to the game Alex was not scheduled to play, but he passed a late fitness test and once again proved to be of great importance to the side. "Anfield was always a lucky ground for me as I had quite a good goalscoring record there at all levels, and I can remember that first game there pretty well. We knew it would be a difficult game as they had some top players, but we were confident we could win.

We did, too, with goals from David Brown and myself," says Alex who scored a penalty to level things up, showing a great coolness under pressure.

Those top stars he refers to were on both sides with Steven Gerrard and Michael Owen playing for Liverpool while Wes Brown was in the United team. "I remember Eric Harrison before the match paying special attention to Michael Owen, knowing if we could keep him quiet then we would win the game. As we used to play against them regularly, we already knew that anyway, you could see that those two were the standout players in the team. Having Wes in our team helped. I used to hate playing against him in training, as he was different class and I knew he would make it at United."

Despite the ability of Brown in the back line and the goalscoring touch of Notman up top, United still succumbed to defeat against Watford in the next round. "It was a big disappointment, we drew in the first game which we should have won, then lost in the replay," says Alex. "We were winning the second game with ten minutes to go and our goalkeeper made two bad errors which got punished and that was us out. We really should have won the cup that year."

Such statements are usually made by eliminated teams who are confident in their own ability yet this United team would back up their talk by the end of the season. Despite the disappointment of the exit, Notman's performances were already drawing comparisons to the player in the first team with a very similar frame, Paul Scholes. So much so, in fact, that he began to be used in other positions to test if he had similar flexibility. "Obviously it was very flattering to be compared to Scholesy, because for me he was the best player that I have ever played with, such an amazing talent and a really great guy," says Alex. "I saw myself at that time as an out-and-out goalscorer, but as I progressed into the reserves at 16-17 years-old, I played a few times in centre midfield, which I enjoyed, but I preferred to be playing up front."

The whole purpose of building a successful youth system is to prepare players to hopefully be first team stars for Manchester United, but embedded in that philosophy is the inherent expectancy to win for every team that you represent. It's been suggested earlier in this book that perhaps Ferguson and Eric Harrison relaxed a little after the success of the class of 1992 and the way they were performing in the first team, but Alex says he doesn't believe that to be the case. "Eric was never one for easing up," he laughs. "No matter what the first team were doing, the demands were still the same, and if the standards dropped he would soon let you know. I loved playing under Eric. If you weren't playing well or not working hard enough you would know about it, and the all the lads had complete respect for him. He had the same aura about him as the Gaffer."

That motivation spurred United on to fantastic success that campaign. The first team won the Premier League, but the Reserves, A and B team all won their respective leagues too. In 122 League games across all those teams, only 18 were lost. If you take away the B team, that figure becomes a frightening 10 in 90.

"Everyone was so proud of that achievement. I never really minded what team I was playing in as long as I was playing well and scoring goals. To have been a part of three teams that won their leagues in the same season was obviously a highlight of my time at United", Alex admits.

In the leagues that Alex represented the club that season, United scored 252 goals in 84 games, an average of three a game. Alex's own record was scattered among the teams that he played for, with five Youth Cup goals, seven for the B team, eight for the A team and a further four for the reserves. Scoring 24 goals over a first campaign was a fantastic achievement when he didn't have a settled team or position. "I was always a confident lad and playing at a higher level never really phased me. It was great to be able to get tested at those levels and prove that I could play well and score goals at any level too," he says. "I always remember waiting at the Cliff training ground on a Friday afternoon for Eric to put up the A and B team squads, hoping that I would be in the A team. As the season went on I was lucky enough to be included in the Reserves too." It was a lot to take in. "It made me more determined to do well in the youth team and get back to playing with the reserves again", Alex says. "It keeps you motivated and you don't take it for granted that you will be involved with the reserves all the time at a young age."

Notman had made such an impression in that first season that at the tender age of seventeen plans were being made to introduce him into the first team. As it transpired, he wouldn't make his debut until December of 1998, but if the manager had his way, Notman would have made his first official appearance for the Manchester United first team in October of 1997. As it goes, Alex did feature with the senior side that month, on the 5th, when United played City in a testimonial for Paul Lake. He made an instant impression coming on as a substitute for the player he had long been compared with. "I remember the occasion so vividly", says Alex. "There were five players that started who were only going to play thirty minutes as they were going away to play for England, I think it was Butt, Scholes, Beckham and the Nevilles. Nearly all of the first team were there that day so to get on for Scholes was an amazing experience that just left me wanting more. I scored the equaliser with just a few minutes to go which was a very proud moment for me, and to top it off it was against City."

The forward realised that the inclusion meant a first team debut was on the cards sooner rather than later. "As I was still really young, I believed if I kept playing and scoring the goals that I was, then my opportunity would come. I did actually have a chance of being involved a lot earlier than I ended up doing," shares Alex. "I remember the Gaffer coming over to me one day in training shortly after that, and he told me I was going to travel with the first team to play Ipswich in the Coca Cola Cup on the 14th. I had to say I couldn't go as I was due to be away playing for one of the Scotland youth sides. I really wanted to be involved in that Ipswich game but there was nothing I could do. So Erik Nevland went instead of me and came on with about 20 mins to go. I remember looking in the paper the next day thinking that it should have been me."

United were eliminated at Portman Road and though Ferguson rotated in the FA Cup games with Walsall and Barnsley, the latter of which resulted in embarrassing defeat, Nevland benefitted from the momentum factor and was selected where Notman might have expected to. When United mathematically conceded the title to Arsenal with two games to play, the Scot was still not selected in dead rubber matches. He had scored eight times in the 1997/98 season for the reserve team.

However, in the summer of 1998, Notman's chances of making the first team suddenly looked a lot better. The first pre-season friendly of the 1998/99 season was at St. Andrews against Birmingham and Alex came on for Andy Cole. Though the game ultimately ended up in a 4-3 defeat with Alex's fellow fledgling, Philip Mulryne, stealing the show by scoring all of United's goals, Notman was just happy to be included with the seniors again. "Just to be involved with first team games was an amazing experience and I really believed if I could keep playing the way I was playing and scoring goals, then I would get my chance in the first team. There were so many world class players in the team at the time it was always going to be difficult, but I really believed I could do it."

The competition, Cole, Teddy Sheringham, and Ole Gunnar Solskjaer, was about to get fiercer as Ferguson hunted for another forward to add a similar presence to that which had been missing since the retirement of Eric Cantona a year earlier. As Patrick Kluivert decided against a move from Barcelona to Old Trafford, speculation intensified that United were about to sign Dwight Yorke from Aston Villa. Prior to that, Notman had one more chance to show what he could do for the first team in a high profile friendly. They don't really come any higher profile than one organised to commemorate the anniversary of the Munich Air Disaster, particularly when Cantona himself was involved. The French legend brought an assembled all-star team and 55,000 supporters packed into Old Trafford to mark 40 years since the tragedy (though the game was held in August, not February).

Not many players can lay claim to have upstaged the man known as the King, especially on a night when Cantona scored his last recognised goal in a United shirt, but Notman did just that, scoring twice in an almost farcical but well-competed 8-4 win. "It was just an amazing experience and to play in front of a full house at Old Trafford, and to get two goals was fantastic", Alex admits. "It's got to be one of the best feelings ever, and to share a pitch with the King made it an even more special occasion. I remember taking some stick off the lads for not leaving the ball for Eric to score for one of my goals, but I wasn't going to pass up the chance to get a goal at Old Trafford on an occasion like that."

It was just as well really because United signed Yorke in the following days, making a direct hit on Notman's chances of senior football. "Of course, after that, it was becoming more and more unlikely that I was going to be involved on a regular basis. When there was Yorke, Cole, Sheringham and Solskjaer ahead of you, it was always going to be difficult. Maybe I was just a little bit unlucky at the time I was trying to break through, as I believe that is the strongest squad that I have ever known United to have."

Few would argue yet strangely enough even with that firepower, Alex would finally make his first team debut that December against Tottenham Hotspur in the League Cup. "I travelled down with the squad and really hoped that I was going to be involved, so I was delighted when I was named as one of the substitutes," says Alex. "We had a strong team playing that night with the likes of Butt, Sheringham and Solskjaer, but Spurs did too and David Ginola was on fire that night. I got asked to go and warm up with about 25 minutes to go and was delighted when I got the wave from the Gaffer that I was coming on. I played up front with Solskjaer and Sheringham and at least with that, I'd done what I had set out to do the minute I had signed for United, and that was to play in the first team."

Alex was encouraged by the breakthrough and his namesake was pleased with his performance. "The next day the gaffer got me in his office and said that I had done really well, and that he thought I could get in front of some players if I kept progressing as I was – but for whatever reason that never really happened," he says. Notman was kept at United for the remainder of the season when the club enjoyed success like never before. If nothing else, he is delighted that his name is down on record as having played for the club in their most remarkable year. "That was another amazing season for United and just to be a part of that is something I will never forget," he confesses. "The buzz around the place at that time was immense, and that went right through the club not just the first team. I will never forget that night in the Nou Camp, I think I went about six rows forward when we scored the winner."

It'd been another profitable season in front of goal for Alex with a hat-trick in his only appearance in the under-19 Premier League, and a decent return of three goals from nine games in a very competitive reserve side, yet that lack of games goes some way to describing how difficult it was to stand out.

Following the European Cup success, United were scheduled to go to Australia for the following pre-season. Alex wasn't included in the travelling squad, instead, he was now wanting first team football and realising he wasn't likely to get it at United in the short term. He went to see the manager with things moving much faster than he'd ever anticipated. "That did not work out the way I had planned it at all", he laughs. "I went to see the gaffer to say I felt it would benefit me maybe getting out on loan and playing some first team football. He agreed and phoned the Aberdeen chairman while I was sitting there. About an hour later it was all done and I was heading up to Aberdeen the next day on a three month loan."

In fairness, it was a gesture made with great intentions and showed great respect by the manager to choose Notman as one of his young stars to send to his former club. Ferguson obviously still had strong connections at Pittodrie and felt that the move would be beneficial for all parties, however it was to prove disastrous. "I really think the Aberdeen manager at that time was told I was coming, rather than him wanting me," says Alex. "We never really had a good relationship and I only ever had two substitute appearances which was really disappointing."

That manager was Ebbe Skovdahl, who had enjoyed incredible success with Danish side Brøndby IF in the 90s, and indeed had coached them against United in the previous season. With the club in debt and expecting Skovdahl to work on a budget, it's possible the coach wanted to exert his own influence and didn't appreciate players being brought in without his knowledge. Whatever the reason, after just two games, Notman returned to United to find another loan club. This time, Ferguson found another United – the Sheffield version – to take the forward.

Though not a top division club, they were well established in the Second Tier and Notman did well there. He played ten times, in one spell scoring three goals in four games against West Brom, QPR and in a Yorkshire derby with Barnsley at Bramall Lane. Under the tutelage of that infamous character Neil Warnock, Notman confesses he really enjoyed his time in Sheffield. "It was a completely different experience than the one I had at Aberdeen. I loved my time there under Neil Warnock. A lot of people don't have too many good things to say about him, but I really enjoyed working with him," Alex says. "I thought I had something to prove after my disastrous time at Aberdeen, so to play in nearly every game when I was there and to score three goals, it was a really successful loan."

So successful in fact that the Blades wanted to sign him, but they were struggling so much financially that they couldn't put up the money. Despite how much he'd enjoyed it, Alex was hoping it would prove to be a springboard to get another opportunity at Old Trafford. "After such a great spell I really wanted to go back to United and push to get into that first team squad," he says. "I always believed if it never happened at United then I would be signed by someone at a decent level."

After giving his career at United another try, and indeed featuring in the first team for the first two pre-season friendlies of the 2000/01 season against York City and Shrewsbury Town, Notman found it ultimately impossible to dislodge the established quartet up front. Even out of his favoured position, looking at the midfield of Beckham, Scholes, Keane and Giggs – arguably the best United have ever had – the Scot accepted it would be time to move on. When Norwich City made an approach in the November of 2000 it seemed the perfect move. "At the time when Norwich wanted to buy me I wasn't even sure where it was," he admits. "But when I went to have a look round the club I could tell it was a real family club just like United. It was made easier as Phil Mulryne was there, and it always makes it easier when you know someone at a new club.

"It didn't really start well for me there though, Brian Hamilton signed me and then left the club seven days later. It turned out alright, as Nigel Worthington, who was his assistant at the time, got the job. I really enjoyed my time under Nigel and the highlight for me there would be getting to the Play-Off Final against Birmingham City in my second season which we unfortunately lost on penalties. I had three great years at Norwich which I will never forget." Oddly for someone who was a great goalscorer, he only managed one senior goal for the Canaries. "I was really disappointed to have only scored one goal for Norwich, as with a little bit more luck I should have had a lot more. The amount of times a goalie pulled off a great save or I hit the bar or post, nevertheless I was playing well and contributing to the team" he says, though adds that part of the reason he didn't get more in the net was because he was playing in a number of roles. "I played a lot of the time on the right wing, which I really enjoyed and on occasion just behind the front two, which was my favourite position. Not a lot of managers like to play that formation though."

With his league career finally taking off, everything was going well for Alex until injury struck in the East Anglian derby at Portman Road in September 2002. "I blocked a free-kick from Mark Venus and when the ball hit my foot it turned my right ankle. At the time I thought it was an ankle sprain as I had done it many times and it felt exactly the same. After about six weeks the swelling wasn't going down and the pain was still there so I went to see a specialist in London, who said I had an extra piece of bone at the back of my ankle which was giving me the pain every time I ran," Alex explains. "So he got me in the next day to remove the piece of bone from my ankle. Everything went well and I was back in the physio room doing my rehab again, but after another two months I was still getting the same pain as I had before.

"This time I went to see a specialist in Sheffield who said it was ligaments that had come detached, and that he would need to operate to re-attach them. I always remember waking up from the op and the surgeon telling me that my physio would be coming in to let me know how it had gone and I knew then that there was something wrong." Alex's premonition was sadly going to be proved right. "Our physio rang to say that when the surgeon went to re-attach my ligaments, there was nothing there to re-attach. After spraining my ankle so many times, my ligament had worn away. They said if I had got it sorted when I was 18 I would have been fine, but I just wasn't to know. I did try to play on and got myself back playing after that, but the demands of training everyday and playing were just too much for my ankle."

In 2003, Notman was forced to announce his premature retirement from the game but found that United were eager to help out where they could. "I received a call from the Gaffer about two weeks after I had to retire, saying he was sorry to hear what had happened and that if there was anything he or Manchester United could do, then I just had to pick up the phone," says Alex. In time he would come to request a favour, but not before at least attempting some kind of comeback. "I was told by the surgeon that I could probably get away with playing part-time as the demands were not as great, so I had an offer from Kings Lynn and I signed there," he says. "I hadn't done anything for about five or six months since retiring so I wasn't very fit at all at the time. I came on in my first game with about 25 minutes to go and I hated every minute of it. Having played at a high level all my career it was a bit of a shock to say the least. The next day they wanted me to play in a reserve game and I told them I hadn't enjoyed it and had decided not to play at all. For some reason they put in the press that I had quit again because of my ankle, but it was down to me not enjoying it, not an injury."

It says a lot about the character of Alex and the impression he made that his two professional clubs were only too willing to help by holding a benefit game in his honour in 2005. Norwich allowed Alex to host it at Carrow Road and he explains that United were equally forthcoming. "I was really grateful to Norwich City for letting me play a benefit game there. I initially wanted to try and get a game against Ipswich Town as Norwich had been promoted to the Premiership and Ipswich were still in the Championship so there were no derbies that season, but the police would not allow it," says Alex. "So I got in contact with Jimmy Ryan and asked if he could speak to the gaffer, to see if there was a chance of getting a team down to Carrow Road. He got back to say that they wouldn't be able to send down a team but they could send down a few players, so it was decided that it would be Norwich City versus an all-stars side. The game went really well and seven thousand people turned up which was good, considering Norwich had just been relegated on the Saturday at Fulham and my game was on the Monday night. United sent down Tim Howard, Guissepe Rossi and Chris Eagles, accompanied by Brian McClair, and I was really grateful for them doing that," he admits.

Even after the wrong move to Kings Lynn, Notman was still in love with the game and in 2007 decided to sign for Boston. "Football is in your blood and it is good to play no matter what level it is. I played on and off for a few years but once you have played professionally, it is very difficult to adapt to the semi-pro game," says Alex. "Tommy Taylor was the manager when I was at Kings Lynn, so that's how the move to Boston came about. I had played about four or five games and was really enjoying my time there, and then I got injured in a game that kept me out for about six weeks. I was playing for nothing at the time, and when they came to offer me something the travelling was too much, so I just never played for them again."

Despite not quite loving the standard, Alex has often toyed with going back into semi-professional football. "Thankfully the ankle doesn't give me any problems, but they did say it may affect me more as I get older. But even when I have been playing semi-pro, the ankle has not given me too many problems, if any," he says. "There were times when I thought about trying to make a comeback professionally, but once you have been out of the game for three or four years it is very difficult to get back to the level you were at."

Alex made the choice to concentrate on a career outside football to provide a stable income for his young family, and showing just how much he enjoyed his time at Norwich, has settled in the area. "I am living in Norwich now, which I have been for the last fourteen years ever since I signed," he says. "I am married and we have an amazing little girl who is five years old. I am now a project engineer for an oil company. If you had told me I was going to be doing that fourteen years ago, I would've said you were mad. It was really difficult to know what to do after football, as that is all I have known since I left school at 15. For the first three years of leaving football I never really did anything, a little bit of coaching and playing part-time on and off. I then got an offer of a job from my wife's uncle at an oil company which I took, but to be honest never thought I would last. Six years later I have worked my way up to where I am now and things are going great."

That hard working and sensible attitude is something he believes United, and Sir Alex, helped instil in him. "There is so much I have taken from my time at United. They taught me discipline, hard work, respect, but just to have been a small part of it's history will be something that I will always be proud of. Being a professional football is millions of people's dreams and I was one of the fortunate ones to have been able to do that."

12

Danny Higginbotham

Many of the accounts and memories of Sir Alex Ferguson in this book feature on his influence as a motivator and a winner. For Danny Higginbotham, the manager's intervention could arguably be said to have saved his very career.

Higginbotham arrived at Manchester United as a schoolboy after he had been training with Manchester City. "After a local game, my dad told me that Brian Kidd had taken him aside and asked 'What colour's your house?'. My dad said red, it's always been red. And Brian said to him, 'Well what the fuck are you doing with them lot then?" laughs Danny. "How ironic that Brian ended up at City but that was that then. I was training one or two nights a week at the Cliff with him, Eric Harrison, Tony Whelan, Nobby Stiles and I loved it. They were my team, so to play for them in tournaments and move up through the ladder was incredible. It's not just about football, they taught you the right way to conduct yourself and carry yourself, as shown by a number of them who have gone on to have great careers."

For Danny to have signed for United at the age of nine means that would have been in the very early days of Sir Alex's tenure, with him being born in 1978, which shows just how early the manager had begun that early recruitment even on an informal basis and underlining how much of a trendsetter he was. "One of my earliest memories was having my picture taken with the FA Cup in 1990, but I'd been at the club for a while by then – it was great to be involved with things like that, especially as a fan," Danny says. "It was unbelievable to see the club transform and how it changed, even with the redevelopment at Old Trafford in the early 90s.

"I think in those early days, we didn't see that much of the manager, but you knew from the coaches and their long history and association with the club that there was very much a strong tradition being restored. Not so much with Eric, but he was the best of the best. There were a lot of people around the club who not only knew the club but knew what it was like to be a footballer, even if not necessarily for United. In recent years you've seen around English football that isn't always the case, you get non-football people involved at football clubs. It shouldn't be the case that clubs have academy managers who have never kicked a ball in their life. I knew that with players who had won the European Cup, like Nobby and Brian, that they could give me advice and I should take it. You idolise these people, and respect their experience. They know what it's like to be a kid starting out, they understand what you're going through."

Danny progressed well but as an apprentice, broke his femur. Thankfully he recovered from that setback. "I had an unbelievable comeback, a great six or seven months when I returned, and ended up getting offered a great contract, a two year deal where most of the other lads were getting a one year offer," he says. "I've been lucky enough to have played most of my career in the Premier League where there might be loads of players in lower leagues with more talent and natural ability than me. But dedication and a good attitude does stand you in good stead so maybe my recovery left a good impression on the manager. I was a late developer, and when I finished my rehab I felt like I'd gone further and past some of the other lads. When I first broke into the youth team I was a left winger, and I was finding it difficult and not really enjoying it so much because I kept getting pushed out of the way. Dave Bushell, who was our manager, put the team up at Littleton Road and said my name after number three. He told me I was playing left back and I never looked back after that. From that, I grew and grew, and really developed. I'd have never said I was a left back in a million years, but it just goes to show what the coaches can see that you can't. My first year as a professional was unbelievable and I made my debut at the end of it."

That was the 1997/98 season, when United had just missed out on the league title to Arsenal. With a couple of dead rubber games, and taking into account the squad (particularly in defence) had been ravaged with injuries, Sir Alex took the opportunity to give some of the youngsters a chance to shine. "It was an amazing week," Danny admits. "Sir Alex called me in on the Monday to say he would give me a new contract, then on the Thursday he spoke to me again and asked me to do him a favour. The team were playing on Sunday and he asked me to 'do an appearance', which I took to mean some kind of publicity appearance at a charity do or something. I said it was no problem at all. But a few seconds later he came into the dressing room and said, 'Danny I'm stupid, sorry – you're travelling with the first team on Sunday'. I couldn't figure it out – did he say it to see how I would react first of all? The game came around at Barnsley, and I went on for the last half hour or so. It was pissing it down, mum and dad were there and got drenched, but they didn't care at all, they got to see their lad play for United."

The 1998/99 season has gone down in history for what United achieved but it was a time that Danny will never forget for different reasons. It began very promisingly with a substitute appearance in the Eric Cantona & Munich testimonial game in August 1998. "That was unbelievable, my first game at Old Trafford," he says. "I'd been involved with the first team quite often and I suppose I didn't fully appreciate it at the time. Their goalkeeper went on a run and I absolutely smashed him in the corner. We got a commemorative statue of a kid with a football, it was great but to be honest it wasn't something I looked back on or dwelled upon."

There was no time for Danny to stand still as part of a new agreement between Manchester United and Belgian club Royal Antwerp, United would send some of their players over to gain first team experience, thereby also helping Antwerp out. Higginbotham saw the move as an opportunity to be seized. "It felt like a great opportunity, having already made my debut in the first team, coming back into pre-season, the club had just established this relationship with Royal Antwerp in Belgium so Jimmy Ryan asked if I wanted to go over there. It was more of a decision taken by the club and I was on my own for three months so it was a big learning curve for me," says Danny.

He was eventually joined by Jamie Wood and Ronnie Wallwork, and began to flourish. "I loved it," he admits. "The whole experience helped me grow up. Their manager was Regi van Acker and he was a brilliant bloke. We got beat in our first three games, and in the third one it was 5-0. I'm not joking, it should have been 10-5 to us. We were on the bus coming back and as we got off, one of the fans went for me, screaming, 'You fucking English bastard, fuck off, you're shit.' Out of nowhere, the manager's wife jumped in front and said, 'Listen he's a kid finding his feet, leave him alone'. Later that night Regi called me and asked if I was okay – I said I wanted to go home, I didn't need it. He convinced me over a meal with his wife that things were going to get better and apologised for the fans but explained how passionate they were. I said I wasn't handling the pressure well, but Regi offered the compromise that if after the next three games I felt the same he would sort out my return to Manchester with his best wishes. He said things were about to change, and we went and won the next 13 games and were top of the league. I became a hero with the fans, and I actually saw the guy who'd abused me – he was crying, singing my name. It was amazing."

With Antwerp doing so well, they headed into a period of crucial games, with a clash against R.A.A. Louviéroise destined to prove a massive moment, propelling a previously relatively unheard of trio of United footballers into the international spotlight. Following an altercation after the game, and allegations by the officials, Higginbotham and Ronnie Wallwork were to find themselves given huge suspensions that made headlines both home and abroad.

Danny puts the record straight. "What upset me was that what was actually being reported was a complete and blatant lie. I was so grateful for Sir Alex's support throughout," he says. "There had been some crowd trouble at a previous game so we were playing against La Louvière behind closed doors and in injury time they scored a goal which knocked us out of the play-offs. He was four or five yards offside and then there was a bit of afters as the clubs were rivals anyway. I kicked one of the advertising hoardings out of frustration, one of those that rotates, but my foot got stuck. It was on national television and I was getting angrier and angrier and it looked as if it was swallowing me up. Then I went into the tunnel and it was carnage. Our dressing room was to the right, but we had to walk down a corridor to get there. The photographers starting taking loads of pictures of the drama and I was with Ronnie and Jamie. Jamie's a lovely lad but hard as nails. I said to him someone needed to stop the photographer so

Jamie went over, and the photographer pulled a knife on him. It was crazy but thankfully someone managed to knock the knife out of his hand. As we're trying to get to the dressing room, I then see the referee has got our goalkeeping coach by the scruff of the neck. You couldn't make it up. Ronnie shoved the coach out of the way and lost his head, I knew he was going to do something to the referee but I dragged him into the dressing room to calm down. He thanked me for doing so but then we got to the team hotel after the game and were given a fax saying we were banned and needed to return to England. We packed our stuff, and flew home after watching the next game.

When we got home we received the news that Ronnie had been banned for life in Belgium and banned for life in England. I'd been given two years in Belgium and one in England. I thought what a great start to my career. Sir Alex was great with me and said the club would appeal the suspension. I had sixteen witnesses to back up that I hadn't done anything and to be fair, Ronnie had some sticking up for him too. We went to the Glass House in Belgium for the hearing and listened to a lady translating the allegations of the officials. They were claiming Ronnie had grabbed the referee by the scruff of his neck and punched him in the face. I then apparently picked him up and head-butted him, knocking him out. He was FIFA listed and untouchable – they claimed to have photographic evidence of the markings on the referee's neck, but guess who took the pictures? The guy with the knife! My ban then went up to life in Belgium and two years in England, Ronnie's couldn't get any worse, obviously.

We went home and Sir Alex was again comforting us saying he would stand by us. Ironically, because Ronnie's ban was so extreme, the club had got his playing registration back and he was allowed to play while their appeal was being held. Because mine wasn't so bad they said it would be okay to remain suspended. We played Liverpool at Anfield at the start of the 1999/2000 season with this all going on, and afterwards the manager said I would have been involved, as it turned out Ronnie was named as a sub and he came on instead". A story so strange had an ending to befit it. "News came through from Belgium that the referee had officiated a game that finished 6-6 or something like that. After, he was interviewed and blamed what Ronnie and I had allegedly done. Two weeks later he made a horrendous error, and the Belgian Association sent him to be evaluated by a psychiatrist and the suspensions ended up being quashed," says Danny.

"One thing I will say about Sir Alex is that he knew all of the lads personally and knew of their character. So he knew, if someone had said something about one of us, whether it was true or not," Danny explains. "He flew over to be our character witnesses and stood up for us. He didn't have to do that. He told us he'd look after us and he was true to his word, and to show even more support he gave us both new contracts. He didn't owe us anything, we were players on the periphery, it was just brilliant. The other coaches were the same with us too when we were suspended. Knowing we couldn't play, they'd arrange little training matches for us to play in, and knowing we had that support was incredible. I could not have asked for anything more, they were the same with my family too."

Free to play, Danny was included in the first team squad on a regular basis in the coming months, and had increased attention accordingly. "It was obviously mentioned quite a lot, 'Danny Higginbotham who was at the centre of that controversy', but it was generally good press to be honest," he confesses. "Without a shadow of a doubt that was down to Sir Alex and the way he handled the press. That's why for me he's the greatest manager this country has ever seen, and will ever see. He would back his players and treat them like family. I'll remember that, and what he did afterwards for me in my career."

Danny started the League Cup defeat at Aston Villa in October 1999 and a few weeks later played against Sturm Graz and Leicester City in the space of a few days. "It was like a gradual progression, included in squads travelling and then named in the squad," he says. "I was named on the bench against Tottenham but didn't play, but then played those next two games. Maybe they thought that they were games they could afford to include me in, both for myself and games that the club could take that chance in. It seemed very well planned by the club."

Following the win over Leicester, Danny's next taste of first team action would come against South Melbourne, in the Club World Cup in January 2000. The competition was the source of much controversy as United had been pressured by the FA to participate in order to assist their bid to host the 2006 World Cup – after having agreed to do so, they were forced to relinquish their place in the FA Cup despite the offer of a compromise whereby United would field a second string side to defend the trophy they'd won as part of the treble in 1999. This was inaccurately reported as United disgracing the competition and withdrawing. As one of the players who would feasibly have been involved in the second string side, Danny prefers to concentrate on what actually happened and enjoy that experience for what it was. "I'd been a part of the travelling squad to Tokyo for the Intercontinental Cup but this was something else, going to Brazil and seeing the Copacabana," says Higginbotham. "I'm sure the results weren't what the club had hoped for but the experience of seeing Brazil, the have's and the have not's so close together, shanty towns across the roads from nice houses, it was another really good learning curve. I played against Melbourne and I'm glad to have had that experience."

Following the trip to Brazil, Higginbotham wasn't included in a game until United had secured the Premier League title, when he came on as substitute at Watford. He was to feature one more time, but not before a surprise twist to the end of the season. His reputation in Belgium, or at least his status amongst Antwerp supporters, had not been harmed by the events in 1999. "Before we were due to play Villa in the last game, Ronnie and I went to Belgium to play a game there at Regi's request. He took us to see the supporters known as the Ultras. Throughout our trouble, the supporters had shown they were behind us with banners saying 'Ronnie and Danny, you'll never walk alone'. They were lighting flares and chanting our names, it was incredible, and Regi said, 'This is what you mean to this football club. If you ever want to come over here and play for us, just let me know and I'll sort it'. Afterwards we went out, didn't get back in until about 5am on the Saturday, and then had to catch our plane. As we landed, I got a call saying I was in the squad for the game against Villa the next day. Ronnie and I played a half each after all that had gone on".

That game would be the last time Danny would play for the club. As a left back, he had a proud record of winning six out of the seven games he'd played for the first team and playing a part in keeping four clean sheets too. "I felt I'd done well, just not well enough to be a regular," he concedes. "I wanted the opportunity to play more often. I had it made up in my mind to give it another year. I was conscious of how many lads had stayed on too long and I didn't want that to be the case for me, just playing reserve team games. I also wanted to be tested. I was glad to play where I had, but theoretically the most competitive game I'd really played was the home game against Leicester City. One morning I got a call from my solicitor saying the manager would call me to let me know a bid from Derby had been accepted, and sure enough, he did. He said I was more than welcome to stay but there was Mikael Silvestre, Denis Irwin and Phil Neville in front of me. That made up my mind right away, the 'but'. If he'd said that he had plans for me that would have been different, but he was straight up and honest. I was only going to give it that year anyway, and my chances of making it there were slim to none." Despite being a supporter of the club, it wasn't a difficult choice to make as a professional. "I had to be selfish, and knew I needed to do something for my career," says Higginbotham. "Leaving when I did gave me the springboard to have the career that I went on to have."

Danny signed for Derby County in 2000 for £2m and went on to have an established career in the top flight with them, Southampton, and Stoke City, with spells at Sunderland and Nottingham Forest as well as Sheffield United, before moving to Chester City in the summer of 2013. That move lasted a few months before a very short lived spell at his hometown club, Altrincham. In early January, 2014, Danny shocked many when he announced his retirement. "Either the second year at Derby, as the first was such a learning experience, or the first few years at Stoke in the Premier League, would have to be the best times of my career," he says. "I missed out on promotion in my first spell with Stoke but when I got back it was great. They upset everyone, we should never have stayed in the league, but we finished 11th and 12th."

Higginbotham has endured a mixed relationship with the FA Cup Final. He was an unused substitute as Southampton lost the 2003 final, and was injured having played his part in getting Stoke to the 2011 final. Despite that hindsight, it doesn't make Danny treasure his Intercontinental Cup medal as a squad member in 1999 any more. "No, my mum and dad have that," he laughs. "If I'm not playing it's not really a medal for me. In 2003 I didn't expect to play as Southampton had done so well to get there. I took Francis Benali's place on the bench and he's a Saints legend and at the end of the game I tried to give him my medal, but he wouldn't take it. He ended up getting one as the club got some more, but I felt like a bit of an impostor. The 2011 game was a bit harder to take as it was a great time for me. I'd scored in the run, my son had just been born, but then I got injured against Chelsea. It was hard to take that I'd be out, especially as I'd been contributing and in the first team at that time."

That wasn't the only professional disappointment Danny had faced. In 2005 he experienced relegation with Southampton at the hands of his boyhood club. "I remember that so well. We played Palace the week before in a six pointer and I equalised in the last minute to take it to the last day when we played United at home," he recalls. "United had just missed out on winning the league so Sir Alex played his strongest side to prove a point. We took the lead and at one time were safe but we ended up losing, and going down – I was gutted. After, I was walking down the tunnel and Sir Alex was waiting for me. He put his arm around me and said, 'Danny, I'm really sorry, that's football, I just had to pick that team today.' He really didn't have to do or say anything but it shows the measure of the man."

Now at the end of his career, Danny is looking at his next steps. "Maybe I'll go into coaching with younger players, but as for management, no chance", he laughs. "I've had a lot of time away from my family in the last ten years and I owe them some time now. I enjoy the media side of it and talking about the game." In November 2013, however, came a huge shock when Danny accepted the call to play for Gibraltar. The country were finally accepted into UEFA ahead of Euro 2016 qualifying, and Higginbotham made history (by virtue of his maternal grandmother's nationality) when he lined up in a creditable 0-0 friendly draw with Slovakia. "The experience has brought me closer to my roots than I ever felt possible. You make mistakes in life but shouldn't have regrets and I'd have regretted turning the opportunity down," he admits.

From over 400 club appearances, Danny's choice of stand-out game might appear odd to some. "That Leicester game at Old Trafford will never be beaten; but the Gibraltar experience has matched it," he says. "After having been in the stands so often and then hearing my name read out on the tannoy alongside the other players to be starting a league game – it's a feeling that will never be beaten. Forget the size of the club, it was my local club, so to make just one appearance for them would have been something never to be beaten."

Danny shares the feeling of many home grown players that Manchester United provide young men with an education on life. "The grounding they give you is phenomenal. The main thing you're taught growing up at that football club is respect, self worth and how to conduct yourself. Giving anything less than 100% is not acceptable. I know that, I know I wasn't the most technically gifted, but giving everything in every single game is not something I picked up throughout my career, it's what I learned at Manchester United. What Sir Alex did speaks for itself. I've a lot to be thankful for personally, from my troubles in Belgium to what he did for me at Southampton. He took a lot of time to look after me and for that I'll be forever grateful."

13

Nick Culkin

Succeeding Peter Schmeichel was never going to be easy. Not until Edwin van der Sar arrived was there a return to the excellence we were used to seeing in the Manchester United goal, an assurance and confidence in that last line of defence on a regular basis. Some even argue that van der Sar was the equal or even better than Schmeichel, citing his European Cup winning contribution and record breaking clean sheet run in the 2008/09 season as examples.

Among the four goalkeepers who played in the early weeks of the 1999/2000 season, one of those was a record breaker too. Not Mark Bosnich (a Fledgling himself who had just returned to the club on a free transfer from Aston Villa), nor Raimond van der Gouw, or even Massimo Taibi, but – as you've most likely guessed by now – the subject of this chapter, Nick Culkin. There were other record breaking or record setting goalkeepers that broke into the first team as fledglings. Gary Walsh was the first goalkeeper, and indeed first Fledgling to be given a debut by Sir Alex Ferguson. Nick Culkin's record, too, is one unlikely to be broken. His substitute appearance for van der Gouw at Highbury in August 1999 was the shortest debut appearance in United history, and barring an unlikely return to Old Trafford following semi-retirement from the game, Culkin also holds the title of the official shortest first team career in the history of the club.

It was a bizarre introduction into United folklore and his very arrival at the club, some four years prior, was a little strange too. "I was at York City and I signed for United the day after York won 3-0 at Old Trafford in the Coca Cola Cup. It was a superb night, an unbelievable night, with great scenes. Obviously Fergie rotated the team but it was unbelievable to turn them over and then go on to progress with an historic win," Nick laughs. "The deal had been done that night between the directors and United without me knowing ... I was there, but I only found out when we got back. Alan Little said he wanted to see me in the morning. I didn't get much sleep but went in and he told me United wanted to sign me. I said, 'Okay, what if I wanted to stay?' And he told me that I couldn't as they needed the money. I went the next morning with my mum, step dad and a PFA representative to meet Fergie, not that I needed anyone to help me sign for United."

If the initial hesitance to leave Bootham Crescent for Old Trafford is confusing then it shouldn't be. "I'm a massive York fan, I always have been and still follow them," says Nick. "They're my hometown club and I just wanted to play for them.

I was only seventeen at the time and Dean Kiely, who's an absolute legend, was our keeper. I was hoping he would move and I would get a chance, but that never happened. I would still love to play for them even now. I do a bit here and there, but I think I'm getting on a bit now. Unbelievable isn't it, I played for United but my biggest regret is not playing for York."

It didn't take long for Culkin to be won over though. "We had a tour around Old Trafford on the day I signed and it was a great day out. You don't really say no to United, do you?" he admits. "There had been rumours that Les Kershaw was watching me and I would hear little things, but Leeds came in for me first. They made a bid but I didn't want to leave and it was turned down. Sunderland were sniffing around but nothing came of that, I just kept my head down and doing as much as I could, and I was playing really well at the time. All I wanted to do was play for my home town club. Unfortunately, or should I say fortunately, Man Utd came in, so that was that. It really is a club you don't turn down. It was a bizarre feeling, celebrating my team beating United one day and signing for them the next.

"I signed there on the Thursday and was training at United on the Monday doing a shooting session with Andy Cole and Eric Cantona. It was ridiculous." It took Nick a while to get to grips with the scale and speed of the change. "At first I was a little over-awed, trying to come to terms with it. Then you see the likes of David Beckham, Ryan Giggs, the Neville brothers, and you just begin to settle in and realise you're part of that."

Culkin had been close to breaking into the first team at York, so his rise in status in terms of clubs was inversely proportional to his chances of senior football, and soon after his arrival at United he was given his Youth Cup debut representing the holders following the 1995 triumph. Culkin remembers it well. "It was against Sunderland at Roker Park. The night before I'd made my debut for the reserves at Newcastle and we'd beaten them, keeping a clean sheet. Maybe because I'd already played for the reserves, and I had already started feeding into the mentality that's given by Sir Alex that every game must be a win, I didn't really feel any pressure in the Youth Cup game,"

Nick confesses, "You have to win at all costs – there's no pressure – you just have to win." They did just that, qualifying to play a strong Norwich City team spearheaded by one Craig Bellamy. Nick helped United get through with a clean sheet. "It was a really strong team we played against; we scored early on but weren't really in control. We were under the cosh for quite some time, but it was great to keep a clean sheet at Old Trafford. It can be overwhelming stepping out at the Theatre of Dreams but you can't afford to let that happen if you want to have a career there, they're the best club ever so you have to enjoy the ride."

Following that win, the Reds faced another big club and a strong team, this time Liverpool at Anfield, with Michael Owen among their ranks as well as David Thompson and Jamie Carragher. "The rivalry between Manchester United and Liverpool is intense throughout the club, whatever level you play at, and the manager saw us before the game to let us know that. United have to beat Liverpool, that's the way it has to be," says Nick. The team were dealt a blow when their build-up was disrupted. "Eric Harrison was ill, so wasn't there," Nick says, "So Neil Bailey took charge. We had loads of chances in the first half but didn't convert any, and then Liverpool started getting into the game and Michael Owen was just unplayable. He turned Ronnie Wallwork inside out for one of the goals and ended up scoring a hat-trick so that was it, out at the quarter final. I'm sure if we'd have got past Liverpool we'd have won it." A Manchester United goalkeeper experiencing the Kop can be an intimidating time, but Nick says he revelled in it. "I enjoyed it, I have to be honest," he says. "I like hostile places and having that response from fans, I like to be riled up as it makes me come out of my shell. It was just a shame that Michael Owen was at his best, he was playing a year younger too."

United were out as holders and after a meteoric rise and swift change in lifestyle, Nick began to settle in to what it meant to be a Manchester United player. "I stayed in Lower Broughton with a lady called Brenda, and Gavin Naylor, David Healy, Ryan Ford and Stuart Brightwell who were already there," he says. "We were well behaved, but you can't be getting into any trouble at United, it was a bunch of good lads who kept themselves to themselves." Nick mixed well with the team but a goalkeeper's education is very different to that of an outfield player when it comes to training. "Alan Hodgkinson was the goalkeeping coach when I arrived, but he wasn't there for that long, maybe the rest of the season. You could barely believe it but after that, we didn't have a goalkeeping coach for eighteen months! I still can't get over that now," he says. "Then we brought in Tony Coton as a player coach."

A year after Coton's return (he had originally signed at the club as a player in January 1996 just three months after Nick had arrived, before moving to Sunderland and returning to Old Trafford in the summer of 1997) Nick was involved in the first team squad for the pre-season tour of Norway. At the age of 20, he was unusually well built and developed for someone of his age and was clearly deemed ready to handle being around the first team squad. "My name was on the list to travel and that was more or less it, we were off on tour. Nothing had been said to me beforehand, that I'd done well or anything and that's why I was going, I'd just kept my head down and tried as hard as I could in training and the reserves," Nick remembers. "I'd played at Birmingham just before we went and although we lost 4-3 the manager kept me with the team. I didn't play in the first two games out in Norway but came on as a sub at half time for Peter Schmeichel against SK Brann. I was quite pleased with how I did." Nick kept a clean sheet – which he recalls clearly – but he does not recall the oddest thing about the game, which was a hat-trick from Denis Irwin that helped the Reds to a 4-0 win. "No way, did he really do that?" Nick laughs. "I can sort of remember him scoring, and

I remember the game really well but I had no idea he scored a hat-trick. I would never have believed that".

Nick's performances and contributions throughout pre-season were rewarded when he was included in the squad for the Charity Shield against Arsenal. "It was a good pre-season, I have to admit, and I really felt part of the squad," says Nick. "The Charity Shield is a fantastic occasion to be involved in. People say bad things about it but you'd rather be involved in it than not. It was just another big game, the rivalry between Arsenal and United was fierce, not like it is now. We all wanted to win, it was great to warm Peter up at Wembley. I'd love to have played in it, unfortunately it wasn't to be, but to experience being in front of 90,000 fans was something else. I might have been an unlucky omen though, involved in two Charity Shields and we lost both".

Nine days later Nick would feature in another friendly, a game that has already been mentioned in this anthology, the 40th anniversary memorial against an Eric Cantona side at Old Trafford. "That was just fantastic. I think Schmeichel was injured, so I played the first 45 minutes with Paul Gibson playing the second half," said Nick. "It was just one of the most incredible occasions. There was lots of build up to it, for everything it was, there was a minute's silence before the game, and so many stars, Jean Pierre Papin, Paul Gascoigne, and Eric of course. I got a video of the game and I think I did quite well. I had to make a point blank save from Mark Hughes. Their keeper, Pascal Olmeta, was a nutcase! They weren't taking it so seriously but it meant a lot to me to play in front of a full house at Old Trafford. I didn't make any mistakes and I didn't let myself down, so I was really pleased with it."

So began one of the most eventful seasons in United's history. Culkin had to make do with a spectator's role as the first team won the Premier League, FA Cup and Champions League with van der Gouw the deputy goalkeeper for Schmeichel. The Danish legend announced in the December that he would retire from English football at the end of the season, leading to much speculation about his successor. Despite that, Nick never felt like he would be destined to be first choice goalkeeper at Old Trafford. "I suppose with how things went with Mark Bosnich and then Taibi, I might have had half a chance", he laughs. "But in reality, I knew that I wasn't close to being number one at that point and eventually, when Fabien Barthez came in, I sort of knew what the situation was. I signed a two year deal just before Peter left but that was more to do with the fact I was progressing well, and the club's long term plan was to send me out on loan." Nick shares an interesting insight into Sir Alex's hopes for the goalkeeping position at United. "When I first signed, I can remember the manager telling me that they wanted a home grown keeper, that Manchester United should be trying to bring one through as they hadn't had a regular British goalkeeper for quite some time."

Culkin didn't feature in the pre-season tour to Australia following the treble win but played in the first friendly back in the UK, in Omagh against Omagh Town in a comprehensive 9-0 win. Again, he'd done enough to be included in the Charity Shield squad, but again, that was a defeat to Arsenal. Three weeks later, he was to be included in the squad to face the same opponents at Highbury following an injury to new signing Bosnich. "I'd been in and around the squad throughout the pre-season and early season, and had experience of travelling around Europe with the team as third choice keeper," says Nick. "Going to Arsenal and being named substitute wasn't really anything out of the ordinary for me. You've been around it for so long that you just don't feel any pressure. The build up was quite intense, we'd lost at Highbury the previous two years, so the Gaffer was making sure all of the tactics were right, and the game went really well. Freddie Ljungberg scored their goal but then Roy Keane equalised and scored in the 88th minute to put us in front. Arsenal were hitting back but I thought we would see the game out. All of a sudden, from a free kick, Martin Keown proper took out Raimond in our goal. I got up to warm up like you do but I didn't think anything of it as Rai's a tough lad, but then Rob Swire, the physio turned to the Gaffer and said he couldn't carry on. The Gaffer turned to me and said 'Alright Nick, on you go mate', just as nonchalant as anything. I thought there were going to be about three or four minutes left of injury time and prepared for it. Steve McClaren came up to me and said 'Just put the free kick on Sylvinho's head'. I ran out on the pitch and Henning Berg was saying 'Nick, I know you've not warmed up, do you want me to take it', but I just said it was no problem.

"I put my head down and walked back as you do, a few Arsenal fans were throwing coins at the back of my head, and as I looked up Marc Overmars and Dennis Bergkamp were trying to encroach. I was thinking, 'Oh god, if I shank this, I'll never be able to get the coach home, they'll absolutely kill me'. I took the kick and the whistle went immediately. If you watch it back, I celebrate and it looks like relief, but it was more about winning – I was looking forward to actually playing and getting involved to show what I could do even in that short time. It wasn't to be, but I maintain that was the best kick ever and I put it exactly where I was told to."

With that, he instantly entered the record books, hasn't been dislodged since, and it seems unlikely he will for quite some time. "Because of the circumstances people remember me more than some people who played ten or fifteen times for United, and despite how brief it was, I have to say I'm really proud of it. A lot of fans would give a lot for that moment. I got a clean sheet bonus too, which I've got to say was pretty nice," he laughs.

Soon afterwards, with the lingering concerns over Bosnich's fitness, Ferguson signed Massimo Taibi for £3.5m. Following the experiences of training with Schmeichel, it was quite a different environment with the likes of Bosnich and Taibi. "For a start, Taibi didn't speak English which made it difficult," says Nick. "There were problems straight away, I didn't really understand the signing at all. They were worried about Bosnich but still I didn't get it. Massimo didn't settle and made a lot of mistakes so didn't last long. He's a nice man but I think he was more suited to the Italian game and he did brilliantly there when he went back.

"I'd be lying if I said I wouldn't have loved the chance to play those games and get that opportunity. Unfortunately I wasn't good enough. If I was, I would have – it's as clean cut as that. That's the way it was and the way it has to be. Manchester United need world class players for every position. I wasn't world class and so I wasn't going to get that chance." Earlier in this book, Kevin Pilkington shared that he felt the experience gained by just observing the practices of Peter Schmeichel was worth more than, say, a first team place on loan somewhere else, but Culkin disagrees. "For me, you've got to want to be playing football", he says. "I watched him train too, I'd never seen anything like it before and I never will again. In training he would be unbeatable, and I mean unbeatable. He's the best goalkeeper ever, the best I've ever seen. It's amazing to watch but trying to copy that would be impossible. Even after he left, and I was competing with other goalkeepers who weren't quite on his level, I have to say I was happy to go on loan and I was quite pleased with how they went."

The first loan spell was at Hull City, before a very successful loan at Bristol Rovers in the 2000/01 season where he was first choice, before a six month period at Livingston in Scotland. Livingston had enjoyed some serious financial injection in the squad and found themselves, for the time that Nick was there, as Scotland's "third" team after Celtic and Rangers. "I had an amazing time there and played over twenty games," he said. "The owner had put a lot of money into it and they'd gone through the leagues quickly. I think there were only about three or four Scottish players, but it was a brilliant team. We beat Hibs 3-0 at Easter Road, I think we beat Hearts away 3-0, and we almost got a point at Celtic on Boxing Day. What an incredible atmosphere, 55,000 drunk Scottish fans in Celtic Park at Christmas. We were drawing 2-2 and I'd been very busy. I remember looking at the clock and there were two minutes left, but then one of the defenders tried and failed to take Alan Thompson out. He set up Henrik Larsson who scored. We would have been the only team to take points away from Celtic Park but regardless, we still ended up finishing third. Third in Scotland is basically winning the league anyway considering the opposition, and we played in Europe which was an amazing achievement."

Despite the progress he'd made, Culkin maintained hope that he would be able to break through back at Old Trafford. "I was only 24, not near my peak, so I was hoping I could get back to United and crack on. To finish third in the SPL was brilliant, though. Sadly the loan was cut short as I broke my finger but the experience was brilliant and it was a great place."

Despite returning to United ready to face the challenge, Nick was instead transferred to QPR. "I was offered a one year extension but QPR offered me three years," says Nick. "Fabien had been there for a while, a World Cup winner, and when I told the manager I'd been offered a deal at Loftus Road, he said all things considered it would probably be best if I did leave the club." It turned out to be the wrong move. "I had a disastrous time down there," Nick admits. "From day one it was a disaster, a nightmare. I was always injured, and I think I might not even have played thirty games for them.

"Just before the season started, Danny Shittu smashed a ball at me from two yards out and I did all my ankle ligaments in. That kept me out for six weeks, and then I was always chasing to get my place back. I got a little run in the second season but then I got a knee problem which I never really recovered from. It's a great club and they have great fans but I was injured through all of the last season there." Nick was forced to announce his retirement from the professional game at just 27. "It was soul destroying," he says. "I probably still haven't got over it, you always look for that adrenalin rush of running out for a game. When I was told I should stop because my knee couldn't cope, when your whole world is football and it comes crashing down in one conversation, it's hard to take. Time to get back to the real world, life goes on – and that was it."

Following the decision to retire, Nick took a couple of months out to consider his options. "I took time out and got myself together. A friend of mine was doing some gardening and asked if I'd like to get involved, so I did, and I've been doing it ever since. I set up my business in 2010," he says. "I fell out with the game for about six or seven years and I've only just started taking my coaching badges. It's a bit annoying because I only want to be a goalkeeping coach but have to do all the outfield stuff too.

"The doctors told me my knee might get better, not good enough for full time training, but good enough to play a few games here and there. Just after I set up my business, my son asked me why I didn't start trying to play again so I thought I'd give it a go, got myself into a half decent condition, and contacted my local team which was Radcliffe Borough. I went there in the pre-season and played nearly a hundred games, it was nice that my two boys could come and watch."

The decision to come back into the game was a good one. "It went really well, I got the players player of the year, the supporters player of the year and the managers player of the year award. The next year I got the players and supporters awards again and got voted in the team of the year by all the other managers, so there's life in the old dog yet. I played a few games for a club called Prescot Cables, a proper old fashioned club, and have helped them out once or twice. It's nice to help the younger lads who are learning and they're always asking me about my time at United. The club might struggle, but to be involved after missing such a long time from the game is nice. If I keep myself in a decent condition there's a good chance I can play at this level until I'm 41 or 42, that's my next ambition anyway. I feel as good, if not better, than I did when I was 21, so maybe my peak is still to come."

Despite the setbacks, Nick looks back on what he achieved with fondness. "I'm proud of what I achieved, even though it was only a short career. There are a lot of people worse off than I am. Playing wise, I had a really good time at Livingston, but at Bristol, even though we got relegated, I kept eighteen clean sheets and was given the player of the year award. I've had a decent relationship with supporters wherever I've been but I'd have to give a special mention to the Bristol Rovers fans as they were fantastic, and I am absolutely over the moon with my place in the United record books. I don't care how short it is, that was my time and a lot of people would have given a lot for what I did."

14

Bojan Djordjic

As we've learned, the inexplicable loss of an immense talent from Manchester United, for whatever the reason, is nothing new. The greatest loss comes not when the club is unable to keep a star name (alà a Pogba) but when that potential does not go on to be fulfilled in the game at any club. Bojan Djordjic is one such case. Once so extravagantly blessed with talent that he had to be refrained from embarrassing United defenders in training, the way he is ultimately remembered by most fans of the Old Trafford club is that he was a "legend" on the Championship Manager simulator computer games. It's a tag he takes lightly yet there is no other way to say it. Djordjic should easily have gone on to become a United first teamer. He had the ability, the strength of character and even his mere existence, born in Belgrade on February 6th 1982 with his home town club being Red Star Belgrade, had eerie nostalgic connections with United.

Playing at IF Brommapojkarna at the time of the interview, it was a potential move to Red Star in the summer of 2013 that made Bojan difficult to track down to do the interview for this book, though he had agreed some months prior. "This week has been a tough one for me," he laughs. "It's been a busy one so I've been avoiding contact. Red Star have shown interest and my contract has a clause in it saying I can leave for free. Brommapojkarna is almost like my home town so everyone thought I would settle down here, but Red Star is my first love, and I'm trying to keep my head down. They're writing in the press that I have had a fight with my coach, and that's not right, but obviously they bring up everything in my past. I'm unsure about moving as I do feel comfortable at home, we've played half of the season, I've played well and found the passion again. I almost lost that. I need to be hungry and have that desire to play, otherwise I'm shit." It's a bluntness and an openness that is typical of Djordjic. "I still have the same highs and lows as I did when I was at United. I could be great one game and terrible the next week. It's just the way I've always been." At the start of 2014, following the expiry of his contract, Djordjic left his club and trained with AIK, though on his 32nd birthday he was without a contract.

It's natural for Djordjic to use United as his point of reference. That is, after all, the point of our discussion, and no matter what he does from here on in, he will more than likely always be more remembered for not quite getting into the team at Old Trafford, with many perhaps unfairly citing his attitude as the reason rather than his talent. "It might be a bit unfair. Look, people can say what they want, it's not like there was Twitter, Facebook, all this social networking about when I was playing at United," he says. "You get the youth players, average youth players, getting more attention than some of the legends and that's not right. It's crazy. I say this kind of stuff and people say 'ahh just because you didn't make it', but I lived a dream, I did what most people dream of doing, being at the same dressing room as some of these players. Because I wasn't in the first team a lot, people think I was shit, but I was far from that, I still believe I was one of the most talented players at that time."

"That time" Bojan refers to is probably around 2000-2001. He arrived at the club in 1999, signing terms on his 17th birthday – the 41st anniversary of the Munich Air Disaster – but had already been playing professionally in Sweden. His father, Ranko, had been a successful professional footballer, so the grounding was there. As a sixteen year old, Djordjic was so advanced that he was playing in the equivalent of the English Championship for Brommapojkarna. His fearless, natural ability to take players on attracted many admirers, though he didn't quite get the move he was hoping for as a child. "Like I said, Red Star were my first love. They were the team I followed from a young age, the team that when they lost a game I cried, so I've always been that," says Bojan. "I don't know if it's because of my birthday, being born in Belgrade, and what happened with United. I don't always believe in superstition and things like that, but it is freaky, and that I went on to play for both as well. United had always been close to me because of that. As a 10 year old boy I was watching Giggsy playing on the left wing every Saturday, then Cantona came and put his collar up. That was just the thing to do, you know."

United's eyes became aware of Djordjic in an under-16 tournament in Slovakia. "We played against England and I've always said that you have to be good in the right games. You can be good all season but when the scouts come you're rubbish and don't get a contract. I think I got caught on the right game," says Bojan. "I was invited to go to United at the end of 1998 for a week's trial, with Kennedy Bakircioglü (who would go on to play for Ajax in a long top-level career) who plays for Hammarby in Stockholm. I remember Dave Williams and Neil Bailey telling me they wanted me to stay. I did really well. I'd had a few trials at different clubs around Europe, United were almost like my last stop on the European tour. I was so tired, I just wanted to go home. People probably think 'How is that the case,' but when you've been away from your family for so long and you have people promising things that don't happen, you get to the place that you wanted to be first of all, and you're so tired. When I first got there I was like, 'What is this?' it seemed not real. Maybe it's because I was so out of it, but I trained like I'd been there for years.

"A few days later we had a trial game. I played with the likes of Danny Webber and Jimmy Davis. I was in midfield. I did really well and was offered a contract on my seventeenth birthday but was loaned back to my old club to see the 1998/99 season out. Sadly that meant I never got to travel to Barcelona when the entire club was there. I look at the pictures and do wish I was there but to be honest it was just one of those things."

In modern age, United signing youngsters from overseas happens on something of a prolific basis but this wasn't the case for Bojan, so his introduction to the English lifestyle was considerably more difficult than others who may have made the trip afterwards. With no compatriots to confide in and a reputation as a 17 year-old who was already used to playing in the first team, being thrust into a United squad that was arguably the most competitive in its history was a substantial challenge. "I wouldn't say I was bullied but I could see in the beginning that something was wrong, I wouldn't get the ball passed to me," he says. "At the same time, maybe they expected me to be a typical quiet Swede. I wasn't one to do that, after all I have Serbian blood in me and we're hotheads! I wanted to keep quiet at the beginning and see how it was and to an extent, I didn't blame them for being cautious. I was there to take a place in the team from someone else, of course, that's how it works. Abroad (from Sweden), it's a completely different mentality. At home, everything's focussed on the group, everybody has to train and play the same, that was impossible for me. A team is full of individuals, some need a hug, some need a slap, we all have different needs."

Gradually, Bojan made his mark. "Obviously I did get some of the ball more often, I was able to show what I could do, what I was made of, and when I had proven my ability, then I was able to speak up and say more things. I was making a point that they'd been a little unfair to me in the beginning, and now I was in a position that I could say something back."

Though later on Djordjic's individuality may have cost him at certain points, in those early days, it did him plenty of favours. "I think the Gaffer liked me because of that," he suggests. "Maybe even the youth team players liked it too, having that cockiness in their team. When I was training with the first team sometimes they'd pass me the ball really hard, or send it too far in the box for me, I don't know if they were looking to get a reaction. The thing was, I didn't care who anybody was, if somebody did something that was wrong according to me, then I would tell them. Because I had that desire to improve, to make something of myself and prove that I wasn't just there to be released after a year, I think the manager was impressed by that. I wanted to be remembered even if I didn't make it. Even though it was hard going, and I would think in the years after 'was that the right way to go', I think that events that happened years later sort of proved that I was at least right to stand up for myself and show that kind of character early on."

Djordjic made an impression throughout the club. Aged just 17, he wasn't included in the Youth Cup, instead making more of an appearance for the reserves, and did so well in his first season that he was awarded the Jimmy Murphy Young Player Of The Year for the 1999/2000 season. "After I'd settled, I was able to really show my talent," says Bojan. "But I have to be honest and say I wasn't training great or properly, I wasn't really pushing to improve myself. I'd still do things right, hit a cross or make the right pass, but there were things I just wouldn't do. I was young and injury free, carefree, and believed in my own ability, I didn't think that I would need to go to the gym or do things like that. Of course, you learn from your next steps, but I would only do things if I really had to. Still, I was doing well. I was called into the reserve team really early on and I was playing so well. This was a team that had plenty of first team players in it, and players that would go on to play for the first team, so I was really happy with how things were going."

Though natural progression dictates that the next step after the reserves is getting into the first team, Bojan feels that was too simplistic a statement for that time. "Believe me, that first team was packed with world class players," he says. "When you're a young kid from Sweden trying to break into a team with Beckham, Keane, Scholes and Giggs in it, you know how difficult it is." Nonetheless, he'd done remarkably well to get to the point that his performance was being recognised with such an accolade, though he very nearly never got the trophy. "When they told me I honestly thought it was a joke," he says. "I had a flight to go back home and it was when we were playing Tottenham in the last home game of the season. There wasn't another flight back home for two or three days and I was so homesick at that time, I'd had a great season and wanted to celebrate with my family. Then I got a phone call saying, 'Listen Bo, you have to be there, you have to be in the tunnel at half time'. My first reaction was 'Oh, what the fuck have I done now?' because the gaffer had a few words with me in the recent weeks about my behaviour in training. I thought I was going to get a telling off so I'd better be there. When I arrived at Old Trafford, I was told to put my suit on and someone said I was going to get a trophy. I said 'It's not just for me is it?' and then I was told what the award was and sent out to collect it. I strolled out in front of fifty thousand people standing up and applauding me. That was one of the proudest moments in my entire life even if I didn't really acknowledge it at the time.

"Looking back, it's something that I'm so proud of doing, something that I achieved that is now a part of history. People might wonder who I was but for me, it meant a lot. Manchester United is perhaps the greatest club ever and the team at that time was maybe the best it ever had. Maybe in the history of football only the Barcelona team from 2009 to 2012 can compare, so to have my name so close to it is something that I am really proud of achieving. Even Juan Sebastian Veron had to sit on the bench when he came so it tells you something about the quality of that team. What chance did I have with one of the best midfielders of all time sitting on the bench."

Veron would arrive in the summer of 2001, by which time Bojan's major chance to break through had seemingly been and gone. His strong year of 2000 continued into the pre-season of 2000/01 when he was included in the squad for the first pre-season friendly, at York City. Bojan Djordjic coming on for Ryan Giggs was probably something that should have been said a lot more over the next few years, though Bojan feels he equipped himself well in that friendly at Bootham Crescent. "I came on for about half an hour and felt like I did really well," he says. "Yes, they were only a lower league team, but I did okay and I was obviously hoping with the way I'd progressed that I'd be seeing more of the first team".

In that pre-season, the usual back up to Giggs, Jesper Blomqvist, suffered a knee injury that meant he would never play for the club again, strengthening the belief that Djordjic would begin to get opportunities. "I just waited for the chance. I trained hard and worked hard, I kept trying to show what I could do, but as a young player, the frustration grows. I was thinking that maybe I should train a little harder. But then you have a lot of time to yourself, and you go through all the names that are in the squad, should I just be happy to train with them? Playing at Gigg Lane for the reserves with good players at the age of 18 or 19 is still a good achievement but I was above that level already. It was an honour at the beginning but I was ready for the next step ... no disrespect to the reserves, I don't know how best to explain it but I'd almost run through what I was going to do in the game beforehand and was able to do it."

Djordjic's frustration could be understood. He wasn't selected for either of the League Cup ties at Watford or Sunderland with the likes of Luke Chadwick, Jonathan Greening and Quinton Fortune being selected in front of him. To further add to his woes, the 2000/01 season was the first in the ultimately unsuccessful expanded Champions League, where teams had to qualify through two group stages before reaching the knock out rounds. It meant more games, and more "dead rubber" matches where the manager could afford to rotate. Still, Djordjic wasn't selected.

Even when United secured the league title with five games left to play, it wasn't until the Celtic legend Tom Boyd's testimonial game in Glasgow after the penultimate game of the season that the Swedish forward would be back in the first team squad. There was a sense of irony about the fact that United were heavily rotating their squad in the league games yet took a full strength team for the game at Celtic Park and in front of 57,000 fans Djordjic had his most memorable moment in a United shirt. "I was happy to be selected for the game and I was warming up through the second half thinking 'Gaffer come on, just put me on!'", says Bojan. "I wanted to play more than half an hour, the atmosphere was brilliant, then the gaffer told me to come on and I began to realise how big it was. All that noise and the opportunity to play with Scholesy and Sheringham, I was thinking 'Oh my God' but when I was on the pitch I just settled down and did my thing."

His thing, it turned out, would be a pretty remarkable, exquisite effort to seal the result in United's favour. "I came on for Giggsy and in the last couple of minutes I scored that chip to make it 2-0, and I think that opened everybody's eyes to what I was really capable of," he says. "Everyone just started talking about me all of a sudden, this teenager from Sweden who scored a wonder goal. It's like I say, if that was to happen in this day, with all the attention, it would have been ten times bigger."

It's one thing having confidence in yourself but demonstrating the ability in such an environment is a pretty big leap. "I've always liked pressure, the best games I've played in recent years are derbies or decisive games", he says. "It's an opportunity to really show I can play. That was what it was like against Celtic. The keeper had come so far out and I thought the only thing I could do was chip him. I remember Butty and Silvestre coming up to congratulate me but I was like, let me go man, I want to celebrate." Such a finish was almost becoming Bojan's trademark in training. "I never had the hardest shot but I was very good at lifting the ball like that, it was my thing. It came unplanned but I just did it more often than not," he says.

There was no way that Ferguson could leave Djordjic out for the final game of the campaign. "We went down to London and when we got there he told me I was going to make my debut. I remember I couldn't sleep in the hotel that night. I couldn't believe it, I knew he was a man who kept his word," he says. "It didn't matter to me if it would be ten seconds or thirty seconds or thirty minutes, or that it was the last game of the season, I was going to pull on that shirt and give everything."

United had lost their two games going into the last league game at Spurs, and after going behind yet again, Ferguson brought Bojan on for Denis Irwin with around quarter of an hour left. "To come on for another legend, Mr Steady Eddie, someone who had made over five hundred appearances for United, was a huge honour for me", says Djordjic. "Just being on the bus, talking to the other guys, and being accepted. There were so many world class players there and I really felt like I belonged. That's why when I speak about United today, I do it with so much passion, because I felt like I belonged there and understood what was required. It always amuses me to hear people have a go at me, they'll say, 'What do you know about United', this will come from someone that was never at the club for a day in their lives, but at least for a while the Gaffer saw something in me and I was accepted for that. I can say that I went back to Sweden that summer very happy and excited."

Sadly, the achievement wasn't quite celebrated in his homeland. "I don't know why, maybe it's because of my Serbian background, but I wasn't really accepted back in Sweden. I suppose I hold a bit of a grudge against them for that," admits Bojan.

Djordjic would go on to feature in the following pre-season, even after the arrival of Ruud van Nistelrooy and Juan Sebastian Veron. He didn't play in the Far East tour but played his first friendly on a day when United sent two teams to play at different clubs on the same day.

Djordjic was with the team that went to Hereford instead of the one that played at Wrexham, and started in a 6-0 win. A few days later he was a used substitute (replacing Fortune) in a comfortable win at Bury. Still, when the real business came around, he found himself behind Fortune and behind the likes of Jonathan Greening, Luke Chadwick and Michael Stewart for opportunities. "It was just the way it was, even if I was more talented than they were, or if I had the potential to change a game more than what they did, maybe it was because I was so hot and cold, or unreliable. At least with the others you knew what you were getting," he admits. "One of my mates came over to watch me for a couple of weeks and after the first game he was saying to me, 'Oh my god what a player, I don't think I've ever seen a young United player like you with so much talent.' The next week he said 'Where is Bo and what have you done with him?' ... I don't know, maybe subconsciously I was getting frustrated with continuously playing for the reserves."

Bojan would get his second, and final, appearance for United in an infamous League Cup game at Arsenal's Highbury Stadium which became more remembered for the fact that Paul Scholes refused to play in it rather than the pretty embarrassing 4-0 defeat. There were mitigating circumstances for the loss, however as only the day before, United had played at Anfield and so were really in no position to field their strongest side even if they had wanted to. Djordjic was named in the starting eleven and felt he did okay. "I hit the post and the bar and I thought I'd played well", he says. "It was mostly the reserve side against a stronger Arsenal team, we might have lost by a lot but I thought we did quite well, creating a lot of chances and missing them. The Gaffer used to say to us that it didn't matter if we lost by a lot as long as we could feel that we had done something to say we had made an impact on the game. If we at least tried to create something instead of taking the handbrake off and feeling sorry about ourselves, then it was something to take away and build on. The result was embarrassing because we were representing the club even though fans understood. I'm not going to lie, I benefitted from the crazy scheduling because otherwise I might not have played and afterwards Sheffield Wednesday said they wanted to take me for a month on loan."

Alongside Bojan in the starting line up at Arsenal was a player making what would ultimately be his only appearance for Manchester United, the late Jimmy Davis. "I always got on really well with him. It was freaky because strangely enough he too was born on the 6th February, 1982", says Bojan. "We were really tight, me, him and Danny Webber would be called the Three Amigos. I was close to John O'Shea as well because we shared digs, too, and it was so good that the four of us started that game. Jimmy was a part of us. He was always happy and pulling jokes with his Brummie accent. He was so fast, gave something extra and could have had a great career. I can still remember hearing about the news when he died and Scholesy rung me up. I was at Red Star on loan, on the way home from a game on the bus. It was a tough time."

Before that loan move, Djordjic spent December 2001 at Hillsborough. "After my first game for Sheffield Wednesday against Millwall the papers were hailing me as the next Ryan Giggs again, it was one of the best games I've ever had in my career", says Bojan. "It was really good, but I was only there for the December because Championship clubs could loan players and in January there was the re-registration for the Champions League at United. I needed first team football".

Once again, despite qualification from the second group stage, Djordjic wasn't called upon and even after a number of injuries set United back late in the season, they didn't use the young winger. He understood he'd probably need a season long loan to really get a chance of proper first team football after another pre-season where he featured for the first team but then wasn't included in competitive squads once the real action began. So he went to Aarhus in Denmark and was a first team regular before returning to Manchester. This time, instead of going on the pre-season, the opportunity arose to go on loan to Red Star Belgrade – it was one Bojan was only too happy to take. "Both of those loan spells went well but of course the Red Star one was special", he admits. "It's probably difficult to explain but Red Star are a huge, huge club. It is similar to United in that they have a history, there is a pressure to win, and the fans are crazy demanding that you win. We won the League and Cup that season, to have my name in the record books of the club that I loved so much growing up, with that special achievement, is something you'll never forget."

In that spell in Belgrade, Bojan shared the dressing room with a future Manchester United captain. "Nemanja Vidic was a hell of a player even in those days," he says. "I was telling people back at United that they needed to be looking at him. We'd speak about United sometimes but even talking to him about it, someone who was one of the youngest captains in Red Star's history, it was hard to think that one day he would be the captain of Manchester United. He was such a great player, he gave everything, putting his feet where I would put my head. You'd look back and see him in your defence and just feel you wouldn't concede any goals."

Though a regular once more, and even managing to score in a Red Star shirt, Bojan feels that the loan moves hampered his chances at United instead of helping them. "If I'd stayed at United through those two years then I probably would have got more chances to play," he says. "By that point, I'd probably spent more time on loan than I actually had at United, but I needed regular football. After the loan spell at Aarhus, they offered United a fair bit of money to sign me on a permanent basis but by that time I'd heard that Red Star wanted me on loan so for me that was a chance I didn't want to turn down. It was not only my boyhood club, the club my dad represented with so much history, but they were also challenging to win things. I couldn't say no to that, and it was better for me to go there than Denmark."

Djordjic's performances with Red Star were impressive enough to ensure he would be taken with United's first team tour of North America in the pre-season for the 2004/05 campaign. "I started alongside Keano against Bayern Munich in Chicago and thought I did well," he says. "But a couple of days I got injured and that was it for the tour and when I got back and fit, the gaffer said Rangers were interested. He was honest with me and told me my chances were limited and that he just didn't see me featuring for the first team on a regular basis. I was 23 or 24, at that age you're either a first team player or you're not, I couldn't play with the reserves any more because it was like playing with little kids. I don't mean that disrespectfully, I just mean that it was a stage of my career that I'd gone past. I'd been playing in front of 70,000 for Red Star against Partizan Belgrade and then came back to play reserve football in front of twenty seven frozen souls at Altrincham."

At the time, there was an interview where it was alleged that Bojan had said that he was at United to play Champions League football and not play with less talented players in the reserves. This was a misinterpretation. "I said words to that effect but I meant it in a different way," he insists. "Yes I could be cocky but I'm not stupid, ignorant or disrespectful. I said I joined United with the hope one day I could accomplish my dream of winning the Champions League What kind of motivation is it to join United and just hope to be a reserve team player? It's not a goal to be a reserve team player, I wanted to achieve the very best and you have to have these goals. Reach for the highest, accept you might sometimes fall a little bit, but if you reach to become a reserve player and don't even become that then you're basically a nobody in the game. I don't think there's anything wrong with wanting the best, you have to do that to succeed."

Another story that would become something in the way of folklore attached to Djordjic's cult status was that burdened with the frustration of not getting his opportunity, he would try and embarrass more established stars in training in an attempt to showcase his talents to the manager. "It's probably accurate but not in any way other than that was just me," says Bojan. "That was the way I always was. On one occasion me and Maysie (David May) nearly came to blows but we now get along really well. We played a friendly and almost had a fight in the dressing room before the game. I guess you could say that I was trying to humiliate them but I wasn't, it was just me. I'm a very straight person and wouldn't do something to create a problem, I'll never be the guy who sticks a knife into someone's back. If I have a problem with someone I'll go right to their face to sort it out."

For a while, that explosive attitude didn't quite sit well with the manager, which might well explain the long spells on loan. "I think maybe the gaffer didn't really appreciate the way I was getting in training and for a while I couldn't really speak to him about it," says Bojan. "I had a decent relationship with Steve McClaren, and then Mike Phelan, and probably had better relationships with Choccy (Brian McClair) and Ricky Sbragia. Choccy would always tell me where I could improve, would listen to me, and would never tell me off. He accepted me as I was. Sometimes I listened, sometimes I didn't. I'd be a bit of a moaner, I can admit. There was a drill we were running in the reserves at one time, they were putting the ball in the box. Someone played a poor ball and I didn't move for it, Mick Phelan asked me why I didn't and I told him it was a shit ball. I said if I was going to go in for that ball I might as well keep walking to the car and go home. He dared me to do it and I did. After five minutes of training I just turned round and went home."

This was not a one off – it happened a few times and Bojan would regularly get fined for the behaviour. "It'd happen everytime, I'd start walking out and then wonder if I was wrong. But then I'd be halfway, I'd made my mind up, and was that strong minded I just kept going. The number of times I should have just turned around and said 'Sorry, I made a mistake, can I come back'. In a way I regret it but at least people can look at it now and laugh. I know people will read this and think what was he doing, throwing away that chance at United, but that was just me and it was the way it was. When you're in there it's very hard to be correct with every single thing you do."

By this point, the club were now being linked to players labelled the next "Ryan Giggs" as Bojan himself once was. It's laughable, knowing what we know now, that Damien Duff and Arjen Robben were hotly tipped to succeed Giggs in the number eleven shirt, but in 2004/05 that was the case and sadly for Djordjic it meant that his own opportunity to at least be back-up for Giggs was close to an end. "Rangers was a massive club and the name still is massive, and I felt fortunate that after leaving United that I still had the chance to play for such a big club. A lot of names leave United and go to lower leagues, especially at the age I was, but I got the chance to go to another of the United Kingdom's biggest clubs," he says.

He was given quite a baptism – only a couple of days after signing he was playing in an Old Firm derby. "I didn't play so many games while I was there but they showed faith in me to start me in the biggest game they possibly could. The atmosphere was incredible. We lost 2-1, a goal in the last few minutes from John Hartson, but Alex McLeish came to me after and said he'd never seen such courage from a player coming into a game like that. He said I should be proud of myself and that was something I'll never forget. It was frustrating, though, I played a handful games and after that I was gone all season. Alex McLeish left, Paul Le Guen came in and didn't want me. I'd only signed a six month contract so was free to find another club at the end of the season. It was annoying. I was now getting injuries when I was seemingly getting my feet on the ground at United and then at Rangers. I'd never complete my fitness programs fully, I'd always come back at 70 or 80 per cent and say I was ready. You can't really do that at the highest level."

Djordjic was 23 in the summer of 2005 when he was unattached to a club. It seemed a huge loss of a talent, someone tipped for the very top who had lost his way. There was an obvious, subsequent result to not featuring at club level often enough, his international career had completely and irrevocably stalled. Once a star for the under 18 national side (indeed, where he had been discovered by United), Bojan feels that his outspoken character had ramifications when it came to being picked for the senior side. "I think they didn't like me. Let's face it, Red Star are a big club and I was playing for them regularly enough, and playing well enough to be considered, but because of my character I think they just tried to ignore me," suggests Bojan. "Maybe it might have helped if I'd been playing in Sweden under their noses, or if I'd have kept my mouth shut until I'd been selected and they could have seen how good I could have been for them. Everything changes if they become dependent on you and see if they can handle the extra. Look at Zlatan Ibrahimovic, he would not have set foot in the national team either. But now he's so big, they cannot touch him, he's just untouchable."

For whatever the reason, Djordjic's next move was completely surprising, signing for Plymouth Argyle and Bobby Williamson. "People said 'why Plymouth?' but I really enjoyed it there, the people really took to me and still remember me. I was a bit of a fans favourite, I'd do that little bit extra, something different, a nutmeg or an inventive pass," says Djordjic. "Bobby was yet another Scot and he probably took advice from Alex McLeish who suggested I'd be a good player. It was nice. You can have bad reports from a manager and it can ruin you, so it was good that people I'd worked with and played for were still saying good things about me."

Things may have been looking rosy for Djordjic, under a manager who clearly thought highly of him, but just two months into the new season Williamson was sacked and replaced by Tony Pulis, a manager whose brand of football was more uncompromising than it was entertaining. "That was completely different. Because I wasn't his kind of player I started becoming a 'super sub' for away games. I'd never start away from home," says Bojan. "If we needed to change a point or nick a point, that's when he'd bring me on. But I respected him. He came in and told me straight, how he saw football, and how I didn't fit in to it. There was me and Ákos Buzsáky who were similar types of player but Tony never had room for us in his team. Obviously it would have been good to play more. I didn't like that style of football, but at least he was honest with us and at the end of the season he left and Ian Holloway came in."

Holloway would turn out to be a completely different character for Bojan to deal with, but the winger brought his frustrations from the 2005/06 season into the next campaign under the new coach. "I was dropped, put on the transfer list and then told to train with the youth team," he says. "I played for the reserves and scored a lot of goals in a few games, and that forced Ian to put me back in the team. I carried on that form in the first team, scoring in three consecutive games against Southend, Leeds and Luton in the Championship. We played West Brom at home and one of my former team-mates at United, Jonathan Greening, broke my cheekbone! I had titanium plates inserted and obviously that was another injury and a setback at a time I was doing well."

Not only that, but he had also won over Holloway and for perhaps the first time felt appreciated by his manager. "We had a special relationship, if that's the right term. He really loved me as a player," says Bojan. "On a professional level it was fantastic but on a personal level it was a bit weird, we didn't always see eye to eye. He would always have to be right and wouldn't always listen to my opinions. At the same time, he was good to me, giving me a chance to prove myself after the first trouble. You do think though, now you've had that problem in the beginning, you'll only need one more problem to be finished."

A run of injuries and spells in and out of the side left Bojan so frustrated that in October 2007, after another disrupted start to a season, he asked to be released from his contract so he could return back to Sweden. Plymouth agreed, and a month later, Bojan had signed a deal with Swedish side AIK, the 'home' club that he had supported as a child. "I didn't want to go to another English team, there were plenty calling when I left I have to stress, although there's a little bit of a bitter aftertaste for the way it ended at Plymouth, I enjoyed my time and remember the club fondly. I just wanted to go back home and start my life and career back on track. When you have had a big talent and didn't make it, you have to deal with that disappointment, and I'm not sure that people can understand that. I had a special ability and I wasn't able to use it fully, I was so disappointed," says Bojan. Putting that behind him, he was able to enjoy success at his new club in Sweden's top division. "We won the treble there, the League, the Cup and the Super Cup, and had a really good rivalry with Gothenburg," he says. "I played every game and was one of the best midfielders in the division in 2009. I know what people will say, they look at me and remember me for my time at United, but I had two successful seasons playing with two of the clubs I adored as a child and I won trophies with them. As a player that's always going to be special, some players go through their careers winning nothing or not getting to play for their favourite clubs."

Following the Championship victory in 2009, AIK struggled the following year and changed their manager. Former Liverpool coach Alex Miller was appointed, and once more Bojan felt a personality clash. "I never wanted to leave AIK but Alex and I didn't get on,". he admits. "To keep the story short, we just never got along and I was gone very quickly. I had four years left on my contract, was very high regarded at the club and was even being named captain sometimes. It was a blow to have to leave but that was my life. Like a rollercoaster, so many clubs, so many countries, so many managers. I've never looked negatively at everything, I've tried to look at the positives from all of my experiences. Sometimes I think maybe if I hadn't done this or that, but all I've done led to another experience I can take some good from."

Djordjic swiftly moved to Hungary to play for Videoton in a short spell that could be described as one of the most bizarre of the many that he had. The director, Alexander Berze, released a public statement saying that the club had been made aware of his statistical record and that they would compare him to Roberto Baggio, only one problem, he'd never actually seen Djordic play. Lofty praise if it wasn't so logically flawed. With such a bewildering approach to signing players, it's barely a surprise to learn that there was turmoil behind the scenes.

"Things happen inside a club that you can't imagine happening in England", says Bojan. "Everything is so political, owners change, bring in managers who want certain players, directors have their input on what they think should happen, there are so many things going on. It's difficult to explain fully but it's so different to clubs even in Sweden, where everything is organised, you know that your wages are coming, you know who the coach is and who is making the decisions. It wasn't like that in Hungary." Djordic left in 2011, after just one year in Hungary, terminating his contract that had a year left on it, and was contacted by Ian Holloway to go back to England, this time at Blackpool who had just been relegated from the Premier League.

"I went over, Ian and I talked about everything and settled our differences, and then I started some pre-season games," says Bojan. "I honestly felt good there, my confidence was back and everything felt rosy. Yet after the pre-season, Ian came up to me and said he didn't think I had a future at the club. He told me I was too negative and that my attitude was spreading to other people, that he didn't think I'd changed from my time at Plymouth. I'd been so positive about the move yet it turned out to be the biggest mistake of my life. If I could take one year or one club out of my career then it would be Blackpool. Not because of the fans, they were unbelievable, not even the club, it was just the problems which surrounded that entire time."

In December, the *Daily Mail* ran a story speculating on the terms of the contract Djordjic had signed at Bloomfield Road. "It was ridiculous – they were claiming that I was in trouble or needed money or something, but I'd just gone there to play and try to resurrect my career," says Bojan. "If I was genuinely in trouble, why would I have left my home in Sweden? None of it made sense. The worst thing was, to clear it up, I actually had to send my contract into the newspaper to prove what it looked like. It didn't matter if I earned £0, or £90, or £100,000 a week, it was my decision to come back and play football. I just couldn't believe that it was being portrayed negatively, and it was so sad that my career in England ended like that. The transfer window had been and gone and there was nowhere to go and nothing I could do."

Though on a professional basis, Djordjic's English career was technically over, he was at least able to leave the country on a very positive note. After hearing of his troubles in Blackpool, Sir Alex Ferguson personally invited Bojan to return to United to train and went to the effort of helping him find a new club. "When I was released by Blackpool, United invited me back to train before I found a new club and that at least said to me that I'd made a positive impression the first time around," says Bojan. "Warren Joyce had been the manager at Royal Antwerp so asked if I would like to go there for the rest of the season – I said why not – and went to Belgium with John Cofie, who was sent from United on loan, and that for me possibly says that I wasn't so bad.

To be allowed back at United after six or seven years was massive, it felt massive, more than being a good player or a talent, that the gaffer liked me for me, for my character, for always being honest. I bought him a bottle of wine as a thank you and could barely believe it when I was back, sitting in his office talking to him after all those years. Not many people can just go back to United if they haven't played five hundred games. I have to say it was only training, but that couple of weeks when I was invited back was very special to me and something I'll always remember. Even when I'm ninety years old I'll remember that."

The move to Antwerp (where Bojan played a few times) and the ten days spent with United at Carrington at least gave a little bit of stability to Djordjic's life and perhaps that influenced his next move –full circle back to his first club, Brommapojkarna. "I went back to the club I was at as a boy," he says. "I was here from ten to the age of seventeen, I was able to help us get promoted. I've been quite lucky to normally have won something wherever I've been. The double with Red Star, trophies with AIK, the league in Scotland, the league in Hungary, and then promoted to the top division in Sweden with the team I'm with now."

Even if Bojan's future does include a move back to Red Star Belgrade, or anywhere else, it appears unlikely that he will fulfil that incredible potential he once exuded. "I scratch my head sometimes and maybe wonder what happened, but that was me, I liked to express myself and my feelings, I like to say when something's wrong. Sometimes it's better not to say anything in football, but that's just not me," he says. "I know people will have their opinion, and it's not like there are a huge amount of people who can stand up and say they saw me play at my best, especially for United. I know people say that he talks about being at United but didn't make it, but you cannot be at a club like that for the length of time I was there and not have the ability. The lowest level I played was the Second Division in Belgium for Antwerp, and when you look at the career of an average professional, that's not bad. You can't be at a club like Rangers or Red Star if you do not have a certain talent, but my problem was that I was in too many different environments and people would then ask questions or just assume that there was a problem. But when you get that negative reception from an early age, it's hard to shake it off. I've been a television pundit in Sweden since the 2002 World Cup, so being that outspoken forms a certain opinion of me."

At the age of 32, though he may not quite achieve what he could and maybe should have, Bojan wants to enjoy the rest of his playing days and have a positive influence on the next generation. "I just want to play football and enjoy the game, and also try and help the kids coming through to help them on the right track," he says. "I'd like to finish my playing career on a really good note, I feel mature and able to express myself in a way that I can play well and also influence others in a better way. Maybe when I was twenty two, I didn't have the same head on in the future. I'd like to be a role model so that people can learn from my mistakes. People don't have to be blessed with the best ability but as long as they've got the right attitude they can go a long way. I hope I could become a good coach because I've experienced highs and lows. I know I will always be reminded of my time at United, that I could've done better. I get people telling me on Twitter all the time that I was the one who should have played more, and asking me what happened."

The other question Bojan is asked about is so frequent that he even referenced it in his "about" section on the social network – "Championship Manager Legend!" – due to his profile on the popular computer simulation game. "Everyone always says that to me. I think they thought I was made up," he laughs. "I played that game myself and I was unbelievable. Without being big headed, I think their researchers got their work spot on, because I really did have the talent. Obviously you do get some negative comments about it, I only put the remark on my account because I thought it was funny, there's no point really listening to the negative opinions though is there?"

The negativity that has clouded some of his career does not make Bojan reflect in a melancholy way. "I've had great times, happy times," he says. "I played for United, the biggest club, and I also won trophies with clubs that I grew up supporting. I cannot put that into words, if you are part of your own team and help them win a trophy, it means more than anything. It brings the ultimate satisfaction to win something if you're a player and a fan."

After such an eventful and varied career, Djordjic's ambition to make a contribution to the game in some form is fantastic, and he admits that even if he had fulfilled his potential at United he still might not have made it. "Before me there was Ben Thornley and then Luke Chadwick and myself who were labelled as the next Ryan Giggs. The first Ryan Giggs was playing in the first team eight years before I went to United and is still playing in the first team eight years after I left," laughs Djordjic. "I had confidence in my ability but I can say with certainty that I knew even when I was young that I could never be better than Ryan Giggs. Doesn't matter how many people I thought I was better than or more talented than, the only one I knew I could never beat was Ryan Giggs, and that still stands today. He's still better than me, he'll still be better than me when he's fifty and I'm forty, that man is unbelievable. To even be on the same pitch as him and watch him go past four or five players and make it look easy. He just made the impossible possible, and it would have been impossible to get in the team ahead of him, I just wanted to learn from him while I had the chance. My goal was basically to just get a few games, even he needs a rest sometimes. To be honest, I always thought I was a better central midfielder than a winger anyway, but because I was left footed I was made to play out there. I was never the quickest on the ground but I was in the mind, and I still am."

Following his return to United for that brief spell in the 2011/12 season, Djordjic has a strong relationship with the club once again. "There was so much warmth from the Gaffer and everyone at the club, even the canteen staff, that they remembered me was so incredible. They were telling me stories about myself and they were all nice, and that gave me a strange sense of fulfilment. That I had been gone for years but people still remembered me fondly, that I had left a mark at a club the size of Manchester United, meant so much."

Djordjic's story has some parallels with that of Jules Maiorana's, in that both were precocious talents who could be said to have had temperament problems. Though Maiorana's stories of his own treatment while at the club means that he is unlikely to ever share a drink with his former manager, perhaps it was the fact that Bojan's own issues were borne out of frustration rather than personal conflict that means he now has a better relationship with Sir Alex. "I really think he appreciated that I was straight up and he knew I would never speak badly of him," says Bojan. "If I had problems I would have knocked on his door. I was like that with anyone. He knew that I could speak for myself and stand up for myself, and a lot of players who were coming through at the time weren't like that, they just lived in a football bubble where that was all they had. I knew that the confidence you would get from football was fake, it wasn't about you, so people forget to be themselves. I would always be myself and I walk the same way today as I did when I was seventeen and just going into United.

"How many people have been at the club and have left and how many get the opportunity to go back? To let that happen for me again, to invite me back to the club – I think that was a bigger deal for me than when I signed for them in the first place. When Sir Alex opens the door of the club to you it's like he was letting you into his house. It let me know I was accepted and that he thought of me as a good human being. That is such an amazing thing to take away from my time at Manchester United."

15

Lee Lawrence

Featuring for the Manchester United youth team, you might figure there's a good chance that you'll get the opportunity to play for the first team at some point. If you are part of a team that actually wins the FA Youth Cup, you would be excused for almost assuming that it would be an inevitability. Lee Lawrence unfortunately missed out through a mixture of misfortune and circumstance.

It was Wigan Athletic where Lee began as a youngster, before United made their move at a very early age. "I was at Wigan from about six years old, and I signed for United when I was nine and was there for about eleven years until I was twenty," he says. "Wigan were in League Two, or the old Division Three, and as soon as a name like United come in, the decision is already made to be honest."

It wasn't just the name. In 1995 Lee's arrival was an indication of just how much the youth system had developed. Scouting the best local lads meant not just the schoolboys and early teens, but even the under-10s were being courted too. United's success in the Youth Cup was there for all to see, with wins and final appearances in the past few years, and it was at least a sign of re-assurance to parents that the club placed a huge amount of emphasis on the development and ability of their younger players. Furthemore, in 1995, there was only one club in Britain who were giving these young players a chance at such a prolific rate, and that was Manchester United.

Still, this was fairly new territory for both clubs and the wider footballing landscape. Whereas before, young players could play for their local small clubs and county sides – with those that represented their region usually standing out – a more pro-active approach was being undertaken to recruit players at a younger age. Perhaps at the age of 13 or 14 you can accurately assess how technically gifted a player is compared to his peers, and how comfortable he finds playing in older age brackets, enough to at least justify any kind of real excitement in a players potential.

With so much in the way of education (in an all-encompassing aspect) concentrating on communication and personal development particularly in infant and junior levels, clubs were taking a bold step in recruiting children to any kind of programme. Lee says that what he can remember of his early days at United showed that they were conscious about the more profound responsibility they were taking on. "Playing football when I first joined was fun and that's all I can really remember, having fun when I was there. There was a really great atmosphere and the coaches made sure that you were just having a good time. From that age to the age of ten or eleven, they don't really know how you're going to develop, but I think it was a good thing because we were so relaxed. We were having a good time and not really aware of the size of the surroundings."

It's an interesting point – perhaps individual aspects of a person's personality such as confidence or determination are difficult to influence or encourage. Yet in giving children the opportunity to naturally progress at their own pace in an environment which may normally prove intimidating for young teenagers, potentially creates a great advantage when thinking about the long term ability to handle pressure. "It's funny because when you grow up with the club, you're more or less used to it and seeing stars day in and day out. The first couple of years it takes a little bit of getting used to, it's like, oh flipping heck, there's Eric Cantona, or Gary Pallister or David Beckham, but as you get older you realise that they're just normal blokes who are good at sport," Lee says.

Lee's development included a trip to the Northern Ireland Milk Cup, which didn't exactly go to plan. "We got to the final but I think we played a team from Paraguay and we were battered," he laughs. "It was the most embarrassing final in the world. The experience was still fantastic though. You go on a trip to a tournament, you're only fourteen and you have people asking for your autograph. I think that's the very first time you start to really hope and believe that it's something you could do for a livelihood."

Another aspect it could be argued that the club were helping to forge or re-create was close friendships and the potential impact they could have on the long term prospects of the club. The 1992 Youth Cup team, or to be more accurate, the members of the academy of that time including the likes of Paul Scholes and Phil Neville, were to make up the bulk of the squad that would be successful for the next generation. That was in no small part thanks to the unity, the willingness to fight for each other, and sometimes the telepathic understanding on the pitch. "Being there for a long time, you obviously made friends. I was close with Ben Collett, Phil Bardsley, David Jones. We all joined around the same time and stayed close throughout our progression," says Lee.

All four were in the squad when Lee made his FA Youth Cup debut at Queens Park Rangers in December 2001, with other local lads Lee Sims and Chris Humphreys in a team that included two hotly tipped stars of the future, Darren Fletcher and Mads Timm. "I was doing so well in the under 17s that I and a few others were called into the Youth Cup squad," says Lee. "It was absolutely brilliant. I think Danny Pugh was injured and because I was doing well, I got the call to play at left back. It gave me a boost of confidence because we knew that we weren't just getting thrown into it, we were being given the opportunity because the club trusted us to perform."

Perform they did and an impressive outing in a 3-1 win meant that Lawrence had done so well that he would retain his number three shirt for the remainder of the cup run that season. "The confidence just flowed to be honest," confesses Lee, "When you're being given the chance and you're doing well, you just feel really good about it. We'd be going back to the under-17 team after the Youth Cup games and we'd be feeling so good that our performances just got better and better, it was almost like a snowball effect." Confidence and togetherness play a part, of that there is no question, yet ultimately you do need talent to succeed and talent was something that one of Lee's team-mates in particular had in abundance. "You could see why the manager had such high hopes for Darren Fletcher," says Lee. "At the age of 13 or 14 when he'd come over from Scotland you'd see how good he was. He really was special, you could see the potential in him. He was head and shoulders above everyone, his technique and passing ability was sometimes scary to watch. Everyone at the club could tell he was destined to make it, and having known him as long as we did, we knew that once he got the chance he was going to take it."

The cup run, helped with Fletcher in the side, saw the team really enjoy their momentum. Another away tie in the fourth round, this time at Birmingham, saw a 3-2 win before the same scoreline brought triumph over Hartlepool United on the anniversary of the Munich disaster. Perhaps in recognition of this, the club decided to host the tie at Old Trafford and Lee says that this again was something the young players took in their stride. "It's weird because when it's all happening, it's not something you're always able to take in. Years later when people tell you about it and you look back and realise what everything meant, it's only really at that point you understand how special it was," admits Lee. "Being honest, I have vivid memories of that first game against QPR because it was my first but after that it feels like a blur. It was a joy to be selected to play. When we lost against Barnsley I'm sure I felt disappointed at the time, but I can't really remember that disappointment, I just remember being so happy to be playing so often." United drew 3-3 with Barnsley in the sixth round but were eliminated on penalties.

Though clearly a setback, Lee was satisfied enough with his progression to have viewed the season a great success. The following year the youngsters who had done well were joined by talented players like Chris Eagles. Lee was an ever-present in the next Youth Cup run as United won at Newcastle United then defeated both Sheffield clubs to get to the sixth round again. Victory over Tranmere Rovers set up a two-legged semi final clash with Charlton Athletic and Lee admits that there was a growing feeling in the camp that United could go all the way. "There was definitely that kind of feeling because we all believed in each other," he says. "I had no doubt that our team would be there or thereabouts, you only have to look at what those players went on to achieve in league football. Kieran Richardson, Phil Bardsley, David Jones and Paul McShane, they have all played lots of times at the top level and they were showing that kind of potential then, so it was no surprise that we were doing so well."

United overcame Charlton to qualify for the final against a team that were really hotly tipped, perhaps even more so than the Reds. Middlesbrough's academy featured names that would go on to play plenty of Premier League games with Ross Turnbull, David Wheater, James Morrison and Chris Brunt to name just four. Lee says everyone was well aware of the task that faced them in the final. "We didn't really have nerves, we knew how good they were, but we had that confidence in each other. We were also made up that Sir Alex came in to the dressing room before the second leg to tell us to keep our heads, that if we played to the best of our ability then he was sure that we would get the right result. He'd said that to us before the first game as well. That just helped us even more, we knew we could beat anyone on our day, pound for pound we were better than them, and we went up to the Riverside and got a great result," he says. Collett and Richardson scored the goals to get a really impressive 2-0 lead to take into the second leg at Old Trafford ten days later. "Having got the win we were buzzing waiting for the second leg, but the coaches kept reeling us in and letting us know that the tie was only really at half time," says Lee. "That helped us to concentrate and not get complacent ahead of the game." Such talk helped ground the players who were not only on the verge of joining much heralded winners of the past but had also benefitted from the experience of losing the previous year.

"The experience the year before really helped us, we knew the club had the faith to play us when we were a little young, so to keep faith in that first run and then give the chance to put things right from the previous year, it was a really good learning curve. It had been mentioned a few times before the game that the club hadn't won the trophy since 1995, so there was a fair bit of pressure to live up to even though we'd put ourselves in a good position," says Lee. "It really was the best feeling ever to win the trophy. There was a lot of talk before the game about what it meant but we never let that get to us in terms of making us nervous. It just prepared us in a great way for the second leg, we were representing Manchester United and we wanted to do ourselves and the club justice." The youngsters drew the second leg 1-1 at Old Trafford to comfortably claim the FA Youth Cup. "I don't know if it was because we were in our normal age group in the second year and so we felt like we were expected to win it, but it definitely felt like a brilliant achievement when we got the win, and we were all so happy for each other," Lee says.

It wasn't just the players that he speaks highly of. "You know you're always going to get first class coaches at a club like United but even so I can't think of a single bad thing to say," he states. "Guys like Tony Whelan, Paul McGuinness, they were absolutely fantastic. Neil Bailey was someone I'd known at Wigan and he really helped me out, they couldn't do enough to help you." The club had really grasped that sense of responsibility in developing and educating the boys into good young men as much as good players. "Definitely, there was a real importance placed on education there. We'd have about two days a week where we could go to Carrington, but even there we'd be doing some classroom work because they were very conscious about preparing you for a life without football as well as giving you all the tools necessary to hopefully become a professional player," says Lee.

Becoming a professional for the first team was the next challenge for Lawrence. "After the cup win, six or seven us were given squad numbers the following season which felt like such a massive accomplishment and an incentive as well," he admits. "You start believing then that you've really got a chance of making it. I was getting games for the reserves and I kept thinking or hoping I'd get the chance."

Though the first team were just about to enter a period of uncertainty, the reserves and young teams were really strong. "You could tell we had a great team because we were winning the league at both age levels, the 17s and the 19s, and the reserves were doing really well too," says Lee. "The potential in the team was massive and when the likes of Gerard Pique and Giuseppe Rossi arrived it really added to it and you got the feeling that a number were going to break through."

It was a logical assumption to make. Lee, an aspiring left-back, could look at his path to the first team and feel he had a genuine chance of making it. With the pedigree of success coming through the ranks, the ability to deal with pressure, and a quick and athletic presence, it seemed only a matter of time until he got his chance. John O'Shea and Mikael Silvestre were the main contenders for the position in the first team but both regularly found themselves playing other positions too, and with no permanent fixture in that left defensive role, nobody could have blamed Lee for feeling he had a good opportunity, however misfortune was about to strike. "I went on loan to Shrewsbury Town which I felt was a good experience to prepare me for first team football but after I returned, I injured my medial ligament and that was a huge setback for me. I never recovered and that's the reason I don't play today," he says.

Lee's star was on the rise and while nobody could place a guarantee on what he would have gone on to achieve, it was inevitable that he would have at least featured in one of the cup games over the next couple of seasons with games against Exeter City and Burton Albion. The denial of such an opportunity is a bitter pill to swallow. "When you've taken everything in your stride and progressed so well, I'd been there for such a long time from a young age and worked so hard. I felt that I was really on the verge of making it, winning the Youth Cup and then getting a squad number. You feel like you're on top of the world one minute and the next it feels like the world has actually ended," admits Lee. "To be honest, at the time I didn't think that much of it. I thought I could come back, but I'd return and play a couple of reserve games and then it would go again. I would be in rehabilitation for sixteen or eighteen weeks, try really hard to get back, literally play one or two games and it would all go again." The spell at Shrewsbury Town would turn out to be the only taste of senior football Lawrence would experience. "I did love it there, it was fantastic. We played in front of decent crowds in the

Youth Cup but to play first team football in front of a proper crowd like that was an experience I'll never forget and I'm so glad that I got that chance," he says.

People often look at the 2003 FA Youth Cup winning team and wonder why more of them didn't quite make the grade at United, but maybe injury has a lot to answer for. There was another player from the Youth Cup team, Ben Collett, who was cruelly injured a week after the success against Middlesbrough, ironically against the same opponents. Gary Smith's tackle broke Collett's leg in two places and after failed attempts to come back from injury, Collett was released in 2006, and when his professional career in New Zealand didn't turn out as planned, he was forced to retire. Subsequently, Collett brought legal action against Smith where both Gary Neville and Sir Alex Ferguson were called to give testimonials about how good Ben could have been. Lee agrees with the plaudits. "I'm sure Ben would have been a top player," he says. "You could ask anyone, he was the hardest working lad at the club. He was always at Carrington looking for ways to improve, the lads would go home, but he would stay behind all of the time. If anyone deserved to make it in the first team it was Ben."

Lawrence was playing in the game that saw disaster strike for Ben. "I was at left back and he was in front of me at left wing," he recalls. "It looked a bad tackle but I honestly didn't realise how bad it was. Obviously, when he came back he was just never the same again. His confidence was gone, it's the same as you see with anyone breaking their leg really, and it was such a shame because he really deserved to make it in the game. I've never known anyone who lived for the game as much as he did."

Like Ben, and to be honest, like many others who suffer the same cruel fate, Lee was given the opportunity to recover from injury at the club. Unfortunately, after he was unable to do so, Sir Alex decided that his contract would not be renewed. "I kind of knew that I'd be getting released, simply because I'd not played in a year," Lee concedes. "The injury had stopped everything and I suppose it was frustrating because the next contract was 'the biggie', the one where we'd have been able to get nice cars and all those things. I was doing okay in training but I just couldn't get a run of games so I wasn't surprised that, after giving me the chance to come back, they decided not to renew my deal. I just have to put it down to one of those things. The manager was really straight with me. He said, 'You've been here for eleven years and you've never once given me any trouble. I'm really sorry but we'll have to let you go. We don't think with your injury that you'll make the first team now.' I thought that was fair and honest and I couldn't have any complaints really, I knew before I went to see him that I was being released."

Considering the position of the first team and how successful the other sides at the club were, does Lawrence feel that maybe more should have broken through into the first team? "I don't know, it's a difficult one to answer," he says. "There were plenty of good players there and so many of that 2003 team have gone on

Sir Alex in his early days with Manchester United
Photo copyright Howard Talbot

The entrance to The Cliff Training Ground

Lee Martin, Tony Gill, David Wilson, Deiniol Graham and Mark Robins surround Eric Harrison in an early publicity photograph as the Fledglings first hit the headlines

Ryan Giggs in a publicity shot, shortly after breaking into the first team squad
Photo copyright Howard Talbot

Giuliano "Jules" Maiorana who, despite showing huge promise, had his professional football career hampered by a serious knee injury
Photo copyright Howard Talbot

Jules Maiorana exiting The Cliff after training
Photo copyright Joanne Morris

Mark Robins broke into the first team in 1988, making regular appearances before joining Norwich City in 1992
Photo copyright Howard Talbot

Gary Walsh, David Wilson, Mark Robins and Russell Beardsmore pick up some tips from a certain United legend

One of the early Fledgling successes, Russell Beardsmore went on to carve out a name for himself at AFC Bournemouth and is now back with The Cherries in a coaching capacity
Photo copyright Howard Talbot

Following a reserve game at Old Trafford, Ryan Giggs on the far left can be seen walking off the pitch
Photo copyright Joanne Morris

Phil Neville and Terry Cooke doing their chores in the youth team dressing room

Tony Gill scores his first Manchester United goal

Tony Gill before a serious injury prematurely ended his career
Photo copyright Howard Talbot

The Manchester United youth side in 2005, including Markus Neumayr (back row, fourth from left) and Bojan Djordjic (back row, furthest right)

Nick Culkin after his comeback from retirement

The old manager and coaches dugout at The Cliff

Located in The Cliff cafeteria, much information is displayed regarding the history of the famous training ground

The training pitch at The Cliff in superb condition

What was formerly the boot room at The Cliff

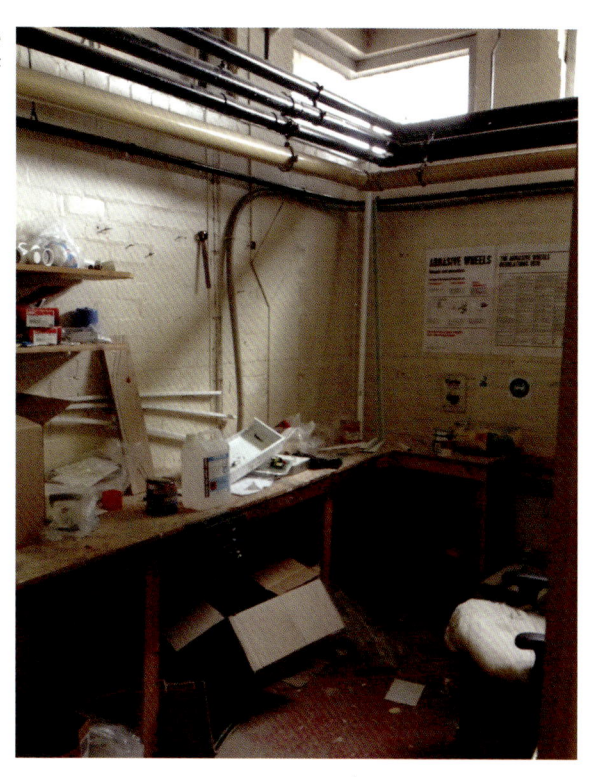

The youth team changing room at The Cliff

Clockwise from above: Lee Martin's shirt and the match ball from the 1990 FA Cup Final in the Manchester United Museum. Ben Amos warms up with David De Gea and Anders Lindegaard in a pre-season training session. Russell Beardsmore, Deiniol Graham and Lee Martin are among many of the Fledglings who take part in "Masters" and "Legends" games. Paul Scholes hits a trademark pass in his testimonial game to successful league careers. United are such a big club that they can get anyone in the world. You're not only competing with players who are the best in the region or in the country, you're doing it with the best in the world and maybe that's the reason why. It sounds a bit weird but maybe we suffered because so many of that 1992 team were still doing so well for the first team. So when I'm asked about whether our side didn't do as well as was hoped for, I think it's a bit harsh, because so many have had really great careers in their own right. It was just a case of bad timing but I feel they've done really well for themselves, spot on."

Lee himself tried to remain in the game. "I had an agent at the time, which I wasn't always comfortable with, but a lot of the lads had them so it was just one of those things you did," he says. "I'd only been with him for a few weeks. He said Tottenham were interested but that fell through. I don't know why, but I have a feeling that the agent was asking for more money than I actually wanted. My dad took over and informed some clubs I was looking for a team. I had a game down at Bristol City and I felt I did really well on a short trial down there, but maybe short is the right term. I'm only 5'6 and they said they were looking for a taller player. I had a trial at Chester, one at Lincoln, and then when I had a trial at Boston my knees went again. I got back and had another trial at Accrington, they were really keen, but I was only there a little while and my knee went again. To be fair to them, they kept me on while I tried to get fit, but it was another four months on the sidelines getting back. We had a game at Morecambe which was my comeback and we agreed that after the game I'd sign a contract with them. After fifteen minutes the knee just went again, it completely went."

This time there were to be no comebacks as the advice Lee received was far more serious. "The doctors said if it went again I might well end up in a wheelchair," Lee confesses. "And that was it. From the biggest club in the world for 11 years and then, with all due respect to the smaller clubs as they are all great with wonderful tradition, scrambling around trying to get a contract at these small clubs and then being rejected because I just couldn't stay fit and get to the same level I was used to playing at was so disheartening, I have to admit, and I knew after Accrington I had to give it in. I don't know if it's any easier to take believing that the reason I didn't make it at United, or in the game, wasn't because I wasn't good enough, but because I was injured. I suppose it's nice to know that it wasn't down to my ability, maybe I might not have made it at United but I was confident enough in my own ability that I would have been able to get a good career at a Championship or Division One side. I've done other things since leaving the game but a couple of years back I thought I'd try and play locally. So I got fit, and everything was going well, but after a couple of games the knee went again! It was incredible. But some things are just not meant to be."

A familiar theme throughout this anthology, particularly with those who have struggled with misfortune, is an appreciation for the things that others may take for granted. "Everything I've been through has given me a different perspective,"

Lee says, "I was out of the game at 21, seven or eight years on I've now got a beautiful wife and two beautiful kids so the way I look at it, it was a blessing in disguise because I might not have met my wife." Lee does have one regret. "Straight after coming out of the game I got the opportunity to go and run an academy in America. I got my coaching badges and was offered the chance to get over there. In my early twenties that was a great opportunity, I even got my work visa through, but I decided to turn it down because of a relationship I was in at the time."

Today, Lee is settled in the North West. "With the money I made at United, I bought my mum's house because I wanted to stay in the Wigan area, but still had a mortgage to pay so I learned the plumbing trade. My dad was a plumber so it was sort of like a natural thing, and then I went into business with a friend and we're both self employed plumbers," Lee says. He does have ambitions of getting back into the game at some point. "I've done my badges so it's something I'd look at in the future but I do have a wife and young family to take care of and stability is important. I did have the conversation with my friend actually, about what we'd do if we weren't in business together. The first thing I said was that I'd love to go and coach, take the family somewhere abroad and coach in an academy. Maybe when my little boy is old enough to get an interest in playing, I might even look at scouting, it'd keep my knees safe, at least!"

With a philosophical outlook, it's no surprise that Lee now only looks at the positive side of his experiences. "I'd much rather have had the opportunity and not made it than not have the opportunity at all, if that makes sense," says Lee. "Being a young kid, growing up at the biggest club in the world, that's an experience to tell the kids and grandkids, and that's not a bad thing to be able to do."

16

Adam Eckersley

There are eight sets of brothers who have played for Manchester United's first team (and twelve if you count Newton Heath). Post-war, there are only six pairs that have represented the club – and only four of those are classed as home grown (though Brian Greenhoff famously was one of the last of the Busby Babes, his brother Jimmy was signed from Stoke some years later). Those four are the Nevilles, the Eckersleys, the Da Silvas, and the most recent, the Keane twins.

When you narrow it down further still to local lads, it makes a select group of three post-war sets of brothers. Adam Eckersley was born in Salford but at the time of writing plays his professional football in Denmark. Despite that local grounding, Adam wasn't a United supporter – well, he was, but the wrong kind! "I actually grew up as a Newcastle fan," he admits. "I was very young and I think I picked them off Teletext. All the teams were up on there and I just said to my mum and dad that I was going to support them, and for my next birthday I got a full Newcastle strip. I was a really big fan of them for about four or five years, during the time when they were doing really well, with the likes of Philip Albert, Darren Peacock and Alan Shearer. I can remember them beating United 5-0 in 1996, when Albert scored that chip over Schmeichel. The good old days," laughs Adam.

"After a while I just sort of stopped supporting one team and followed football in general. It's strange as my dad's a massive Man Utd fan but won't admit it, especially now me and my brother have left. He's never actually said he's a United fan, he's strange like that, but we know he is and he always wanted to make sure that we played for the club." It's a little known fact that there were actually three Eckersley brothers at United as youngsters. As well as Adam's younger brother Richard, who also eventually made the first team, there was eldest brother Mike who was released without making an appearance.

Ironically, Adam was already at Old Trafford while enjoying watching the Magpies stuff his own club. He began training at United as a nine year old in 1994. "I think it was Paul McGuiness who scouted me. I was training with the under-nines, everyone had a red kit on but he gave me a blue one," he says. "I stood out like a sore thumb. I hope they did that to all the new players and not just me but obviously I must have done enough for them to like me."

For the first time, United's youth scouting had really dug deep. Instead of finding kids that were fourteen or fifteen, the step further to recruit children who hadn't even reached puberty was pretty bold. On the one hand it was a risky step taking on so many that hadn't properly developed as it was difficult to judge their potential fairly. On the other, it was a calculated move designed to facilitate an environment where promising players of the same age group could learn an understanding, thereby increasing your chances of creating a better team from a much earlier age. There can be no denying that by it's very nature it's a forced environment, however that does not mean that normal friendships and bonds do not naturally develop. That was the case for Adam.

"There were four or five of us that were really close like Mark Howard, Phil Picken, and Steven Hogg. We were really close, but we got even closer when we were about twelve because the club took us out to play in the Dallas Cup in Texas." That tournament was held in 1998 and United faced a group consisting of Californian side Hotspurs Elite, Costa Rican side LD Alajuelense and one of the home teams for the tournament, Texas Longhorns. "We absolutely smashed it and won the tournament, which was great because I can remember hearing that no United side had ever won it, so it felt like a massive achievement for the club and for us as well to win our first major tournament." For such young heads, it's reasonable to imagine such an experience being daunting to say the least. "It was huge," Adam confesses. "Being twelve and going to the States – United are huge at any level, so we had people who were coming just to watch us.

"There was so much hype and it was very much an introduction to the kind of thing we might expect if we progressed, another level. A first little taste of stardom in a way. We were signing autographs, which was a surreal feeling, but we got a major boost from it at the time. It's funny because you probably won't find a footballer who's older who says they enjoy doing autographs, it's something they have to do, but at the time it feels like a really big thing."

With that in mind, the coaches had an important role to play in keeping the players grounded. "Before we went on the trip we stayed at Manchester Castlefield Hotel and we had a three hour meeting on team building. The white board was out and we were talking about the structure, what makes up a team, things that weren't concentrated on football but just about being a team of people and understanding our responsibilities to each other. We even made a song, a motto, called the Chain. Paul McGuinness made it into a song, so C was Compact, H was Hard to Beat, A was Attack the Ball, I was In Position and N was Never Switch Off. Don't ask me how I remember that though. I'm sure if he ever reads this he'll be so impressed that I remember it, I'm impressed myself," he laughs. "The talk really got us to focus and concentrate on being professional, reminding us about what it means to represent the club. That's drummed into you from day one anyway but I can really remember that meeting sticking out."

Adam's experience of the personal development is something of a bridge between the more robust early approach to bringing up younger players to the modern day where everything is catered for. Being there from 1994, Adam's own experience was of that very transition. "I got both sides of it," he says. "When we trained at the Cliff, Eric Harrison was training us. Paul McGuinness would coach us and stress the importance of being a team, but Eric would be saying to us from the age of twelve, thirteen, 'Come on lads, no more time to be boys now, you have to be men'. It was the perfect education. Everything had been put in place by the manager to ensure that all different personalities could be understood by the coaches."

Rene Meulensteen is described by others in this book as being one who took a personal interest in their well-being, however Adam doesn't believe it's as straightforward as that. "I don't think coaches were allocated like that, like a good cop-bad cop," he says. "For me I think it was an individual thing, people respond differently to everyone really, so the club had enough in place to make sure that we were all happy. We had a guy called Neil Bailey who ruled with an iron rod just like Eric, Tony Whelan was great, but a different character. They all had different ways of encouraging and motivating. Neil and Eric might get on your back but Tony and Paul would be more like encouraging us to look at different aspects of our game and see if we could do things differently to get better."

Adam made his Youth Cup bow aged eighteen in the 2003/04 season but was actually included in one of the squads in the successful run the season before. "Lee Lawrence was the left back in front of me so I never really got a chance that year," Adam says. The inclusion to even be a substitute for the game at Newcastle in the Youth Cup was a reward for Adam's season, as he had been excelling for the under 18s in their league campaign. He was involved from the very first game of the Youth Cup the following year. Far from feeling the pressure of following in the footsteps of success both traditional and recent, Adam was bullish about their chances of victory as defending holders. "Honestly, we didn't feel any pressure. I actually expected us to win it that year," he says. "We had a great team, it was really strong." The confidence was unfounded, however, because after they knocked out Manchester City and Norwich City they came up against Blackburn Rovers at Ewood Park. "It was a horrible game where nothing went right for us, but football comes with defeat and victories, you have to take them both and learn from what went wrong so you can come back better," says Adam.

Unfortunately, he never got the opportunity to right the wrongs in the Youth Cup as United were knocked out at home to Stoke City in the third round. However, with the absence of Lee Lawrence who was due to leave the club, Eckersley's chances of being used by Sir Alex Ferguson greatly improved. "Though I obviously saw more of him as I moved up the levels, he'd always taken an interest and an involvement in our progression. He'd never let you forget about how important it was for Manchester United to have young players and he'd especially make that known to the local lads," Adam says. "I can remember when we were really young, we had this promotional shoot at McDonalds. I was there, Mark Howard and Phil Bardsley, and I can always remember him saying 'This will be the next class of 1992. He would sometimes come and watch us playing even at the under-nines to under-twelves."

As well as the group of players with whom he had shared adolescence, there was also the small factor of possibly playing for the club with his brothers. "That was something we thought about and talked about," he says. "We hoped at least two of us would get to play for the first team. Unfortunately it never quite worked out for my older brother who was let go at under-nineteen level. We took what we did in our stride and it wasn't like we were thinking of the future as there's no point putting the pressure on yourself of 'Oh, we'll be the next Neville's.' We played football and enjoyed playing for Manchester United, that's the way I took it, anyway."

Perhaps the mature outlook was influenced by the events of the day following the Manchester City Youth Cup game in January 2004, a game in which Adam had played left wing. "The accident had a huge impact on everything at the club," Adam says. "Everyone knows what a force Sir Alex was at Manchester United and from that day on he stopped all the Youth players driving a car above a 1.2 litre engine. It was a strange day. We'd just beaten City 2-0 and were buzzing from that, but everything went flat afterwards, completely flat. It rocked us all quite hard."

Coming so soon after the Jimmy Davis tragedy, it proved an immensely testing time for the young group of players. Adam feels that the club's reaction was the right one to help them all recover and develop. "They basically cut the risk factor out and that was the right way to do it. Nothing was really done after Jimmy died. I remember going down to the funeral in Birmingham, everyone was there, all the first teamers made the journey, even David Beckham was there. There wasn't a dry eye in the house but the thing was, after that, I think the club just wanted to allow everything to settle before they put new rules in place. When the accident happened they reacted straight away," he says.

"Mark Howard and I were in the car behind Callum Flanagan and Phil Marsh, so we had a week off where we had to make our statements and lots of people asking us what really happened. After that, everyone had to do a driving school. The club had a police officer come around once a week to show us how to drive safely, how to watch for traffic." While Phil Marsh recovered in hospital and began his recuperation, the rest of the young group tried their best to get back to business as normal. "You do want to concentrate on your football, you're a young lad and although you care, you naturally look on these extra things that you're having to do as a bit of a pain", admits Adam. "As far as Callum was concerned, it wasn't like we all hung him out to dry. In that kind of environment, there's a lot of piss taking, so when it had settled down we were laughing and joking about the possibility of him going to prison.

Obviously for the first couple of weeks no-one wanted to say anything at all, but in a football dressing room things are said and jokes are made, that was just typical of the time. It wasn't nasty or anything and I'm sure Callum and Mads knew that." Since that time, a number of first team players have allegedly been involved in car accidents – Cristiano Ronaldo and Anderson the most high profile – while youngster Ryan Tunnicliffe was charged with drink driving and banned from driving for 18 months in October 2012. "I think it's probably just something that comes from the culture of being at football clubs, not just United, but any football club," says Adam. "As a kid, you look at the top players with the flash cars, and that's what you aspire to have. They've got big fast powerful cars, you want what they have. It doesn't help, and something more should probably be put in place. I don't have all the answers but maybe it should be put into contracts that they don't have these £60,000 cars until they reach the first team or have played a few games there. I fell into that same trap, driving Bentleys and Mercedes Benz cars when I was 17 or 18 years-old. I was forever getting pulled by the police because I looked so young driving, looking back I wish I'd left the money in the bank and concentrated on playing football."

Adam's progression was going quite well. Throughout 2004/05, he was featured quite often with the reserve side, and after Lee Lawrence's departure in 2005, he was going to be the regular left back for the second string. In the pre-season of the 2005/06 campaign, he came on as substitute in the first two friendlies, playing full second halves in the comprehensive wins at Clyde and Peterborough. His good form through the season was one of the reasons that the reserve side of that year did so incredibly well. Mikael Silvestre and Gabriel Heinze were the club's regular left backs, with John O'Shea also deputising there from time to time. With Silvestre and O'Shea both preferring other positions in the team, and Heinze's erratic form, Eckersley was arguably one fair crack at the first team away from being established in the latter part of 2005.

He and three others were rewarded for their fine form when United were drawn to face Barnet at Old Trafford in the League Cup 3rd round. "There was me, Lee Martin, Ritchie Jones and Darron Gibson who made our debuts that night. It was one of the best nights of my life," says Adam. "We went to the Lowry before the game and I can just remember being so nervous. I spoke to Wes Brown, who was playing, and asked if he was nervous thinking that might calm me down if someone as experienced as he felt the same, but he said, 'nah not at all mate.' It didn't help me a bit.

"Before kick off, Carlos Queiroz came and said 'We've got a young team out there tonight. Just go out and enjoy yourself. Enjoy playing football with your mates on this great stage.' And that was that – the nerves just went." It was a young side and a United team with an average age of twenty went to town in a convincing 4-1 win with Adam impressing more than anyone. "I had a great game and was named MUTV's man of the match. I was flying and came off thinking that I'd get another chance soon."

An unavoidable set of circumstances that followed was to have severe consequences for Adam's future at United. That win over Barnet had secured a fourth round tie with West Bromwich Albion, again at Old Trafford, in a game that Adam would almost certainly have featured in. Tragically, five days prior to the tie, United legend George Best passed away and the game then took on extra significance as the first to be played at Old Trafford after his death. "To honour George Best, Sir Alex put out a first team squad. They won, and after that, he never put the kids back in. He really made a point of trying to win the League Cup that year," says Adam. Additionally, immediately after the game against Barnet, United faced crisis when Roy Keane sensationally left the club following an outburst against some of the players he felt were underachieving. In an attempt to maintain stability, Ferguson kept the squad together and playing, and possibly felt he needed to make a statement in the transfer market to show United were still a force. That, too, was to have a direct hit on Adam's chances.

"With the team doing so well that was the first real time I started to think that not just me, but a few of the team, could break through and get into that first team," he says. "We had a real interest from supporters because of the way that we played football. Maybe even some weeks the fans preferred to watch us rather than the first team. We had Gerard Pique, Jonny Evans, Rossi, Markus Neumayr and people would always say great things to us so it was only natural that we believed we'd get our chances. The problem is that United have got the money to bring in whoever they want if they're not doing so well, and that's what proved difficult for us."

Christmas 2005 would prove to be a turning point in Adam's career at the club. "At our Christmas party, Gabriel Heinze came up to me and said that if I kept going the way I was, I had a great chance at making the first team. I was so encouraged by that, but a couple of days later we signed Patrice Evra, and that was it, I was back to third choice. From then I suppose I always felt like I was forever skiing uphill, trying hard to show what I could do but going nowhere. Part of me just thinks my timing was absolutely awful."

Riding the crest of a wave with great form and not wanting to be restricted by the obvious lack of opportunities that now remained for him in the 2005/06 season, Adam was faced with a decision over a move. In truth, perhaps this was an acknowledgement of the misfortune that surrounded Eckersley's current predicament from the management. "I was called into the office early one morning in the January and asked if I wanted to go on loan to Antwerp," he says. "I was like, 'Okay, sure', and by the afternoon I was on a plane to Belgium. A few of the lads like John O'Shea had gone there and I thought it was the next step on the ladder to getting into the team. I felt it was something that all the players had to go through. I most definitely felt it was a step in the right direction. United were watching Antwerp closely and I thought if I had a good six months there that doors would open for me when I got back. Obviously I wasn't exactly over the moon about going to Belgium when I'd been so close to the first team.

To be fair though, I had a great few months there. United sent five of us over I think, me, Lee Martin, Tom Heaton, Sylvan Ebanks-Blake, and Danny Simpson. Antwerp were really struggling at the time, close to relegation, and by the end of the season we'd got them three goals from the playoffs on goal difference. We'd won eleven or twelve games on the bounce and did really well."

Little did he know it at the time but the strange set of circumstances that had contrived to send Adam to experience football abroad was to have a huge impact on his later choices. "I was so young but I liked playing in the first team and the foreign atmospheres were really great. It wasn't ideal living out of an hotel for half a year but at the same time I coped with it really well. Maybe that kind of control benefitted me as well. I learned that I could go and play football and live abroad and cope with it, so it was a real eye-opening experience for me," he explains. "After that, Rene Meulensteen had just left United to coach Brondby, so he took me for a few games at the start of the 2006/07 season. It was a great experience and I absolutely loved it. The fans are crazy, the stadium was great. It went so good that I could see myself signing there and playing for them full time but then Rene left because he couldn't get full control as manager. The directors were signing players behind his back and making decisions without him knowing. Unfortunately, I picked up an injury and had to come back before the end of my loan."

Adam had quite an eventful 2006 but found himself no closer to getting into the first team at Old Trafford. "United were still looking after me at the time but when I came back I knew I'd have to go out again," he says. "I was called into the manager's office and he asked how I'd feel about going to Barnsley. I thought it would be another step in the right direction, a team in the Championship where United would be able to keep updates on me. What people don't realise sometimes is how profound the mentality of playing for Manchester United is. It's different to other clubs. So you go to one of these other clubs, and the mentality isn't to be the best, it's survival football, and I wasn't suited to that kind of game. It didn't go well for me and I picked up an injury.

"It was really frustrating for me as the injuries were coming at the wrong time." Adam's 2006/07 season was cut short by those injuries but being back at United meant he was propelled back into the first team reckoning for the start of the following season. With injuries in defence and around the squad, Adam was used in the pre-season friendlies at Doncaster Rovers and again at Peterborough. Both games were won, with Adam finding the net at Peterborough in the 3-1 win. His final first team appearance would come in the next friendly, against Dunfermline, as a substitute for Wes Brown.

As United's players recovered from injury, Adam was out on loan again in October 2007, this time at Port Vale. "I had a bit of a crazy debut – I won man of the match against Brighton and was sent off," he laughs. "When I got home after the game, I felt something wasn't quite right in my knee. I played another game, but then I did the meniscus in my knee and was back at United on the treatment table."

At the age of 22, Adam had suffered a couple of unlucky years with regards his first team chances. "I felt my career at United was stalling and I was getting frustrated so much with my injuries. When the manager sends you on loan he looks for progression. Mine had been okay but had ended with injury, apart from the one at Barnsley which just went awful. Maybe the manager looked at that and thought if I can't handle it there how can I handle it at United?" says Eckersley. "That frustration and irritation caused me to make a couple of rash decisions. I talked it over with my mum, telling her I was sick of playing reserve team football. and she said I should go speak to the manager. I did, and told him I felt I was going nowhere so I sealed my own fate, really, because I said I wasn't happy. I still had a year on my contract. Sir Alex was good, though, and said that if I found a club that wanted me, then I could move without a fee. I can remember his words like it was yesterday – he said, 'Adam you're a fantastic player and you're going to have a great career.' Because Port Vale had just seen me and liked me, I went back there and signed a six month deal. It was a rush decision, one that I made overnight. Vale had just got a new manager in and it was a really tough six months. I learned a lot from it and it helped in terms of experience but looking back, if I had the choice again I don't think I'd make the same decision. I'd gone into it thinking I'd do six months there and move on somewhere bigger. Vale got relegated. They were bottom when I went there and didn't get out of it."

Finally, Adam was about to get a bit of good luck. "At the end of the season, just by chance, I got a call from Kent Nielsen, the former Aston Villa and Denmark defender who'd seen me playing for Brondby. He was managing AC Horsens, who were in the Danish Superliga, and there was no chance I wanted to play in League Two," confesses Adam. "No disrespect to Horsens but it wasn't like they were a big club. But I'd seen them play a game before, when they won 3-1 against Copenhagen who had only recently beaten Manchester United themselves. I thought they must be a decent team. It wasn't a great standard of football, though. I had another injury and then Horsens got relegated too. It hadn't been a great couple of years to be fair."

Still, now settled abroad and an established first teamer, Adam was about to finally start enjoying his football. "It started with a tattoo," he laughs. "It was such a tough time, I was in a dark place, literally. The apartment I was in had no furniture in it, I always kept the blinds shut and after the relegation with Horsens I kept dwelling on it, how had my career come to this when I was on the verge of the United first team. I felt rock bottom. Then the love of my life came along and she gave me a talking to, a few home truths, reminding me why football was just a game. She said that everything happened for a reason – she would say that, because that's how we met – but it was really a change in mindset that I needed to make sure I wasn't taking everything so seriously.

"I played the next season injury free and did really well, helping the team get promoted back to the Superliga. After that, I felt I'd done my time at Horsens, it wasn't the right club for me. Mark Howard was at Aarhus and said they needed a left back. They'd just been relegated back to the Danish second division. Mark convinced me that the team was good, they'd just had a really unfortunate year, so I signed a two year contract and we got promoted in the first season."

Since getting back on track Adam's exploits have been picked up back home. "There have been quite a few Premier League clubs coming to watch me, and some other European clubs too," he says. "I think the change in mentality that comes with playing for a team that wants to win and challenge has made a huge difference to me. It's important that we're up there competing at the top of the league – for my game, it had to be that I'm playing for that kind of team."

Following the promotion in 2011, Adam's form back in the Superliga was superb. "I've flourished and it's nice to hear everyone saying nice things. They award 'half year' awards here and I was winning them, so that's been nice, but I still look at everything as that progression to get back to where I want to be, at the very top of the game," says Eckersley. "I admit it's not my ambition to stay here forever. The Premier League is the best league in the world for me but I now know I can go to play football in another country and survive and do well."

Adam's story is a refreshing one both in the context of this anthology and that of Englishmen playing overseas. All too often do we hear the stories of young foreign players restricting the opportunities for home grown talent to succeed and it is rare to hear of a success story from one of our own players in a foreign league. Adam feels that United's participation in that area, with the set up with Antwerp, was a very important stepping stone in that development. "For young players to have that opportunity, it helps them stand on their own two feet and gain their independence," says Adam. "Not to mention that football is different abroad, it's not the same as back in England. It's not quite as physical, it's a little more tactical. The maturity I've got from going away from home and living in a different country, becoming a more rounded person away from the game, that's been better for me than it would have been playing in the lower leagues, with all due respect. As preparation for the Man Utd first team, it's one of the best paths, and you can see why so many did it when they were younger. Other clubs are only starting to set up the same kind of thing now, Aarhus have a new partnership with Manchester City, so they're all cottoning on to it being a great development opportunity."

Though United have a prolific rate of youth players who go on to have successful careers in the English leagues, few can claim to have their name in the club's record books for something unique, and arguably even fewer can claim to have made an impression in the game overseas. "I have plenty of people ringing me up interested about how I'm doing in Denmark and wanting to talk about our players abroad", says Adam. "I've got a lot of time for it and enjoy talking about it, because a lot of the younger players don't understand that there are huge benefits to it. It's a good standard of football, a good living as well. You don't have to be afraid to get on a plane and try something new. England might be the best place to play but it isn't the only place."

The other questions that Adam has had to deal with since the summer of 2013 have been those about his relationship with Sir Alex Ferguson. "I was doing an interview shortly after his retirement was announced but the guy was asking me all kinds of questions, really strange things that I wouldn't know unless I knew him on a personal level, it was strange," he says. However, there are some things that he believes he has learned from the manager which are evident in his personality. "His determination and motivation to succeed has definitely worn off on me a little bit. Not just that, but having to be a winner. He wasn't happy with merely a good performance. I always remember that after we beat Barnet we were all really happy with how we'd done. He came in to the dressing room after and said 'If you were all in school now, I'd give you all a D!' We all thought 'What the hell' – thinking that we'd done so well and we'd been good. But what he meant was that he didn't want us just to be good, he wanted us to be remarkable and to stand out. That's what made him the manager he was."

Such a remark is not uncommon and unexpected as Ferguson's will to win has been well documented and is universally appreciated, even begrudgingly by rivals. What isn't as well documented, however, is the groundwork done by United through Ferguson in giving young British footballers an alternative path if they don't make it in the first team at Old Trafford. It's something that's been understated yet something that many have been crying out for – the opportunity for British players to further their technical footballing education by playing abroad.

Despite the potential long term benefits, Adam believes that the manager might never get the credit he deserves for his work. "It's a strange one because I don't believe that English clubs focus enough on it. The media only seem to go on about the Italian and Spanish players coming to England and it restricting the opportunities at home, they don't look at the other side of it. I don't think it will get recognised, which is a shame as I think it's such a great thing to do. But, in terms of Sir Alex getting a pat on the back for it, I don't think that will happen."

It's probably no coincidence that Adam's younger brother Richard, (who himself looked to show remarkable promise when appearing for United's under 17s in a Manchester derby at the tender age of just 14), plays in Canada for Toronto at the time of writing. Richard made four substitute appearances for United in the second half of the 2008/09 season and was on the bench for the Carling Cup Final victory of 2009, earning a winners medal in the process, something which made Adam extremely proud.

Though the two never managed to play together in the first team, Adam is delighted that they both made appearances for the club. "It actually brings a smile to my face every time someone says it to me. It would have been great to have run out alongside my little brother, the only thing that I'd change if I could. You can't ask for everything though," he beams. "Obviously, we'd known about it all along and talked about it, but it was great one night when I was in a pub and it came up in a pub quiz. Name five sets of brothers who have played for United (before the Keanes played) and I could name them off the top of my head. It's great to know that the family name is going down in history because of something that we achieved together and no matter how bad some of the years have been, I know that one day I'll be able to take my kids to the museum at Old Trafford and say 'Look at what dad achieved'. It's a great story and I'm proud to be a part of an incredible history at an incredible club."

17

Phil Marsh

Stories of misfortune and differing degrees of tragedy dog the stories of some of the players in this compendium. The very inclusion of the term 'tragedy' in footballing lexicon doesn't always sit easy on the palate yet it was so very nearly appropriate in every sense in the word for Phil Marsh in 2004.

In many ways, the fact that Phil's story doesn't conclude with him playing in Champions League Finals for Manchester United barely matters. The determination to recover and the faith, patience and eventual reward that came from Sir Alex Ferguson in return sums up so much about the character of the manager and the identity of the club that he had helped to shape. It's true that if Ferguson has had enough of a player or personality for whatever reason, that invariably the player departed sooner rather than later. Paul Ince or Andrei Kanchelskis, for example. Or, more recently and perhaps more relevant to the narrative, Ravel Morrison.

Yet as well as that brutal record of dispensing with players, Ferguson also demonstrated remarkable humanity and patience when trying to help those who fell on hard times or misfortune. Owen Hargreaves, for one, was given every opportunity to recover from the injury nightmare that would ruin his career. Maybe most famously of all, patience was afforded to Ole Gunnar Solskjaer, who eventually returned from chronic knee injuries to have a wonderful swan-song to his career at Old Trafford in the 2006/07 season. The original plans were for Solskjaer to replace David Beckham in the wide right position following Beckham's move to Real Madrid in 2003, however a knee injury early in the season was to have a crippling impact on the remainder of the Norwegian's career. His three year road to redemption would be shared by Phil Marsh, whose personal journey would prove to be just as, if not more, significant and poignant than even Solskjaer's.

Phil's first connection with Manchester United came in 1997 when he was just eleven. "I was playing at the centre of excellence in Wigan and for a Sunday League team called Pilkington's. The game I was first scouted at was in a final at St Annes Town against Whiston," says Phil. "I scored the winner running from the halfway line and beating a couple of players. When I got home my sister told me a scout from Man Utd had asked if he could speak to my dad. It turned out it was Walter Joyce, Warren Joyce's father. I was offered a two week trial at United and because it was only a centre of excellence at Wigan rather than a club, I spoke to the staff who were really understanding about it. The trial went well and United decided to take me on a two year contract from the age of twelve to fourteen."

Alongside the likes of Danny Simpson and Ritchie Jones, Phil impressed enough to earn another two year deal and that put him in a good position to become an apprentice. "There was only us three who were kept on. There were other good players like Danny Guthrie (who was subsequently signed up by Liverpool) and Ashley Grimes who weren't kept on," he says. "There were quite a few talented lads who didn't get through, which was a bit of a shame as that group were pretty close as friends go. I don't know why. Maybe it was down to the pressure. Being around Carrington and around the first team players, I just got used to it and it became second nature, but the expectation level was huge and maybe that's what made a difference."

There is a marked change in the words of Marsh to, say, Chris Casper's experiences in the early nineties. The worlds could not have been more different. In Casper's time, under Harrison et al, life was hard. The education was tough but had to be so. Those who survived the cuts went on to invariably have strong and long careers at high levels, but they were pressured by a personal will to win. United's culture of excellence was historical in the early nineties and it was a comprehensive task to try and restore those glories. By the time that Phil Marsh was at the club, everything had changed.

The basic facilities at the Cliff were succeeded by first class options at Carrington, while the culture of excellence was very much the here and now. The Youth Cup successes of 1992 and 1995 were recent enough to illustrate what was demanded of the players to follow in order to prepare them for, hopefully, an even more demanding spell in the first team. And just the year before, in 2003, United's latest crop of youngsters had enjoyed their own success in the competition. The expectations were the same but the context in which they now stood could hardly be more different. The constant standard of excellence was a change from how it was at the start of the Nineties, where walking in the shadows of these greats was now a literal rather than figurative phrase, as was the amount of money in the game that was available for players just for signing their first professional contracts.

So the attitude of how to nurture these precocious talents inevitably had to roll with the times too. "The way everything was done at the club was exceptional, from the football side to off the pitch and they offered everything in terms of diet to make sure you were in the best shape you could be," says Phil. "There wouldn't be the need to say you were a good player – you were at Manchester United after all, and that said it everything. The coaches would place emphasis on expressing ourselves and provide us with the incentive to train with the first team players which brought its own pressures and expectance."

Phil's hard work paid off when in November 2003, he was given his first taste of FA Youth Cup action at the age of just 17 and was named in the squad for the Manchester Derby in the next round. "I was doing really well, captaining the under 17s and I'd just been selected for my first reserve team game as well against

Nottingham Forest," says Phil. "Then I got to play at Old Trafford, coming on as a substitute in the Youth Cup against City. We won, everyone was buzzing and on a high. It's unbelievable to think of what happened next – it went to show me that you just never know what's going to happen in life."

For Phil, the events of Wednesday, 14th January 2004 were to completely change everything. "Looking back, you can't help but wonder. I was playing so well, everything was going great, and then there was a massive setback. I was lucky to have survived, really," he admits. "The day after the Youth Cup game we went into training for a cool down. I used to stay in digs with Ritchie Jones and two of the older lads, Callum Flanagan and James Jowsey. Some of the lads would have schoolwork and if they got behind they'd have to come in during the week. I'd been up to date with all of mine and I was ready to go after training.

"The first year YT's would get picked up by a minibus because the club wouldn't allow us to drive or get lifts off of any of the older lads unless it was an emergency or a one-off. Because I was waiting for a couple of the others who were doing their school work, rather than have the minibus wait around for an hour, I went and asked if it would be okay if I could get a lift home with Callum as we shared digs. On the way home, Mads Timm, who was in the reserve team, sped down past us in his big flash sports car. Callum drove a Civic, a fairly fast car, and as young lads do he chased after him. It wasn't anything extreme, he was just trying to play catch up. This carried on as we went past City's training ground which follows a sort of 'S' bend in the road. The last thing I remember is going round a turn and the car spinning over itself out of control. When I woke up I was in a right mess, tangled in the car."

The car crashed and suffered the majority of its damage on impact on the left hand side, where Phil had been sitting as a passenger. He suffered a multitude of injuries down his left. His left leg was broken, he had cracked his shoulder blade, and suffered injuries to his head which required stitches and would leave scars. In the immediate aftermath of the accident, it was not just Phil's football career but his life that hung in the balance. "I was lucky that I had friends and family to support me. The club were really good, too. Some of the first team players came to see me in hospital and when I was allowed home, the manager paid a personal visit to see that I was okay. He re-assured me, telling me everything would be okay, everyone had setbacks. You do try to be optimistic but you also have to be realistic and in those early weeks, when you've suffered such a setback, you wonder if you'll ever get back at all let alone to the level that you were at. To receive a visit and such support from the manager showed me that the club believed I could do it."

It wasn't just support from the club that served to give Phil motivation. Due to the accident making local and national news, he was now in the public eye and Manchester United supporters were quick to give their own moral support. "I got quite a lot of fan mail in the weeks after the accident," says Phil. "There were people all over the world telling me they'd heard about what happened and wishing me a speedy recovery. That kind of thing really helps you find the determination to get back to where you were previously."

Of course, the club and its supporters were well aware of the perils of motor accidents. Less than half a year had passed since Jimmy Davis – the United player on loan to Watford – was killed in a car crash. It is one of those sad tales of fate. United were in the process of implementing new rules and policies for their young players driving which included the use of the minibus. "For those of us under the age of 18, we weren't allowed flash cars or anything like that. When players reached 18, they had to speak with the manager to reach an agreement on what would be the best step going forward for them," says Phil. "It was something that was being done anyway, because as far as the manager was concerned, he was reading far too much about accidents with players from other clubs, but when Jimmy's accident happened there was a clampdown. After what happened to me, there was a total shut down and none of the younger players were allowed lifts with the older ones whatsoever. We all had to go on the minibus."

Put into that kind of perspective, Phil could consider himself fortunate he had escaped at all, and with the support of the fans and the personal encouragement from Sir Alex, he set about getting on the road to recovery. "For a few months I was in a cast so I just had to stay at home for a while. Once I managed to get the cast off, I went into Carrington to have the physiotherapists checking on me. I had a brace put on my leg for support and stimulation so I could put some more pressure on it, and I was able to get about a bit better," explains Phil. "I went into the club quite often for treatment, with having the cast on for such a long time I'd lost quite a lot of weight from my leg so that was looked at. Mostly it was a waiting game, going through that routine, as it was very difficult. I'd go on little walks around Carrington, little walks around the side of the pitch. I had a limp but was trying to walk as straight as I could. Once I could walk on it comfortably, I tried to build it up to a jog and then started on the weights to really try and build the muscle back up. After about eight months, and after I'd started some sprint and running work, I was finally back to working with the balls and gradually I was involved in some of the warm ups with the other players. Small things at first, such as pig in the middle where I could just pass the ball without any challenge, little drills like that."

The coaches were mindful of the extent and severity of Phil's injuries and so cautiously approached the prospect of him involving himself more in the contact side of the sport. Phil's physical recovery had gone better than anyone expected but there was, of course, the mental effects of the accident and the damage done to his body that was yet to really be tested. "They were great like that, wanting the physical side to come gradually, and I think that was best. They were very safe with me, and once I got back into the swing of things, I felt fine playing with the ball. I was a little bit frightened coming back, though," admits Phil. "I did have it on my mind, thinking about people coming in for tackles. An injury would have been the last thing I needed. After a couple of weeks, I felt fine, my biggest issue was my sharpness and fitness and maybe a little bit of being out of sorts, as I'd not trained with the lads for such a long time. I was just keen to get myself back to the level I was at."

A consequence of the encouragement and well wishing that Phil received was that, for better or worse, there was an inevitable and unavoidable increase in attention on his recovery and development. It's a fine line between encouragement and expectation but, perhaps fortunately for Phil, he was already well versed in that thanks to his surroundings. "At United, things are always expected of you anyway, and I was doing so well before the accident," says Phil. "It was amazing to receive the support I did and it gave me extra motivation to fulfil my potential. After everything, I was really determined to do the best for myself, my friends and my family and also for all of the supporters who had taken the time to wish me well."

2004 had been a year-long journey for Phil on both a personal and professional level. January had seen almost everything taken away from him, and by December he was back in the frame for another FA Youth Cup tie. After the win over Manchester City in January, United had defeated Norwich City before being beaten by Blackburn Rovers in the sixth round and relinquishing their grasp on the trophy as a result. When the following year's competition began and United entered in the third round, they were given a favourable tie against Stoke City. Phil was given a start in the number eight shirt in an incredibly strong United side that included Jonny Evans, Ryan Shawcross, Gerard Pique, Darron Gibson and Giuseppe Rossi, all of whom would go on to become successful and established players at the top level.

The omens were good – the teams had faced each other at under-18 league level the previous weekend with Phil getting two goals, which made it all the more surprising that United were unable to get going. "To lose 1-0 was a real surprise, I still can't believe we lost that game to be honest," laughs Phil. "I was speaking about it recently to one of my friends who was in the Stoke side that day and he agreed. The talent that was on show was unbelievable, our record in the league was so good, but that was just one of those games where nothing goes in. We really thought that we had such a good chance of winning it, so good in fact that we kept hearing that this was the best youth team United had had for many a year. I suppose that's football isn't it? The 2003 winning team didn't have that many players who played at the top level, well, nowhere near as many as the side that we had," observes Phil.

Defeat on the pitch then, yet something of a spiritual victory for Phil. Having lost a year of natural development and progression, the comeback was significant and profound. As he had just turned 18, his sights were set on advancing past the age bracket sides and into the reserves, and he was given yet further personal encouragement from Ferguson. "The manager was really good and not just with keeping in touch and saying that I was doing really well," says Phil. "He acknowledged that I'd basically lost a year and so granted an extra year on my contract, which was something that he didn't have to do, but was something that I really appreciated. He said that I'd lost time through no fault of my own but he'd been so impressed by the work and dedication I'd shown that he was willing to keep observing to see just how much I wanted to play for the club. It was great for him to say that, because he didn't have to do that either." Did that year out of development weigh on his mind?. "Sometimes, well, it was something that I thought about. Matches, training, interaction, there were things I missed out on, but I didn't dwell on it, because I'd got myself back into a good position," says Phil.

Ferguson's words about determination seemed to resonate deeply with Marsh. A different way of looking at the "lost year" is to observe the increase in maturity and accountability, an extra awareness and appreciation for the chance that Phil was blessed with, which perhaps maybe even placed him at an advantage. It certainly helped that Phil showed the professional maturity associated with many United players of the modern era when it came to receiving his next break.

A striker of a good standard, a completely unexpected direction began to open up for Phil's development. "Rene Meulensteen had just started taking over the reserve side and in training there was an increase in the number of drills we did that exercised and worked our technique," Phil says. "For some reason, I don't know what it was, but Rene always got on well with me. Sometimes people just take a liking to you and I was happy that Rene did. He was observing how I was doing in the technical drills and one of them was a play where we'd have to practice a long diagonal ball to the winger. I was quite good at hitting the passes, and one day Rene came up to me in a training session and said 'Phil, can you come and play right back for us today? I just want to have a look at something in your game'.

"At the time, there were a lot of injuries in defence and I think Danny Simpson was on loan at Antwerp, which meant there was an opening in the reserves at right back. I agreed and did quite well in the training game at right back, so well that Rene asked me if I wanted to play in the same position for a game against Leeds at home for the reserves. He said he thought I would do really well. I said that was fine and I'd be happy to do that for him. I was just so happy to get the chance anyway, as up front there were some really good strikers, Giuseppe, Sylvan Ebanks-Blake too, Frazier Campbell. That's not to mention players like Louis Saha who would feature for the reserves."

It may come as no surprise that Phil seized his opportunity with both hands. "I did really well and I think I got man of the match against Leeds, Rene was smiling afterwards telling me how fantastic I was," laughs Phil. "He said I looked like I'd been playing there all my life! So I stayed there for a couple of months, playing at full back, and took to it really well. Rene asked if I would ever consider changing my position. I'd played as a striker all my life, that's where I'd been picked up and scouted, and I'd always done well in scoring lots of goals. It was lovely for Rene to say I was capable of playing in another position but I was honest and said although it was a privilege and honour to play at right back, what I really wanted was to play up front. Rene said to me that it might be best to have a think about it, as there weren't that many players demonstrating the flexibility I was, so it might be best to keep an open mind. I think he said I was a blessing in disguise."

With the encouragement and reminder about determination from Ferguson and the blatant ego-stroking from Meulensteen, Marsh was understandably in such high spirits that he carried on with the wish of his coaches and continued that professional sacrifice of what he preferred doing in order to help out his team. It might have helped somewhat that the team were doing so well. "It was such a good team, the reserve side had so many quality players who were doing so well. Not many teams got near us because we were so talented," says Phil of the side that swept the board at reserve team level in 2006.

Marsh's progression since his return from the accident had accelerated since his positional shift. As the 2006/07 season began, and a couple of dark years at the club finally seemed to be over, Phil's star appeared to shine brightly too. "After being with the reserves for a while, I was now training with the first team on a fairly regular basis too," Phil says. "When you'd be told that you were training with the first team again, it's a bit of a weird feeling. You're thinking and hoping that you'll get involved, even on the bench."

In late October in 2006, with a League Cup tie at Crewe Alexandra on the horizon, Phil's hard work, determination and sacrifice was about to get the ultimate reward – a first team appearance, and better still, a start in his favoured position. "I was training with the first team again and going through the drills when Mick Phelan called me over to one side and said 'You're going to be starting this week.' I don't even know what the word is to describe how I was feeling. I was like, 'Oh, right'. We carried on training through the week and I had that on my mind. It was an odd feeling, I really can't describe it".

At Gresty Road, United had their fair share of debutants – five, in total – and complemented that with some fine experience. Wes Brown and Mikael Silvestre had played over five hundred times combined, with Gabriel Heinze, Alan Smith and Kieran Richardson all having a fair amount of first team experience too. Marsh was to partner a real club legend up front. "I was in attack with Ole Gunnar Solskjaer," he recalls with all the eagerness as if he's just been told for the first time. "Getting on the coach was again a weird feeling. Amazing, weird – you get to the ground and the dressing room and you see a Manchester United shirt hanging from the peg with your name and number. It feels like you're dreaming, but I'll never ever forget anything from that day because it was amazing. The fans were great."

The start was most certainly a symbolic reward for the incredible spirit shown by Marsh but, more importantly, it was a stunning achievement and example of overcoming adversity. "Honestly, I don't know if it felt like it was a reward to me," he admits. "It just felt as if all of that hard work had paid off. That was my ultimate goal when I first signed for United, so all of the hours I'd put in before, and then all the hours to get myself back, had made it all the more special before kick off.

"Sir Alex said 'You lads have all got this chance to play because you have been doing so well for the reserves. You've earned the chance, so there's no pressure whatsoever. You just go and play your game, that's all you need to do.' No matter what anyone says, when you're about to play for one of the biggest clubs in the world for the first time you do have a few butterflies but his words of reassurance in that way took a big weight off of our shoulders. I felt like I could go and enjoy myself, and I really made sure I did, it was one of the best days of my life."

United won 2-1 at Crewe, Solskjaer's early goal had United ahead at half time. At the break, Marsh was substituted for Michael Barnes to give Barnes his debut out wide and tighten it up. Crewe levelled to take the game to extra time but a goal from another debutant, Kieran Lee, in the last minute of extra time sent United into the next round and another away tie at a lower league ground, this time, Roots Hall and Southend United. Marsh was pencilled in for involvement. "I think I was going to play because before the game they said that although they were taking more first team players, they were also going to keep some of the younger lads too. I picked up an injury, nothing serious, the weekend before, and because I didn't train I was one of those that had to drop out. I was obviously gutted but that was just how it was."

As it turned out, Marsh's instincts in the box might well have been necessary against Southend, as United looked poor despite only one outfield player having played less than fifty times for the club. An experienced side went down 1-0 and were eliminated from the competition. Thankfully, the result was a hiccup as United broke through that transitional period they were in to taste Premier League glory for the first time in four years, as well as reach the FA Cup Final and the Champions League semi finals. Still, Phil may feel aggrieved at not adding to the sole first team start he got, particularly at a time of transition when Ferguson remained true to the philosophies he'd adopted for all of his time at United. "Perhaps", he admits, "You do think with the club you're at and after you do get a chance that you might get another. But with it being United, and the resources they do have, you understand it is always going to be difficult for anyone trying to break through unless you're absolutely exceptional or you're fortunate."

Not that Phil has any sense of entitlement. "Maybe I didn't get a big enough chance or the right break, but no matter what, it wouldn't have taken it away from me that I represented the biggest club in the world," he says. "At least I know I can always look at myself in the mirror and say with no shame that I gave it my best and I got to play for the club. There's no shame in admitting that you weren't good enough to play there more often, or make it, because there are literally hundreds and thousands of lads who have been in a similar situation."

Perhaps in that regard, Phil is doing himself a huge disservice. It's true to say that plenty of young players have found themselves realising they may not be able to make it at Manchester United, but not many show the courage and determination on the same level that he did. One can look back at those with talent who just throw away their opportunities and suggest if they had shown the same kind of character and determination that Phil had, then they may have had a glittering career at United. After all the history books, the ghosts that cast the shadows, and the names that are remembered so fondly at Manchester United, are just as often grafters as they are mercurial talents.

Unfortunately for Phil, his path to the first team was blocked by players with both abilities, with Wayne Rooney and Cristiano Ronaldo starring. And so in the summer of 2007 it was time for him to find a new club. Showing a respectful acknowledgement for all of his efforts, Sir Alex spoke to Phil about his future with the season barely over. "He called me into his office and said that he could quite easily keep me and give me a year or two years," Phil says. "He said I would get lots of reserve team football and I would be in and around the first team in case of injuries. I might get the odd game in the cup, but he advised that at the age I was, 21, I ought to be out playing first team football in order to progress my career. Whether that be in League One or the Championship, he said I would be in a better position for my career if I did that to prove myself. It was a decision that we sat down and spoke about and I really appreciated what he said and the advice he gave. I considered myself fortunate for the opportunity I had been given."

Phil found himself searching for a club and had a trial with Blackpool. "I signed for a year with another year option up there," he says. "I did start quite well in pre-season and got a couple of goals but because there were a lot of senior strikers there I found it difficult to get a chance when the season started, I don't know if that's because Simon Grayson, who the manager was, didn't really trust a young lad to lead the line. In a reserve game at Tranmere, I had a big setback when I broke a metatarsal and that kept me out for four months."

The injury essentially ended his season and though Marsh returned before the end of the campaign, he wasn't able to get the sufficient match practice to force himself back into contention. When Grayson decided to make a cull of 16 squad members, Phil was among those to be free-transferred. "It was hard to motivate myself after that. I have to be honest and say that I felt like I'd lost another year, but this was a little bit harder to take. I'd done well and felt I deserved the chance, then I got the cruel luck of the injury which just ruled the season out," he confesses. "It was frustrating. I know all managers are different and Simon obviously wanted a consistent and experienced squad. When you sign at a club you don't know these things, or future plans, I just thought it was a Championship club that I could get a chance at and then hopefully get a Premier League club seeing me and liking what they saw. After the injury, it felt like one setback after another but I felt good when Bury gave me an opportunity."

Phil had a trial at Gigg Lane and felt it went well. "I was scoring goals and against some big clubs, too," he says. "I think we played Sheffield United, Sheffield Wednesday, Huddersfield, I scored four or five goals in those games. The manager seemed dead keen on signing me but all of a sudden there was an issue when they said they couldn't afford me. I didn't understand that as I'd told my agent that money wasn't a problem, I just wanted to be playing somewhere to prove myself. That just killed all my momentum. The pre-season had gone, I'd earned a contract, but by the time the chairman came back to sort it out it fizzled out and nothing came of it.

"The season had begun and most clubs had already done all of their buying, clubs who were interested weren't any longer because they'd signed someone else. I felt like I'd plummeted in a way. I'd really tried to be positive when I left United because I didn't want to think it was a bad thing, I felt I'd done well to do what I did do while I was there and I'd get a chance to prove myself again. But now I was feeling that nothing was going right, and I wasn't getting the luck and breaks that I maybe deserved. Sometimes you just need someone to take a shine to you and it was hard to take."

It was with a heavy heart that Phil made a bold choice to move out of the Football League and sign for Northwich Victoria. Was it coincidence that it was yet another Northern club? "I did have a couple of offers from down south, and a club in the league, but it wasn't that different to the level that Northwich were at and to be honest I knew a few of the lads there," Phil says. "I felt it was a decent standard, a place I would play regularly, get some goals, get my confidence up and kick-start my career again."

The Northwich move didn't work out. A short spell at Leigh Genesis was followed by a transfer to FC United of Manchester, the club which was established and created by disgruntled supporters in the wake of the Glazer takeover of Manchester United in 2005. The move had significance – Phil was the first player that had played for United to sign for FC United. "I knew there was a bit of buzz about it, but it was just me moving to a normal club where again, the focus was playing at a decent level where I could creep back up the ladder," he says. "I was playing all kinds of different positions at this point. I wanted to play up front, so people look at my record of 11 goals in 43 games and say it isn't a decent return for a striker, but a lot of the time I was right back, midfield, I really was all over the place. I think I played a dozen games at full back."

In the summer of 2010, Phil decided to leave FC United and sign a contract with Stalybridge Celtic, then of the Conference North, where he enjoyed a successful two year spell. "I was happy and got back to a level of performance I knew I was capable of," Phil says, "I had a really strong first season scoring about twenty five goals."

Overall, Marsh scored forty goals in seventy five appearances for Stalybridge, earning him a move to Forest Green Rovers who were spending big in an attempt to get into the League. "They had ambitions, but after I signed, they signed another three or four strikers which meant they had seven overall at the club," says Phil. "I didn't get a chance so tried to get an immediate loan and went to Hereford. I scored on my debut but then started getting moved around in position again. I returned to Forest Green and it wasn't going anywhere so my contract was cancelled, and I eventually signed for Guiseley in Leeds to hopefully get some first team football."

At the age of twenty seven at the time of writing, Phil is hopeful that he can still enjoy his peak years in League football. "Of course, ideally that's what I want to do. At the end of the day as long as I'm playing, I'm happy. If I can do well from those performances to help get noticed or get my club into the league then that's what's important," he says.

There is still time for Phil to make his mark on the game and as long as he continues to show the determination that he showed in his time at Old Trafford then you wouldn't bet against him eventually achieving his ambition of playing in League football and scoring a few goals too. Unsurprisingly, for all that went on in his spell at United, he still has a strong relationship with the club and returns there occasionally. "I couldn't speak any higher of what the staff were doing for us, and more than that, it's always evolving and improving. I've been back since I left to catch up with some of the lads I used to know or those a little younger than me, and just to have a look around at what they're doing is eye opening," says Phil. "It really is like a bubble when you're at Carrington and at United. When you leave and see what other clubs do, you understand just how lucky you were to have been there."

He has natural emotions as a result of what he went through. "Obviously, you have regrets, but you can't hold on to them forever. The incident with Callum and Mads was a huge setback for me and if that hadn't have happened, who'd have known. I don't hold any grudges though. I've spoken to Callum since and he apologised. Everyone makes mistakes and everyone's entitled to second chances but you can't avoid the truth, it did have a massive impact."

Marsh now has a young family and takes a different perspective on the way that the accident impacted his life. "To still be alive was lucky," says Phil. "On the one hand I could say sometimes I'm gutted about my career, if only about the unknown and what might have been. But to have done what I did do, and to have my family and my little girl, I feel very lucky."

The philosophical outlook has already got Phil preparing for the long term while appreciating today. "I've still got quite a while left playing but I'm taking the first steps towards doing my badges," he laughs. "I want to stay in the game as long as possible in whatever role. I don't know what specific route my life will go but I do hope it is in the game as you have your ambitions about what you want to achieve in the game. I would like to play in the League, I feel I'm more than capable of getting there, and if I'm being honest I do feel I've earned a bit of luck so it'd be great if I do. You never know, even being remembered for something like scoring in the FA Cup is something that would be great. Longer term, perhaps a coach, but after all the help I received and everything I went through, even a role as a youth development officer, or someone helping those who do suffer setbacks, could be something I would be able to make a difference". In terms of showing remarkable determination and strength of character, Phil would certainly make a wonderful example.

18

Markus Neumayr

In the summer of 2003, Sir Alex Ferguson decided to sell David Beckham to Real Madrid. Manchester United were losing a home grown talent, their "superstar" in the team, and arguably the best taker of a set piece in world football. On the eve of the 2003/04 season after a pre-season friendly against Sporting Lisbon, United's players urged Ferguson to sign the tricky teenage opponent they'd faced immediately. He obliged. Cristiano Ronaldo arrived at Old Trafford within days for a fee of just over £12 million. Ronaldo would go on to become arguably the greatest player the club had ever seen, winning the Ballon D'or in 2008 (also winning it in 2014 for his incredible 2013), but in the early days of his stint at United, he had to deal with comparisons to Beckham after he inherited the number seven shirt.

There was another player who arrived at United the same summer, under less of a spotlight. Markus Neumayr, a 17 year old German midfielder, drew a natural comparison to those who saw him in his early days at the club. Unlike Ronaldo, Neumayr almost fitted the Beckham mould. A similar frame at the same age, floppy blond hair and good looks gave a physical resemblance. The similarities didn't end there. Markus even struck the ball like Beckham, though the man himself insists that was a result of the natural action of a young player imitating an idol. "Obviously there was a little bit of me that imitated his shooting technique but not in a way that wasn't normal for any young footballer. You watch the great players and when you are younger you try to make these special abilities part of your own game," says Markus. "That's how you develop your own style. When I signed at United I tried to create my own image, my own style, and it was always compared to David Beckham."

The reputation of the England captain meant such a comparison might have been daunting, yet Neumayr was able to put a realistic perspective on things. "It was never a big issue," he insists. "Of course people try to compare you with big players to identify your playing style. I never saw myself as a second Beckham, and I couldn't control or influence what other people said or thought, so I just wanted to create my own image."

There was nothing familiar about the path Markus took to Old Trafford. No German player had played for the senior team at Manchester United before he made the move. Markus was a fan of the club, though he grew up in Hösbach, a village with a population of under 15,000 around 50km from Frankfurt. From the age of 6, he played for the local side Hösbach Bahnhof. "My father played there and that was my first experience in football. I was there for three or four years before my parents saw I had a bit of talent," says Markus. "The decision was made to take me to Aschaffenburg, which is about 5km away from Hösbach, to play for the local club there, Viktoria Aschaffenburg, which is a lower league club in Germany. It was a higher level and the club had signed some of the best talent in the area so it was a good chance to test myself. I was one of the best in the three or four years I spent learning the game there. In one tournament there were a lot of scouts present and after I impressed there, I was invited to go to Eintracht Frankfurt who are a very good club with an impressive track record of bringing through young players."

Thomas Berthold, Manfred Binz, Jürgen Grabowski and Bernd Nickel were all famous and long serving names for Frankfurt who had come through the youth system there and so, as one of the more highly rated prospects in Germany, the move to Frankfurt was a logical one. "It was a big step to make as I still went to school in Aschaffenburg, was doing quite well with my studies and was doing the highest degree you could do in the school system. I would be at school until 2:30pm, and afterwards my parents would have to drive me the 50 or 60km to Frankfurt for training and then back afterwards. It took a lot of time and cost for them so it must have been hard for them to do it over the time I was there."

The dedication of Markus and his parents was rewarded when he was called up to the German youth team. "I was 16 and got to play plenty of games in tournaments – it was great and a real honour," admits Markus. "The higher level brought in scouts from bigger clubs. Chelsea and Arsenal wanted to sign me but then Manchester United came in for me. That was possibly the biggest thing that could happen as I was such a big fan of English football. Beckham was great, Wayne Rooney was breaking through at Everton, and at United, Ryan Giggs, Paul Scholes, Nicky Butt, Ruud van Nistelrooy, all these great players. United were playing brilliant football and as soon as I knew they were interested I never had a doubt, not even for a minute, that I wanted to go there. I had a trial over in Manchester, the club were impressed with me, and when I turned seventeen in March 2003, I signed a contract with them for three years."

Neumayr moved to Manchester but concedes that initially, it was difficult to settle. "I wasn't an independent kind of guy. I was still looked after a lot by my parents and with all the travelling I'd done with them I'd obviously spent a lot of time with them as a teenager. The relationship with them was very strong and I'd never really been away from home before so it was a massive task for me. I tried not to think about it at the beginning. I was at Manchester United, such a big club, and I was so excited to have the chance, but after some time I realised how difficult and how big a task it would be. I tried to push the thoughts away and concentrate solely on football but life isn't just football and especially when you've moved to another country and another culture," confesses Markus. "It got even tougher. After only two or three months I suffered an injury, a broken collarbone, that put me on the sidelines for three or four months. It was the first big injury I'd had in my career. My parents flew over to be there for me, but it felt like a real blow for my career. I hadn't even thought about getting injured and, with it happening so early on, it made me worried that I might not be able to make the step up."

It was a significant setback, exacerbated by the fact that Markus was in alien surroundings. "United tried to help me as much as they could but I had to try and help myself first and it was very difficult. I saw it as the biggest task of my life." In order to get into a more positive frame of mind, Neumayr returned home until he recuperated from his injury. "I returned in March, and got fit again, but by then the season was already over and that was it for my first year."

Perhaps United's policy in the early years after the turn of the century to recruit a lot of talented young players from overseas was also counting against them in terms of settling in. This was proven by the cosmopolitan background of the people Markus found himself sharing his time with in the early months. "I was in digs with Florent N'Galula who became a good friend. I couldn't speak the language properly but he helped me settle as much as possible, and Danny Simpson came into digs as well and he really helped. When I returned after the summer holiday in 2004, Gerard Pique was living next door to me. From the first moment we had a great connection, we were similar characters and in a similar position. He really helped me, as did Giuseppe Rossi, and those two became my biggest friends and have remained so ever since."

British football culture and the behavioural culture of teenagers in the country is much different to how it is on the continent, yet Markus insists that this presented no significant obstacle. "The only weird thing was the cars driving on the other side of the road," Markus laughs. "Other than that everything was fine, as England is a great place to live and not that different to Germany. There were plenty of things to see and do, particularly in a city like Manchester. I absolutely loved the city from the first minute, though I did have some trouble learning the language and understanding the Mancunian accent. I got to terms with it after the first year and saw that as possibly the biggest thing I ever achieved."

It showed great character for Markus not to give in – others in the same situation might well have found it easier to stay at home and not return at all. The club stood by him after the early setback, but this wasn't a surprise given their commitment to bringing through young players. "Everyone told me when I signed that I was joining a list of great players who came through the ranks and it was always something I wanted to follow, something I wanted to achieve. Nowadays it's more difficult to achieve something like that because the game has changed so much, the step from youth team to professional football is much tougher. There'll always be one or two breaking through if it's a good year but you'll never see the likes of 1992 again. The ones breaking through now don't immediately go into the first team, they must have loan spells to develop. Even when they get back to the club, they need to be lucky that they're there at the right time and play in the right position. Things have changed, the pace of the game has got quicker, but even so I knew that being at United, with their tradition, it was something special."

Markus also has fond memories of those tasked with the development of the next generation. "I was with Choccy (Brian McClair) and it wasn't easy understanding his Scottish accent, you know," he laughs. "But he was great as he let us express ourselves and find our own way as players. He wasn't pushing us to play in a certain way which was great for us to be able to develop naturally, make our own mistakes and learn from them."

Rene Meulensteen and Paul McGuinness were also helping to look after the younger players. "Rene was like a father to me, we had a special connection. He was completely different to Choccy. It's quite hard to be warm with a guy like Choccy, but it was very different with Rene. Rene would always tell me what he thought of me as a player and a human being and I really appreciated that. Unfortunately, I only spent a year with him and I would have liked to have spent more time with him but that's football, you can't choose your coaches. I'm still in touch with him to this day which shows how great he is as a person," says Markus.

Having suffered the injury, Markus bypassed an academy education at United almost by default, featuring in only one Youth Cup game, as a substitute in a win over Norwich City in February 2004. Instead being more or less thrust right onto the periphery of the reserves, but with concerns over the injury still dogging him, he felt as if his second year didn't go as well as it could or should have. "I had to find my form and develop my own style of play. Before, I'd never really thought about it, I just played naturally, but after I came back I started to think about things more. Things like 'What did I do before my injury?' That is the worst thing you can do in football, question yourself, because you make decisions late and it doesn't go well. It was frustrating for most of the second year. I felt as if my football talent wasn't there anymore, or that I couldn't play the same way I did before I got injured."

At the end of the season, United and Neumayr went to play in the Blue Star tournament in Zurich. "I just played without thinking. We won the tournament and I was really happy with my contribution. My form felt good, I'd got my natural body shape back to what I wanted it to be. I came back after that summer and Rene was in charge of the reserve team, because Ricky Sbragia had left to go to Bolton. As I've said, I had a good connection with Rene. David Fox left, and he was captain of the reserves, so I was given the honour and it was a massive, massive boost for me. It was an achievement for the hard work I'd done in the second year and it inspired me to play well."

The Manchester United reserve team of 2005/06 was full of talent and rightly swept the board in terms of trophies. Gerard Pique, Jonny Evans, Kieron Richardson, Darron Gibson, Giuseppe Rossi were all part of the team that Markus captained and in the early stages of that campaign, Markus was often the best player on the pitch, directing and running the play with an intelligence and composure rarely seen in a 19 year-old. "Gerard and Giuseppe were brilliant for us as we won everything we possibly could," says Neumayr. "We played fantastic football, often winning with big margins, and it was a great experience to play in a team full of players you knew would go on to play in the Premier League and, in Gerard's case, become one of the best in the world in his position."

2005 had become gradually better for Markus on the pitch but it was very much an "annus horribilis" for Manchester United. Having witnessed a newly-rich Chelsea storm to the Premier League title, the club suffered the blow of an FA Cup penalty shoot-out defeat to Arsenal in a game they dominated and should have won. Off the pitch, there was a controversial takeover that was met with opposition and caused much division, while later in the year, Roy Keane would be shown the door after criticising the ability of the younger players at the club in a never shown interview with the club's internal television studio.

To an observer it could, and did, appear to be a tumultuous time, but Markus insists it didn't affect the mood inside the club or with the players Keane allegedly tore into. "As a young player you honestly don't let that kind of thing affect you, you don't think about those things," insists Markus. "You think about your own development, you don't concentrate on the business side. We realised there was a lot of tension around the club but it didn't play on our minds. To us inside the club, it didn't affect the way we approached our games or anything like that. We were professional footballers but not players for the first team, maybe it might have been different to those in the first team." On Keane? "Every person has their own perspective and opinion of others but again, it wasn't anything we could control. I'm not sure what he said, only what he was supposed to have said, so it's difficult to say it would cause any issue and I didn't pay too much attention to that. There was no bigger picture for me, I was only concerned with myself."

Keane's departure highlighted a growing concern for United. Not long after the Irishman left, Paul Scholes suffered an eye injury and there was doubt whether he would return at all, never mind to the level he had played at. Darren Fletcher was growing but was used on the right side as often as he was in the middle of the pitch and United would line up with John O'Shea and Ryan Giggs as their central midfield pairing on a number of occasions. In that circumstance, with Neumayr performing well as captain in a reserve team regularly scoring four or more goals, he understandably felt he might get a chance to step up. "I was training with the first team regularly, everyone was encouraging me with my development and the senior players were saying that they hoped I got my chance," says Markus.

That chance almost came against West Ham United in March 2006. Neumayr was called into the squad after a season he'd been almost ever present in the reserves but didn't even make the bench as O'Shea, nominally a defender, was called to play in the centre of midfield. Neumayr is philosophical about the decision on the night. "I wasn't frustrated, just happy to be a part of the team for the first time. The gaffer unfortunately didn't have the confidence in me to give me a run out that night, but these are decisions you have to accept," says Markus.

A meeting with Ferguson late in the season, with Neumayr's contract up for renewal, led to a parting of the ways for player and club. "He was honest and said for the next year it might be difficult for me to get into the first team and get that kind of practice. I said that I felt I had achieved all I could in the reserves and had proven myself, that I deserved the chance to step into the first team or at least have a go. Sir Alex said that it would be difficult for me to break into the middle, as on the right there was Ronaldo, Fletcher and Chris Eagles, so I would have been number four there too. At the end of the day if you're behind Ronaldo and Fletcher it will be difficult for you to get minutes at all. I had a really good offer from Germany so we both decided it would be best for my progression if I was to leave."

That offer came from Duisburg, a good club who had just suffered relegation but were favourites to be promoted back into the Bundesliga. "I was very disappointed as I didn't want to leave but I had to in order to get football. I actually hoped that things would go so well for me that I would end up back at United one day," he admits. "That's life, sometimes you make the wrong decision. Maybe I could have stuck it out for one more year in the reserves or even got a loan spell in the Championship".

Nonetheless, Markus doesn't regret his decision. "No, there are no regrets, everything in life happens for a reason. Sometimes you make good choices, sometimes you make bad ones. You have to live with it and it doesn't make sense to talk about it as a regret years later. It was a decision that made sense at the time. Sir Alex did say he was disappointed to see me leave but wished me the best".

The immediate future following Neumayr's departure didn't go well for him. A few appearances in the first team at Duisburg were undermined by the pressure he was under, and then he suffered another injury that kept him out for almost a year. "After I left United, I carried their 'shadow'. People expected me to be the perfect player, and when I couldn't meet that expectation and then got injured with an infection that just wouldn't heal, I had a spell where I thought of quitting football altogether. I had a baby girl who was just born while I was out with injury and it was a difficult time to make choices. I wasn't able to do what I loved. I couldn't even walk properly, I had a terrible pain in my right foot, so I began to think whether it was worth having all these problems, having bad moods as a consequence and I didn't want my daughter to see her dad like this.

"Thankfully I met a guy who helped me overcome my injury and it was comfortable for me to play on. I had a desire to play and I had talent that was given to me by God and my parents so it would have been a waste to not work hard, a waste to throw it away. It's not easy, A lot of people do throw things away and take the easy way out. I had to start playing again in the lower leagues in Germany for Rot-Weiß Essen and I could hear people laughing at me, the fact I'd played for Manchester United and here I was making my way back into the game again. People thought I was finished but I believed in myself and so did my wife and that, to me, was the most important thing."

Neumayr keeps in touch with many of the people he played with at United, with those long standing relationships with Rene Meulensteen and Gerard Pique the two most valuable things he will take from his time at Old Trafford. "I meet Gerard regularly and have been to watch him a few times for Barcelona," says Markus. "These are friendships that I'll have and cherish for my lifetime. Gerard was like a brother to me in Manchester and that hasn't changed. He's a great person, he's gone so far up the football ladder but is still the same guy. And as for United, they were my favourite team when I grew up and they'll always have a special place in my heart."

Markus managed to get his career back on track with a move to Swiss side FC Thun where he scored twice in thirteen appearances, before a transfer to AC Bellinzona in June of 2011. "I was playing the best football of my career and still think I have six or seven years left. I feel I can play at a higher level and I'm determined to do that," he says. The renewed drive and effort from Neumayr paid dividends with his on pitch performances. Spectacular long range goals for Bellinzona renewed those old Beckham comparisons, and his form was so great that in 2012 he was linked with a transfer to FC Basel, who had recently knocked United out of the Champions League.

In the summer of 2013, Neumayr transferred to FC Vaduz, where at long last he made his European debut in a Europa League qualifier. "You have to try and give it all. Even though I had thoughts of giving it in, I had a love for the game that made me not want to give it in. It was sad for me that things didn't work out at United, but maybe I was given the difficulties I've had to show that it's always possible to turn your life around. Mads Timm and Florent both stopped playing football, many others I've played with who didn't make it at United have struggled because of the expectations on you when you leave the club. The best thing to do, as long as you have love in your body for the game, is to do the best you can to fulfil your own potential and not that of what people expect just because you played for this massive club. I just hope I stay healthy and enjoy the next six or seven years in the game. Whether I play Champions League, or don't play Champions League, for me it doesn't matter. I achieved everything I set out to by just getting myself back into the game and everything else that comes from now on is just a bonus. Perhaps it's even better to have been on the floor and have picked myself back up, it gives me the opportunity to enjoy the highs forever more. That will be something I teach to my kids – if you stop fighting, you always lose."

19

Sam Hewson

If you played in the centre of midfield and were the captain of the Manchester United reserve side at any point in the last six or seven years of Sir Alex Ferguson's reign as manager, you might well have thought you'd get more of an opportunity in the first team. Particularly if, as Sam Hewson did, you were having the best spell of your career in terms of form. Yet Manchester United have produced many quality players in midfield who just couldn't break in as we've already discussed. Markus Neumayr (who, incidentally, Sam succeeded as full time skipper of the second string) left in search of playing in the first team to aid his development after seeing John O'Shea and Ryan Giggs preferred as a midfield pairing in the run in at the end of the 2005/06 campaign. Rarely have supporters of the youth and reserve sides been fortunate enough to see someone play with the authority and composure that Hewson seemed to ooze at that level, making it all the more sad that he didn't ever make a first team appearance. The fact of the matter is though, that the only time that Ferguson seriously beefed up the middle of the park in those last six or seven years was the summer of 2007, slap bang in the middle of Hewson's annus mirabilis.

Hewson's association with the club was a long one, joining before he was even ten years of age with the new concentration on recruiting local talent early on. Sam was a bit of a star at many sports at school and might not even have gone into football. "I was into cricket at school. We had a good team and won quite a few tournaments. I was an all rounder and could bat and bowl which was good," he says. "I also liked cross country running and used to run for the school. When I was growing up though, I always really knew I liked football the most. We used to have matches with a tennis ball, about 30 of us. There was no room at all to play but everyone enjoyed it and it was very competitive."

Even with that concentration on playing football there was no guarantee he'd end up as a United player, as he supported one of their biggest local rivals. "I was a massive Bolton fan growing up, it was great to have a season ticket at Bolton and watch the different styles of playing. I'd go with my dad to watch Bolton and it was so good," he admits. "I started off playing for a team called AFC Bolton because my best mate at school used to play for them and his dad watched us playing in the school playground. He mentioned to the manager I was quite good so he told me to come down the following week." That happened out of the blue but it was swiftly about to get much bigger.

"I was there for three weeks then luckily, one game, a United scout was there and he asked me and two other players to go down to United to have a six week trial," Sam says. Being a Bolton lad and a fan, was there any hope that he could have signed for his boyhood club? "Obviously, Bolton is the team I supported, but as a kid if United ask you to go there then you go. It's such a big club that no kid would turn that down," he confesses. "People will probably say it would have been easier to make it at Bolton. To be fair, that may be true, but I can remember how jealous all the other kids got when you said you were trialling with United."

After his first impressions of the size of the club, Sam could probably appreciate that jealousy. "I was very impressed when I first went for a trial to realise how big it was," he says. "Initially as a kid I didn't really think of that stuff. I just went to enjoy the game and to impress the managers. It wasn't until I was there for a while that I began to understand more about the tradition and how big the youth set up is there."

There's no magic formula to it. Manchester United legend Gordon Hill describes the class of 1992 as a "lottery ticket" and there is certainly sense in the logic. You cannot guarantee talent but what you can do to improve your chances is try to manipulate an environment which is conducive to the development of talent of that nature. There is no substitute for hard work but if you have the ability, training and playing in an environment with other young players of similar quality improves team-work (naturally) and the apparent telepathy in some partnerships that can follow after a long time. It goes to show just how much of a one-off the class of 1992 was that even with the "forced" methods adopted by professional clubs around the country, no-one has quite managed to replicate or, in fairness, get close. Even if they don't quite have the natural ability, what is guaranteed is the best possible education in the game.

Sam can remember the people he was friends with in those early days. "There were about five of us who were there for quite a long while and in that time it's only natural to become close friends with some of them, like James Chester, Tom Cleverley, Febian Brandy and Richard Eckersley," says Sam. He says that the emphasis on keeping a bunch of players together from such an early age had its benefits on the group. "We went away a lot when we were younger to different tournaments so we were with each other a lot," he says. "Also, the coaches would make you do things together to make sure you were developing the bonds within the group, too."

As the team got older together and prepared for their first collective steps into some serious competitive action – namely for Sam, his FA Youth Cup debut at Birmingham City in 2005 – the staff at the club, as well as some older players, made them aware of the path they were treading. "We were told about the history of the Youth Cup, and the big effect it has on players who have gone onto better things. We watched a lot of videos and got told stories by past players about it," he says. "I felt a little nervous going out for the first game but I also knew we had a really good team at the time so I was confident."

That team included the likes of Jonny Evans and Darron Gibson. "We had a really good team then. Obviously Jonny and Darron were the standouts," says Hewson. "The thing that stood out most about those two was that they both hated to lose and demanded a lot from the other lads. They would tell you when you weren't doing your job. Obviously you can see they both have quality. They could use both feet which is very important and also they were both leaders which helped me too as a young player." Sam feels that there were others, too, who perhaps went under the radar because of the talent of the other two. "Ryan Shawcross and Danny Rose were in that team and they also were very good players. I thought Danny Rose didn't get the credit he deserved because he was a very good player to play with."

United won Sam's first Youth Cup game to set up a tie against Sunderland in a really competitive atmosphere – Sam made a real difference, scoring a penalty in the win. "I was very proud of that. It was a tough game that was! Tough conditions and it was a very hard fought win. I was glad to put the penalty away and get my first goal in the competition," he says. United navigated their way past Charlton and faced City in the next round. Though probably the better team on the night in the setting of the Etihad Stadium, United's youngsters just couldn't make the breakthrough and were knocked out. "We knew there were still tough games to come. But with the team we had we were very confident and a lot of people thought we would win it, me included," Sam says. "We knew it would be a tough game against City though and so it proved. It's always disappointing to lose to City never mind in the cup, and especially that game when we played so well throughout. It was a very hard result to take because we believed we would go all the way."

If there's one thing that is written into the DNA of Manchester United as much as the glamour and the excitement, certainly under Sir Alex Ferguson, it's the ability to triumph after adversity, the record at any level of the club of bouncing back after not winning a trophy, or suffering a cruel exit, to make amends the following year or shortly after. A defeat in intense circumstances can do much to strengthen the character of a player and that seemed to help Hewson. Defeat in the 2005/06 FA Youth Cup was a bitter pill to swallow but his personal development had been aided no end by the experience.

Influenced by the drive and determination of the likes of Gibson and Evans, Hewson was now seen by team-mates as one of the most experienced and important members of the youth team. Though able to run proceedings best from a conventional central midfield role, at times the way he was deployed in the team was akin to a young Matthias Sammer, the German midfielder of the late 80s and early 90s who was able to play all the way through the spine of his team. Sam was comfortable defending his back line and also supporting the front men which not only made him a valuable player to the coaches, so much so that he was now used in the reserve team, but also an indispensable team-mate particularly to those in the same age group.

Going into the 2006/07 season and the attempt to achieve Youth Cup glory, Sam knew that he would be seen as one of the main players. "I felt I had a bit more responsibility because I had been there the season before and knew what it was all about," he admits. "Also, I'd been playing with the reserves a lot that season which meant I was always improving. I suppose I thought of myself as one of the main players and that I needed to perform to help us get through."

There was plenty of talent in the 2006/07 team. Ben Amos, Tom Cleverley and Danny Welbeck would all feature in the Youth Cup run, as the first signs of Rene Meulensteen's training techniques straight from the methods of Wiel Coerver, the legendary Dutch innovator, were beginning to bear fruit in the visual on-pitch performances. Sam enjoyed the approach of the different coaches at the time. "We worked with Rene a lot when we were younger, with the skills and touch part of our game, and he would help with different moves to get out of a certain situation," says Sam. "He was very good at helping you get out of tight situations and for me being a midfielder, that was a big help. To be able to have the different tricks to get out of tight spots was a great advantage. I have to say, though, that Paul McGuiness had the biggest influence on me because he always believed in me from a very young age, and he would always help the young players out a lot with extra training and talking to you a lot about your game."

Far from feeling the pressure of his increased importance to the side, Sam flourished throughout the winter of 2006 and into 2007. There was a strong Youth Cup run. Hewson scored in the fourth round win over Southampton, again in the next round against Crystal Palace, and then scored both goals in the win over Birmingham in the quarter final. "I felt like my season was just kicking on and I couldn't have been in better form," he says. "Scoring goals always gave me that boost of confidence every player needs. But it was good, because I was coming from midfield and helping the strikers out. The main importance, though, was getting through each round. It was a good team to be in because everyone played for each other and if someone else was in a better position to score they would give it to them. I was lucky to be there."

United were drawn to face Arsenal in the semi final, meaning a trip to the Emirates Stadium and a second leg at Old Trafford. Though they hadn't been to a final since 2001, Arsenal were widely lauded for their development of young players under Arsene Wenger, perhaps too much so. However the initial consequence of any kind of hype is pure and simply that people become aware of you if they weren't before. That naturally leads to curiosity, and then a subsequent desire to prove yourself against them, especially in games that were going to have a fair bit of media attention. "Everything was talked about before the game and we knew that it would be a tough one. They had some young players but so did we," says Sam.

He has fond memories of playing in such stadiums on those occasions. "The

Emirates was unreal, one of the best stadiums I've played in, if not the best. The pitch was like a bowling green, there was no grass out of place. They also let kids in the ground for free which made the atmosphere very good that evening. By this time I'd played at Old Trafford a couple of times but every time is always special. It's every young lad's dream to play at Old Trafford and a semi final made it extra special." Arsenal's decision to let children in for nothing led to a record attendance at the time of just over 38,000 and that big crowd inspired the home side to a slender 1-0 win they scarcely deserved.

Rarely for Sir Alex Ferguson, he commented prior to the second leg – using mind games even at Youth Level – when he stated that "Arsenal's young players get credit for being the best in the world but they're not as good as ours." That comment had the desired effect on Hewson and his team-mates. "Obviously when the manager says that, it's got to give you a confidence boost. For him to say what he did showed what he thought of us as young players and it definitely gave us the thought of wanting to go out there and prove to him that he was right. He would speak to us after every game saying well done. He came in before the game saying good luck and just relax and enjoy it and we will be fine. That's all he needed to say really." In that second leg, United took a while to get going, but after some exceptional football and the nerves of extra time, Danny Welbeck made it 4-2 on the night, and 4-3 on aggregate. There could be no denying that it was the determination, inherent from the likes of Hewson and inspired by the comments of Ferguson, that made the difference.

The youngsters had shown they could handle pressure, the pressure of playing in big stadiums in front of big crowds, and putting on good performances too. The final, however, was to provide a completely unique kind of pressure – a two legged tie with Liverpool. United's first team had only recently gone to Anfield and snatched a dramatic, famous win thanks to an injury time goal from John O'Shea at the Kop End which was to prove valuable in the pursuit of a first league title for four years. You couldn't write the script. The team struggled to get to grips in the first half of the first leg of the final and Liverpool went ahead early on. An own goal had levelled things up when, fifteen minutes from time, United won a penalty in front of the Kop. Hewson was United's designated taker and had done well from the spot previously. "I always felt confident when taking a penalty because I thought if I hit the ball with power and in the corner then it's going to take some save to stop it," Sam says. "So I was quite confident stepping up, but I have to say my adrenalin was going standing there in front of the Kop End with all their fans trying to put me off. I did know it was a big penalty and it would be good to take the advantage back to Old Trafford and luckily for me the keeper went the wrong way."

Hewson had once again led by example and steered his team into a strong position going into the second leg. The professional pride he felt from such a wonderful season was about to take a hit in the most cruel of circumstances. In the second leg of the final, Liverpool won 1-0 after extra time to take the game to penalties. This time, instead of the Kop, the teams would be facing the Stretford End. Magnus Eikrem missed the first penalty, and Liverpool scored their next four, meaning that when Hewson, who was saved until last because of his proven ability to handle such pressure, stepped up to take the last of five United penalties needing to score to keep his team in the final. "It really was the worst feeling I've ever felt," Sam admits. "It was more anger at myself for missing the penalty because before that, I didn't want to change the way I normally took it. But then I thought the keeper would know were I was going, so I tried to lift it higher and unfortunately got too much on it. It was hard to take because we really thought it was our year."

Earlier in this chapter, retribution and fulfilment was discussed after the exit to City the previous year. It certainly didn't come against Liverpool, with defeat even more sadistic. However, as a team, that United side finally achieved some of the success they were probably due, in the Champions Youth Cup tournament in Malaysia. United defeated Porto, Barcelona, Flamengo of Brazil, where Hewson scored the winner, and in the final overcame Juventus to win the inaugural tournament.

Sam has good memories of Malaysia, not least because it came in a summer when he was selected for the England under-19 team and also signed his first professional contract at United. "The tournament in Malaysia was full of really good teams so we went knowing it would be hard for us but played really well as a group", says Sam. "It was an awesome feeling. Then to get the call that I was going to be picked for England was the proudest moment of my life, knowing that telling my mum and dad would make them the proudest parents ever. That had always been my aim, to try and break into the England Youth set up. The year was going great and finally, when I got told about getting a professional contract, it couldn't have been any better."

Being awarded a squad number in the summer of 2007, and then being kept at the club instead of going out on loan looked like a hugely promising step for Hewson, despite the newly crowned Champions adding to their squad with Nani, Carlos Tevez, and the midfielders Owen Hargreaves and Anderson. With the latter pair providing an obstruction to the first team, Hewson would have been content to go out on loan. "I was feeling very encouraged. Even though I did want to go out on loan and get experience, I thought they must be keeping me here for a reason, so I kept going and working hard to see if I could get my chance. I was getting encouragement in the reserves working with Brian McClair. He was totally different to Paul or Rene, more of a sit back, watch and see how you progress kind of thing. But he gave me the captaincy of the reserve team so obviously I liked him for that. I was very proud of that too." says Sam.

Injuries in the squad and difficulties in acclimatisation meant that when the Carling Cup tie against Coventry City came around in September, Hewson, who would normally have felt that he had a good chance of playing in such a game, was not even considered. Instead, Anderson and Nani were given the opportunity to get some more experience. "I admit I was very annoyed, these players were brought in to be playing the bigger games, so I thought I definitely had a chance of being picked for that squad and thought this could be my chance," says Sam. "I suppose things were going too well, something had to go not so well. I just wanted the chance to prove to the manager that I could handle it."

Hewson's patience was rewarded, at least slightly, when he was included in the squad to play against Roma in the final Champions League group game. It's not unusual for the club to take a number of younger players along to such occasions to get the experience, though in this particular game, as United had already qualified, a few stood to get more than just a sight-seeing trip. Sam can recall what happened quite vividly. "A few of the reserve lads were training with the first team all week leading up to this game and Mike Phelan had said to us the Gaffer was thinking about taking a few of us to the game, so obviously that gave us extra motivation to try really hard in training to impress," he says. "The day before we travelled Mike Phelan put the squad up in the reserves changing room and I couldn't believe it when my name was on it. Not just mine, but a couple of the other reserve lads which made it a lot better knowing you've got good friends with you too. That experience was awesome. Running out to warm up and the Roma fans booing us felt unreal, I can't explain the buzz I got from that. Although I didn't get on the pitch, the whole experience of being with the first team and seeing how it worked and how people were on match days helped me a lot and gave me the desire to improve and want to be there every game."

It was now a tough choice for Sam. Having had pretty much a non-stop year of progression up until the autumn of 2007, he was now faced with the choice of persevering with trying to break into a team that was packed with experience, or going on loan. "I thought I might have progressed more that season. It was strange because once again, in January, I had a couple of loan offers, but I never went, I stayed with the reserves which for me shouldn't have happened," he admits. "There were young lads coming through and I thought I was in their way to improve so I wanted to go out, not just for me but for them too."

Staying at United had a benefit. Sam was able to train day in, day out with the man who would be named the best player in the world in 2008. "I think every kid in the world would have been jealous of me at that time, training with Cristiano Ronaldo," he says. "He was fast becoming the best player in the world and to be training with him was an honour really. But at the time you don't really feel it, because you just think it's normal everyday going in seeing players like that and training with them. Obviously when you see players like that who are top of the game and they are still trying and working hard to improve it only gives you that boost to improve yourself."

Perhaps it was that professionalism and dedication to self-improvement as well as selflessness that made Sir Alex keep Sam around. He was a wonderful example for younger players to follow, and a sensible influence to have around. Though he didn't feature for the first team in the duration of the 2007/08 season, in the summer of 2008 he was "upgraded" in shirt number from 43 to 33, and featured in the first game United played after becoming European Champions in Moscow, a friendly in Aberdeen. "It was really good to be involved so early in the year," he says. "I loved the whole experience. It was my first proper game for United and I came on for Rooney! Couldn't have been any better. I was thinking though, if the manager has brought me here then I may have a chance, so I just had to knuckle down and keep proving that I'm a good player each day in training. It gave me a lot of confidence, that trip."

Ironically, with a new resolve to proving his ability, Sam would find himself going on loan for the first time after a difficult start to the season where nothing seemed to improve. "It was getting to the stage were I was just staying around the reserve team and thought my progress wasn't going anywhere, so I wanted to taste league football. When I was asked to go to Hereford I was thrilled to go," insists Sam. "After ten games and three goals, it felt good, but doesn't tell the whole story. When I made my debut we won five nil at home, which was a good start but I also remember making a challenge and something pulled in my groin. I was thinking, no this can't happen. I carried on for a few weeks with this groin problem when really I should have gone and had it sorted but because it was my first time out on loan I wanted to carry on. Even though I was injured, I thought I did well. I wasn't at my best and later had to go back to United and get an operation on it which kept me out for a few months."

Moving into the 2009/10 season, Hewson knew he would need to find another club and went on loan to Bury. "Bury was a good club, I felt really good there and it was just up the road from me in Bolton. I enjoyed it though I didn't really play much because I struggled with fitness and injuries," says Sam. Those injuries, and the stalling they added to his already stunted progression, meant that his contract was not renewed at United in 2010. Typically though, Hewson had done enough with his attitude to impress at Bury so they had no hesitation in offering for him a return. "The manager at the time, Alan Knill, said to come back at pre-season to prove my fitness and if I did, I'd have a contract," he says. "I did do that and things seemed to be going well, even though I had a feeling I wasn't in his starting eleven and that kind of played on my mind a little. I thought I was training hard to sit on the bench which I didn't like. Saying that, I then made the wrong decision of leaving Bury to go on trial at Yeovil Town after some bad advice from an agent. Looking back now, I should have stayed at Bury where I would have had a contract but then the Yeovil thing didn't work and I had no offers on the table."

It is unfortunate that such an uncharacteristically rash decision would have such a profound impact on an incredibly important time in Sam's career. With the season already underway, he needed to find a club fast. "Things just seemed to be going wrong at this time, with nothing going right for me. Grimsby did offer me a deal but it wasn't enough to move away from home and live on so that's why I didn't end up there", he says. "I had to make a decision then because the season was starting and I had no income coming in. My girlfriend and I had just moved house so needed income. Altrincham, who were in non-league, asked me a few times to sign for them and at this time it was either keep going on trial at clubs or go to Altrincham. I thought I have to start somewhere now and work my way back up. It was a shock to the system I have to admit but was something I had to do at the time."

Sam signed for Altrincham in the September of 2010, and after making nineteen appearances was granted a free transfer in March of the following year. Again, in need of a club, his next career move was one that barely anyone would have predicted. "I got a call saying I could go out to Iceland and play there, which at first I couldn't believe because I had never thought about Iceland before really in my life," he admits. "I sat down with my family and talked about it and came to the conclusion of why not, I've got nothing to lose so I may as well give it a try. I went out there two weeks later and signed with Fram." It was a bold move by anyone's standards, but Sam believes he has learned from the experience. "I do feel the experience has helped me a lot and it suits my style of play. A lot of teams try to play it on the floor. It's an easy way of living because there is no real language barrier as they all speak English, too. I'm improving all the time and trying to be better. There are a lot of scouts from Scandinavian countries watching so I'm trying to impress all the time."

That is the next step, he hopes. "I'm not looking too far in the future, at the moment I'm just enjoying playing and seeing what happens. One day I do hopefully want to play in England again but that seems hard now because there's so many players trying to get clubs. I'm settled here now, I'm trying to get on with life and if I keep playing well who knows what could happen. The next aim for me is maybe move to a Scandinavian team and see from there."

Sam still keeps in touch with some of the players he grew up with. "I still try to speak to them when I can, but obviously they have gone on to their own things. Me and Febian are still good friends, we see each other a lot and still meet up," he says. "All in all, my time at United were the best years of my life. I learnt so much and did so many things with the club that it's something I will never forget. I would like to say thanks to all the coaches helping me since I was a young player at the club, they brought me on so much and made me the player I am today. I don't have any regrets about it, things worked out how they did for a reason, and for me it was just not meant to be. Yes I feel it would have been better if I got a chance to prove myself in a first team game, it could have been different if so, but it didn't happen. Now I have to make the most of life and what I have been given and to make it work in Iceland."

20

Ben Amos

And so we reach the end of the journey for this anthology, completion of the Sir Alex Ferguson era, and a look into the future. In keeping with United's local recruitment policy, Ben Amos has been at Old Trafford since the tender age of eleven and has been at the club throughout one of the most successful periods in its history. Amos is almost the very prototype of what the club expects from an academy product in the modern era – a player who, influenced by the greats he has seen, will give his all to try and perform for the first team, and a young man who is articulate and well rounded.

The path may be tried and tested yet may not have been travelled by Amos at all had fate taken a twist on the day United decided to take a chance on him. At the age of eleven, Ben was a goalkeeper training with Crewe Alexandra, but when United took the plunge he was playing outfield for his local team. "I was playing for Priory County in midfield and then our goalkeeper got injured and I had to go in goal," says Ben. "I was our normal penalty taker and when we got one I went up, took it and scored! I think that won us the league as well. Added to that story was the fact we got lost en route to the game so we had to ring my Nan to ask her to find Sparkle Cleaning Company in the Yellow Pages. One of the players' parents owned that company so, after all that drama, we got there just before kick off. I was offered a six week trial at United and they signed me after two weeks."

On arriving at United, and Carrington, Ben shares the commonly held view in recent years that the club placed a huge emphasis on personal development and credits many individuals. "A man called Dave Bushell, who is still at the club, was great with me in terms of encouraging my education forward," admits Ben. "He knew I was an intelligent lad and nudged me towards doing my English Language A Level, alongside the business diploma that a lot of the lads were doing. That involved a hell of a lot of work in my own time, but, with the help of my tutor Marian Digweed, I achieved an A.

"The coach who inspired me most at that age was a man called Rich Hartis, who since moved on with Ole Gunnar Solskjaer at Molde FK and then went with him to Cardiff City in January 2014. It was him who signed me at 11 years-old. I was his first signing and he laid the majority of my foundations and nurtured me mentally to deal with life in football." After all the time he had been in charge at United, and even taking into account the staggering expansion of the club and number of employees they now had, it was still a personal standard set by Ferguson that he would ensure he was personally involved and available to youngsters – something that Ben was initially intimidated by. "With Sir Alex, he used to scare the shit out of me," he laughs. "He'd say something to you and you'd be thinking 'Is he joking or not?'. But you daren't smile because you genuinely thought he could rip your head off at any moment. Then of course he would smile, rub your hair vigorously, say something like 'well done son' and walk off. I think it was his way of keeping you grounded, and it certainly worked with me. I used to think he didn't take me seriously when he did things like that, which drove me on to do what I had to do to get in his first team."

If Sir Alex was seen, and still is seen, as a father figure to many Fledglings, then Ben was fortunate in that he had another to give him guidance. Edwin van der Sar joined United at what many would consider to be the twilight of his career, but went on to win eight major honours in just six years including four league titles. He made such an impact that many now think he is the second-best goalkeeper in United's history, and Ben's experiences of working alongside "the Flying Dutchman" certainly compare to those of the young goalkeepers who were fortunate enough to observe Peter Schmeichel in the 1990s. "Working with Edwin really was like having your Dad around the place," says Ben. "To this day he's great with me and back when he was at the club I would be chewing his ear off about his career and trying to get to the bottom of what made him tick. I loved working with him and admiring his calm demeanour and style, though he always had a fiery temperament bubbling away underneath. He had a massive impact on my progression and development and I've been lucky to have worked with him."

Ben's own development was tested because as well as him, United had Ron-Robert Zieler, the highly rated German stopper. Both were contending for a place in goal in the academy and in the 2006/07 FA Youth Cup run, it seemed as if Amos had done enough to have established himself as number one, until disaster struck in the semi final. "I was devastated. I had worked tirelessly to get myself above Zieler in the pecking order, although he was more physically matured and more powerful than me at the time," Ben admits. "I made up for that in aggression and kept my place, only to dislocate my shoulder in the tenth minute against Arsenal. I had to step aside and heard about us eventually winning in extra time whilst in hospital. If I said I was happy for the boys I'd be partly lying, because whilst I was, I was also gutted about how this might affect my career. I knew winning the Youth Cup would mean Sir Alex would give me opportunities at some point, and I had six months on the sidelines to think about that." Zieler would go on to represent Germany, though like Markus Neumayr before him, he would ultimately fail in his quest to become the first German to play for the United first team. He was also unable to stop Liverpool winning the Youth Cup Final of 2007 on penalties at Old Trafford.

When he returned from injury, Ben was regularly selected for the academy side in the 2007/08 season and when the next season rolled around, he was elevated to the big time – somewhat unexpectedly being taken on the pre-season tour to South Africa with the newly crowned European Champions. It was a step that Amos concedes was a little frightening at first. It is true to say that the first team squad was littered with academy products such as Darren Fletcher, John O'Shea and Wes Brown, but also those older heads like Ryan Giggs, Paul Scholes and Gary Neville. "To be honest with you, back then at 18 years-old, I still looked and felt like a teenager playing with men," says Ben. "Not just physically but mentally too. That team was studded with the best players in the world, many of them in their thirties, with only Danny Welbeck that I really knew and I'm not sure he was even involved at that point."

Ben shares that those senior members of the squad still displayed the benefit of their own education, and demanded the same standards from their team-mates as was expected by them way back under the tutelage of Eric Harrison. "I'm talking about real cold-hearted winners," laughs Ben. "I'm sure Gary Neville wouldn't mind me saying that he would fucking rip my head off if I did something wrong in training and would still be talking about it two days later. If he did something wrong and I said anything to him it would be 'fuck off and save the fucking ball.' That was it, he was Gary Neville and I was new boy Ben Amos, so what could I say. They were winners and didn't care who they upset, every training session was a match."

If Ben thought introduction to the first team was a hard road then his potential was at least recognised higher up when he was given a chance of first team action in the bizarre friendly against Portsmouth in Nigeria. United were 2-0 up when he was brought on to replace Tomasz Kuszczak in front of 30,000 supporters in Abuja, but was powerless to stop Jermain Defoe grabbing a consolation in the final minute. Less than two months later and Ben was to make his senior debut at the tender age of 18 in the League Cup game against Middlesbrough, a huge pat on the back from Sir Alex, though Ben himself puts it down to fortune. "I remember every keeper ahead of me dropping like flies the week before until, as the day of the game came, I was finally going to be on the bench for United. I thought, surely Ron was going to start being the older and more mature keeper, so I spent all afternoon in the hotel preparing myself as if I was playing, just in case. I thought sod it, I'm going to give it a right good go, and if I don't do well then I can live with knowing I didn't cower from the challenge. So 5.30pm came and the manager called me into his office at Old Trafford. He said 'Right son, I'm going to start you tonight, concentration for ninety minutes, OK? You're a good goalkeeper so go and enjoy it.' That was it, and by that point I was smiling and excited. The game went well, I dealt with everything positively and the goal I conceded was a deflected effort from Adam Johnson from 20 yards in a 3-1 win."

Ben was kept around the squad for the rest of the season, aside from a very short loan spell at Peterborough as cover in October 2008, and was part of the travelling squad for the Club World Cup in December 2008. He was also named as a substitute for the League Cup Final of 2009 where Ben Foster kept goal and decided the game in United's favour against Tottenham Hotspur in a penalty shoot out. Ben typically shrugs off the medals he won for his inclusion in the squads. "Of course, my long term goal is that I want to win Premier League and Champions League medals and you have to play a certain amount of games if you are to achieve that. I don't count the Club World Cup medal to honest, because even though it was great to be a part of it all I didn't feature," he says.

With Edwin still not quite ready to retire despite being almost forty, Amos sought first team football and got some in a three month loan spell at Molde in Norway. Ahead of the 2010/11 season, Ben Foster was sold and so Amos was promoted to third choice goalkeeper. In October 2010 he played in the League Cup win over Wolves at Old Trafford and then six weeks later found himself making his Champions League debut in the final group game against Valencia.

When Danish goalkeeper Anders Lindegaard joined shortly after Christmas, Amos went on loan to Oldham Athletic with a view to staying there for the rest of the season, yet two months later he was recalled to United following an injury to Lindegaard. In the 2011/12 season Amos was third choice again. Van der Sar had retired, but United signed Spanish goalkeeper David De Gea as his long term replacement. As De Gea and Lindegaard contested for the number one spot, Amos found himself as the regular goalkeeper for the League Cup ties, starting with wins over Leeds and Aldershot where he kept his first clean sheets, but he was helpless to stop either Crystal Palace goal in the shock quarter final defeat that season.

After six competitive appearances for United, five in the League Cup and one in the Champions League, Ben was finally given his league debut on the last day of January 2012 at Old Trafford against Stoke City. It was a proud moment. "It was amazing. Again it was down to injury to Anders Lindegaard the previous day with David already injured," he says. "I'd been impressive in training and believed in myself, knowing I could handle what was thrown at me. I didn't have a great deal to do but it was an assured and composed performance. Obviously my family and I were very proud after the years of graft." Stoke came with a physical presence but Ben impressed to keep a clean sheet.

Though De Gea would come through what was a difficult spell for him to firmly establish himself as the number one goalkeeper, there was genuine debate as to whether Ben should retain his place, particularly given the unconvincing form of Lindegaard at the time. However, he wouldn't feature for the remainder of that season and after signing a contract extension at the end of the campaign, heading into the 2012/13 season, Ben went to Hull City. He impressed, starting 19 games for the Tigers as their number one choice before being recalled in January 2013. Hull would go on to be promoted to the Premier League while Ben returned to United to contend with Sam Johnstone for the position of United's third choice goalkeeper going into the 2013/14 season.

It's a new world at Old Trafford following the retirement of Sir Alex Ferguson and the appointment of David Moyes, but Ben feels the impact of his former manager will linger on at the club for another generation. "I absolutely believe that," he says. "I think it gives the players in the youth teams a real belief seeing other academy graduates like Jonny Evans, Danny Welbeck, and myself in the first team. If we can do it then so can they, and that can only have a positive impact on the future of the club. Sir Alex will have known that, and I expect the club will introduce more youth team players over the coming years, it's what Manchester United is all about."

Ben would like to personally thank Sir Alex for the impact he had on his life. "I'd like to say thank you for the opportunities he gave me, plain and simple," he says. "He put faith in me at a time when I needed it and I know that he could see how desperate I was to play for Manchester United from the desire I showed in training to keep the ball out. I know that because Rich Hartis told me that's why he played me pre-season against Portsmouth in Nigeria in 2008. It's not handed to you because of talent, which you obviously need, but you need more than that. He taught me that hard work really can get you what you desire and dream of, and playing for Manchester United is a privilege that you have to earn."

Appendix 1

Reserves and FA Youth Cup Statistics under Sir Alex Ferguson

Note: although complete season statistics are included for the season 1986/87, Sir Alex Ferguson did not become manager at Manchester United until 6th November 1986.

Season 1986/87

MANCHESTER UNITED RESERVES 1986/87: CENTRAL LEAGUE

Date	Opponents	Comp	Venue	Res	Att	1	2	3	4	5	6	7	8	9	10	11	12	14
27-Aug	Newcastle United	League	Away	1-2		Digby	Sivebaek	Martin	Murphy	Garton	Hogg	Russell	Gidman	Hanrahan	T Gibson	Olsen 1	Ratcliffe	Wood
03-Sep	Blackburn Rovers	League	Home	2-0		Walsh	Gidman	Martin	Murphy	Garton	Hogg	Harvey	Ratcliffe	Wood 1	Hanrahan	Cronin 1	Russell 1	Bottomley (8)
13-Sep	Aston Villa	League	Away	7-0		Walsh	Gidman	Martin	Duxbury 1	Garton	Ratcliffe	Moses	Wood 2	Blackmore 1	Hanrahan 1	Barnes	Cronin 1 (8)	Russell
27-Sep	Everton	League	Home	1-0		Walsh	Gidman	Martin	Duxbury	Garton	Hogg	Blackmore	Ratcliffe	Wood	Barnes 1	Cronin	Murphy (7)	Todd
04-Oct	Manchester City	League	Home	2-0	741	Walsh	Gill	C Gibson	Moses	Ratcliffe	Hogg	Harvey	T Gibson 1	Wood 1	Barnes	Cronin	Todd	
10-Oct	Nottingham Forest	League	Away	1-0		Walsh	Gill	C Gibson	Duxbury	Garton	Blackmore	Russell	Ratcliffe	Wood 1	Bottomley	Todd	Gill	Harvey
14-Oct	Oldham Athletic	League	Away	1-2		Walsh	Duxbury 1	C Gibson	Duxbury	Garton	Moran	Harvey	Ratcliffe	Cronin 1	Wood 1	Blackmore	Cronin (6)	Gill
21-Oct	Sheffield Wed	League	Home	1-2		Walsh	Gill 1	C Gibson	Moses	Scott	Blackmore	Ratcliffe	O'Brien	Cronin	Wood 1	Olsen	Russell	O'Brien (8)
28-Oct	Sunderland	League	Away	4-2		Walsh	Gill	C Gibson	Garton	Moran	Hogg	Ratcliffe	O'Brien	Wood 1	Hanrahan 2	Russell	Harvey	Cronin
05-Nov	Coventry City	League	Home	1-0		Walsh	Gill	Martin	Brazil	Ratcliffe	Hogg	Blackmore	T Gibson	Hanrahan	Harvey 1	Barnes	Hopley	Hutchinson
08-Nov	Liverpool	League	Away	1-3		Walsh	Gill	Martin	Gardner	Brazil	Hogg	Scott	O'Brien	Hanrahan 1	Scott	Todd	Beardsmore	
11-Nov	Middlesbrough	League	Home	3-1		Walsh	Gill 1	Martin	Ratcliffe	Garton	Hogg	Harvey	O'Brien 1	Wood 1	Hanrahan 1	Wood	Todd (7)	Gardner
25-Nov	Leeds United	League	Home	3-0		Walsh	Gill	Albiston	Garton	Garton	Hogg	Scott	O'Brien	Whiteside	Cronin	Murphy	Harvey (7)	Murphy
03-Dec	Leicester City	League	Away	2-1		Walsh	Gill	Martin	O'Brien 1	Gardner	Hogg	Robson 1	Strachan	Wood	Barnes 1	Cronin	Hanrahan (4)	Hanrahan (11)
09-Dec	Sheffield United	League	Home	4-2		Walsh	Scott	Harvey	Murphy	Garton	Hogg	Blackmore	O'Brien	T Gibson 1	Hanrahan	Gill	Scott (7)	Scott (7)
16-Dec	Middlesbrough	League	Away	2-0		Bailey	Martin	Blackmore	Garton	Hogg	Robson 1	O'Brien	Bottomley	Stapleton 2	Hanrahan 1	Todd (7)	Gardner	
11-Feb	Hull City	League	Away	3-1		Walsh	Gill	Albiston	McGrath	O'Brien	Gill 1	Murphy	Davenport	Hanrahan	C Gibson 1	Ratcliffe (7)	Cronin (9)	
17-Feb	Derby County	League	Away	1-5		Walsh	Sivebaek	Albiston	Ratcliffe	Gardner	Hogg	O'Brien	Wood	T Gibson	C Gibson	Cronin (9)	Scott (10)	
21-Feb	Liverpool	League	Home	0-0		O'Donnell	Gill	Albiston	Moses	Blackmore	Hogg	O'Brien	Stapleton	Cronin	Russell	Martin (5)	Bottomley (10)	
24-Feb	Leeds United	League	Away	1-1		Tiplady	Gill	Albiston	Martin	Ratcliffe	Hogg	Blackmore	Stapleton	Cronin	Russell	Bottomley (10)	Graham (4)	
03-Mar	Sheffield Wed	League	Away	1-2		O'Donnell	Sivebaek	Albiston	Moses	Martin	Ratcliffe	Blackmore 1	O'Brien	Hanrahan	Russell	Gill		
14-Mar	Oldham Athletic	League	Home	1-0		Walsh	Garton	Martin	Moses	Stapleton	Hogg	Blackmore 1	Ratcliffe 1	Bottomley	Russell	Harvey (8)	Harvey	
17-Mar	Nottingham Forest	League	Home	2-1		Walsh	Gill	Albiston 1	Martin	Hogg	Gardner	Blackmore 1	Ratcliffe	T Gibson	Bottomley	Russell	Harvey (9)	Graham
21-Mar	Aston Villa	League	Home	5-0		Walsh	Martin	Albiston 1	Moses	Hogg	Ratcliffe	Blackmore 1	Ratcliffe	Bottomley 1	Wood 1	Russell 1	Harvey (9)	Brazil
28-Mar	Manchester City	League	Away	1-3	694	Turner	Scott	Martin	Ratcliffe	Garton	Hogg	Blackmore	O'Brien	Davenport	T Gibson	Gill	Todd (4)	Graham
31-Mar	Coventry City	League	Away	2-1		Turner	Gill 1	Albiston	Ratcliffe	Garton	Hogg	Harvey	Martin	Graham 1	Davenport	Brazil	Todd	Scott
09-Apr	Hull City	League	Home	1-1		Walsh	Gill	Albiston	Brazil	Garton	Hogg	Ratcliffe	Martin	Wood	Davenport	Martin	Harvey (4)	Scott (2)
11-Apr	Sunderland	League	Home	2-2		Turner	Garton	Albiston	Moran	Hogg	Ratcliffe	Strachan	T Gibson	Graham	O'Brien 1	Wood 1	Gill	Martin
14-Apr	Leicester City	League	Home	1-0		Turner	Gill	Martin	Ratcliffe	Garton	Hogg	Harvey 1	Blackmore	Bottomley	Whiteside	Olsen	Todd (7)	Scott
22-Apr	Blackburn Rovers	League	Home	0-1		Turner	Gill	Martin	Ratcliffe	Garton	Hogg	Blackmore	T Gibson	Bottomley	Stapleton 1	Olsen 1	Murphy	Todd (4)
25-Apr	Everton	League	Home	4-1		Turner	Gill	Blackmore 1	Ratcliffe	Garton	Hogg	Blackmore	T Gibson 1	Stapleton 1	Bottomley	Todd	Scott	
29-Apr	Derby County	League	Home	1-1		Turner	Gill	Martin	Murphy	Garton	Hogg	Harvey	Ratcliffe	T Gibson 1	Bottomley	Olsen	Hanrahan (10)	Kirkham (9)
04-May	Newcastle United	League	Home	2-0		Turner	Gill	Martin	Brazil	Gardner	Todd	Harvey	O'Brien	Stapleton 1	Hanrahan	Todd 1	Davenport	Scott
06-May	Sheffield United	League	Away	1-0		Turner	Gill	Martin	Brazil	Gardner	Todd	Wilson 1	McBride	Hanrahan	Hopley	Beardsmore	Scott	Hutchinson

208

Season 1986/87

RESERVES APPEARANCES AND GOALS 1986/87

Name	League Apps	League Gls	Youth Cup Apps	Youth Cup Gls	Season Total Apps	Season Total Gls
Arthur Albiston	11	2			11	2
Gary Bailey	1				1	0
Peter Barnes	5	2			5	2
Russell Beardsmore	1		2		3	0
Clayton Blackmore	22	7			22	7
Jon Bottomley	8 (3)	1			8 (3)	1
Derek Brazil	6		2		8	0
Denis Cronin	6 (5)	2			6 (5)	2
Peter Davenport	4				4	0
Fraser Digby	1				1	0
Mike Duxbury	5	2			5	2
Steve Gardner	5	1			5	1
Billy Garton	23	1			23	1
Colin Gibson	7	1			7	1
Terry Gibson	14	4			14	4
John Gidman	5				5	0
Tony Gill	25	5			25	5
Deiniol Graham	2 (1)	1	0 (1)		2 (2)	1
Joe Hanrahan	13 (3)	6			13 (6)	6
Paul Harvey	12 (5)	3	2	1	14 (5)	4
Wayne Heseltine			2	1	2	1
Mark Higgins	2				2	0
Graeme Hogg	21				21	0
Tony Hopley	1		1	0	2	0
Simon Hutchison			2	1	2	1
Paul Kirkham	(1)				0 (1)	0
Andrew McBride	1		2	0	3	0
Paul McGrath	1				1	0
Lee Martin	24 (1)				24 (1)	0
Kevin Moran	3				3	0
Remi Moses	8				8	0
Aidan Murphy	6 (1)				6 (1)	0
Liam O'Brien	15 (1)	4			15 (1)	4
Jim O'Donnell	2		2		4	0
Jesper Olsen	6	2			6	2
Simon Ratcliffe	23 (1)	1			23 (1)	1
Mark Robins			1 (1)	2	1 (1)	2
Bryan Robson	2	2			2	2
Martin Russell	11	2			11	2
Ian Scott			1		1	0
Ken Scott	8 (3)				8 (3)	0
John Sivebaek	3				3	0
Frank Stapleton	7	4			7	4
Phil Steer			2		2	0
Gordon Strachan	2				2	0
Gary Tiplady	1				1	0
Mark Todd	3 (5)	1			3 (5)	1
Chris Turner	9				9	0
Gary Walsh	20				20	0
Dyfan Williams			0 (1)		0 (1)	0
Norman Whiteside	2				2	0
David Wilson	1	1	2		3	1
Nicky Wood	16	10			16	10

YOUTH CUP GAMES 1986/87

Date	Opponents	Rnd	Venue	Res	Att	1	2	3	4	5	6	7	8	9	10	11	12	14
02-Dec	Wrexham	R 2	Away	4-0	721	O'Donnell	Beardsmore	Heseltine 1	Scott	Brazil	Hutchinson	Wilson	McBride	Harvey 1	Robins 2	Steer	Graham (6)	Williams (3)
26-Jan	Leicester City	R 3	Home	1-2	1002	O'Donnell	Scott	Brazil	Brazil	Heseltine	Hutchinson 1	Wilson	McBride	Hopley	Harvey	Steer	Robins (11)	Graham (8)

Season 1987/88

MANCHESTER UNITED RESERVES 1987/88: CENTRAL LEAGUE

Date	Opponents	Venue	Res	Att	1	2	3	4	5	6	7	8	9	10	11	12	14
22-Aug	Everton	Le Away	3-1		Turner	Martin	Gibson	Gill	Garton	Hogg	Blackmore 1	O'Brien 1	Hanrahan	Wilson 1	Wood	Graham	Bottomley (4)
26-Aug	Leicester City	Le Away	2-2		Turner	Albiston	Gibson	Gill 1	Martin	Hogg	Blackmore	O'Brien	Hanrahan	Wood 1	Davenport	Wilson (8)	Heseltine
05-Sep	Huddersfield Town	Le Home	0-1		Turner	Garton	Martin	Beardsmore	Brazil	Hogg	Blackmore	O'Brien	Wood	Wilson	Graham (4)	Heseltine (9)
23-Sep	Hull City	Le Away	5-2		Turner	Beardsmore	Blackmore 1	Wilson	Martin	Hogg	Hutchinson	O'Brien 1	Graham 2	Robins 1	Gill	McBride	Bullimore
06-Oct	Nottingham Forest	Le Away	2-2		Turner	Beardsmore	Albiston	Moran	Brazil 1	Hogg	Robins	Wilson	Davenport 1	Graham	Gill	Heseltine	McBride (11)
13-Oct	Sheffield United	Le Home	3-0		Turner	Beardsmore	Albiston	Garton	Martin 1	Hogg	Hutchinson	Wilson	Davenport 1	Robins 1	Gill	Heseltine (6)	Brazil (4)
03-Nov	Coventry City	Le Away	0-0		O'Donnell	Martin	Albiston	Wilson	Brazil	Hogg	Beardsmore	O'Brien	Blackmore	Robins	Gill	McBride	Hutchinson (11)
21-Nov	Sheffield Wed	Le Home	1-1		Turner	Martin	Beardsmore	Wilson	Brazil	Hogg	Hutchinson	Wratten	Hanson	Robins 1	Bullimore	Andrews (9)	Jackson
28-Nov	Liverpool	Le Away	0-2		Turner	Martin	Beardsmore	Moses	Brazil	Heseltine	Hutchinson	O'Brien	Graham	Gill	Andrews	Bullimore (11)	Wratten (1)
01-Dec	Aston Villa	Le Home	3-0		O'Donnell	Martin	Albiston	Wilson	Brazil	Heseltine	Hutchinson	O'Brien	Robins 2	Wratten 1	Gill	Bullimore	Mortimer (7)
17-Dec	Derby County	Le Home	1-0		O'Donnell	Martin	Albiston	Wilson	Sulonen	Heseltine	Blackmore 1	O'Brien	Graham	Beardsmore	Wratten	Hutchinson (4)	Brazil (10)
19-Dec	Sunderland	Le Home	2-0		O'Donnell	Martin	Heseltine	Brazil	Hogg	Hutchinson	Wilson	Robins	Blackmore 1	Wratten	Mortimer 1 (7)
22-Dec	Bradford City	Le Home	1-2		O'Donnell	Albiston	Wilson	Sulonen	Hogg	Beardsmore	Robins 1	Graham	Brazil (5)	Hutchinson (4)
05-Jan	Blackpool	Le Home	1-1		Walsh	Albiston	Moses	Brazil	Hogg	Wilson	O'Brien	Robins	Beardsmore	Mortimer
12-Jan	Leicester City	Le Home	3-0		Walsh	Martin	Wilson	Brazil	Hogg	Hutchinson	O'Brien	Robins	Gill	Robins (7)	Heseltine (11)
23-Jan	Everton	Le Home	0-3		O'Donnell	Beardsmore	Martin	Wilson	Brazil	Heseltine	Hutchinson 1	Wratten	Davenport 1	Blackmore 1	McBride	Robins (7)	Andrews
02-Feb	Coventry City	Le Away	1-3		Walsh	Martin	Albiston	Brazil	Garton	Wilson	Hutchinson	O'Brien	Robins	Graham	Beardsmore	Mortimer (3)	Graham 1 (9)
09-Feb	Hull City	Le Home	0-1		O'Donnell	Martin	Albiston	Wilson	Moran	Garton	Hutchinson	Wratten	Hanson	Davenport	Beardsmore	Mortimer (4)	Graham (10)
11-Feb	Grimsby Town	Le Home	1-0		O'Donnell	Martin	Blackmore	Wilson	Brazil	Heseltine	Hutchinson	O'Brien	Robins	Hanson	Beardsmore	Brazil (5)	Mortimer (4)
16-Feb	Bradford City	Le Away	4-3		O'Donnell	Albiston	Martin	Wratten	Garton	Heseltine	Wilson	O'Brien	Graham 1	Graham 1	Beardsmore	McBride (7)	Brazil (5)
20-Feb	Huddersfield Town	Le Home	2-4		O'Donnell	Mortimer	Martin	Wilson	Brazil	Beardsmore	Wratten	O'Brien 1	Robins 2	Graham	McBride	Bullimore (3)	Andrews (11)
24-Feb	Sheffield United	Le Away	1-2		Hughes	Mortimer	Albiston	Moran	Blackmore	Wratten	O'Brien 1	Robins	Andrews	Olsen 1	Wilson (10)	McBride
02-Mar	Nottingham Forest	Le Home	2-1		O'Donnell	Mortimer	Beardsmore	Brazil	Hutchinson	Wilson	Blackmore	Robins	Graham 1	Olsen 1	Andrews	Hutchinson
05-Mar	Manchester City	Le Home	0-1	861	O'Donnell	Mortimer	Brazil	Wratten	Beardsmore	Hutchinson	Bullimore	Moses	Robins	Graham	McBride	Wilson (9)	McBride
22-Mar	Derby County	Le Home	1-0		O'Donnell	Martin	Albiston	Garton 1	McGrath	Hogg	Moses	Hanson	Robins	Graham	Andrews
29-Mar	Sheffield Wed	Le Home	1-1		O'Donnell	Martin	Albiston	Garton	Moran	Hogg	Hutchinson	Graham	Robins	Beardsmore	McBride
04-Apr	Liverpool	Le Home	0-2		O'Donnell	Martin	Albiston	Moses	Moran	Hogg	Hutchinson	Wilson	Robins	Olsen	Beardsmore	Graham (4)
07-Apr	Grimsby Town	Le Away	1-1		O'Donnell	Martin	Albiston	Moran	Hogg	Whiteside 1	O'Brien	Robins	Graham	Olsen	Beardsmore (9)	Wilson (10)
16-Apr	Manchester City	Le Away	1-6	3,022	O'Donnell	Mortimer	Brazil	Hutchinson	Martin	Jackson	Robins	Graham	McBride	Hanson (10)	Bullimore (4)
19-Apr	Leeds United	Le Away	3-1		O'Donnell	Martin	Albiston	Hesseltine	Martin	Beardsmore 1	O'Brien 1	Blackmore 1	Robins	McBride	Olsen (9)	Graham (10)
23-Apr	Blackpool	Le Home	1-1		O'Donnell	Martin	Albiston	Moses	Moran	Hogg	Beardsmore	O'Brien	Robins	Graham 1	McBride	Brazil (5)	Heseltine (10)
27-Apr	Sunderland	Le Away	0-1		Walsh	Albiston	Brazil	Moses	Martin	Hogg	O'Brien	Blackmore	Robins	Wratten	McBride	Mortimer (10)	Hutchinson (6)
04-May	Aston Villa	Le Away	3-2		O'Donnell	Martin	Albiston	Moran	Heseltine	Hogg	Dalton 1	O'Brien	Graham	Blackmore 1	Wratten	Graham (8)	McBride (5)
09-May	Leeds United	Le Away	0-1		Walsh	Mortimer	Jackson	Wratten	Brazil	Heseltine	Dalton	Graham	Robins 1	Bullimore	McBride	Hutchinson (10)	Andrews (9)

Season 1987/88

RESERVES APPEARANCES AND GOALS 1987/88

Name	League Apps	League Gls	Youth Cup Apps	Youth Cup Gls	Season Total Apps	Season Total Gls
Arthur Albiston	20				20	0
Simon Andrews	1 (3)		1		2 (3)	0
Russell Beardsmore	28 (1)	2			28 (1)	2
Clayton Blackmore	15	7			15	7
Jon Bottomley	(1)				0 (1)	0
Derek Brazil	19 (5)	1			19 (5)	1
Wayne Bullimore	3 (3)		0 (1)		3 (4)	0
Paul Dalton	3	1			3	1
Peter Davenport	5	3			5	3
Billy Garton	10	1			10	1
Colin Gibson	3				3	0
Tony Gill	8	1			8	1
Deiniol Graham	18 (6)	7	1	1	19 (6)	8
Joe Hanrahan	3				3	0
David Hanson	3 (2)				3 (2)	0
Wayne Heseltine	14 (4)		1		15 (4)	0
Graeme Hogg	15				15	0
Brett Hughes	1				1	0
Simon Hutchinson	16 (5)	1			16 (5)	1
Craig Lawton			1		1	0
Jason Lydiate			1		1	0
Tony Jackson	2		1		3	0
Andrew McBride	6 (4)				6 (4)	0
Paul McGrath	1				1	0
Lee Martin	30	1			30	1
Kevin Moran	9				9	0
John Mortimer	6 (6)	1	1		7 (6)	1
Remi Moses	9				9	0
Liam O'Brien	20	6			20	6
Jim O'Donnell	20				20	0
Jesper Olsen	3	1			3	1
Mike Pollitt			1		1	0
Mark Robins	30 (1)	12	1		31 (1)	12
Petri Sulonen	3				3	0
Chris Turner	8				8	0
Gary Walsh	5				5	0
Norman Whiteside	1	1			1	1
David Wilson	21 (5)	1			21 (5)	1
Nicky Wood	3	1			3	1
Paul Wratten	12 (1)	1	1		13 (1)	1

YOUTH CUP GAMES 1987/88

Date	Opponents	Rnd	Venue	Res	Att	1	2	3	4	5	6	7	8	9	10	11	12	14
12-Aug	Mansfield Town	R2	Home	1-2	561	Pollitt	Mortimer	Jackson	Lydiate	Heseltine	Hutchinson	Wratten	Robins	Graham 1	Andrews	Lawton	Bullimore (11)	Sixmith

Season 1988/89

MANCHESTER UNITED RESERVES 1988/89: CENTRAL LEAGUE

Date	Opponents	Comp	Venue	Res	Att	1	2	3	4	5	6	7	8	9	10	11	12	14
31-Aug	Barnsley	League	Home	4-2		Turner	Lydiate	Gill	Wilson 1	Brazil	Heseltine	Hutchinson	O'Brien	Robins 2	Graham 1	Dalton	Bullimore	Goater (11)
06-Sep	Manchester City	League	Away	0-1	1,879	Turner	Gill	Sharpe	Garton	McGrath	Dalton	Dalton	O'Brien	Robins	Graham	Hutchinson	Goater (10)	Brazil
13-Sep	Huddersfield Town	League	Home	1-2		Bosnich	Gill	Sharpe	Brazil	Lydiate	Hutchinson	O'Brien	Beardsmore	Robins	Graham	Dalton	Sixsmith	Rodlund (11)
20-Sep	Liverpool	League	Away	3-1		Bosnich	Beardsmore	Gill	Brazil	Martin	Hutchinson	Bullimore	Robins 3	Graham 1	Dalton	Bullimore	Lawton (11)
27-Sep	Sunderland	League	Home	0-1		Bosnich	Gill	Gill	Brazil	Anderson	Beardsmore	Dalton	O'Brien	Robins	Graham	Bullimore	Heseltine (3)	Rodlund (9)
05-Oct	Nottingham Forest	League	Away	1-5		O'Donnell	Beardsmore	Gill	Wilson	Anderson	Heseltine	Hutchinson	O'Brien	Robins	Graham	Dalton	Heseltine (3)	Harris (8)
18-Oct	Sheffield Wed	League	Home	5-1		O'Donnell	Hutchinson	Gill 1	Grimshaw	Heseltine	Dalton	Rodlund 1	Robins 2	Davenport 1	Olsen	Whitehouse
26-Oct	Aston Villa	League	Away	2-1		Gill	Gibson	Grimshaw	Brazil	Heseltine	Hutchinson	Beardsmore	Robins 1	Graham	Bullimore	Whitehouse
02-Nov	Newcastle United	League	Away	2-1		Gill	Donaghy	Grimshaw	Brazil	Heseltine	Rodlund 1	Graham 1	Dalton	Lydiate (3)	Bullimore (7)
12-Nov	Everton	League	Home	1-1		Hucker	Gill	Wilson	Brazil	Heseltine	Dalton	Bullimore	Goater	Graham 1	Wood 1	Lydiate (9)	Lawton (7)
15-Nov	Coventry City	League	Away	2-3		Hucker	Gill	Sharpe	Brazil	Heseltine	Milne	Goater	Graham	Wood 1	Lydiate (3)	Dalton (8)
24-Nov	Derby County	League	Home	2-3		Hucker	Gill	Martin 1	Wilson	Heseltine	Dalton	Grimshaw	Robins	Goater	Beardsmore	Graham (9)	Lydiate
30-Nov	West Brom°	League	Away	3-3		Bosnich	Lydiate	Brazil	Wilson	Beardsmore	Dalton	Robins	Goater	Sharpe	Goater 1 (2)
06-Dec	Leicester City	League	Home	1-2		Walsh	Gill 1	Beardsmore	Wilson	Brazil	Heseltine	Dalton	Martin	Robins	Wood	Maiorana	Sallis (10)	Bullimore (11)
14-Dec	Blackburn Rovers°	League	Home	2-1		Dalton	Brazil	Beardsmore	McAuley	Heseltine	Milne 1	Graham	Robins	Graham	Lydiate	Maiorana	Goater (9)	Bullimore
21-Dec	Sheffield United	League	Away	2-6		Bosnich	Brazil	Beardsmore 1	Gill	Lydiate	Hutchinson	Graham	Robins 1	Martin	Maiorana	Sallis (3)	Wilson (2)
04-Jan	Manchester City	League	Home	3-4	2,770	O'Donnell	Hutchinson	Gill	Heseltine	Beardsmore 1	Dalton	Hutchinson	Robins 1	Goater	Maiorana 1	Sallis (3)	Lawton (10)
19-Jan	West Brom°	League	Home	7-1		O'Donnell	Sallis	McGuinness	Brazil	Wilson	Lydiate	Dalton 1	Robins 3	Goater 2	Maiorana	Dalton (7)	Tonge (11)
25-Jan	Leeds United	League	Away	1-4		O'Donnell	Gill	Wilson	McGuinness	McGrath	Brazil	Strachan 1	Wilson	Robins 1	Graham	Maiorana	Dalton (7)	Sallis
31-Jan	Sunderland	League	Away	0-0		O'Donnell	Brazil	Heseltine	McGrath	Beardsmore	Wilson	Dalton	Graham	Robins	Maiorana	Sallis	Goater
07-Feb	Nottingham Forest	League	Home	0-0		Hucker	Brazil	Heseltine	Duxbury	Wilson	McGuinness	Gill	Robins	Graham	Goater	Dalton 1	Dalton (4)	Sallis (10)
14-Feb	Sheffield Wed	League	Away	3-0		Sallis	Brazil	Gill	Gill	Hutchinson	Wilson	Graham 2	Beardsmore	Graham	Bullimore	Goater (9)
23-Feb	Aston Villa	League	Home	0-3		Bosnich	Brazil	Beardsmore	Gill	Wilson	Hutchinson	McGuinness	Goater 1	Dalton	Sallis (10)	Tonge (5)
04-Mar	Everton	League	Away	2-2		O'Donnell	Gill	Martin	Heseltine	Brazil	Dalton	Robins	Goater 1	Whiteside	Sharpe	Andrews
07-Mar	Newcastle United°	League	Home	1-1		O'Donnell	Martin	Bruce	Brazil	Wilson	Hutchinson	Blackmore	Robins 1	Whiteside	Lawton	Tonge (5)	Andrews (11)
14-Mar	Liverpool	League	Home	2-1		O'Donnell	Gill 1	Brazil	Heseltine	Wilson	Blackmore	Robins 1	Goater	Maiorana	Tonge (2)	D Ferguson (7)
29-Mar	Huddersfield Town	League	Away	2-2		Bosnich	Martin	Anderson	Brazil	Heseltine	Wilson	Blackmore	Robins 1	Goater	Maiorana	Lawton	Andrews
05-Apr	Sheffield United	League	Home	0-0		Bosnich	Martin	Martin	Heseltine	Brazil	Wilson	Blackmore	Robins	Goater	Whiteside 1	Maiorana	D Ferguson (8)	Tonge
12-Apr	Leicester City♦	League	Away	0-0		Bosnich	Gill	Martin	Heseltine	Brazil	McGrath	Wilson	Robins	D Ferguson	Goater	Maiorana	Lydiate	Tonge
25-Apr	Derby County	League	Away	0-1		Bosnich	Gill	Duxbury	Heseltine	Bruce	Brazil	McClair	Robins	Milne	D Ferguson	Maiorana	Andrews 1 (6)	D Ferguson (11)
27-Apr	Blackburn Rovers	League	Away	1-3		Bosnich	Duxbury	Lydiate	Heseltine	Tonge	D Ferguson	Lawton	Milne	Robins 1	Goater 1	Dalton	Jackson (4)
04-May	Leeds United	League	Home	3-3		Bosnich	Brazil	Sharpe	Brazil	McGuinness	Heseltine	Blackmore 1	Milne	Goater 1	Andrews	Bullimore (11)
08-May	Barnsley	League	Away	0-0		Bosnich	Tonge	Jackson	Lydiate	McGuinness	Carter	D Ferguson	Andrews	McAuley	Sixsmith	Taylor
15-May	Leicester City	League	Away	1-3		Bosnich	Duxbury	Sharpe	Martin	Blackmore	Donaghy	Robson 1	Beardsmore	McClair	Hughes	Milne	Brazil	Robins (11)

° Own goals: Goodall v West Bromwich Albion (away), Hill v Blackburn Rovers (home), Rogers v West Bromwich Albion (home), Thorn v Newcastle United (home)

♦ Abandoned after 70 minutes due to waterlogged pitch

Season 1988/89

RESERVES APPEARANCES AND GOALS 1988/89

Name	League Apps	League Gls	Youth Cup Apps	Youth Cup Gls	Season Total Apps	Season Total Gls
Viv Anderson	3				3	0
Simon Andrews	1 (2)	1	2 (3)		3 (5)	1
Russell Beardsmore	14 (1)	3			14 (1)	3
Clayton Blackmore	5	2			5	2
Mark Bosnich	16		5		21	0
Derek Brazil	31				31	0
Steve Bruce	3	1			3	1
Wayne Bullimore	7 (5)		4	4	11 (5)	4
Stephen Carter	1				1	0
Lee Costa			4		4	0
Paul Dalton	19 (4)	2			19 (4)	2
Peter Davenport	1	1			1	1
Mal Donaghy	2				2	0
Mike Duxbury	4				4	0
Darren Ferguson	2 (4)		5		7 (4)	0
Billy Garton	1				1	0
Colin Gibson	1				1	0
Tony Gill	23	3			23	3
Shaun Goater	13 (7)	5			13 (7)	5
Deiniol Graham	20 (1)	5			20 (1)	5
Andrew Grimshaw	4				4	0
Richard Harris	(1)				0 (1)	0
Wayne Heseltine	26 (1)				26 (1)	0
Peter Hucker	5				5	0
Mark Hughes	1				1	0
Simon Hutchinson	19	1			19	1
Tony Jackson	1 (1)		4		5 (1)	0
Craig Lawton	2 (4)		5	2	7 (4)	2
Jason Lydiate	7 (3)		4 (1)		11 (4)	0
Sean McAuley	2		0 (1)		2 (1)	0
Brian McClair	3				3	0
Steven McGavin	1				1	0
Paul McGrath	4				4	0
Paul McGuinness	6				6	0
Giuliano Maiorana	14	1			14	1
Lee Martin	11	1			11	1
Ralph Milne	8	1			8	1
Liam O'Brien	4				4	0
Jim O'Donnell	9				9	0
Jesper Olsen	1				1	0
Mark Robins	29 (1)	22			29 (1)	22
Bryan Robson	1	1			1	1
John Rudlund	1 (2)	1	3 (1)	1	4 (3)	2
Roger Sallis	2 (4)		5		7 (4)	0
Lee Sharpe	8		1 (1)		9 (1)	0
John Shotton			4	3	4	3
Gordon Strachan	1	1			1	1
Kieran Toal			1 (1)	1	1 (1)	1
Alan Tonge	2 (5)		5		7 (5)	0
Chris Turner	2				2	0
Gary Walsh	2				2	0
Norman Whiteside	3	1			3	1
David Wilson	24 (1)	1			24 (1)	1
Nicky Wood	4	3			4	3

YOUTH CUP GAMES 1988/89

Date	Opponents	Rnd	Venue	Res	Att	1	2	3	4	5	6	7	8	9	10	11	12	14
13-Dec	Darlington	R 2	Away	5-2	885	Bosnich	Sallis	Jackson	Tonge	Lydiate	Toal	Bullimore 2	Ferguson	Rodlund 1	Shotton 2	Lawton	Andrews (3)	Sharpe (6)
09-Jan	Sheffield Wed	R 3	Away	0-0	538	Bosnich	Sallis	Jackson	Tonge	Lydiate	Costa	Toal	Ferguson	Rodlund	Shotton	Lawton	McAuley (7)	Andrews (12)
17-Jan	Sheffield Wed	R 3R	Home	2-0	1550	Bosnich	Sallis	Jackson	Tonge	Lydiate	Costa	Bullimore 1	Ferguson	Rodlund	Shotton 1	Lawton	Andrews 1 (9)	Sharpe
31-Jan	Ipswich Town	R 4	Home	4-1	1834	Bosnich	Sallis	Jackson	Sharpe 1		Costa	Bullimore 1	Ferguson	Andrews	Rodlund	Lawton	Lydiate (6)	Rodlund (10)
01-Mar	Brentford	R 5	Away	1-2	2567	Bosnich	Sallis	Sharpe	Lydiate		Costa	Bullimore	Ferguson	Andrews	Rodlund	Lawton	Jackson	Toal (10)

Season 1989/90

MANCHESTER UNITED RESERVES 1989/90: CENTRAL LEAGUE

Date	Opponents	Comp	Venue	Res	Att	1	2	3	4	5	6	7	8	9	10	11	12	14
23-Aug	Sheffield United	League	Away	1-0		Bosnich	Beardsmore	Martin	Carey	Brazil	Ferguson	Milne	McGuinness	Robins 1	Graham	Maiorana	Heseltine	Tonge
30-Aug	Blackburn Rovers	League	Away	0-1		Bosnich	Anderson	Heseltine	Brazil	Ferguson	Milne	McGuinness	Graham	Bullimore	Maiorana	Tonge (1)	Shotton (11)
09-Sep	Oldham Athletic	League	Home	2-1		Bosnich	Brazil	Heseltine	Carey	Bullimore	Goater	McGuinness	Robins	Graham 1	Maiorana 1	Gordon
12-Sep	Derby County	League	Away	0-2		Bosnich	Brazil	Carey	Lydiate	Blackmore	Graham	McGuinness	Robins	Graham	Maiorana	Brammeld
23-Sep	Everton	League	Home	1-2		Bosnich	Tonge	Martin	Carey	Ferguson	Graham	McGuinness	Robins	Bullimore	Maiorana	Brameld
03-Oct	Hull City	League	Away	1-1		Bosnich	Martin	Gibson	Heseltine	McGuinness	Graham	Bullimore	Robins	Rammell 1	Maiorana	Goater	R Wilson (11)
11-Oct	Nottingham Forest	League	Away	1-0		Bosnich	Gibson	Brazil	Heseltine	McGuinness	Graham	Rammell	Robins 1	Sharpe	Maiorana	Tonge
24-Oct	Bradford City	League	Away	3-1		Bosnich	Blackmore	Carey	Brazil	McGuinness	Graham	Rammell 1	Robins 2	Ferguson	Bullimore	Bullimore
31-Oct	Coventry City	League	Home	3-2		Bosnich	Duxbury	Heseltine	Carey	McGuinness	Beardsmore	Rammell	Robins 2	Blackmore	Maiorana	Graham (11)	Lawton
04-Nov	Liverpool	League	Home	1-2		Bosnich	Anderson	Brazil	Carey	McGuinness	Beardsmore 1	Rammell 1	Robins 1	Duxbury	Milne	Ferguson (5)	Bullimore
08-Nov	Newcastle United	League	Away	3-0		Bosnich	Anderson	Heseltine	Brazil	Blackmore	Milne 1	Rammell	Robins 2	Duxbury	Wallace	Milne (6)	Bullimore
14-Nov	Leeds United	League	Home	0-4		Bosnich	Anderson	Heseltine	Duxbury	Sharpe	Beardsmore	Rammell	Robins	McGuinness	Milne	Graham (4)	McGuinness
20-Nov	Leicester City	League	Away	4-0		Bosnich	Anderson	Brazil 1	Donaghy	Duxbury	Milne	Graham	Robins 3	Sharpe	Maiorana	Graham (11)	Heseltine
29-Nov	Notts County	League	Home	2-1		Bosnich	Anderson	Sharpe	Brazil	Duxbury	Milne 1	Rammell	Robins 1	Beardsmore	Maiorana	Heseltine (3)	McGuinness (8)
05-Dec	Huddersfield Town	League	Home	1-0		Bosnich	Anderson	Donaghy	Brazil	Duxbury	Milne	Rammell	Robins	Beardsmore	Maiorana	Duxbury	Hodge (8)
09-Dec	Manchester City	League	Away	1-0	862	Bosnich	Heseltine	Donaghy	Brazil	Duxbury	Blackmore	Graham 1	Robins	Beardsmore	Maiorana	Wratten (9)	Bullimore
19-Dec	Aston Villa	League	Home	2-2		Sealey	Anderson	Sharpe	Martin	Wratten	Beardsmore	Robins 1	Blackmore 1	McGuinness	McGuinness (11)	Lawton (7)
02-Jan	Oldham Athletic	League	Away	3-0		Sealey	Duxbury	Beardsmore	Carey	Brazil	McGuinness	Milne 1	Graham 2	D Wilson	Maiorana	Brameld	Bullimore
16-Jan	Sheffield United	League	Home	1-0		Crossley	Duxbury	Sharpe	Carey	McGuinness	Milne	Wratten	Graham	Wratten	Maiorana	D Wilson (8)	Bullimore
03-Feb	Everton	League	Away	2-1		Crossley	Brazil	Duxbury	Brazil	D Wilson	McGuinness	Rammell 1	Graham 1	Beardsmore	Maiorana	Brameld	Sixsmith (7)
06-Feb	Leicester City°	League	Home	3-0		Crossley	Duxbury	Carey	Lydiate	Bullimore	McGuinness	Rammell	Robins 1	Beardsmore	Milne	Doherty	Smyth
14-Feb	Notts County	League	Away	1-1		Bosnich	Ince 1	Brazil	Carey	Beardsmore	Bullimore	Rammell	Robins 2	Bullimore	Shields	Lydiate
20-Feb	Blackburn Rovers	League	Home	0-2		Bosnich	Beardsmore	Brazil	Gibson	Bruce	D Wilson	McGuinness	Graham	Rammell	McAuley (7)	D Wilson
28-Feb	Hull City	League	Home	3-0		Bosnich	Donaghy	Gibson	Brazil 1	Gibson	Milne	Ince	Robins 1	Rammell	Maiorana	Carey	Bullimore (4)
06-Mar	Nottingham Forest	League	Home	1-2		Bosnich	Blackmore 1	Gibson	Brazil	McGuinness	Duxbury	Bullimore	Graham	Rammell	Maiorana	Taylor	Wratten (8)
17-Mar	Liverpool	League	Away	1-2		Bosnich	McGuinness	Gibson	Brazil	Donaghy	Webb 1	McGuinness	D Wilson	Rammell	Robins 2	D Wilson	Maiorana (9)
20-Mar	Bradford City	League	Home	1-1		Bosnich	Brazil	McGuinness	Carey	McAuley	Milne	Webb	Graham	Rammell	Lawton	Maiorana 1 (11)	D Wilson (10)
27-Mar	Coventry City	League	Away	2-4		Sealey	Anderson	Blackmore 1	Dunbury	Beardsmore	Webb	Beardsmore	Maiorana	Robins 1	Graham	McGuinness	Rammell (5)
04-Apr	Huddersfield Town	League	Away	3-0		Bosnich	Blackmore	Carey	Carey	McGuinness	Robson	Beardsmore	Graham 1	Rammell 1	Maiorana	Bullimore (7)	Brameld (8)
14-Apr	Manchester City	League	Away	2-3		Bosnich	Anderson	Duxbury	Brazil	McGuinness	Beardsmore	Bullimore	Graham 1	Rammell 1	Lawton	McAuley (5)	Tonge
18-Apr	Aston Villa	League	Home	3-0		Bosnich	Duxbury	McAuley	Brazil	D Wilson	Blackmore	Blackmore	Rammell 1	Robins 1	Lawton	Lawton	McGuinness
24-Apr	Newcastle United	League	Home	1-1		Bosnich	Blackmore 1	Brazil	McAuley	D Wilson	Duxbury	Bullimore	Blackmore 1	Robins 1	Graham	Rammell (5)	McGuinness (2)
26-Apr	Derby County	League	Home	2-1		Sealey	Duxbury	Gibson	Lydiate	Brazil	McGuinness	Beardsmore	Maiorana	Graham 1	Rammell	Ferguson (3)	D Wilson
02-May	Leeds United	League	Away	2-2		Sealey	Donaghy	Sharpe 1	Brazil	Carey	McGuinness	Doherty	Graham 1	Lydiate	Maiorana	Ferguson (7)	Lawton (11)

°Own goal: James

214

Season 1989/90

RESERVES APPEARANCES AND GOALS 1989/90

Name	League Apps	League Gls	Youth Cup Apps	Youth Cup Gls	Season Total Apps	Season Total Gls
Viv Anderson	13				13	0
Russell Beardsmore	19	2			19	2
Clayton Blackmore	9	4			9	4
Mark Bosnich	24		4		28	0
Marcus Brameld	(1)				0 (1)	0
Derek Brazil	32	2			32	2
Steve Bruce	1				1	0
Wayne Bullimore	11 (3)	1			11 (3)	1
Brian Carey	21				21	0
Steve Carter			0 (3)		0 (3)	0
Lee Costa	(1)		6	4	6 (1)	4
Mark Crossley	3				3	0
Adrian Doherty	1		6	2	7	2
Mal Donaghy	9				9	0
Mike Duxbury	18				18	0
Darren Ferguson	4 (3)				4 (3)	0
Colin Gibson	7				7	0
Shaun Goater	2 (1)				2 (1)	0
Mark Gordon			2		2	0
Deiniol Graham	26 (3)	10			26 (3)	10
Wayne Heseltine	12 (1)				12 (1)	0
John Hodge	(1)				0 (1)	0
Paul Ince	3	1			3	1
Craig Lawton	3 (3)		4	1	7 (3)	1
Jason Lydiate	7		6		13	0
Sean McAuley	4 (2)		6		10 (2)	0
Paul McGuinness	24 (4)				24 (2)	0
Alan McReavie			2		2	0
Colin McKee			6	2	6	2
Giuliano Maiorana	28 (2)	2			28 (2)	2
Lee Martin	5				5	0
Ralph Milne	13	4			13	4
Mike Pollitt			2		2	0
Andy Rammell	21 (2)	6			21 (2)	6
Mark Robins	20	19			20	19
Bryan Robson	2				2	0
Les Sealey	7				7	0
Lee Sharpe	8	1			8	1
John Sharples			4	1	4	1
Jimmy Shields			0 (1)		0 (1)	0
John Shotton	(1)				0 (1)	0
Paul Sixsmith	(1)		5		5 (1)	0
Alan Tonge	1 (1)				1 (1)	0
Danny Wallace	1				1	0
Neil Webb	3	1			3	1
David Wilson	9 (2)				9 (2)	0
Ryan Wilson	(1)		6	3	6 (1)	3
Paul Wratten	3 (2)				3 (2)	0

YOUTH CUP GAMES 1989/90

Date	Opponents	Rnd	Venue	Res	Att	1	2	3	4	5	6	7	8	9	10	11	12	14
03-Jan	Burnley	R 2	Away	4-1	1614	Pollitt	McReavie	McAuley	Tonge	Lydiate	Doherty	Costa 2	Sixsmith	Sharples 1	McKee	Wilson 1	Smyth	Taylor (9)
17-Jan	Port Vale	R 3	Away	3-0	1017	Bosnich	Tonge	McAuley	Sharples	Lydiate	Doherty	Costa 1	Sixsmith	McKee	Lawton	Wilson 2	Smyth	Taylor
08-Feb	Sheffield Wed	R 4	Home	3-1	3451	Bosnich	McReavie	McAuley	Sharples	Lydiate	Sixsmith	Doherty 1	Costa 1	McKee 1	Taylor	Wilson	Gordon	Shields
05-Mar	Leicester City	R 5	Home	2-0	1354	Bosnich	Tonge	McAuley	Lydiate	Sharples	Doherty	Costa	Gordon	McKee 1	Lawton 1	Wilson	Carter (9)	Shields (2)
04-Apr	Tottenham Hotspur	SF1	Away	0-2	2874	Bosnich	Tonge	McAuley	Sixsmith	Lydiate	Costa	Doherty	Ferguson	Gordon	Lawton	Wilson	Carter (11)	McKee (6)
04-Jan	Tottenham Hotspur	SF2	Home	1-1			Tonge	McAuley	Sixsmith	Lydiate	Costa	Doherty 1	Ferguson	McKee	Lawton	Wilson	Carter (9)	Gordon

Season 1990/91

MANCHESTER UNITED RESERVES 1990/91: CENTRAL LEAGUE

Date	Opponents	Comp	Venue	Res	Att	1	2	3	4	5	6	7	8	9	10	11	12	14
29-Aug	Blackburn Rovers	League	Home	3-1		Leighton	Anderson	Lydiate	Brazil	Gibson	Milne	Beardsmore	Wratten	Rammell	Ferguson 1	Wilson (7)	Maiorana (6)	
04-Sep	Coventry City	League	Away	1-0		Walsh	Anderson	Lydiate	Brazil	Gibson	Wratten	Milne	Ferguson	Martin	Rammell 1	Wallace	Wilson	
11-Sep	Sunderland	League	Home	1-1		Walsh	Martin	Anderson	Gibson	Wilson	Doherty	Wilson	Graham	Rammell	Wallace	Ferguson (3)	Maiorana (7)	
20-Sep	Leeds United	League	Away	1-1		Leighton	Martin	Donaghy	Brazil	Milne	Martin	Sharpe	Graham 1	Graham (8)	McGuinness (8)	Lydiate (3)		
27-Sep	Nottingham Forest	League	Away	0-2		Leighton	Anderson	Whitworth	Anderson	Wratten	Sharpe	Ferguson	Martin	Graham 1	Wilson (2)	Maiorana (11)		
04-Oct	Wolves	League	Home	2-1		Leighton	Brazil	Carey	Beardsmore	Ferguson	Ince	Graham 1	Robins 2	Russo	Wratten	Milne (9)		
06-Oct	Liverpool	League	Home	3-0		Leighton	Brazil	Lydiate	Beardsmore	Wratten	Sharpe	Ferguson	Robins 2	Russo	Wallace 1	Wratten (10)		
13-Oct	Huddersfield United	League	Home	1-2		Leighton	Anderson	Brazil	Irwin	Beardsmore 1	Sharpe	Ferguson	Graham	Graham	Wallace	Wilson (6)	Milne	
16-Oct	Sheffield Wed	League	Away	0-1		Bosnich	Anderson	Beardsmore	Lydiate	Palister	Ferguson	Ince	Giggs	Graham	Wallace	Lydiate (3)	Wratten (10)	
25-Oct	Newcastle United	League	Home	0-0		Wilkinson	Brazil	Whitworth	Donaghy	Milne	Sharpe	Ferguson	Giggs	Robins	Graham	Wratten (8)	Wilson (10)	
31-Oct	Wolves	League	Away	3-0		Bosnich	Whitworth	Carey	Beardsmore	Wratten	Ferguson	Milne	Robins 1	Giggs	Giggs	Wilson (8)	Wratten (7)	
17-Nov	Manchester City	League	Away	2-2	1,200	Leighton	Anderson 1	Martin	Lydiate	Ferguson	Beardsmore	Wratten	Lawton 1	Giggs 1	Giggs 1	Gibson	Brazil	
19-Nov	Leicester City	League	Away	4-0		Leighton	Brazil	Whitworth 1	Donaghy	Beardsmore	Ferguson 1	Wratten 1	Martin	Lawton	Robins 1	Maiorana	Lawton (11)	
01-Dec	Everton	League	Home	2-3		Walsh	Whitworth	Carey	Wratten	Beardsmore	Ferguson	Robson	Lawton	Robins 2	Giggs	McGuinness (4)	Sixsmith (8)	
04-Dec	Derby County	League	Away	1-0		Walsh	Martin 1	Anderson	Donaghy	Beardsmore	Wilson	Lawton	Robins	Giggs	Gibson	McGuinness (7)	Graham (8)	
12-Dec	Rotherham United	League	Home	4-2		Walsh	Anderson	Whitworth	Donaghy	Beardsmore	Wilson 1	Martin	Robins	Lawton	Giggs	Wratten (10)	Maiorana	
15-Dec	Coventry City	League	Home	1-0		Walsh	Anderson	Martin	Lydiate	Sixsmith	Ferguson	Lawton	Robins	Gibson 1	Lawton	Sixsmith 1	Lydiate	
09-Jan	Blackburn Rovers	League	Away	3-0		Walsh	Phelan	Brazil	Donaghy	Beardsmore	Wilson	Ferguson	Robins 1	Milne	Wallace 1	Graham (11)	Lawton (9)	
15-Jan	Leeds United	League	Home	1-0		Walsh	Carey	Whitworth 1	McAuley	Beardsmore	Wilson	Ferguson	Graham	Sixsmith	Giggs	Wratten	Doherty (5)	
23-Jan	Sunderland	League	Away	2-1		Walsh	Brazil	Whitworth	McAuley	Beardsmore	Wilson	Ferguson	Graham 2	Sixsmith	Giggs	Wallace	Wratten	
29-Jan	Rotherham United	League	Away	1-3		Leighton	Brazil	Whitworth	Donaghy	Beardsmore	Martin	Ferguson	Robins 1	Graham 1	Giggs (9)	Lydiate	Wilson	
05-Feb	Derby County	League	Home	2-1		Leighton	Brazil	Lydiate	Martin	Sixsmith	Wilson	Ferguson 1	Ince	Robins	Graham	McAuley (11)	Wilson	
16-Feb	Manchester City	League	Home	0-1	3,579	Walsh	Whitworth	Lydiate	Beardsmore	Sixsmith	Wilson	Ferguson 1	Robins	Graham	Maiorana	Giggs (7)	McAuley	
23-Feb	Liverpool	League	Away	2-1		Walsh	Brazil	Carey	Lydiate	Beardsmore	Whitworth	Ferguson	Robins 1	Wratten	Maiorana	Sixsmith (5)	Maiorana (12)	
02-Mar	Everton	League	Away	2-3		Leighton	Carey	Lydiate	Tonge	Wratten	Wilson	McKee	Graham 1	Bullimore 1	Giggs	Maiorana (8)	McGuinness (5)	
07-Mar	Leicester City	League	Home	1-0		Bosnich	Sixsmith	Brazil	Carey	Wratten	Kanchelskis	Ferguson	Robins 1	Sixsmith	Maiorana 1	Giggs (9)	Wilson	
18-Mar	Aston Villa°	League	Away	1-0		Bosnich	Carey	Whitworth	Lydiate	Wratten	Wilson	McKee	Graham	Lawton	Maiorana	Sixsmith	Wilson	
26-Mar	Huddersfield Town	League	Home	0-1		Walsh	Brazil	Carey	Sixsmith	Beardsmore	Wilson	Ferguson	Robins 1	Giggs	Maiorana	Sixsmith (11)	Toal	
04-Apr	Aston Villa	League	Home	2-0		Walsh	Whitworth	Lydiate	Brazil	Beardsmore	Ferguson	Wratten	Robins 1	Giggs	Maiorana	Tonge	McKee (7)	
11-Apr	Huddersfield Town	League	Away	1-1		Bosnich	Whitworth	Carey	Sixsmith	Beardsmore	Ferguson	Toal	Graham 1	Graham	Tonge	Gordon (3)	Toal (11)	
13-Apr	Sheffield Wed	League	Home	1-4		Bosnich	Carey	Lydiate	Carey	Beardsmore	Wratten	Toal	Robins 1	Graham	Maiorana	Sallis (11)	Tonge (4)	
25-Apr	Newcastle United	League	Home	2-1		Walsh	Beardsmore	Sixsmith	Brazil	Lydiate	Kanchelskis	Wratten	Sixsmith	Robins 2	Graham	Wallace	Carey (11)	
27-Apr	Nottingham Forest	League	Away	1-0		Brazil	Brazil	Lydiate	Sixsmith	Beardsmore	Smyth	Kanchelskis	Ferguson	Robins 1	Milne	Brameld	O'Kane	
01-May	Sheffield United°	League	Home	4-2		Bosnich	Brazil	Carey	Lydiate	Sixsmith	Wratten	Milne 1	Costa	Ferguson	Robins 1	Tonge	Graham (8)	Sallis (11)

°Own goals: Ormondroyd v Aston Villa (away), Morris v Sheffield United (home)

216

Season 1990/91

RESERVES APPEARANCES AND GOALS 1990/91

Name	League Apps	League Gls	Youth Cup Apps	Youth Cup Gls	Season Total Apps	Season Total Gls
Viv Anderson	11	2			11	2
Russell Beardsmore	28	1			28	1
Mark Bosnich	6				6	0
Markus Brameld			1 (3)		1 (3)	0
Derek Brazil	27 (1)				27 (1)	0
Raphael Burke			3		3	0
Wayne Bullimore	1	1			1	1
Brian Carey	14 (1)				14 (1)	0
Lee Costa	1				1	0
Simon Davies	1		7	1	8	1
Adrian Doherty	2 (2)		4	1	6 (2)	1
Mal Donaghy	7				7	0
Darren Ferguson	27 (1)	5			27 (1)	5
Colin Gibson	9	1			9	1
Ryan Giggs	12 (2)	2	6	7	18 (2)	9
Mark Gordon	(1)		7	1	7 (1)	1
Deiniol Graham	20 (3)	7			20 (3)	7
Paul Ince	3				3	0
Denis Irwin	1				1	0
Craig Lawton	6 (2)	1			6 (2)	1
Jim Leighton	10				10	0
Jason Lydiate	23 (2)				23 (2)	0
Andrei Kanchelskis	3				3	0
Sean McAuley	2 (1)				2 (1)	0
Colin McKee	1 (1)		7	2	8 (1)	2
Paul McGuinness	(4)				0 (4)	0
Alan McReavie			7		7	0
Giuliano Maiorana	7 (8)	1			7 (8)	1
Lee Martin	13	2			13	2
Ralph Milne	8 (1)	1			8 (1)	1
John O'Kane			0 (1)		0 (1)	0
Gary Pallister	1				1	0
Mike Phelan	1				1	0
Les Potts			7		7	0
Andy Rammell	3	1			3	1
Mark Robins	21	19			21	19
Bryan Robson	1				1	0
Alexandro Russo	2				2	0
Roger Sallis	(2)				0 (2)	0
Lee Sharpe	4				4	0
John Sharples			7	1	7	1
Jimmy Shields			7		7	0
Paul Sixsmith	14 (3)	1			14 (3)	1
Peter Smyth	1		7	2	8	2
Ben Thornley			0 (2)	0	0 (2)	0
Kieran Toal	1 (1)				1 (1)	0
Alan Tonge	3 (1)				3 (1)	0
Danny Wallace	11	4			11	4
Gary Walsh	16				16	0
Neil Whitworth	19	2			19	2
Ian Wilkinson	2		7		9	0
David Wilson	14 (5)	1			14 (5)	1
Paul Wratten	17 (2)	1			17 (2)	1

YOUTH CUP GAMES 1990/91

Date	Opponents	Rnd	Venue	Res	Att	1	2	3	4	5	6	7	8	9	10	11	12	14
26-Nov	Darlington	R 2	Away	6-0	544	Wilkinson	McReavie	Potts	Gordon	Shields	Sharples	Doherty	Smyth	McKee	Giggs 4	Davies 1	Brameld	O'Kane
03-Jan	Everton	R 3	Home	1-1	1618	Wilkinson	McReavie	Potts	Shields	Sharples	Gordon	Doherty 1	Smyth	McKee	Giggs	Davies	Brameld	O'Kane
10-Jan	Everton	R 3R	Away	2-1		Wilkinson	McReavie	Potts	Shields	Sharples	Gordon	Doherty	Smyth 1	McKee 1	Giggs 1	Davies	Brameld (9)	O'Kane
05-Feb	Liverpool	R 4	Away	3-1	1155	Wilkinson	McReavie	Potts	Shields	Sharples	Gordon 1	Burke	Smyth 1	McKee	Giggs 1	Davies	Brameld (7)	Noone
22-Mar	Southampton	R 5	Away	0-3	1,976	Wilkinson	McReavie	Potts	Shields	Sharples 1	Gordon	Burke	Smyth	McKee	Brameld	Davies	O'Kane (7)	Thornley (10)
08-Apr	Sheffield Wed	SF1	Away	1-1		Wilkinson	McReavie	Potts	Shields	Sharples	Gordon	Burke	Smyth	McKee	Giggs	Davies 1	Brameld	Thornley (7)
18-Apr	Sheffield Wed	SF2	Home	0-1														

Season 1991/92

MANCHESTER UNITED RESERVES 1991/92: CENTRAL LEAGUE

Date	Opponents	Comp	Venue	Res	Att	1	2	3	4	5	6	7	8	9	10	11	12	14
17-Aug	Aston Villa	League	Away	0-0		Leighton	Donaghy	Martin	Whitworth	Brazil	McAuley	Toal	Beardsmore	Robins	Wallace	Sixsmith	Lydiate	Gordon (7)
28-Aug	Bolton Wanderers	League	Home	1-1		Walsh	Donaghy	Phelan	Brazil	Whitworth	Beardsmore	Toal	Robins 1	Wallace	Sixsmith	McAuley (11)	Carey
03-Sep	Bradford City	League	Away	3-2		Walsh	McAuley 1	Martin	Brazil	Whitworth	Sixsmith	Beardsmore 1	Ferguson	Robins 1	Wallace 2	Carey (4)	Lydiate (11)
10-Sep	Newcastle United	League	Home	2-1		Leighton	Martin	McAuley	Toal	Brazil	Carey	Beardsmore	Ferguson	Robins 1	Sixsmith	Wallace	Sixsmith
14-Sep	Everton	League	Home	1-3		Walsh	Gordon	McAuley	Wratten 1	Carey	Whitworth	Beardsmore	Ince	Robins 1	Ferguson	Wallace	Smyth (2)
26-Sep	Sheffield United	League	Home	0-0		Leighton	Donaghy	McAuley	Carey	Whitworth	Ferguson	Toal	Robins 2	Sixsmith	Wallace	Sixsmith (11)	Smyth
03-Oct	Barnsley	League	Away	2-4		Walsh	Whitworth	Blackmore	McAuley	Wratten	Beardsmore	Ferguson	Robins 3	Sixsmith	Wallace	Toal (10)
12-Oct	Leeds United	League	Home	3-2		Wilkinson	Blackmore	Martin	Webb	Whitworth	Carey	Beardsmore	Wratten	Robins	Sixsmith	McAuley	Sixsmith (4)
16-Oct	West Brom	League	Away	1-0		Leighton	Blackmore	Martin	Carey	Whitworth	Beardsmore 1	Wratten	Robins	Wallace	McAuley	McKee 1 (10)
24-Oct	Sheffield Wed	League	Home	3-2		Walsh	Gordon	Martin	Donaghy	Sixsmith	Beardsmore	Wratten	McKee 2	Toal 1	Davies	Thornley (3)
07-Nov	Nottingham Forest	League	Away	1-5		Wilkinson	Gordon	Martin	Donaghy	Carey	Beardsmore	McKee	Toal	McAuley	Lydiate	Davies 1 (6)
12-Nov	Rotherham United	League	Home	3-0		Walsh	Martin	Wratten	Carey 1	Lydiate	Beardsmore	Wratten	Robins 1	Sixsmith	Wallace 1	Lawton (6)
23-Nov	Manchester City	League	Away	6-1		Walsh	Martin	Sixsmith	Donaghy	Carey	Beardsmore 1	McKee 3	Robins 1	Lawton	Wallace 1	Toal
26-Nov	Sunderland	League	Home	3-1		Walsh	Martin	Sixsmith	Donaghy	Carey	Beardsmore	Wratten	Robins 1	Lawton	Wallace 1	Lydiate	Noone
07-Dec	Liverpool	League	Away	1-2		Walsh	Phelan	Martin	Whitworth	Carey	Beardsmore	Wallace	McKee	Robins 1	Lawton	Toal	Gordon
10-Dec	Coventry City	League	Home	0-1		Walsh	Phelan	Irwin	Donaghy	Carey	Blackmore	Beardsmore	Wratten	Robins 1	Sharpe	Whitworth	McKee (10)
13-Jan	Bolton Wanderers	League	Home	1-1		Walsh	Martin	Phelan	Brazil	Donaghy	Robson 1	Whitworth	McKee 1	Wallace	Sharpe	Lydiate (3)	Thornley (11)
21-Jan	Everton	League	Away	3-1		Walsh	Beardsmore	Martin	Lawton	Brazil	Sharpe	Robson 1	Toal	Robins 2	McKee	Gordon	Wratten
28-Jan	West Brom	League	Home	3-0		Walsh	Beardsmore	Martin	Lydiate	Phelan	Wallace 2	Toal	McKee	Robins 1	Wallace 1	Sharpe	Lawton
01-Feb	Manchester City	League	Home	3-2		Walsh	Beardsmore	McAuley	Brazil	Lydiate	G Neville	Wallace 2	Beardsmore	Robins 1	Wallace	Sharpe 1	Ferguson (10)	Gordon
06-Feb	Sheffield Wed	League	Away	0-2		Walsh	Martin	McAuley	Wratten	Brazil	Lydiate	Beardsmore	Toal	Robins	Ferguson	Lawton (9)	Smyth (8)
19-Feb	Sunderland	League	Away	1-0		Walsh	Beardsmore	Martin	Wratten	Whitworth	Phelan	Ferguson	Robins	Wallace 2	Sharpe	Lawton (11)	McKee (7)
29-Feb	Liverpool	League	Home	3-4		Pilkington	Martin	McAuley	Brazil	Lydiate	Ferguson	Wratten	McKee 1	Lawton	Wallace 2	Toal (4)	Thornley (3)
05-Mar	Coventry City	League	Away	1-3		Walsh	Beardsmore	Martin 1	Bruce	Blackmore	Wallace	Phelan	Robins	Lawton	Sharpe	Toal (4)	Lawton
17-Mar	Rotherham United	League	Away	0-0		Walsh	Smyth	Sixsmith	Lydiate	Wratten	Wallace	Ferguson	Robins	McKee	Maiorana (10)	G Neville (4)
25-Mar	Newcastle United	League	Away	0-2		Walsh	Smyth	McAuley	Donaghy	Blackmore	Wratten	Ferguson	Robins 1	McKee	Maiorana	Noone (2)	Gough (11)
01-Apr	Bradford City	League	Home	4-0		Walsh	O'Kane	McAuley	Toal	Casper	Brazil	Ferguson	Robins 1	Wallace 1	Maiorana 1	Wratten (11)	Sixsmith
04-Apr	Blackburn Rovers	League	Home	1-3		Walsh	O'Kane	McAuley	Carey	Brazil	Webb	Ferguson	McKee 1	Wallace	Maiorana	Toal (10)	Davies (4)
09-Apr	Sheffield United	League	Home	1-1		Walsh	Parker	McAuley 1	Phelan	Smyth	McKee	Toal	Blackmore	Ferguson	Sixsmith	Davies	Beckham (6)
13-Apr	Nottingham Forest	League	Home	0-1		Walsh	Donaghy	Sixsmith	Brazil	Carey	Wallace	Phelan	McKee	Ferguson	Sixsmith	McKee 1	Gillespie (8)
21-Apr	Barnsley	League	Home	3-0		Leighton	O'Kane	Sixsmith	Brazil	Carey	McGibbon	Toal	Wallace	Blackmore	Maiorana	Thornley 1	Burke (11)
23-Apr	Aston Villa	League	Away	1-2		Walsh	O'Kane	Sixsmith	Butt	Brazil	Whitworth	Wallace 2	Savage	McKee 1	Toal	Gough	Brazil
25-Apr	Leeds United	League	Away	0-1		Walsh	Gordon	Switzer	Beckham	Brazil	Wratten 2	Beardsmore	McKee	Roberts	Thornley (7)	Smyth (5)
02-May	Blackburn Rovers	League	Away	0-2		Wilkinson	Smyth	Sixsmith	Toal	Carey	Beardsmore	Ferguson	McKee	Wallace	Maiorana	Wratten (11)	Gordon

Season 1991/92

RESERVES APPEARANCES AND GOALS 1991/92

Name	League Apps	League Gls	Youth Cup Apps	Youth Cup Gls	Season Total Apps	Season Total Gls
Russell Beardsmore	27	3			27	3
David Beckham	1 (1)		3 (4)	1	4 (5)	1
Clayton Blackmore	7				7	0
Derek Brazil	15				15	0
Steve Bruce	1				1	0
Raphael Burke	(1)		1 (2)		1 (3)	0
Nicky Butt	1		8	4	9	4
Brian Carey	19 (1)	1			19 (1)	1
Chris Casper	1		6		7	0
Simon Davies	1 (2)	1	8	1	9 (2)	2
Mal Donaghy	12				12	0
Darren Ferguson	15 (1)				15 (1)	0
Ryan Giggs			3 (1)	4	3 (1)	4
Keith Gillespie	(1)		3 (1)	1	3 (2)	1
Mark Gordon	5 (1)		2		7 (1)	0
Paul Gough	(1)				0 (1)	0
Paul Ince	2				2	0
Denis Irwin	1				1	0
Craig Lawton	7 (2)				7 (2)	0
Jim Leighton	4				4	0
Jason Lydiate	7 (2)				7 (2)	0
Sean McAuley	17 (2)	2			17 (2)	2
Colin McKee	17 (3)	11	7	3	24 (3)	14
Pat McGibbon	1				1	0
Giuliano Maiorana	5 (1)	1			5 (1)	1
Lee Martin	20	1			20	1
Gary Neville	1 (1)		8		9 (1)	0
Andy Noone	(1)				0 (1)	0
John O'Kane	3		6	1	9	1
Paul Parker	1				1	0
Mike Phelan	9				9	0
Kevin Pilkington	1		8		9	0
Joe Roberts	1		0 (2)		1 (2)	0
Mark Robins	24	14			24	14
Bryan Robson	2	1			2	1
Robbie Savage	2		7 (1)	1	9 (1)	1
Lee Sharpe	8	1			8	1
Paul Sixsmith	17 (2)				17 (2)	0
Peter Smyth	6 (3)				6 (3)	0
George Switzer	1		8		9	0
Leonard Taylor			0 (1)		0 (1)	0
Ben Thornley	1 (3)	1	8	5	9 (3)	6
Kieran Toal	17 (4)	2			17 (4)	2
Danny Wallace	27	13			27	13
Gary Walsh	26				26	0
Neil Webb	3				3	0
Neil Whitworth	13				13	0
Ian Wilkinson	3				3	0
Paul Wratten	22 (3)	3			22 (3)	3

YOUTH CUP GAMES 1991/92

Date	Opponents	Rnd	Venue	Res	Att	1	2	3	4	5	6	7	8	9	10	11	12	14
27-Nov	Sunderland	R 2	Away	4-2	5410	Pilkington	Gordon	Switzer	O'Kane	G. Neville	Gillespie 1	Butt	Davies	McKee 2	Savage 1	Thornley	Beckham (7)	Casper
17-Dec	Walsall	R 3	Home	2-1	5424	Pilkington	Gordon	Switzer	O'Kane	G. Neville	Gillespie	Butt 1	Davies	McKee	Savage	Thornley 1	Casper	Giggs (10)
06-Feb	Manchester City	R 4	Away	3-1	8708	Pilkington	O'Kane 1	Switzer	Casper	G. Neville	Gillespie	Butt	Davies	Savage	Burke	Thornley 2	Beckham (6)	Gordon
13-Feb	Tranmere Rovers	R 5	Home	2-0	7633	Pilkington	O'Kane	Switzer	Casper	G. Neville	McKee	Butt	Davies	Savage	Giggs 2	Thornley	Beckham (6)	Burke (11)
07-Mar	Tottenham Hotspur[a]	SF1	Home	3-0	967	Pilkington	O'Kane	Switzer	Casper	G. Neville	McKee	Butt 1	Davies	Savage	Giggs 2	Thornley 1	Beckham (8)	Burke (6)
25-Mar	Tottenham Hotspur	SF2	Away	2-1	7825	Pilkington	O'Kane	Switzer	Casper	G. Neville	Beckham	Butt 2	Davies	Mckee	Savage	Thornley	Roberts (10)	Taylor (11)
14-Apr	Crystal Palace	F1	Away	3-1		Pilkington	O'Kane	Switzer	Casper	G. Neville	Beckham 1	Butt	Davies	McKee	Savage	Thornley	Roberts (10)	Taylor
15-May	Crystal Palace	F2	Home	3-2	14681	Pilkington	O'Kane	Switzer	Casper	G. Neville	Beckham	Butt	Davies 1	McKee 1	Giggs	Thornley 1	Gillespie (11)	Savage (8)

[a] Own goal: Jordan

Season 1992/93

MANCHESTER UNITED RESERVES 1992/93: PONTINS LEAGUE

Date	Opponents	Comp	Venue	Res	Att	1	2	3	4	5	6	7	8	9	10	11	12	14
17-Aug	Leeds United	League	Away	1-1		Walsh	Beardsmore	Switzer	Carey	Webb	Lawton	Dublin	Wallace	Davies	Telford	McKee (11)
26-Aug	Aston Villa	League	Home	0-0		Walsh	McGibbon	Davies	Toal	Carey	Beardsmore	Webb	McKee	Wallace	Lawton	Telford (5)	Rawlinson
03-Sep	Leicester City	League	Away	0-0		Walsh	Martin	Switzer	Butt	Carey	Beardsmore	McKee	Toal	Davies	McGibbon	Casper
09-Sep	Nottingham Forest	League	Home	4-2		Walsh	Martin	Switzer	Webb	G Neville	Beardsmore	McKee 1	Wallace 3	Lawton (11)	Casper
17-Sep	Wolves	League	Home	3-3		Walsh	G Neville	Switzer	Butt	Carey	Beardsmore 1	Toal	McKee 2	Savage	Whitworth (5)	Davies (4)
21-Sep	Rotherham United°	League	Away	3-2		Pilkington	G Neville	Switzer	Butt 1	Casper	Beardsmore	Beckham	McKee	Scholes 1	Lawton	Toal (7)	Whitworth (6)
01-Oct	Sunderland	League	Home	4-1		Walsh	G Neville 2	Switzer	G Neville	Carey 1	Gillespie	McKee 1	Wallace	Savage	Scholes (10)	Whitworth (7)
06-Oct	Notts County	League	Away	0-2		Walsh	Phelan	Switzer	Toal	Whitworth	Beardsmore	Scholes	McKee	Wallace	Lawton	McGibbon
14-Oct	Blackburn Roversφ	League	Away	0-1		Pilkington	G Neville	Switzer	Beckham	Carey	Beardsmore	Webb	Wallace 1	Sharpe	Thornley	Whitworth (1)	Burke (11)
28-Oct	Barnsley	League	Away	2-6		Pierce	Martin	Whitworth	Carey	Beardsmore	Robson	Phelan	Wallace 1	Sharpe 1	Butt	Davies (11)	Lawton (10)
12-Nov	Sheffield United	League	Home	2-1		Digby	O'Kane	Switzer	Toal	McGibbon	Carey	Beardsmore 1	McKee	Dahlum 1	Lawton	McGibbon (5)	Burke (4)
14-Nov	Sheffield United	League	Away	1-1		Digby	O'Kane	Switzer	Phelan	Carey	Gillespie	Beardsmore	McKee	Roberts	Sharpe	Burke	Rawlinson (11)
18-Nov	Bolton Wanderers	League	Away	1-1		Digby	O'Kane	Martin	Phelan	Carey	Gillespie	Scholes 1	Wallace	Wallace	Thornley	Switzer	Savage (11)
25-Nov	Newcastle United	League	Away	3-2		Digby	Martin	Switzer	Butt	Casper	Kanchelskis	Toal	McKee 2	Wallace	Rawlinson	O'Kane	Roberts
03-Dec	Sheffield Wed	League	Home	0-2		Digby	Martin	Switzer	Butt	McGibbon	Scholes	Scholes	McKee 1	Wallace 1	Thornley	O'Kane	Roberts
16-Dec	Manchester City	League	Away	1-2		Digby	Martin	Switzer	Phelan	McGibbon	Kanchelskis	Appleton	McKee	Wallace	Toal	Burke (6)	Kirovski (10)
03-Jan	Stoke City	League	Home	1-2		Digby	Martin	Blackmore	Phelan	Carey	Blackmore	McKee 1	Wallace	Toal	Davies	Burke
06-Jan	Wolves	League	Away	3-2		Sealey	Blackmore 1	Blackmore	Carey	Whitworth	Ferguson	McKee 1	Wallace	Lawton 1	Switzer	Davies (11)
13-Jan	Rotherham United	League	Home	3-1		Sealey	Martin	Blackmore	Carey	Whitworth	Beardsmore	Phelan	McKee 1	Wallace	Davies	Switzer (6)	Roberts (3)
19-Jan	Leicester City	League	Home	0-2		Pilkington	Martin	Toal	Carey	McGibbon	Scholes	Davies	Lawton 2	Wallace	Davies	G Neville (11)	Beckham (4)
30-Jan	Aston Villa	League	Away	2-1		Sealey	Martin	Switzer	Carey	McGibbon	Lawton 1	Ferguson	Savage	Wallace 1	Riley	Brown (9)
10-Feb	Leeds United	League	Home	1-2		Sealey	Martin	Switzer	Carey	McGibbon	Lawton 1	Ferguson	McKee	Wallace 1	Thornley	Switzer	Savage (11)
17-Feb	Nottingham Forest	League	Away	1-1		Sealey	Phelan	Switzer	Toal	McGibbon	Phelan	Davies	Wallace	Wallace 1	Lawton	Davies (10)	Ferguson (6)
24-Feb	Sunderland	League	Away	3-1		Sealey	Martin	Phelan	McGibbon	Switzer	Toal	McKee	Wallace	Wallace	McKee	Ferguson (6)	O'Kane (4)
03-Mar	Notts County	League	Home	3-1		Sealey	Martin	Switzer	McGibbon	Davies	Gillespie	Phelan	Ferguson 1	Dublin 2	Wallace	Toal
18-Mar	Sheffield Wed	League	Away	1-1		Sealey	Martin	Switzer	McGibbon	Davies	McKee 2	Ferguson 1	Lawton	Dublin 1	Lawton	McKee	Davies
27-Mar	Liverpool°	League	Home	1-0		Sealey	Martin	Blackmore	Phelan	Carey	McGibbon	Robson	Gillespie 1	Dublin	Lawton	Toal	Switzer (7)
31-Mar	Newcastle United	League	Home	1-1		Sealey	Blackmore	Martin	Phelan	Carey	McKee	Robson	McKee	Dublin 1	Davies	Thornley	Switzer	Irving
07-Apr	Bolton Wanderers	League	Home	2-2		Wilkinson	Blackmore	Phelan	Carey	McGibbon	McKee	Gillespie	Dublin 1	Davies	Thornley	Doherty (8)
13-Apr	Stoke City	League	Away	3-3		Wilkinson	Martin	Phelan	Phelan	Blackmore	McGibbon	Rawlinson	Blackmore 1	Dublin 1	Rawlinson	Davies	Cooke (7)	Riley (7)
21-Apr	Manchester City	League	Home	4-1		Wilkinson	Martin 1	Switzer	Ferguson	Whitworth	Blackmore	Doherty	McKee 1	Dublin 1	Lawton 1	Davies	G Neville (5)	Beckham (10)
28-Apr	Barnsley	League	Home	3-1		Wilkinson	Blackmore	Switzer	Phelan	Carey	McGibbon	Thornley	McKee 1	Dublin	Lawton	Davies	McGibbon	Davies
01-May	Liverpool	League	Away	3-1		Sealey	Martin 1	Switzer	Carey	Whitworth	Robson	McKee	Ferguson 1	Dublin	Ferguson	Lawton	McGibbon	Savage (9)
03-May	Blackburn Rovers	League	Home	1-1		Wilkinson	Martin	Switzer	Butt	Carey	McGibbon	Savage	McKee	Dublin	Davies	Thornley 1	Whitworth (4)	Gillespie (8)

°Own goals: Pickering v Rotherham United (away), Brydon v Liverpool (home)
φCarey replaced Pilkington in goal

Season 1992/93

RESERVES APPEARANCES AND GOALS 1992/93

Name	League Apps	League Gls	Youth Cup Apps	Youth Cup Gls	Season Total Apps	Season Total Gls
Michael Appleton	1				1	0
Russell Beardsmore	13	2			13	2
David Beckham	4 (2)		8	2	12 (2)	2
Clayton Blackmore	8	2			8	2
Karl Brown	(1)		0 (1)		0 (2)	0
Raphael Burke	(3)				0 (3)	0
Nicky Butt	8	1			8	1
Brian Carey	32	1			32	1
Chris Casper	3		8		11	0
Terry Cooke	(1)				0 (1)	0
Tore Andre Dahlum	1	1			1	1
Simon Davies	18 (5)	1			18 (5)	1
Fraser Digby	7				7	0
Adrian Doherty	1 (2)				1 (2)	0
Dion Dublin	13	7			13	7
Darren Ferguson	8 (1)	3			8 (1)	3
Keith Gillespie	7 (1)	1	8		15 (1)	1
Richard Irving			7 (1)	5	7 (1)	5
Andrei Kanchelskis	3				3	0
Jovan Kirovski	(1)		0 (2)	1	0 (3)	1
Craig Lawton	19 (2)	6			19 (2)	6
Colin McKee	26 (1)	14			26 (1)	14
Pat McGibbon	19 (2)				19 (2)	0
Lee Martin	26	2			26	2
Colin Murdock			0 (2)		0 (2)	0
Adam Ndlovu	1				1	0
Gary Neville	6 (2)	2	8	2	14 (2)	4
Phil Neville			4	0	4	0
John O'Kane	3 (1)		7	1	10 (1)	1
Mike Phelan	18				18	0
David Pierce	1				1	0
Kevin Pilkington	3				3	0
Mark Rawlinson	3 (1)		0 (3)		3 (4)	0
Steven Riley	(1)		5		5 (1)	0
Joe Roberts	1 (1)		1 (1)		2 (2)	0
Bryan Robson	5				5	0
Robbie Savage	6 (2)		3 (2)	1	9 (4)	1
Les Sealey	12				12	0
Paul Scholes	7 (1)	2	8	4	15 (1)	6
Lee Sharpe	2	1			2	1
George Switzer	26 (2)				26 (2)	0
Colin Telford	(1)				0 (1)	0
Ben Thornley	6	1	7 (1)	1	13 (1)	2
Kieran Toal	16 (1)	1			16 (1)	1
Danny Wallace	16	8			16	8
Gary Walsh	7				7	0
Neil Webb	4				4	0
Darren Whitmarsh			8		8	0
Neil Whitworth	10 (4)				10 (4)	0
Ian Wilkinson	4				4	0

YOUTH CUP GAMES 1992/93

Date	Opponents	Rnd	Venue	Res	Att	1	2	3	4	5	6	7	8	9	10	11	12	14
08-Dec	Blackburn Rovers	R 2	Home	4-1	1268	Whitmarsh	O'Kane	Riley	Casper	G.Neville	Gillespie 1	Scholes 1	Beckham	Roberts	Savage	Thornley	Irving 2 (10)	Rawlinson (7)
12-Jan	Notts County	R 3	Home	3-1	2.565	Whitmarsh	O'Kane	P.Neville	Casper	G.Neville 1	Gillespie	Butt	Beckham	Irving 1	Savage	Scholes 1	Rawlinson (8)	Roberts (10)
02-Feb	Wimbledon	R 4	Home	3-0	3225	Whitmarsh	O'Kane	P.Neville	Casper	G.Neville	Gillespie	Scholes 1	Beckham 1	Irving 1	Roberts	Thornley	Rawlinson (10)	Riley
08-Mar	York City	R 5	Home	5-0	4937	Whitmarsh	O'Kane 1	Riley	Casper	G.Neville	Gillespie	Rawlinson	Beckham 1	Irving 1	Scholes	Thornley 1	Brown (2)	Savage 1 (7)
06-Apr	Millwall	SF1	Home	1-2	7678	Whitmarsh	O'Kane	P.Neville	Casper	G.Neville	Gillespie	Butt 1	Beckham	Irving	Scholes	Thornley	Kirovski (8)	Riley
13-Apr	Millwall	SF2	Away	2-0	6276	Whitmarsh	O'Kane	Riley	Casper	G.Neville	Gillespie	Butt	Beckham	Irving	Scholes	Thornley	Kirovski 1 (9)	Murdock
10-May	Leeds United	F1	Home	0-2	30562	Whitmarsh	O'Kane	Riley	Casper	G.Neville	Gillespie	Butt	Beckham	Irving	Scholes	Thornley	Murdock (9)	Savage (8)
13-May	Leeds United	F2	Away	1-2	31037	Whitmarsh	P.Neville	Riley	Casper	G.Neville	Gillespie	Scholes 1	Beckham	Irving	Savage	Thornley	Murdock (9)	Rawlinson

Season 1993/94

MANCHESTER UNITED RESERVES 1993/94: PONTINS LEAGUE AND LANCASHIRE CUP

Date	Opponents	Comp	Venue	Res	Att	1	2	3	4	5	6	7	8	9	10	11	12	14	15	16	17
24-Jul	Preston North End	LSC	Away	1-3		Sealey	Riley	Murdock	Rawlinson	McGibbon	Gillespie	Roberts 1	Davies	Wallace	Thornley	Brown	Savage	Irving			
27-Jul	Bury	LSC	Away	5-1	1,783	Sealey	Riley	Martin	Butt	Whitworth	Pallister	Davies 2	Dublin	Wallace 1	Ferguson	Sharpe 2	Irving (7)	Murdock			
31-Jul	Wigan Athletic	LSC	Away	2-0	1,773	Sealey	O'Kane	Martin	G Neville	Whitworth	Beckham	Scholes	Dublin	Wallace	Ince	Sharpe	Murdock	Rawlinson			
10-Aug	Blackpool	LSC Fin	Away	0-1		Sealey	Martin	Blackmore	Phelan	Whitworth	McGibbon	Ferguson	Dublin	Wallace	Sharpe	Scholes (10)	Butt (4)	Riley			
19-Aug	Blackburn Rovers	League	Away	1-0		Walsh	Blackmore	G Neville	Phelan	McGibbon	Casper	McKee	Dublin	Ferguson	Sharpe 1	Butt (7)	Davies				
26-Aug	Notts County°	League	Home	5-0		Walsh	G Neville	Martin	Phelan	Whitworth	Butt	McKee 3	Dublin 1	Wallace	Ferguson	Davies (4)	Gillespie (10)				
04-Sep	Leeds United	League	Away	3-1		Walsh	G Neville	Martin	Casper	Whitworth	Phelan	Robson	Dublin 1	Wallace	Ferguson	McKee	Thornley (11)				
08-Sep	Newcastle United	League	Home	3-2		Sealey	G Neville	Martin 2	Phelan	McGibbon	Casper	Butt	McClair	Dublin	Dublin 1	McKee 1 (11)	Beckham (8)				
13-Sep	Leicester City	League	Home	4-3		Sealey	O'Kane 1	G Neville	Beckham	McGibbon	Casper	Butt	Ferguson	Dublin	McCair	Thornley	McGibbon	Butt 1 (4)			
23-Sep	Nottingham Forest	League	Away	3-2		Walsh	G Neville	Blackmore 1	Casper	McGibbon	Butt	Ferguson	Scholes 1	Davies	McKee	Thornley	McGibbon	Beckham			
02-Oct	Everton	League	Home	2-0		Walsh	Martin	Blackmore	Ferguson	Whitworth	Casper 1	O'Kane	Davies	Wallace	Thornley	Riley					
13-Oct	Aston Villa	League	Away	1-1	9,000	Sealey	O'Kane	Martin	Davies	G Neville	O'Kane	Butt	McKee	Dublin	Wallace 1	Thornley	Beckham (11)	P Neville (4)			
27-Oct	Wolves	League	Away	3-2	1,369	Walsh	O'Kane	Blackmore	Beckham	G Neville	Casper	Butt	Dublin	Davies	Ferguson	Thornley 1	Ferguson (10)	Scholes (2)			
10-Nov	Liverpool	League	Away	0-0		Sealey	O'Kane	P Neville	Phelan	G Neville	Casper	Butt	Dublin 1	Savage 2	McKee	Thornley	O'Kane	Davies (11)			
13-Nov	Sheffield United	League	Home	2-1		Sealey	Phelan	Blackmore	Beckham	G Neville	Casper	McKee	Dublin 1	Ferguson	Davies	Thornley	McGibbon	Scholes (4)			
17-Nov	Coventry City	League	Home	2-1		Sealey	Martin	Blackmore	Beckham 1	G Neville	Casper	Butt	Dublin 1	Ferguson	McClair	Thornley	Davies (8)	McKee 1 (2)			
25-Nov	Bolton Wanderers	League	Away	4-2		Pilkington	O'Kane	Blackmore	Phelan	G Neville	Casper	Butt 1	Dublin 1	Giggs	McKee 1	Thornley	Rawlinson (7)	Gillespie (11)			
30-Nov	Derby County	League	Away	2-3		Sealey	Martin	Blackmore	G Neville	McGibbon	Robson	McKee 1	Dublin 1	Ferguson	McClair	Thornley	Davies (8)	McKee 1 (2)			
05-Jan	Sheffield Wed	League	Home	1-0		Sealey	Blackmore	Martin	Phelan	G Neville	Beckham	Robson	Dublin 1	Ferguson	Davies	Thornley	McKee (11)				
25-Jan	Wolves	League	Home	1-0		Walsh	O'Kane	Blackmore	Phelan	McGibbon	Casper	Beckham	McKee	Scholes 1	Davies	Thornley	Rawlinson (4)	Whitworth			
29-Jan	Everton	League	Home	2-1		Walsh	Blackmore	Blackmore	Rawlinson	Whitworth	Casper	Irving 1	McKee 1	Scholes 1	Thornley	Roberts	P Neville				
01-Feb	Sheffield United	League	Away	4-0		Walsh	G Neville	Riley	Whitworth	Whitworth	Casper	Beckham	McKee 2	Scholes	Thornley 1	Rawlinson (9)	P Neville				
09-Feb	Leicester City	League	Away	1-3	14,419	Walsh	G Neville	Riley	Casper	Gillespie	Butt	McClair	Dublin 1	Scholes	Thornley	McKee (10)	Beckham (6)				
02-Mar	York City	League	Away	0-0		Sealey	O'Kane	P Neville	Whitworth	Casper	Gillespie	Butt	Dublin	Scholes	Davies	Thornley	Gillespie (11)				
09-Mar	Derby County	League	Home	0-2		Sealey	G Neville	P Neville	Phelan	McGibbon	Casper	McKee	Dublin	Beckham	Davies	Scholes (10)	Thornley (8)				
14-Mar	Notts County	League	Away	2-1		Walsh	G Neville	Davies	Phelan	Whitworth	Casper	Robson	Dublin 2	Scholes 1	Thornley 1	Beckham	McKee				
23-Mar	Leeds United	League	Away	7-0	4,640	Sealey	O'Kane	Blackmore 1	Phelan	McGibbon	Davies 1	Butt	Scholes 3	Dublin 2	Thornley 1	Beckham	McKee				
31-Mar	Sheffield Wed	League	Away	6-0		Walsh	Blackmore	Blackmore	Phelan	McGibbon	Butt 2	Robson	Dublin 2	Ferguson	Thornley 1	McKee (8)	Beckham 1 (4)				
06-Apr	Blackburn Rovers°	League	Home	3-0		Walsh	Blackmore	Blackmore	Butt 2	McGibbon	Casper	Butt	McClair	Phelan	Thornley	McKee (8)	Beckham (6)				
13-Apr	Sunderland	League	Home	1-3		Walsh	G Neville	Blackmore	Phelan	McGibbon	Casper	Irving	McClair	Dublin 2	Phelan	Thornley	Rawlinson	Irving (9)			
19-Apr	Liverpool	League	Away	1-0		Walsh	G Neville	Riley	Phelan	McGibbon	Casper	Butt	Beckham	McKee	Davies	Thornley	McKee (6)	P Neville (7)			
23-Apr	Nottingham Forest	League	Home	2-1		Sealey	G Neville	Blackmore	Phelan 1	Whitworth	Casper 1	Butt	Dublin 1	McKee	Davies	Beckham (7)	O'Kane (3)				
25-Apr	Aston Villa	League	Home	1-1		Sealey	G Neville	Blackmore	Beckham	McGibbon	Casper	McKee	Dublin 1	McKee	Davies	Lawton	Lawton (8)				
27-Apr	Bolton Wanderers°	League	Home	3-0		Sealey	P Neville	Beckham	Beckham	G Neville	McKee	Rawlinson	Scholes 1	Davies	Johnson	Irving	Rawlinson (11)				
03-May	Coventry City	League	Away	1-1		Pilkington	P Neville	O'Kane	Phelan	G Neville	McKee	Butt	McClair	Dublin 1	Davies	O'Kane	Lawton (8)				
05-May	York City	League	Home	2-2		Pilkington	Riley	Dean	Rawlinson	McGibbon	Lawton	Beckham	Scholes 1	Davies	Maiorana 1	Riley (1)	Lawton (11)				
09-May	Sunderland	League	Away	1-2		Pilkington	Riley	Dean	Whitworth	McGibbon	O'Kane	Lawton	Kirovski	Dublin 1	Lawton	Maiorana	Rawlinson (3)	Irving (4)			
16-May	Newcastle United	League	Away	3-3		Pilkington	Clegg	McGibbon	G Neville	Mustoe	Davies	Lawton	Scholes 2	Dublin	Maiorana 1	D Hall	Gardner (5)	Baker			

° Own goals: Gallagher v Notts County (home), Morrison v Blackburn Rovers (home), Spooner v Bolton Wanderers (home)

15: Ryan, Appleton (4)
16: McGibbon (6), Brown
17: Roberts, Brown

Season 1993/94

RESERVES APPEARANCES AND GOALS 1993/94

Name	League Apps	League Gls	LSC Apps	LSC Gls	Youth Cup Apps	Youth Cup Gls	Season Total Apps	Season Total Gls
Michael Appleton			(1)		1		0 (1)	0
David Beckham	16 (5)	2	1				17 (5)	2
Clayton Blackmore	15	2	1				16	2
Nicky Butt	16 (3)	6	1 (1)				17 (4)	6
Chris Casper	27	2					27	2
Richard Clegg	1						1	0
Terry Cooke	(1)				1		1 (1)	0
Simon Davies	21 (3)	1	3	2			24 (3)	3
Craig Dean	1						1	0
Dion Dublin	23	16	1				24	16
Darren Ferguson	10 (1)		1				11 (1)	0
David Gardner	(1)						0 (1)	0
Ryan Giggs	1						1	0
Keith Gillespie	5 (3)		2				7 (3)	0
Danny Hall	1						1	0
Paul Ince			1				1	0
Richard Irving	2 (2)	1	(1)		1		3 (3)	1
David Johnson	1				0 (1)		1 (1)	0
Jovan Kirovski	1				1		2	0
Craig Lawton	4 (3)						4 (3)	0
Brian McClair	8	1					8	1
Colin McKee	22 (9)	14					22 (9)	14
Pat McGibbon	12		2 (1)				14 (1)	0
Giuliano Maiorana	2	1					2	1
Lee Martin	9	2	3				12	2
Matthew Monaghan					1		1	0
Colin Murdock			1				1	0
Neil Mustoe	1						1	0
Gary Neville	29		1				30	0
Phil Neville	6 (2)				1		7 (2)	0
John O'Kane	12 (1)	1	1				13 (1)	1
Gary Pallister			1				1	0
Mike Phelan	19	2	2				21	2
David Pierce					1		1	0
Kevin Pilkington	5						5	0
Mark Rawlinson	4 (5)		1				5 (5)	0
Steven Riley	5 (1)		2				7 (1)	0
Joe Roberts			1	1			1	1
Bryan Robson	6	1					6	1
Mark Ryan					1		1	0
Robbie Savage	1	2	1				2	2
Les Sealey	10		4				14	0
Paul Scholes	18 (4)	13	1 (1)				19 (5)	13
Lee Sharpe	1	1	3	3			4	4
Ben Thornley	22 (2)	4	1				23 (2)	4
Gary Twynham					1		1	0
Danny Wallace	3	2	4	2			7	4
Gary Walsh	19						19	0
Ashley Westwood					1		1	0
Philip Whittam					1		1	0
Neil Whitworth	15		4				19	0

YOUTH CUP GAMES 1993/94

Date	Opponents	Rnd	Venue	Res	Att	1	2	3	4	5	6	7	8	9	10	11	12	14
22-Nov	Bradford City	R 2	Away	0-2	739	Pierce	P.Neville	Monaghan	Ryan	Westwood	Cooke	Appleton	Twynham	Irving	Kirovski	Whittam	Barnes	Johnson (11)

Season 1994/95

MANCHESTER UNITED RESERVES 1994/95: PONTINS LEAGUE AND LANCASHIRE CUP

Date	Opponents	Comp	Venue	Res	Att	1	2	3	4	5	6	7	8	9	10	11	12	13	14	15
23-Jul	Rochdale	LSC	Away	2-3		Pilkington	G Neville	O'Kane	Beckham 2	Whitworth	Casper	Butt	Gillespie	Tomlinson	Scholes	Davies	McGibbon	Rawlinson	Irving	
26-Jul	Burnley	LSC	Away	3-2		Pilkington	G Neville	O'Kane	Beckham	May	Casper	Butt	Scholes 1	Tomlinson	Davies 1	Sharpe 1	Rawlinson (10)	McGibbon	Johnson	
31-Jul	Bury	LSC	Away	0-4		Pilkington	G Neville	O'Kane	Beckham	Whitworth	McGibbon	Butt	Davies	Tomlinson	Scholes	Gillespie	Twynham	Rawlinson (7)		
17-Aug	Leeds United	League	Away	1-2	3,930	Pilkington	G Neville	O'Kane 1	Casper	Rawlinson	Beckham	Gillespie	McKee	Dublin	McKee	Johnson	Scholes (6)	McGibbon (11)		
23-Aug	Aston Villa	League	Home	2-0		Pilkington	Parker	P Neville	Keane	McGibbon	Butt	Scholes	Dublin	Scholes 2	Gillespie	G Neville (4)	Davies (11)			
01-Sep	Wolves	League	Away	1-0		Pilkington	P Neville	O'Kane	Beckham	Whitworth	Butt	McKee	Scholes	Johnson	Scholes	Rawlinson	Johnson (4)	Westwood (2)		
03-Sep	Blackburn Rovers	League	Home	3-0		Pilkington	Gillespie 1	P Neville	O'Kane	G Neville	O'Kane	Butt 1	McGibbon	Tomlinson 1	Davies 1	Gibson	Johnson (4)	Westwood (2)		
07-Sep	Liverpool	League	Home	1-3		Pilkington	Westwood	O'Kane	Beckham	G Neville	Rawlinson	G Neville	Johnson	Tomlinson	Scholes	Davies	Rawlinson (7)	Casper		
22-Sep	Nottingham Forest	League	Away	0-2		Pilkington	Westwood	O'Kane	Appleton	McGibbon	Casper	Rawlinson	Scholes 2	Johnson	Irving	Dean				
11-Oct	Notts County	League	Away	3-1		Walsh	O'Kane	O'Kane	McGibbon	McGibbon	Butt	Scholes 1	Tomlinson 1	Johnson	Davies	Irving	Pilkington	Appleton		Kirovski (9)
17-Oct	Coventry City	League	Home	3-0		Pilkington	Westwood	Appleton	Beckham	McGibbon	Casper	Irving 2	Tomlinson	McClair	Cooke 1	Kirovski (10)	Johnson			
24-Oct	Derby County	League	Home	2-3		Pilkington	Westwood	Clegg	Kirovski	McGibbon	Casper	Gillespie	Appleton	Tomlinson 1	Irving 1	Johnson	Rawlinson (4)	Thornley (11)		
03-Nov	Rotherham United	League	Home	0-1		Pilkington	Westwood	O'Kane	Beckham	McGibbon	Rawlinson	Gillespie	Scholes	Tomlinson	Davies	Cooke	Irving (8)	Appleton (7)		
08-Nov	Bolton Wanderers	League	Away	1-3		Pilkington	G Neville	O'Kane	Beckham	McGibbon	Casper	Gillespie	Kirovski	Johnson	Cooke	Appleton (2)	Tomlinson (9)			
16-Nov	Sunderland	League	Home	2-1		Pilkington	G Neville	O'Kane	May	McGibbon	Casper	Butt 1	Scholes	Irving	Davies	Johnson 1	McGibbon	Rawlinson (11)		
24-Nov	Tranmere Rovers	League	Home	1-1	4,872	Pilkington	P Neville	O'Kane	Beckham	McGibbon	Casper	Scholes	Cooke	Irving	Rawlinson	Davies	Tomlinson (11)	Appleton (7)		
30-Nov	Coventry City	League	Away	1-0		Pilkington	P Neville	P Neville	Beckham	McGibbon	Westwood	Gillespie	Rawlinson	Irving	Scholes	Davies 1	Appleton (11)	Tomlinson (7)		
08-Dec	Leeds United	League	Home	0-1	4,487	Pilkington	P Neville	O'Kane	Rawlinson	McGibbon	Gillespie	Gillespie	Scholes	Irving	Johnson	Thornley	Cooke (7)	Appleton (8)		
11-Jan	Everton	League	Away	0-3		Pilkington	G Neville	O'Kane	Beckham	McGibbon	Casper	Thornley	Davies	Irving	Scholes	Sharpe	Kirovski (7)	Dean		
19-Jan	Stoke City	League	Home	2-1		Walsh	Westwood	P Neville	Beckham	McGibbon	Casper	Ince 1	Butt	Irving	Davies	Davies	Johnson (9)	Pilkington	Rawlinson (8)	
24-Jan	Derby County	League	Away	2-2		Walsh	G Neville 1	P Neville	McGibbon	McGibbon	Cooke	Cooke	Davies	Kirovski 1	Kirovski 1	Thornley	Irving 1 (11)	Pilkington	Westwood (5)	
01-Feb	Bolton Wanderers	League	Home	2-4		Walsh	G Neville	May	Beckham	McGibbon	Casper	Cooke	Kirovski	Johnson	Davies	Thornley	Rawlinson (11)	Gibson	McGibbon	
08-Feb	Sunderland	League	Away	2-3		Pilkington	O'Kane	O'Kane	Beckham	Tohill	Kanchelskis	Butt 2	Appleton	Kirovski	Kirovski	Davies 2	McGibbon	Pilkington	Thornley (3)	
15-Feb	Tranmere Rovers	League	Home	2-1		Walsh	G Neville	Beckham 1	May	Casper	Butt	Kirovski	Davies	Hughes 1	Cooke	Casper (3)	Pilkington	Appleton (10)		
20-Feb	Blackburn Rovers	League	Away	0-2		Pilkington	Appleton	Westwood	Dean	McGibbon	Butt	Irving	Kirovski	Davies	Thornley	Rawlinson (8)	Pilkington	Flash (11)		
15-Mar	Sheffield United	League	Home	1-1		Pilkington	Westwood	P Neville	Casper	Cooke	Cooke 1	Appleton	Davies	Scholes	Rawlinson (11)	Maxon	Flash			
17-Mar	Bolton Wanderers	League	Home	1-1		Pilkington	Westwood	Casper	McGibbon	Davies	Rawlinson	Appleton	Kirovski	Davies	Thornley	Rawlinson (11)	Maxon	Dean (3)		
21-Mar	Wolves	League	Home	0-0		Pilkington	D Hall	Dean	Casper	Davies	Rawlinson	Butt	Appleton	Irving	Kirovski	Flash	Gibson	Tomlinson (11)		
04-Apr	Sheffield United	League	Away	1-1		Pilkington	Appleton	O'Kane	Casper	McGibbon	Davies	Butt	Irving	Kirovski 1	Scholes	Thornley	Rawlinson	Gibson	Tomlinson	
10-Apr	Nottingham Forest	League	Away	1-1		Pilkington	Appleton	O'Kane	Casper	McGibbon	Appleton	Cooke 1	Irving 1	Tomlinson	Kirovski	Thornley	Johnson (9)	Gibson	Rawlinson	
12-Apr	West Brom	League	Home	0-0		Pilkington	Westwood	O'Kane	Casper	McGibbon	Cooke	Appleton	Irving 1	Irving	Kirovski	Thornley	Johnson (9)	Gibson	Tomlinson (8)	
20-Apr	West Brom	League	Away	0-1		Pilkington	P Neville	O'Kane	Casper	McGibbon	Rawlinson	Appleton	Scholes	Irving	Davies	Thornley	Westwood (9)	Gibson	Appleton (11)	
22-Apr	Everton	League	Home	1-0	3,098	Pilkington	P Neville	O'Kane	Casper	McGibbon	Rawlinson	Cooke	Scholes	Johnson	Davies	Tomlinson 1	Westwood	Gibson	Appleton (10)	
29-Apr	Liverpool	League	Away	1-0		Pilkington	Casper	O'Kane	McGibbon	May	Beckham 1	Cooke	Rawlinson	Tomlinson 1	Scholes	Thornley	Flash	Gibson	Johnson	
02-May	Rotherham United	League	Away	3-0		Pilkington	Casper	O'Kane	Casper	McGibbon 1	Beckham 1	Cooke	Tomlinson	Johnson	Davies	Thornley	Davies (11)		Teather	Dean
05-May	West Brom	League	Home	2-3	3,174	Pilkington	Casper	O'Kane	Casper	McGibbon 1	Beckham	Rawlinson 1	Rawlinson	Tomlinson 1	Kirovski	Thornley	Kirovski 1 (7)	Pilkington	Davies (8)	
11-May	Notts County	League	Home	2-2		Walsh	Pilkington	O'Kane	Casper	Beckham	Scholes 1	Irving	Irving	Tomlinson	Davies	Dean				

224

Season 1994/95

RESERVES APPEARANCES AND GOALS 1994/95

Name	League Apps	League Gls	LSC Apps	LSC Gls	Youth Cup Apps	Youth Cup Gls	Season Total Apps	Season Total Gls
Michael Appleton	14 (9)						14 (9)	0
Des Baker					5 (2)		5 (2)	0
David Beckham	20	2	3	2			23	4
Grant Brebner					4		4	0
Nicky Butt	10	5	2				12	5
Chris Casper	28 (1)		2				30 (1)	0
Michael Clegg	1				6		7	0
Terry Cooke	16 (1)	2			9	9	25 (1)	11
John Curtis					2 (2)		2 (2)	0
Simon Davies	23 (3)	4	3	1			26 (3)	5
Craig Dean	2 (2)						2 (2)	0
Dion Dublin	3						3	0
Richard Flash	(1)						0 (1)	0
David Gardner					2 (3)		2 (3)	0
Paul Gibson					9		9	0
Keith Gillespie	7	1	3				10	1
Danny Hall	1				5 (1)		5 (1)	0
Paul Heckingbottom					5	1	5	1
David Hilton					2 (1)		2 (1)	0
John Hudson					2 (1)	3	2 (1)	3
Mark Hughes	1	1					1	1
Paul Ince	1	1					1	1
Richard Irving	23 (3)	8					23 (3)	8
David Johnson	11 (4)	1			6 (1)	4	17 (5)	5
Andrei Kanchelskis	1						1	0
Roy Keane	1						1	0
Jovan Kirovski	15 (4)	3					15 (4)	3
Paul Lyons					1		1	0
Brian McClair	1						1	0
Colin McKee	3						3	0
Pat McGibbon	27 (1)	2	1				28 (1)	2
David May	4		1				5	0
Phil Mulryne					9	2	9	2
Neil Mustoe					8	1	8	1
Gary Neville	14 (1)	1	3				17 (1)	1
Phil Neville	12				9	1	21	1
John O'Kane	25	1	3				28	1
Paul Parker	1						1	0
Kevin Pilkington	26		3				29	0
Mark Rawlinson	13 (7)	1	(2)				13 (9)	1
Paul Scholes	16 (1)	5	3	1			19 (1)	6
Lee Sharpe	1		1	1			2	1
Ben Thornley	16 (2)						16 (2)	0
Anthony Tohill	2						2	0
Graeme Tomlinson	14 (5)	7	3				17 (5)	7
Michael Twiss					0 (1)		0 (1)	0
Ronnie Wallwork					8	1	8	1
Gary Walsh	8						8	0
Ashley Westwood	11 (3)				9		20 (3)	0
Neil Whitworth	2		2				4	0

YOUTH CUP GAMES 1994/95

Date	Opponents	Rnd	Venue	Res	Att	1	2	3	4	5	6	7	8	9	10	11	12	13	14
28-Nov	Wrexham	R 2	Home	4-1	1240	Gibson	P.Neville	Whittam	Westwood	Wallwork	Mustoe	Gardner	Heckingbottom	Johnson 2	Cooke 2	D. Hilton	Hudson	Maxon	Baker
21-Dec	Charlton Athletic	R 3	Home	1-1	1430	Gibson	Hall	Lyons	Westwood	Wallwork	Gardner	P.Neville	Heckingbottom	Johnson	Cooke	D. Hilton	Hudson 1 (11)	Maxon	Baker (6)
12-Jan	Charlton Athletic	R 3R	Away	5-2	3515	Gibson	P.Neville	Hall	Westwood	Clegg	Mustoe	Hudson 1	Brebner	Johnson 2	Cooke 1	Heckingbottom 1	Curtis (3)	Maxon	Gardner (11)
31-Jan	Arsenal	R 4	Home	2-1	2701	Gibson	P.Neville	P.Neville	Westwood	Clegg	Mustoe 1	Hudson 1	Brebner	Johnson	Cooke 1	Mulryne	Wallwork	Maxon	Baker (11)
28-Feb	Aston Villa	R 5	Away	3-2	4323	Gibson	P.Neville	Wallwork 1	Westwood	Clegg	Mustoe	Brebner	Heckingbottom	Baker	Cooke 1	Mulryne 1	Hall	Maxon	Twiss (11)
25-Mar	Wimbledon	SF1	Home	2-1	6167	Gibson	P.Neville 1	Wallwork	Westwood	Clegg	Hall	Mustoe	Johnson	Baker	Cooke 1	Mulryne 1	Johnson (7)	Maxon	Hall (8)
08-Apr	Wimbledon	SF2	Away	3-0	4441	Gibson	P.Neville	Wallwork	Westwood	Clegg	Hall	Mustoe	Johnson	Baker	Cooke 2	Mulryne 1	Curtis	Maxon	Brebner
11-May	Tottenham Hotspur*	F1	Away	1-2	3503	Gibson	P.Neville	Wallwork	Westwood	Clegg	Hall	Mustoe	Brebner	Baker	Cooke 1	Mulryne	Curtis (9)	Maxon	Gardner (11)
15-May	Tottenham Hotspur*	F2	Home	1-0	20190	Gibson	Curtis	P.Neville	Westwood	Wallwork	Hall	Mustoe	Brebner	Baker	Cooke 1	Mulryne	D. Hilton (11)	Maxon	Gardner (6)

*Won 4-3 on penalties

Season 1995/96

MANCHESTER UNITED RESERVES 1995/96: PONTINS LEAGUE

Date	Opponents	Comp	Venue	Res	Att	1	2	3	4	5	6	7	8	9	10	11	12	13	14	15
16-Aug	Bolton Wanderers	League	Home	1-0		Pilkington	Casper	Clegg	McGibbon	May	Mulryne	Appleton	Tomlinson 1	Baker	Thornley	Smith (7)	Twiss (10)	Hilton		
30-Aug	Notts County	League	Home	2-2	3,950	Pilkington	Parker	O'Kane	McGibbon 1	Appleton	Tomlinson	Giggs 1	Davies	Thornley	Mustoe	P Neville (3)	Clegg (10)			
02-Sep	Liverpool	League	Away	2-3		Pilkington	Clegg	O'Kane	McGibbon	Wallwork	Appleton 1	Tomlinson	Giggs 1	Davies	Thornley	Brebner	Baker			
06-Sep	Blackburn Rovers	League	Away	1-1		Pilkington	P Neville	O'Kane	McGibbon	Mustoe	Cooke	Tomlinson	McClair 1	Mulryne	Wallwork 1 (8)	Clegg (3)				
27-Sep	Oldham Athletic	League	Home	2-0		Pilkington	Clegg	O'Kane	Casper 1	McGibbon	Mustoe	Cooke	Tomlinson 1	Davies	Mulryne	Baker (9)	Whittam			
07-Oct	Leeds United	League	Home	2-0	21,502	Pilkington	Clegg	P Neville	Casper	Wallwork	Sharpe	Cantona	Cooke 1	Tomlinson 1	Scholes	Davies	Baker (7)	Gibson	Mustoe (10)	Curtis
11-Oct	West Brom	League	Away	4-2		Pilkington	Parker	Appleton	Clegg	Mustoe	McClair	Cooke 1	Tomlinson 1	Kirovski 3	Davies	Baker	Thornley			
18-Oct	Birmingham City	League	Home	3-0		Pilkington	Irwin	Casper	Cooke 1	Davies	Cooke 1	Tomlinson 2	McClair	Kirovski	Scholes	Appleton (3)	Mustoe (10)			
25-Oct	Nottingham Forest	League	Away	1-1		Pilkington	Clegg	Casper	McGibbon	Sharpe 1	Cooke 1	Beckham	McClair	Davies	Kirovski	Thornley	Appleton (6)	Gibson	Baker	
01-Nov	Sheffield Wed	League	Away	3-5		Pilkington	P Neville	May	Casper	Sharpe	Cooke	Tomlinson	McClair	Kirovski 2	Davies	Thornley	Beckham 1 (7)			
15-Nov	Sheffield United°	League	Home	6-0		Pilkington	Clegg	Casper	May	Baker	Cooke 1	Beckham	McClair 1	Kirovski 1	Appleton	McGibbon	Clegg (9)	Appleton (11)	Thornley (6)	
20-Nov	Wolves	League	Home	2-0		Pilkington .	Clegg	O'Kane	McGibbon	Davies	Sharpe 1	Tomlinson	Beckham	McClair	Kirovski 1	Davies	Mustoe (6)		Casper	Wood
29-Nov	Tranmere Rovers	League	Away	3-1	2,597	Gibson	P Neville	O'Kane	Casper	May	Appleton	Kirovski	Tomlinson 1	Appleton	Scholes	Sharpe	Clegg (11)		Brebner	Appleton 1 (6)
06-Dec	Leeds United	League	Away	2-1		Gibson	Clegg	O'Kane	Casper	McGibbon	Davies	Cooke 1	Tomlinson 1	Kirovski 1	Davies	Mustoe	Murdock		Brebner	
14-Dec	Oldham Athletic	League	Home	2-2		Pilkington	Keane	O'Kane	Casper	McGibbon	Baker	Cooke	Tomlinson 1	Davies	Kirovski 2	Thornley	Murdock (9)		Baker 1 (2)	
20-Dec	Derby County°	League	Home	3-1		Pilkington	Parker	Prunier	Casper	Appleton	Mustoe	Butt	Tomlinson	Kirovski 1	Mustoe 1	McGibbon	Baker		Clegg	
03-Jan	Newcastle United	League	Away	0-2		Pilkington	Clegg	O'Kane	Casper	Appleton	Scholes	Scholes	Tomlinson	Davies	Sharpe	Baker (9)	Mustoe (10)		Wallwork	
09-Jan	Everton	League	Away	1-0		Culkin	Parker	Clegg	McGibbon	Davies	Cooke	Tomlinson	McClair	Kirovski	Scholes	Appleton	Mustoe (6)		Murdock	
17-Jan	Liverpool	League	Home	2-1		Pilkington	Clegg	O'Kane	McGibbon 1	Murdock	Cooke	Tomlinson	McClair	Davies	Sharpe	Mustoe	Wallwork (4)		Baker	
24-Jan	Bolton Wanderers	League	Away	2-0		Coton	Parker	O'Kane	Murdock	Beckham 1	Cooke	Tomlinson	McClair	Kirovski 1	Scholes	Thornley 1	Clegg (4)	Pilkington	Mustoe	
31-Jan	Blackburn Rovers	League	Home	2-1		Coton	Clegg	O'Kane	Wallwork	Davies	Beckham 1	Kirovski 1	McClair	Kirovski	Scholes	Appleton (7)	Mustoe (6)	Gibson	Tomlinson	
15-Feb	Everton	League	Home	2-0		Coton	Clegg	Appleton	Murdock	Davies	Scholes	Tomlinson	McClair	Kirovski 1	Thornley 1	Mustoe (6)	Tomlinson	Gibson		
26-Feb	Sheffield United	League	Away	3-0		Coton	Parker	G Neville 1	May	Appleton	Mustoe	Beckham	McClair	Kirovski	Davies 2	Tomlinson (8)	Clegg			
07-Mar	Sheffield Wed	League	Home	2-1		Pilkington	Parker	O'Kane 1	McGibbon	Beckham	Cooke	Scholes 1	Kirovski	Scholes	Davies	Mustoe (9)	Baker	Pilkington	Tomlinson	
19-Mar	Derby County	League	Home	1-2		Coton	Parker	Clegg	Casper	Appleton 1	Cooke 2	Kirovski 1	Davies	Scholes	Mulryne	Murdock (7)	Hall (7)	Pilkington	Murdock (11)	
28-Mar	Stoke City	League	Away	1-1		Pilkington	Clegg	O'Kane	McGibbon	Mustoe	Cooke 1	Kirovski 2	McClair	O'Kane	Baker	Appleton (9)	Wood (11)	Pilkington	Mulryne (6)	Wallwork
04-Apr	Notts County	League	Away	1-1		Coton	Hall	O'Kane	Clegg	Beckham	O'Kane	Kirovski	Baker	Ford	Naylor	Baker	Cooke (2)		Curtis (2)	Murdock (11)
10-Apr	West Brom	League	Away	4-1		Coton	Parker	Clegg	McGibbon	Murdock	Mustoe	Appleton	Davies	Scholes	Notman	Cooke	Hall		Baker	Mustoe (2)
20-Apr	Nottingham Forest	League	Home	4-0		Pilkington	Parker	Clegg	Casper	Wallwork	Appleton 1	Cooke 1	Appleton	Davies	Wood 1	Baker	Pilkington		Byers (6)	Wood (10)
22-Apr	Birmingham City	League	Home	0-1		Pilkington	Parker	Clegg	Casper	Murdock	Mustoe	O'Kane	Baker 1	McClair	Davies	Mulryne	Baker		McGibbon	
24-Apr	Newcastle United	League	Away	2-0		Pilkington	Clegg	O'Kane	Casper	Mustoe	Appleton 1	Cooke	Kirovski 1	Baker	Scholes	Appleton (6)	Wood (2)	Gibson	Hall (6)	
29-Apr	Stoke City	League	Home	1-0		Pilkington	Hall	O'Kane	Casper	Appleton	Cooke	Kirovski 1	McClair	Davies	Gibson	Gibson	Notman			
01-May	Tranmere Rovers	League	Home	2-3		Pilkington	Hall	Whittam	Clegg	Cooke	Appleton	O'Kane	Kirovski 2	McClair	Davies	Gibson	Gibson		Notman	
06-May	Wolves	League	Away	2-3		Pilkington	McGibbon	Whittam	Casper	Clegg	Mustoe	Appleton	Davies	Cooke	Kirovski 1	O'Kane 1	Murdock (2)	Gibson	Hall (3)	

° Own goals: Blount v Sheffield United (home), Sutton v Derby County (home)

226

Season 1995/96

RESERVES APPEARANCES AND GOALS 1995/96

Name	League Apps	League Gls	Youth Cup Apps	Youth Cup Gls	Season Total Apps	Season Total Gls
Michael Appleton	20 (8)	3			20 (8)	3
Des Baker	8 (5)	2	4	3	12 (5)	5
David Beckham	5 (1)	2			5 (1)	2
Grant Brebner			3 (1)	2	3 (1)	2
Stuart Brightwell			3 (1)		3 (1)	0
David Brown			0 (2)	1	0 (2)	1
Nicky Butt	1				1	0
Jamie Byers	(1)				0 (1)	0
Eric Cantona	1				1	0
Chris Casper	24	2			24	2
Michael Clegg	24 (5)				24 (5)	0
Terry Cooke	28 (1)	10			28 (1)	10
Tony Coton	8				8	0
Nick Culkin	2		4		6	0
John Curtis	(1)		4		4 (1)	0
Simon Davies	26	2			26	2
Andy Duncan			3		3	0
Ryan Ford	1		1		2	0
Paul Gibson	3				3	0
Ryan Giggs	2	2			2	2
Danny Hall	4 (3)		2		6 (3)	0
David Hilton			0 (1)	1	0 (1)	1
Denis Irwin	1				1	0
Roy Keane	1				1	0
Jovan Kirovski	22	20			22	20
Brian McClair	17	1			17	1
Pat McGibbon	24	3			24	3
Jon Macken			1		1	0
David May	6				6	0
Phil Mulryne	4 (1)		3		7 (1)	0
Colin Murdock	7 (4)				7 (4)	0
Neil Mustoe	12 (7)	1			12 (7)	1
Gavin Naylor	1				1	0
Gary Neville	1	1			1	1
Phil Neville	7 (1)				7 (1)	0
Alex Notman	1				1	0
John O'Kane	24	3			24	3
Paul Parker	12				12	0
Kevin Pilkington	21				21	0
William Prunier	1				1	0
Paul Scholes	12	3			12	3
Lee Sharpe	7	2			7	2
Tommy Smith	(1)		2		2 (1)	0
Paul Teather			3		3	0
Robert Trees			1		1	0
Ben Thornley	8 (1)	2			8 (1)	2
Graeme Tomlinson	21 (1)	8			21 (1)	8
Michael Twiss	(1)		4	1	4 (1)	1
Ronnie Wallwork	4 (2)	1	4	1	8 (2)	2
Phil Whittam	2				2	0
Mark Wilson			4	1	4	1
Jamie Wood	1 (2)	1			1 (2)	1

YOUTH CUP GAMES 1995/96

Date	Opponents	Rnd	Venue	Res	Att	1	2	3	4	5	6	7	8	9	10	11	12	13	14
21-Nov	Rotherham United	R 2	Home	3-1	1222	Culkin	Curtis	Teather	Smith	Wallwork 1	Brightwell	Brebner	Mulryne	Macken	Baker 1	Twiss	D. Hilton (9)	Maxon	Trees (4)
10-Jan	Sunderland	R 3	Away	4-1		Culkin	Curtis	Hall	Duncan	Wallwork	Brightwell	Brebner	Mulryne	Baker 2	Wilson 1	Twiss	Smith	Maxon	D. Brown 1 (7)
13-Feb	Norwich City	R 4	Home	1-0	2545	Culkin	Curtis	Teather	Duncan	Wallwork	Hall	Ford	Smith	Baker	Wilson 1	Twiss	Brightwell (6)	Maxon	Brebner (10)
05-Mar	Liverpool	R 5	Away	2-3	5221	Culkin	Curtis	Teather	Duncan	Wallwork	Brightwell	Brebner 1	Mulryne	Baker	Wilson	Twiss 1	D. Brown (6)	Maxon	Smith

Season 1996/97

MANCHESTER UNITED RESERVES 1996/97: PONTINS LEAGUE

Date	Opponents	Comp	Venue	Res	Att	1	2	3	4	5	6	7	8	9	10	11	12	13	14	15
21-Aug	Oldham Athletic	League	Away	3-1		Pilkington	Clegg	O'Kane	Casper	Wallwork	Appleton	Cooke 1	Mulryne	Davies	Solskjaer 2	Twiss	Macken (8)	Gibson	Teather	
28-Aug	Everton	League	Home	5-2		Van der Gouw	Curtis	O'Kane 1	Clegg	Appleton	Cooke	Poborsky 1	Cole 2	Scholes 1	Thornley	Davies	Mulryne	Pilkington		
10-Sep	Derby County	League	Away	2-1		Pilkington	Curtis	Clegg	McGibbon	Teather	Mulryne	Cole 2	O'Kane	Macken 1	Twiss 1	Wallwork (8)	Wood (9)	Pilkington		
18-Sep	Tranmere Rovers	League	Home	5-1		Van der Gouw	Appleton	Wallwork	May	Casper	Cooke	Mulryne	Scholes	Davies	Thornley	McGibbon	Mulryne			
26-Sep	Sheffield Wed	League	Away	1-2		Van der Gouw	Clegg	Casper	Wallwork	McClair	Keane	Cooke	O'Kane	Cole 3	McClair 1	Thornley	Davies			
30-Sep	Bolton Wanderers	League	Home	0-0		Van der Gouw	Curtis	Wallwork	Casper	Appleton	Cooke	Davies	Mulryne	Cole	Scholes 1	Thornley	Mulryne			
04-Oct	Liverpool	League	Away	3-0		O'Kane	Clegg	Curtis	Wallwork	Casper	Appleton	Cooke	McClair	Mulryne	Scholes 1	Thornley 1	D Brown (8)	Pilkington		
21-Oct	Stoke City	League	Away	0-2	8,968	Van der Gouw	O'Kane	Wallwork	Murdock	Appleton	Cooke	McClair	Cole	Macken	McClair	Mulryne	Pilkington	Murdock		
09-Nov	Nottingham Forest	League	Away	4-0		Pilkington	Curtis	O'Kane	Casper	Wallwork	Brebner	Mulryne	Twiss	Macken 1	Davies	Teather	Duncan (5)	Ford (3)		
04-Dec	Birmingham City	League	Away	4-2		Culkin	Clegg	O'Kane	Duncan	Murdock	Appleton 1	Cooke	Newland 3	McClair	Giggs	Thornley	Mulryne	Macken	Naylor	
18-Dec	Leeds United	League	Away	3-3		Gibson	Teather	Curtis	Wallwork	Casper	Appleton	Brebner 1	Notman 1	Wilson	Davies 1	Teather	Hilton	Wilson 1 (9)	W Brown	Hilton (10)
23-Dec	Derby County	League	Home	2-2		Pilkington	Teather	O'Kane	Casper	Wallwork	Appleton	Brebner	McClair	Cole 1	Macken 1	Thornley	Twiss (8)	Duncan (2)	Wilson 1 (9)	Twiss (8)
08-Jan	Sheffield Wed	League	Home	3-0		Pilkington	Teather	O'Kane	Casper	Wallwork	Appleton	Cruyff	McClair	Cole 1	Davies	Thornley 2	Macken	Duncan (2)	Teather (6)	Wellens (7)
22-Jan	Tranmere Rovers	League	Away	3-2		Van der Gouw	Clegg	Curtis	Wallwork	Wallwork	Cooke	Cruyff 1	Mulryne	Macken	Mulryne 1	Twiss	Macken (9)	Duncan (4)	Teather (6)	Twiss (8)
26-Feb	Nottingham Forest	League	Home	4-0		Van der Gouw	Clegg	P Neville 1	McGibbon	May	Cooke	Cole 2	Cruyff 1	Cole 2	Davies	Thornley	Brebner (8)	Duncan (4)	Teather (6)	Mulryne (3)
17-Mar	Birmingham City	League	Home	2-1		Van der Gouw	Clegg	O'Kane	Casper	Casper	Cooke	Cooke	Scholes	Tomlinson 2	Davies	Thornley	Brebner	Macken		Twiss (3)
25-Mar	Everton	League	Away	3-2		Van der Gouw	Clegg	O'Kane	Casper	Duncan	Cooke	Cooke	Scholes 1	Cruyff 2	Davies	Thornley	Brebner	Macken		Teather
29-Mar	Bolton Wanderers	League	Home	1-0		Gibson	Clegg	O'Kane	Casper	Wallwork	McClair	Cooke	Scholes	Tomlinson	Davies	Thornley	Macken (9)			Duncan
02-Apr	Oldham Athletic	League	Home	1-1		Gibson	Clegg	O'Kane	Wallwork	Wallwork	Curtis	Cooke 2	Appleton	Cole 1	Cruyff	Mulryne	Davies (9)	Macken		Teather (8)
14-Apr	Liverpool	League	Home	4-0		Gibson	Clegg 1	O'Kane	Casper	Murdock	Appleton	Cooke	McClair	Tomlinson 1	Davies	Mulryne	Macken 1 (9)	Macken		Teather (8)
26-Apr	Leeds United	League	Home	1-2		Van der Gouw	Clegg	Wallwork	Casper	Murdock	Appleton	Cooke	Teather	Tomlinson 1	Davies	Macken	Brebner	Duncan	Twiss (7)	Teather
01-May	Blackburn Rovers	League	Home	0-0		Pilkington	Clegg	O'Kane	Casper	Wallwork	Cooke	Cooke	McClair	Cole 1	Davies	Twiss	Brebner (11)	Duncan		Notman
05-May	Blackburn Rovers	League	Away	1-0		Pilkington	Curtis	O'Kane	Murdock	Duncan	Appleton	Brebner 1	Mulryne	Macken	Thornley	Mustoe	Teather		
13-May	Stoke City	League	Home	0-0		Pilkington	Twiss	Teather	Murdock	Wallwork	Mulryne	Appleton	Appleton	Macken	Davies	Thornley	Mustoe		Clegg

Season 1996/97

RESERVES APPEARANCES AND GOALS 1996/97

Name	League Apps	League Gls	Youth Cup Apps	Youth Cup Gls	Season Total Apps	Season Total Gls
Michael Appleton	15	1			15	1
Grant Brebner	5 (2)	2			5 (2)	2
Stuart Brightwell			4	1	4	1
David Brown	1 (1)		4	2	5 (1)	2
Wes Brown			4		4	0
Jamie Byers			0 (1)		0 (1)	0
Chris Casper	18				18	0
Michael Clegg	17	1			17	1
Andy Cole	9	10			9	10
Terry Cooke	17	3			17	3
Jordi Cruyff	5	4			5	4
Nick Culkin	1				1	0
John Curtis	11		4		15	0
Simon Davies	16 (1)	1			16 (1)	1
Andrew Duncan	5 (3)				5 (3)	0
Ryan Ford	(1)		4		4 (1)	0
Paul Gibson	3				3	0
Ryan Giggs	1				1	0
David Healy			0 (2)		0 (2)	0
Danny Higginbotham			4		4	0
David Hilton	(1)				0 (1)	0
Roy Keane	1				1	0
Brian McClair	12	1			12	1
Pat McGibbon	2				2	0
Jonathan Macken	7 (5)	2			7 (5)	2
Leon Milla			0 (1)		0 (1)	0
David May	2				2	0
Phil Mulryne	10	1			10	1
Colin Murdock	4				4	0
Gavin Naylor			1 (1)	1	1 (1)	1
Phil Neville	1	1			1	1
Erik Nevland	1	3			1	3
Alex Notman	2 (1)	4	4	6	6 (1)	10
John O'Kane	15	1			15	1
Kevin Pilkington	8				8	0
Karel Poborsky	1	1			1	1
Adam Sadler			4		4	0
Paul Scholes	9	5			9	5
Ole Gunnar Solskjaer	1	2			1	2
Paul Teather	7 (2)				7 (2)	0
Ben Thornley	16	4			16	4
Graeme Tomlinson	5	5			5	5
Michael Twiss	5 (4)	1			5 (4)	1
Raimond van der Gouw	12				12	0
Ronnie Wallwork	18 (1)	1			18 (1)	1
Richie Wellens	(1)		4		4 (1)	0
Mark Wilson	1 (1)	1	4		5 (1)	1
Jamie Wood	(1)		1 (3)	2	1 (4)	2

YOUTH CUP GAMES 1996/97

Date	Opponents	Rnd	Venue	Res	Att	1	2	3	4	5	6	7	8	9	10	11	12	13	14
25-Nov	Wrexham	R 2	Home	7-0	941	Sadler	Ford	Higginbotham	Curtis	W. Brown	Brightwell 1	Wilson	Wellens	Brown	Notman 4	Naylor 1	Wood 1 (9)	Mills (2)	Healy (6)
07-Jan	Liverpool	R 3	Away	2-1	4931	Sadler	Ford	Higginbotham	Curtis	W. Brown	Brightwell	Wellens	Wilson	D.Brown 1	Wood	Notman 1	Naylor (10)	Rachubka	Mills
15-Feb	Watford	R 4	Home	1-1	4366	Sadler	Ford	Higginbotham	Curtis	W. Brown	Brightwell	Wellens	Wilson	D.Brown	Notman 1	Naylor	Wood (8)	Healy (11)	Byers (9)
06-Mar	Watford	R 4 R	Away	2-3	3781	Sadler	Ford	Higginbotham	Curtis	W. Brown	Brightwell	Wellens	Wilson	D.Brown	Notman 1	Naylor	Wood 1 (11)	Byers	Millard

Season 1997/98

MANCHESTER UNITED RESERVES 1997/98: PONTINS LEAGUE

Date	Opponents	Comp	Venue	Res	Att	1	2	3	4	5	6	7	8	9	10	11	12	13	14	15
14-Aug	Leeds United	League	Away	0-3		Pilkington	G Neville	Wallwork	Curtis	Mulryne	Cooke	Beckham	McClair	Twiss	Thornley	Brebner			Notman (10)	Teather
20-Aug	Blackburn Rovers	League	Home	2-2		Van der Gouw	O'Kane	Casper	Wallwork	Teather	Cooke	Twiss	McClair	Notman 1	Thornley	Mustoe			Higginbotham	D Brown
25-Aug	Aston Villa	League	Home	1-0		Van der Gouw	Curtis	Casper	Wallwork	Teather	Cooke	Twiss	McClair	Mulryne	Thornley 1	Brebner			Higginbotham	Notman (6)
10-Sep	Sheffield Wed	League	Home	4-0		Van der Gouw	O'Kane	Higginbotham	Clegg	Wallwork	Teather	Cooke 1	Cole 1	Poborsky 1	Thornley 1	Notman			Twiss (3)	Mustoe (7)
22-Sep	Derby County	League	Away	4-0		Pilkington	Curtis	O'Kane	Clegg	Wallwork	Teather	Mulryne 1	Nevland	McClair	Solskjaer 2	Thornley 1	Brebner (10)		Twiss (8)	
29-Sep	Tranmere Rovers	League	Home	1-2	625	Van der Gouw	Clegg	Curtis	Wallwork	Teather	Mulryne	Nevland	McClair	Solskjaer 1	Thornley	O'Kane (8)	Brebner (10)		D Brown (6)	Mustoe
07-Oct	Everton	League	Away	2-3		Van der Gouw	O'Kane	May	Wallwork	Teather	Mulryne	Mustoe	Twiss	Notman 1	Nevland	Thornley 1	D Brown (10)		Higginbotham	Brightwell
13-Oct	Nottingham Forest	League	Home	1-1		Pilkington	O'Kane	Twiss	May	Wallwork	Teather	Mustoe	Brebner	Notman 1	Tomlinson	Thornley	D Brown (10)		Smith (4)	Brightwell (11)
27-Oct	Liverpool	League	Away	2-2		Pilkington	Twiss	Duncan	Wallwork	Mulryne	Mustoe	Brebner	McClair 1	Tomlinson	Nevland	Thornley	Teather (4)		D Brown (10)	Wilson
12-Nov	Stoke City	League	Home	4-2		Pilkington	O'Kane	Wallwork	Casper	Johnsen	Mulryne	Poborsky	Notman 1	McClair 1	Solskjaer 2	Thornley 1	Duncan		Brebner (3)	Wilson
24-Nov	Preston North End	League	Home	5-2		Pilkington	Clegg	Curtis	May	Wallwork	Teather	Wilson	Nevland 2	McClair 1	Poborsky	Thornley 1	Notman (7)		Twiss	Ford (8)
02-Dec	Tranmere Rovers	League	Away	1-0		Van der Gouw	Clegg	Curtis	Casper	May	Teather	Twiss	McClair	Nevland 1	Notman 2	Thornley	Wallwork		Teather (6)	O'Kane (9)
11-Dec	Blackburn Rovers	League	Away	1-3		Pilkington	Curtis	Clegg	Casper	Wallwork	Teather	Mulryne	Twiss	D Brown	Nevland 1	Thornley	Tomlinson (10)		Wilson (6)	Tomlinson (8)
30-Dec	Leeds United	League	Home	1-1		Pilkington	Curtis	Irwin	Clegg	Clegg	O'Kane	Twiss	Nevland 1	McClair	Tomlinson	Thornley	Twiss		Brebner	Wilson
07-Jan	Aston Villa	League	Away	1-0		Pilkington	Clegg	O'Kane	Berg	Casper	Twiss	Mulryne	Nevland 1	McClair	Tomlinson	Thornley	Brebner		Notman (10)	Curtis
14-Jan	Birmingham City	League	Away	3-4	12,300	Van der Gouw	Clegg	P Neville	Casper 1	W Brown	Wellens	Cruyff 1	Tomlinson	McClair	Wood	Thornley	Higginbotham		Notman 1 (10)	Twiss (11)
04-Feb	Sheffield Wed	League	Away	2-0		Pilkington	Wallwork	Higginbotham	W Brown	W Brown	Twiss	Brightwell	Mulryne	D Brown	Notman	Thornley	Wood 1 (4)		Ford (8)	Smith
09-Mar	Stoke City	League	Away	2-1	3,507	Pilkington	W Brown	Higginbotham	May	Casper	Wellens	Cruyff 1	Nevland	Notman 2	Tomlinson	Thornley	Tomlinson (8)		Wood (12)	Wilson (9)
21-Mar	Derby County	League	Home	2-1		Pilkington	Higginbotham	May	Casper	Ford	Twiss	Cruyff	Nevland	McClair	Notman 2	Thornley 1	D Brown		Brightwell	Tomlinson
25-Mar	Liverpool	League	Home	0-1		Pilkington	Ryan	Higginbotham	Casper	W Brown	Ford	Cruyff	Twiss	McClair	Notman	Thornley 1			Brightwell	Ford
30-Mar	Preston North End	League	Away	6-1	9,072	Pilkington	Curtis	Higginbotham	May	W Brown	Twiss 2	Mulryne	Cruyff 1	McClair	Notman 2	Thornley 1	Nevland (6)		Wood	Brightwell
14-Apr	Birmingham City	League	Away	2-0		Clegg	Higginbotham	Casper	May	Berg	Mulryne 1	Cruyff	Solskjaer 1	McClair	Sheringham	Thornley	Notman 1		Ford (4)	Healy (8)
22-Apr	Everton	League	Home	7-0		Van der Gouw	Clegg	Clegg	Berg	Curtis	Ford	Cruyff	Twiss 1	McClair 1	Solskjaer 4	Thornley 1	Notman	Van der Gouw (1)	Brightwell	Wellens
29-Apr	Nottingham Forest°	League	Away	1-0		Van der Gouw	Clegg	Curtis	Casper	Berg	Twiss	Mulryne	Mulryne	Solskjaer	Solskjaer	Thornley	Notman		W Brown (5)	Ford (3)

° Own goal: Lyttle

Season 1997/98

RESERVES APPEARANCES AND GOALS 1997/98

Name	League Apps	League Gls	Youth Cup Apps	Youth Cup Gls	Season Total Apps	Season Total Gls
David Beckham	1				1	0
Henning Berg	3				3	0
Grant Brebner	1 (2)				1 (2)	0
Stuart Brightwell	1 (1)				1 (1)	0
David Brown	3 (4)	1			3 (4)	1
Wes Brown	4 (1)		2		6 (1)	0
Chris Casper	15	1			15	1
Luke Chadwick			1		1	0
George Clegg			1		1	0
Michael Clegg	13				13	0
Andy Cole	1	1			1	1
Terry Cooke	4	1			4	1
Jordi Cruyff	6	2			6	2
Nick Culkin	2				2	0
John Curtis	15				15	0
Andrew Duncan	2				2	0
Wayne Evans			2		2	0
Ian Fitzpatrick			0 (1)		0 (1)	0
Ryan Ford	2 (4)				2 (4)	0
David Healy	1 (1)		2	2	3 (1)	2
Danny Higginbotham	6				6	0
Kirk Hilton			0 (1)		0 (1)	0
Denis Irwin	1				1	0
Ronny Johnsen	1				1	0
Brian McClair	19	4			19	4
David May	7				7	0
Phil Mulryne	17	3			17	3
Neil Mustoe	2 (1)				2 (1)	0
Gary Neville	1				1	0
Phil Neville	1				1	0
Erik Nevland	11 (1)	8			11 (1)	8
Alex Notman	10 (7)	11	2		12 (7)	11
John O'Kane	10 (2)	1			10 (2)	1
Kevin Pilkington	12				12	0
Karel Poborsky	2	1			2	1
Paul Rachubka			2		2	0
Lee Roche			2	1	2	1
Stephen Rose			2		2	0
Michael Ryan	1		2		3	0
Teddy Sheringham	1				1	0
Tommy Smith	(1)				0 (1)	0
Ole Gunnar Solskjaer	5	9			5	9
Paul Teather	10 (2)				10 (2)	0
John Thorrington			2		2	0
Ben Thornley	22	6			22	6
Graeme Tomlinson	6 (5)				6 (5)	0
Michael Twiss	18 (4)	4			18 (4)	4
Raimond van der Gouw	10 (1)				10 (1)	0
Ronnie Wallwork	13				13	0
Richie Wellens	1		2		3	0
Paul Wheatcroft			0 (2)		0 (2)	0
Mark Wilson	3 (2)				3 (2)	0
Jamie Wood	1 (2)		1		1 (2)	1

YOUTH CUP GAMES 1997/98

Date	Opponents	Rnd	Venue	Res	Att	1	2	3	4	5	6	7	8	9	10	11	12	13	14
02-Dec	Blackburn Rovers	R 2	Away	1-1	1257	Rachubka	Roche	S.Rose	Ryan	W. Brown	Evans	Wellens	Thorrington	Healy 1	Notman	Chadwick	K.Hilton (4)	Sadler	Wheatcroft (8)
08-Dec	Blackburn Rovers	R 2R	Home	2-3	3170	Rachubka	Roche 1	S.Rose	Ryan	W. Brown	Evans	Thorrington	Wellens	Healy 1	Notman	G. Clegg	K. Hilton	Fitzpatrick (6)	Wheatcroft (7)

Season 1998/99

MANCHESTER UNITED RESERVES 1998/99: PONTINS LEAGUE AND MANCHESTER SENIOR CUP

Date	Opponents	Comp	Venue	Res	Att	1	2	3	4	5	6	7	8	9	10	11	12	13	14	15	16	17
20-Aug	Sunderland	League	Home	0-0		Gibson	M Clegg	Curtis	Casper	Wallwork	Wilson	Wellens	Greening	Notman	Higginbotham	Teather			Wood (9)	Nevland (7)		
02-Sep	Aston Villa°	League	Home	4-0		Van der Gouw	M Clegg	Curtis	Wallwork	Teather	Ford	Wilson 2	Greening 1	Cruyff	Notman	Wood			Healy (11)	Best (5)		
05-Sep	Everton	League	Away	2-0	2,527	Van der Gouw	M Clegg	Higginbotham	May	Cooke	Teather	Wilson	Greening 1	Cruyff 1	Notman	Blomqvist			Wood (9)	Healy		
17-Sep	Birmingham City	League	Home	3-2		Van der Gouw	M Clegg	May	Brown	Casper	Cooke	Butt	Cole	Cruyff 1	Cruyff 1	Wallwork			Nevland (9)	Cooke (10)	Wilson (6)	
25-Sep	Liverpool	League	Away	2-0		Van der Gouw	M Clegg	Curtis	May	Wallwork	Mulryne	Cruyff 1	Butt	Nevland	Sheringham 2	Blomqvist			Greening (9)	Wood		
01-Oct	Nottingham Forest	League	Home	1-0		Culkin	M Clegg	Curtis	Brown	Wallwork	Wilson	Cooke 1	Wellens	Nevland	Notman 1	Mulryne			Culkin	Greening (9)		
14-Oct	Blackburn Rovers	League	Home	3-2		Gibson	M Clegg	Curtis	Wallwork	Greening 2	Cooke	Mulryne	Cruyff	Greening	Notman	Ford			Gibson	Best	Roche (4)	
03-Nov	Stoke City	League	Home	4-1		Gibson	M Clegg	D Studley	Wallwork	Wilson 1	Cooke	Mulryne	Wellens	Greening 2	Cruyff	Wellens (3)			Rachubka	Healy	Thorrington	
16-Nov	Leicester City	League	Away	6-2	14,326	Van der Gouw	M Clegg 1	Roche	May	Wallwork	Teather	Wellens 1	Nevland	Greening 1	Notman 1	Wood 1 (10)			Culkin	Ford (8)	Teather (3)	
24-Nov	Leeds United	League	Away	1-5		Culkin	Stewart	O'Shea	Johnsen	Wallwork	Wellens	Mulryne	Nevland	Greening 3	Sheringham 1	Wood			Culkin	Ryan	Chadwick (6)	
17-Dec	Sunderland	League	Away	0-2	20,583	Van der Gouw	M Clegg	Roche	O'Shea	Wallwork	Thorrington	Wellens	Nevland	Greening 1	Sheringham	Greening			Nevland	Notman	Ford	Chadwick
06-Jan	Aston Villa	League	Away	5-1		Culkin	M Clegg	Curtis	May	P Neville	Teather	Mulryne	Mulryne	Nevland	Cruyff	Greening 1			Culkin	Ryan	M Rose	
19-Jan	Derby County	League	Away	2-2	2,531	Van der Gouw	M Clegg	Curtis	May	O'Shea	Ford	Mulryne 1	Wilson 1	Nevland 1	Soiskjaer 2	Greening 1			Gibson	McDermott	Healy	
27-Jan	Derby County	League	Home	4-0		Van der Gouw	M Clegg	Curtis	May	Brown	P Neville	Mulryne 1	Wilson 1	Nevland 1	Bakircioglu	Greening 1	Wilson (9)	Culkin	S Rose (2)	Chadwick 1 (10)	Wellens	
03-Feb	Birmingham City	League	Away	1-1		Culkin	M Clegg	S Rose	Brown	Wilson	Mulryne	Wilson	Mulryne	Nevland	Healy 1	Ford	Healy (10)	Gibson	Hilton	Ford	Ryan	
08-Feb	Preston North End	League	Away	1-0	2,478	Van der Gouw	S Rose	May	O'Shea	Ford	Wellens	Wilson	Notman	Fitzpatrick	Mulryne 1	Greening	Thorrington	Gibson	G Clegg	Stewart	Ryan (10)	
24-Feb	Nottingham Forest	League	Away	1-1		Van der Gouw	M Clegg 1	Curtis	May	O'Shea	Ford 1	Wilson	Healy	Stewart	Healy	Greening	Wilson (9)	Culkin	Ryan	G Clegg	Cosgrove	
10-Mar	Oldham Athletic	MSC	Away	3-2		Gibson	M Clegg	S Rose	Brown	Ford	Stewart	Mulryne	Stewart	Fitzpatrick	Greening 1	Greening	Culkin	Culkin	Notman (9)	Cosgrove		
15-Mar	Blackburn Rovers	League	Away	0-1		Culkin	M Clegg	Curtis	May	Brown	Ford	Mulryne	Wilson	Healy	Chadwick	Greening		Gibson	Hilton	Chadwick 1 (10)	Ford	
22-Mar	Stoke City	League	Away	1-3		Culkin	M Clegg	Roche	May 1	O'Shea	Ford	Wilson	Wilson	Healy	Sheringham	Chadwick			O'Shea (5)	Wellens (6)	Stewart	Roche
27-Mar	Everton	League	Home	3-0	15,646	Culkin	M Clegg	Curtis	O'Shea 1	Brown	Wellens	Mulryne	Fitzpatrick 2	Stewart	Sheringham	S Rose			Hilton	Cosgrove	Wellens (6)	
31-Mar	Bury	MSC	Home	4-1		Van der Gouw	M Clegg	Curtis	May 1	Brown	Wellens	Wilson 1	Fitzpatrick 1	Stewart	Greening	O'Shea 1 (5)			Hilton	Evans	Howard	
06-Apr	Manchester City	MSC	Away	5-1	3,457	Culkin	M Clegg	Curtis	May	O'Shea	Ford 1	Wilson 1	Healy 1	Stewart	Greening 1	Fitzpatrick		Marsh	Wheatcroft (9)	Wheatcroft	Hilton	
13-Apr	Leicester City	MSC	Away	0-2		Culkin	Ford	Curtis	O'Shea	Stewart	Wellens	Wellens	Healy	Healy	Stewart	Cosgrove		Marsh	Evans	Howard	Howard	
16-Apr	Bury	MSC	Home	2-4		Marsh	Strange	Gaff	Jones	Ford	Stewart	M Rose	Healy 1	Fitzpatrick	Wood 1	Chadwick		Hickson	Wheatcroft (9)	Walker	Lynch	
19-Apr	Manchester City°	MSC	Home	2-2		Culkin	M Studley	May	Curtis	Ford	Wellens	Wilson	Healy* 1	Greening 1	Stewart	O'Shea (5)		Rachubka	Whiteley (4)	Hickson	Strange (10)	
22-Apr	Liverpool	League	Home	0-1		Hoie	May	Brown	Brown	Ford	Wellens	Wilson	Healy	P Neville	Greening	Greening		Culkin	Fitzpatrick	Howard	G Clegg (6)	
28-Apr	Leeds United	League	Home	4-1		Van der Gouw	S Rose	G Clegg	O'Shea	Ford	Wellens	M Rose	Wilson 2	Thorrington	Chadwick 1	Greening		Culkin	Cosgrove	Howard	Howard	
03-May	Preston North End	League	Home	0-1		Culkin	M Clegg	Curtis	O'Shea	Ford	Wellens	Wilson	Healy 1	Fitzpatrick	Thorrington	Chadwick		Fitzpatrick	Wheatcroft	Cosgrove	Howard	
05-May	Oldham Athletic	MSC	Home	0-1		Culkin	G Clegg	S Rose	O'Shea	Ford	Wellens	Thorrington	Wilson 1	Healy 1	Fitzpatrick (9)	Chadwick		Chadwick	Thorrington (11)	Hilton	Cosgrove	
13-May	Oldham Athletic	MSC Fin	Away	3-0		Culkin	M Clegg	O'Shea	Brown	Ford	Wellens	Wilson 1	Thorrington	Wheatcroft	Fitzpatrick	S Rose		Marsh	Thorrington	Stewart	Fitzpatrick	G Clegg

°Own goals: Jaszczun
¹Lost 1-4 on penalties

Season 1998/99

RESERVES APPEARANCES AND GOALS 1998/99

Name	League Apps	Gls	MSC Apps	Gls	Youth Cup Apps	Gls	Season Total Apps	Gls
Kennedy Bakircioglu	1						1	0
Russell Best	(1)						0 (1)	0
Henning Berg	2						2	0
Jesper Blomqvist	3						3	0
Wes Brown	7		2				9	0
Nicky Butt	2						2	0
Chris Casper	2						2	0
Luke Chadwick	6 (2)	2	2 (1)	1	2	2	10 (3)	5
George Clegg	1 (1)		1		2		4 (1)	0
Michael Clegg	21	2	6	2			27	4
Andy Cole	1						1	0
Terry Cooke	6 (1)	1					6 (1)	1
Stephen Cosgrove					0 (1)		0 (1)	0
Jordi Cruyff	7	4					7	4
Nick Culkin	9		4				13	0
John Curtis	16		5				21	0
Wayne Evans					2		2	0
Ian Fitzpatrick	3 (1)	2	2	1	2		7 (1)	3
Ryan Ford	12 (1)		7	1			19 (1)	1
Gerard Gaff			1				1	0
Paul Gibson	3		1				4	0
Jonathan Greening	18 (1)	9	5	3			23 (1)	12
David Healy	8 (4)	2	5	4			13 (4)	6
Danny Higginbotham	3						3	0
Kirk Hilton					2		2	0
Kenneth Hoie	1						1	0
Josh Howard	(1)		(1)				0 (2)	0
Ronny Johnsen	1						1	0
Rhodri Jones			1				1	0
Mark Lynch					2		2	0
Allan Marsh			1				1	0
David May	15	1	3	1			18	2
Phil Mulryne	14	2					14	2
Phil Neville	3						3	0
Erik Nevland	7 (2)	2					7 (2)	2
Alex Notman	8 (1)	3					8 (1)	3
John O'Shea	11 (2)	1	4 (1)	1	2		17 (3)	2
Paul Rachubka					2		2	0
Lee Roche	3 (1)				2		5 (1)	0
Michael Rose			1				1	0
Stephen Rose	4 (1)		2		2		8 (1)	0
Michael Ryan	1 (1)						1 (1)	0
Teddy Sheringham	3	3	1	1			4	4
Ole Gunnar Solskjaer	1	2					1	2
Michael Stewart	4		5		2		11	0
Gareth Strange			1 (1)				1 (1)	0
Dominic Studley	1				0 (1)		1 (1)	0
Mark Studley			2				2	0
Paul Teather	6 (2)						6 (2)	0
John Thorrington	2 (2)		1				3 (2)	0
Raimond van der Gouw	11		1				12	0
Ronnie Wallwork	7 (1)						7 (1)	0
Danny Webber					0 (1)		0 (1)	0
Richie Wellens	10 (3)	1	6				16 (3)	1
Paul Wheatcroft	(1)		1		2		3 (1)	0
Lee Whiteley			(2)				0 (2)	0
Mark Wilson	20 (2)	9	5	3			25 (2)	12
Jamie Wood	(3)		1	1			1 (3)	2

YOUTH CUP GAMES 1998/99

Date	Opponents	Rnd	Venue	Res	Att	1	2	3	4	5	6	7	8	9	10	11	SUB	SUB	SUB
19-Dec	Everton	R 3	Home	2-2	271	Rachubka	Lynch	Hilton	Roche	O'Shea	G.Clegg	Evans	Stewart	Wheatcroft	Fitzpatrick	Chadwick	12 S Rose (2)	14 Studley (7)	16 Webber (10)
06-Jan	Everton	R 3 R	Away	0-4	1563	Rachubka	Lynch	Hilton	Roche	O'Shea	G.Clegg	Evans	Stewart	Wheatcroft	Fitzpatrick	Chadwick 2	14 Cosgrove (6)		

Season 1999/2000

MANCHESTER UNITED RESERVES 1999/00: FA PREMIER RESERVE LEAGUE (NORTH) AND MANCHESTER SENIOR CUP

Date	Opponents	Comp	Venue	Res	Att	1	2	3	4	5	6	7	8	9	10	11	12	13	14	15	16	17
18-Aug	Sheffield Wed	League	Home	3-1		Culkin	Clegg	Curtis	Roche	O'Shea	Stewart	Wellens	Greening 2	Notman	Chadwick	Howard	S Rose	Hilton (5)	Davis (8)			
25-Aug	Bury	MSC	Away	5-0		Rachubka	G Neville	Curtis	Roche	Twiss 2	Healy	Wilson	Greening 1	Notman 2	Chadwick	S Rose (2)	Rachubka	Hilton (3)	Howard (6)			
07-Sep	Leeds United	League	Away	1-2		Culkin	Clegg	Hilton	Wallwork	Roche	Ford	Wilson	Fortune	Notman 1	Twiss	Fitzpatrick (6)	Rachubka	Ford (7)	O'Shea	Stewart		
15-Sep	Liverpool	League	Away	0-0		Bosnich	Roche	Wallwork	O'Shea	Healy	Cruyff	Butt	Greening	Notman	Chadwick	Nevland (10)	Culkin	Hilton (3)				
23-Sep	Aston Villa	League	Home	2-3		Culkin	Roche	Curtis	Wallwork	O'Shea	Healy 1	Wellens	Greening 1	Notman	Chadwick	Notman (9)	Ford	Nevland (10)				
30-Sep	Sunderland	League	Home	1-1		Rachubka	Clegg	Higginbotham	Curtis	Wallwork	Cruyff	Greening	Fortune	Chadwick	Roche	Twiss	O'Shea	Twiss (6)				
21-Oct	Bolton Wanderers	League	Away	2-0		Culkin	Clegg	Higginbotham	May	G Neville	Fortune	Wilson	Greening*	Notman 1	Chadwick 1	Notman (9)	Curtis					
28-Oct	Manchester City*	MSC	Home	1-1		Culkin	G Neville*	Higginbotham	Curtis	Wilson 1	Wilson*1	Greening*	Notman 1	Chadwick	Curtis	Healy (6)						
09-Nov	Newcastle United	League	Away	0-2		Taibi	Higginbotham	O'Shea	Roche	Wilson	Greening	Healy	Twiss	Chadwick	Clegg	S Rose	O'Shea					
13-Nov	Everton	League	Home	4-2		Culkin	Clegg	Higginbotham	O'Shea	Cruyff	Fortune	Wilson	Healy 3	Notman	Healy	Twiss	Culkin	Roche	Webber			
16-Nov	Blackburn Rovers	League	Home	1-1		Clegg	Higginbotham	Curtis	O'Shea	Wilson	Sheringham	Fortune 1	Greening 1	Notman	Twiss (10)	Marsh	Cosgrove	Stewart				
25-Nov	Bradford City	League	Away	3-1		Taibi	Higginbotham	Roche	Wallwork	Wilson	Healy 1	Notman 1	Fortune 1	Twiss	Twiss	Culkin	Roche	Ford	Wellens			
01-Dec	Barnsley	League	Home	3-1		Van der Gouw	Clegg	S Rose	O'Shea	Stewart	Chadwick	Wilson	Healy 1	Notman 1	Twiss	Nevland (9)	Culkin	Webber (7)	Ford (6)	S Rose		
17-Jan	Middlesbrough°	League	Home	1-2		Van der Gouw	Clegg	Higginbotham	Roche	Ford	Wellens	Fletcher	Healy	Notman 1	Twiss	Wheatcroft	Rachubka	Stewart (7)	S Rose	D Studley (10)		
25-Jan	Everton	League	Away	1-2		Rachubka	Clegg	Higginbotham	Roche	Berg	Cruyff	Wilson	Fitzpatrick 1	Healy	Soskjaer 1	Djordjic	Rachubka	Healy (9)	Stewart (8)	Wellens	Roche	
03-Feb	Newcastle United	League	Home	3-0		Van der Gouw	Clegg	Higginbotham	Wallwork	Fletcher	Wilson	Healy 2	Greening	Soskjaer 1	Scholes	Stewart (6)	S Rose	Webber (12)	Cosgrove			
08-Feb	Manchester City	MSC	Away	3-1	3,447	Van der Gouw	Clegg	Higginbotham	Roche	Webber	Wilson	Healy	Greening	Djordjic 1	Twiss 1	Cosgrove (7)	Rachubka	S Rose	Fletcher 1 (6)			
16-Feb	Blackburn Rovers	League	Away	1-2		Culkin	Roche	Higginbotham	Berg	P Neville	Stewart	Wilson	Greening	Cruyff	Nevland (9)	Djordjic	Rachubka	Howard	Davis (9)			
23-Feb	Bradford City	League	Home	5-1	5,100	Rachubka	Lynch	Higginbotham 1	Wallwork	Stewart	Wilson 1	Fortune 2	Fitzpatrick 1	Greening 1	Djordjic	Teather (8)	Culkin	Howard	Fitzpatrick (11)	Wheatcroft (7)		
28-Feb	Bury	League	Home	4-0		Van der Gouw	Lynch	Higginbotham	Wallwork	Teather	Stewart	Davis 1	Greening 2	Healy	Djordjic 1	Howard (5)	Rachubka	Evans	M Studley (3)			
02-Mar	Barnsley	MSC	Away	1-2		Culkin	Lynch	Higginbotham	Berg	Teather	Stewart	Wilson	Davis	Greening 1	Fortune	Rachubka	Rachubka	M Studley (7)				
23-Mar	Oldham Athletic	MSC	Away	2-1		Culkin	Higginbotham	Johnsen	Teather	Stewart	Wilson	Greening	Soskjaer	Stewart	O'Shea (5)	Notman 1 (10)	Cosgrove (7)					
27-Mar	Sunderland	League	Away	1-2	25,787	Culkin	Roche	Higginbotham	Wallwork	Wallwork 1	Johnsen	Evans	Wilson 1	Greening	Davis	Teather (7)	Rachubka	Cosgrove	S Rose	D Studley		
30-Mar	Sheffield Wed	League	Away	5-2		Culkin	Clegg	Roche	Wallwork	Wallwork	Teather	Stewart	Evans	Greening 1	Notman 4	D Studley (6)	Rachubka	Cosgrove	S Rose (2)	Davis		
03-Apr	Aston Villa°	League	Away	2-1		Culkin	Lynch	Higginbotham	Johnsen	Johnsen	Teather	Stewart	Evans	Greening	Notman 1	D Studley	Rachubka	Howard	Howard	Sampson (11)		
05-Apr	Oldham Athletic	MSC	Home	0-2		Rachubka	Tiemey	McDermott	Tate	Stewart	Howard	D Studley	Murhead	Molloy	M Rose	Davis (7)	Pugh (8)	S Clegg	Howard			
12-Apr	Bolton Wanderers	League	Home	4-0		Van der Gouw	Higginbotham	Roche	Wallwork	Johnsen	Stewart	Evans	Greening 3	Notman	Twiss	D Studley	Culkin	Howard	O'Shea			
17-Apr	Liverpool	League	Home	0-2		Culkin	Higginbotham	Roche	Wallwork	Johnsen	Stewart	Evans	Greening	Notman	Twiss	Wheatcroft	Rachubka	S Rose	Cosgrove (11)	Howard (7)		
26-Apr	Middlesbrough	League	Away	0-2		Culkin	Higginbotham	Roche	S Rose	O'Shea	Stewart	Evans	Greening	Fortune	Twiss	Cosgrove (9)	Rachubka	Evans	Tierney (7)	Coates (10)		
02-May	Oldham Athletic°	MSC Fin	Away	2-0		Culkin	Higginbotham	Roche	O'Shea	Stewart	Wilson 1	Greening	Notman	Djordjic	Twiss	Rachubka	Evans	Cosgrove	Davis (7)			
04-May	Leeds United	League	Home	2-0		Culkin	Higginbotham	Wallwork	O'Shea	Stewart	Wilson	Greening 1	Notman	Djordjic	Fletcher (9)	Rachubka	Evans	Cosgrove (8)				

° Own goals: Cooper v Middlesbrough (home), Bowers v Aston Villa (away), Smith v Oldham Athletic (MSC Final away)
* Won 5-4 on penalties

Season 1999/2000

RESERVES APPEARANCES AND GOALS 1999/2000

Name	League Apps	League Gls	MSC Apps	MSC Gls	Youth Cup Apps	Youth Cup Gls	Season Total Apps	Season Total Gls
Henning Berg	3						3	0
Mark Bosnich	1						1	0
Nicky Butt	1						1	0
Luke Chadwick	7	2	2				9	2
Michael Clegg	12		1				13	0
Craig Coates	(1)						0 (1)	0
Steven Cosgrove	(3)		(2)				0 (5)	0
Jordi Cruyff	6		1				7	0
Nick Culkin	13		3				16	0
John Curtis	6		1				7	0
Jimmy Davis	4 (2)	2	1 (2)		1		5 (4)	2
Bojan Djordjic	4		2	1			6	1
Wayne Evans	7		1				8	0
Ian Fitzpatrick	(2)		1 (1)	1			1 (3)	1
Darren Fletcher	3 (1)		1 (1)	1			4 (2)	1
Ryan Ford	2 (2)						2 (2)	0
Quinton Fortune	9	3					9	3
Jonathan Greening	19	12	6	4			25	16
David Healy	11 (2)	8	2				13 (2)	8
Danny Higginbotham	19	1	5				24	1
Kirk Hilton	1 (2)		1				2 (2)	0
Josh Howard	(1)		1 (3)				1 (4)	0
Ronny Johnsen	3		1				4	0
Mark Lynch	3		1		1		5	0
Alan McDermott			1				1	0
David May	1		1				2	0
Eric Molloy			1				1	0
Ben Muirhead			1				1	0
Daniel Nardiello					0 (1)		0 (1)	0
Gary Neville	1		2		1		4	0
Phil Neville	2						2	0
Erik Nevland	(4)						0 (4)	0
Alex Notman	13 (3)	9	3 (1)	3			16 (4)	12
John O'Shea	9		2 (1)				11 (1)	0
Danny Pugh			(1)				0 (1)	0
Paul Rachubka	2		2				4	0
Lee Roche	16		5				21	0
Michael Rose			1		1		2	0
Steven Rose	2 (1)		(1)				2 (2)	0
Gary Sampson	(1)		(1)				0 (2)	0
Paul Scholes	1						1	0
Teddy Sheringham	1						1	0
Ole Gunnar Solskjaer	1	1	1				2	1
Michael Stewart	12 (3)		3				15 (3)	0
Gareth Strange					1		1	0
Dominic Studley	(2)		1		1		0	0
Mark Studley	(1)		(1)				0 (2)	0
Massimo Taibi	2		1				3	0
Alan Tate			1				1	0
Paul Teather	2 (2)		2				4 (2)	0
Paul Tierney	(1)		1				0	0
Michael Twiss	13 (3)	2	2 (1)	2			15 (4)	4
Raimond van der Gouw	6		1				7	0
Josh Walker			1				1	0
Ronnie Wallwork	17		4	1	1		22	1
Ben Williams					1		1	0
Danny Webber	(2)		1		1	1	0	1
Richie Wellens	9		2	1			11	1
Paul Wheatcroft	(1)		(1)				0 (2)	0
Mark Wilson	20	4	6	2			26	6
Neil Wood					1		1	0

YOUTH CUP GAMES 1999/00

Date	Opponents	Rnd	Venue	Res	Att	1	2	3	4	5	6	7	8	9	10	11	SUB
02-Dec	Nottingham Forest	R 3	Home	1-2	210	B. Williams	Lynch	Studley	Strange	Szmid	Walker	Muirhead	M.Rose	Webber	Davis	Wood	Nardiello (6)

Season 2000/01

MANCHESTER UNITED RESERVES 2000/01: FA PREMIER RESERVE LEAGUE (NORTH) AND MANCHESTER SENIOR CUP

Date	Opponents	Comp	Venue	Res	Att	1	2	3	4	5	6	7	8	9	10	11	12	13	14	15	16	17
24-Aug	Bradford City	League	Home	3-2		Bostnich	Lynch	Studley	Tate	Stewart	Davis	Greening	Healy	Norman 2	Djordjic 1	Evans	Rachubka	Cosgrove	Webber (8)	G Clegg		
07-Sep	Sunderland	League	Away	0-4		Rachubka	M Clegg	Studley	O'Shea	Stewart	G Clegg	Davis	Healy	Norman	Djordjic	Webber (7)	B Williams	Lynch (4)	Cosgrove (9)	Szmid		
14-Sep	Blackburn Rovers	League	Home	0-0		Van der Gouw	M Clegg	Studley	Wallwork	Stewart	Stewart	Greening	Webber	Norman	Djordjic	Pugh	Rachubka	Cosgrove (6)	Lynch	Szmid		
21-Sep	Aston Villa	League	Away	1-0		Rachubka	Lynch	Studley	O'Shea	Stewart 1	Davis	Greening	Healy	Norman	Djordjic	Webber (7)	B Williams	Walker (9)	Tate	Pugh		
28-Sep	Bury	MSC	Home	8-1		Rachubka	M Clegg	Studley 1	M Clegg 1	Stewart 2	Webber 1	Fortune	Healy 1	Norman 1	Davis 1 (9)	Djordjic			Lynch	Cosgrove	Evans (10)	Szmid (8)
02-Oct	Liverpool	League	Away	2-4	5,236	Rachubka	M Clegg	Studley	O'Shea	Wallwork	Stewart	Fortune	Soskjaer 1	Yorke	Djordjic	Webber (9)			Lynch	Cosgrove	Szmid	Evans
12-Oct	Oldham Athletic*	MSC	Home	2-2		Rachubka	Lynch	Tate	Jones	Wallwork	Evans*	Cosgrove*	Webber*1	G Clegg*1	Norman	Walker	Rachubka	B Williams	Dodd	Rose	Whiteman	
19-Oct	Sheffield Wed	League	Home	1-0		Bostnich	M Clegg	May	O'Shea	Jones	Wallwork	Greening 1	Wallwork	Healy	Djordjic	Webber			Davis (8)	Lynch (4)		
26-Oct	Manchester City	MSC	Home	5-1		Rachubka	M Clegg	May	O'Shea	Stewart	O'Shea	Fortune	Greening	Norman 2	Chadwick	Lynch	Rachubka	Jowsey	G Clegg	Djordjic 1 (8)		
15-Nov	Middlesbrough	League	Away	3-4		Rachubka	M Clegg	May	Wallwork	Stewart	Chadwick	Greening 1	Healy 1	Norman 2	Djordjic	Webber (3)			Evans	G Clegg		Evans
23-Nov	Newcastle United	League	Home	4-0		Van der Gouw	M Clegg	Studley	O'Shea	Wallwork 1	Stewart 1	Chadwick	Greening 1	Healy	Djordjic	Webber	Rachubka	Jowsey	Lynch (4)	G Clegg		
29-Nov	Bury	MSC	Away	3-2		Van der Gouw	M Clegg	McDermott	May	Stewart	Cosgrove	Evans	Wilson	Healy 2	Davis 1	Szmid (10)			Rachubka	Rose	Strange	Walker
05-Dec	Manchester City	League	Away	1-2	2,016	Rachubka	M Clegg	Studley	May	Madou-Kah	Szmid	Chadwick	Webber	Davis	Djordjic 1	G Clegg			Cosgrove (3)	Jones	Lynch (4)	Wood (8)
16-Jan	Bradford City	League	Away	3-2		Bostnich	M Clegg	Studley	May	Wallwork	Cosgrove	Chadwick	Wilson 2	Stewart 1	Djordjic	Evans	B Williams		Lynch (3)	Rose		
25-Jan	Sunderland	League	Home	540		Rachubka	M Clegg	Pugh	May	Wallwork	Cosgrove	Chadwick	Greening	Greening	Djordjic	Wood (6)			Evans	G Clegg		Jones
01-Feb	Leeds United	League	Home	3-0		Van der Gouw	M Clegg	Pugh	May	Wallwork	Cosgrove	Greening	G Clegg 2	Stewart	Djordjic	Rose (10)	Rachubka		Lynch (7)	Dodd	Jones (5)	
15-Feb	Aston Villa	League	Home	4-2		Rachubka	M Clegg	Studley	May	Jones	Stewart	Chadwick 1	Wilson 1	Yorke 2	Djordjic	Lynch			G Clegg	Webber (9)	Rose	
22-Feb	Blackburn Rovers	League	Away	0-2	2,360	Rachubka	P Neville	May	May	Wallwork	Greening	Wilson	Webber	Greening 1	Yorke	Szmid (10)			Cosgrove (3)	Dodd		
08-Mar	Sheffield Wed	League	Away	3-1		Rachubka	M Clegg	Pugh	May	Wallwork	Chadwick 1	Wilson	Fortune 1	Greening 1	Djordjic	Webber (9)			Cosgrove	Tate (4)	Lynch (7)	
20-Mar	Leeds United	League	Away	0-2	4,190	B Williams	M Clegg	May	Lynch	Cosgrove	Muirhead	Wallwork	Webber	Fortune	Djordjic	Pugh***	Moran		Tate	M Williams	Sampson	
27-Mar	Manchester City*	MSC	Away	1-1		Rachubka	M Clegg*	Studley	May	Wallwork**	Stewart	Muirhead**	M Williams**1	Nardiello**(10)	Pugh (11)			B Williams	Tate (4)	Sampson (6)	Tierney	
29-Mar	Everton	League	Home	2-3		Rachubka	M Clegg	May	Tate 1	Wallwork	Muirhead**	Djordjic	M Williams	Fortune	Djordjic	Davis (7)	B Williams (1)	Rachubka	Nardiello (9)	Nardiello (5)	Cosgrove	
09-Apr	Newcastle United*	League	Away	1-2		Rachubka	Van der Gouw	Tierney	Lynch	Johnsen	Wilson	Wilson	M Williams	Webber	Djordjic	Fortune	B Williams	Rachubka	Tate	Sampson		
19-Apr	Everton	League	Away	3-0		Van der Gouw	Lynch	May	Johnsen	Wallwork	Davis 1	Wilson	Webber 1	Stewart 1	Djordjic (11)		B Williams	Tate	Cosgrove			
23-Apr	Oldham Athletic	MSC	Away	2-0		Rachubka	Lynch	Tierney	May	Jones	Cosgrove	Muirhead	Wilson 1	Webber 1	Rose	Fortune	B Williams	Sampson	Strange	Heath		
26-Apr	Manchester City	League	Home	2-1	Goram	M Clegg	Tierney	Tate	Wallwork	Muirhead	Wilson 1	Webber 1	Nardiello	Studley	Rachubka	Lynch (7)	M Williams					
30-Apr	Middlesbrough	League	Home	0-3		Rachubka	M Clegg	May	Tate	Davis	Greening	Wilson	Webber	Nardiello	Djordjic	Studley	B Williams	Cosgrove	Lynch (7)	M Williams (10)	Rose (6)	
07-May	Liverpool	League	Home	2-2		Rachubka	M Clegg	Tierney	May	Wallwork	Sampson	Wilson	Webber	Nardiello	Djordjic	Lynch (10)	B Williams	Nardiello (9)	Cosgrove	Muirhead (7)		
11-May	Manchester City	MSC Fin	Home	1-4	3,132	Rachubka	Lynch	Studley	Tate	Sampson	Muirhead	Cosgrove	Wilson	Webber 1	Nardiello (7)		B Williams	Nardiello	G Clegg	Strange	Szmid	

*Own goal: Caldwell
*Won 4-2 on penalties
**Won 6-5 on penalties

Season 2000/01

RESERVES APPEARANCES AND GOALS 2000/01

Name	League Apps	League Gls	MSC Apps	MSC Gls	Youth Cup Apps	Youth Cup Gls	Season Total Apps	Season Total Gls
Neil Baxter					0 (1)		0 (1)	0
Mark Bosnich	3						3	0
Wes Brown	1						1	0
Luke Chadwick	7	3	1				8	3
George Clegg	3 (1)	2	1 (1)	1			4 (2)	3
Michael Clegg	21		3				24	0
Steven Clegg					3		3	0
Steven Cosgrove	4 (5)		4				8 (5)	0
Jimmy Davis	8 (2)	2	2 (1)	2			10 (3)	4
Bojan Djordjic	20 (1)	3	5 (1)	1			25 (2)	4
Wayne Evans			2 (1)				2 (1)	0
Quinton Fortune	6	2	3				9	2
David Fox					0 (1)		0 (1)	0
Andy Goram	1						1	0
Jonathan Greening	11	3	1				12	3
David Healy	6	2	3	5			9	7
Colin Heath					0 (1)		0 (1)	0
Chris Humphreys					0 (1)		0 (1)	0
Ronny Johnsen	2						2	0
Rhodri Jones	1 (1)		3				4 (1)	0
Mark Lynch	5 (9)		4				9 (9)	0
Alan McDermott			1				1	0
Pa Madou-Kah	1						1	0
David May	15		2				17	0
David Moran					2		2	0
Ben Muirhead	4 (1)		3		3		10 (1)	0
Daniel Nardiello	2 (3)		1 (2)	1	2	5	5 (5)	6
Phil Neville	1						1	0
Alex Notman	8	5	2	3			10	8
John O'Shea	6		2	1			8	1
Danny Pugh	4 (2)		2		2		8 (2)	0
Paul Rachubka	12		7				19	0
John Rankin					3	1	3	1
Michael Rose	(2)		1				1 (2)	0
Gary Sampson	1		1 (1)		3		5 (1)	0
Ole Gunnar Solskjaer	1	1					1	1
Michael Stewart	16	3	4	2			20	5
Mark Studley	12		5				17	0
Marek Szmid	1		1 (2)				2 (2)	0
Alan Tate	5 (1)	1	3 (1)		3		11 (2)	1
Andy Taylor					0 (1)		0 (1)	0
Kris Taylor					1		1	0
Paul Tierney	6		2		3		11	0
Raimond van der Gouw	4						4	0
Josh Walker	(1)						0 (1)	0
Ronnie Wallwork	16		3	1			19	2
Danny Webber	9 (7)	2	4	4			13 (7)	6
Marc Whiteman					0 (1)		0 (1)	0
Ben Williams	2 (1)						2 (1)	0
Matty Williams	1 (1)		1	1	3	3	5 (1)	4
Mark Wilson	13	6					13	6
Neil Wood	(2)				3	1	3 (2)	1
Dwight Yorke	3	2					3	2

YOUTH CUP GAMES 2000/01

Date	Opponents	Rnd	Venue	Res	Att	1	2	3	4	5	6	7	8	9	10	11	SUB	SUB	SUB	SUB
29-Nov	Reading	R3	Away	1-0	8894	Jowsey	S.Clegg	K. Taylor	Sampson	Tate	Tierney	Muirhead	M. Williams	Nardiello 1	Wood	Rankin	12 A. Taylor (11)	13 Baxter (1)	14 Whiteman (12)	
22-Jan	Scunthorpe[9]	R4	Home	8-0	2357	Moran	S.Clegg	Pugh	Sampson	Tate	Tierney	Muirhead	M. Williams	Nardiello 4	Wood 1	Rankin 1	12 Coates (8)	15 Fox (4)	16 Humphreys (9)	
14-Feb	Nottingham Forest	R5	Home	1-2	3008	Moran	S.Clegg	Pugh	Sampson	Tate	Tierney	Muirhead	Coates	M.Williams 1	Wood	Rankin	16 Heath (8)			

[9]Own goal: Butler

237

Season 2001/02

MANCHESTER UNITED RESERVES 2001/02: FA PREMIER RESERVE LEAGUE (NORTH) AND MANCHESTER SENIOR CUP

Date	Opponents	Comp	Venue	Res	Att	1	2	3	4	5	6	7	8	9	10	11	12	13	14	15	16
29-Aug	Middlesbrough	League	Away	2-2		Culkin	Roche	Tierney	Wallwork	May	Yorke	Lynch 1	Stewart	Webber	Davis	Fortune 1	Tate	B Williams	Sampson	Nardiello (3)	Muirhead
03-Sep	Manchester City	MSC	Away	0-5	2,035	B Williams	M Clegg	McDermott	Tate		Lynch	Sampson	Davis	Nardiello	Blomqvist	Tierney (3)	Moran	K Taylor	Heath (4)	Richardson (11)	
06-Sep	Sunderland	League	Home	3-0		Van der Gouw	Roche	Tierney	May	Wallwork	Butt	Webber	Yorke 3	Fortune	Lynch (11)	Nardiello (10)	Roche	Davis	Nardiello (10)	Davis (8)	
13-Sep	Liverpool	League	Home	3-2		Carroll	M Clegg	Irwin	May	Wallwork 1	Chadwick	Butt	Solskjaer 1	Webber	Yorke (3)	Fortune	Roche (4)	Culkin	Webber	Djordjic (8)	
18-Oct	Bradford City	League	Away	7-2		Van der Gouw	Lynch	O'Shea 1	May 1	Wallwork	Chadwick	Stewart 1	Fortune 2	Webber 1	Blomqvist	Webber 1 (3)	B Williams	Culkin	Roche	Tate	
25-Oct	Aston Villa	League	Home	1-0		Van der Gouw	Roche	M Clegg	P Neville	Wallwork	Fortune	Butt	Webber 1	P Neville	Davis (7)	B Williams	Djordjic (5)	Djordjic	Tate	Fox (8)	
01-Nov	Sheffield Wed°	League	Home	5-1		Van der Gouw	Roche	Tierney	M Clegg	Tate	Stewart	Wood	Webber 2	Davis 2	Djordjic	B Williams	Davis (7)	Nardiello (9)	Timm (7)	K Taylor	
13-Nov	Everton	League	Away	3-1		Rachubka	Roche	Tierney	M Clegg	Wallwork	Davis	Stewart	Nardiello 1	Fletcher	Djordjic 1	B Williams	Wood 1 (8)	Fox (6)	Heath	Muirhead (7)	
22-Nov	Manchester City	League	Home	1-1		Carroll	Roche	O'Shea	M Clegg	Yorke	Chadwick	Stewart	Webber	Nardiello 1	Solskjaer	B Williams	Davis	Nardiello (6)	Timm (7)	K Taylor	
06-Dec	Blackburn Rovers	League	Away	3-1		Carroll	Roche	Tate	O'Shea	Wallwork	Muirhead 1	Stewart	Webber 1	Nardiello	Davis 1	B Williams	Pugh (6)	Nardiello (10)	Tate	Sampson (6)	
20-Dec	Bolton Wanderers	League	Home	2-4		Van der Gouw	Roche	Tierney	Wallwork	Wood	Chadwick 2	Stewart	Cole	Fortune	Yorke	B Williams	Tate (2)	Nardiello (6)	Pugh (10)	M Williams (9)	
17-Jan	Middlesbrough	League	Home	1-0		Carroll	Roche	Irwin	Tierney	Wallwork	Davis 1	Pugh	Webber	Nardiello	Djordjic	Tate (2)	S Clegg	B Williams	Rankin (3)	Muirhead	
21-Jan	Sunderland	League	Away	0-0		Carroll	Roche	Pugh	M Clegg	Tierney	Rankin	Stewart	Webber	Nardiello	Djordjic 1	Fortune	Muirhead (9)	B Williams	Sampson	Rankin (3)	M Williams
24-Jan	Oldham Athletic	League	Home	4-1		Carroll	Roche	Pugh	M Clegg	Brown	Chadwick	Davis 1	Stewart 1	Webber 1 (3)	Nardiello	S Clegg	Muirhead (10)	M Williams	Nardiello	Muirhead (7)	McDermott (5)
31-Jan	Manchester City*	MSC	Home	1-1	737	Carroll	Brown	Irwin*	O'Shea	M Clegg	Wallwork	Davis*	Webber 1	Fortan	Djordjic*	McDermott	B Williams	Baxter	Pugh	Rankin (3)	Rankin
13-Feb	Bolton Wanderers	League	Away	3-0		B Williams	Roche	O'Shea	Johnsen	Wallwork 1	Davis 1	Stewart	Fortan 1	Yorke	Fortune	Muirhead (10)	B Williams	M Clegg	Tierney	Nardiello (3)	
21-Feb	Aston Villa	League	Away	0-1		Van der Gouw	Pugh	Wallwork	O'Shea	Fox	Stewart	Webber	Nardiello	Djordjic	McDermott (4)	B Williams	Rankin	M Williams (10)			
28-Feb	Bradford City	League	Home	1-1		Carroll	Roche	Pugh	Wallwork	Fortune	Davis	Webber	Nardiello	Djordjic 1	Webber (9)	McDermott (4)	B Williams	M Williams (6)	McDermott (2)		
04-Mar	Newcastle United	League	Away	2-5		Rachubka	Pugh	O'Shea	Tierney	Fortune 1	Davis	Webber 1	Yorke	Davis*	McDermott	B Williams	Fox (6)	M Williams (7)	Fox (6)	Muirhead (10)	
07-Mar	Bury°**	Home	1-1	229	Carroll	Pugh	O'Shea	Tierney	Muirhead	Davis**	Yorke	Djordjic	McDermott	B Williams	Nardiello (10)	Jowsey	Nardiello***(7)	Fox			
11-Mar	Oldham Athletic	MSC	Away	1-2		Steele	Pugh	McDermott	Fox	Stewart	Webber	M Williams	Davis 1	Djordjic 1	K Taylor	B Williams	Jowsey	M Clegg	Tierney	Nardiello (3)	
14-Mar	Blackburn Rovers	League	Home	1-2		Steele	P Neville	Tierney	Tierney	Fortune	Butt	Nardiello	M Williams	Fortune	Djordjic	K Taylor	B Williams	Rankin	Sampson (8)	Fox (10)	M Williams (10)
20-Mar	Liverpool	League	Away	1-1		Carroll	Irwin	Pugh 1	O'Shea	Brown	Muirhead	Davis	Webber 1	Nardiello	Fortune	McDermott	B Williams	M Williams (7)	Sampson	Fox (10)	McDermott (7)
26-Mar	Sheffield Wed	League	Away	2-0		Rachubka	Brown	Pugh 1	Tierney	May 1	Fox	Davis	Stewart	Webber	Nardiello	Rankin	B Williams	M Williams (6)	Muirhead (7)	Tierney (5)	Muirhead (7)
04-Apr	Newcastle United	League	Home	0-0		Carroll	Brown	Pugh	Tierney	May	Stewart	Davis	Stewart	Webber	Nardiello	Richardson	B Williams	Tate (9)	Wood	Muirhead (7)	Rankin
09-Apr	Manchester City	League	Away	1-1		Van der Gouw	Roche	Pugh	May	Wallwork	Wood	Richardson 1	M Williams	Webber 1 (3)	Davis 2	Djordjic	B Williams	Sims (4)	Wood	Fox (7)	
15-Apr	Bury	MSC	Home	1-0		B Williams	S Clegg	Rankin	Tate	Cogger	Sampson	Moonaruck	Humphreys	Fortan	Richardson	K Taylor	B Williams	Poole (9)	Jowsey	Johnson (7)	
18-Apr	Everton	League	Home	2-1		Williams	Roche	Rankin	May	May	Wallwork	Chadwick	Djordjic	Muirhead 1	Richardson	Tate	B Williams	Tate (9)	Moran	Muirhead	
25-Apr	Leeds United	League	Away	2-0	2,954	Van der Gouw	Roche	Rankin	Tierney	May	Wallwork 1	Chadwick 1	Djordjic	Nardiello	Davis 1	Richardson	B Williams	M Williams (7)	Wood (7)	M Williams (11)	Muirhead
06-May	Leeds United	League	Home	1-2		Rachubka	S Clegg	Rankin	Roche	May	Wallwork	Lynch	Stewart	Muirhead 1	Nardiello	Djordjic	M Williams	B Williams (11)	Tate (2)	Wood	Fox (7)

° Own goals: Rand v Sheffield Wednesday (home); Thompson v Bury (MSC home)
* Lost 3-4 on penalties
** Lost 2-3 on penalties

Season 2001/02

RESERVES APPEARANCES AND GOALS 2001/02

Name	League Apps	League Gls	MSC Apps	MSC Gls	Youth Cup Apps	Youth Cup Gls	Season Total Apps	Season Total Gls
Phil Bardsley					4		4	0
Danny Byrne			1				1	0
Jesper Blomqvist	1		1				2	0
Wes Brown	3		2				5	0
Nicky Butt	3						3	0
Roy Carroll	8		2				10	0
Luke Chadwick	7	3	1				8	3
Michael Clegg	10		3				13	0
Steven Clegg	1		1				2	0
John Cogger			1 (1)		1 (2)		2 (3)	0
Ben Collett					0 (2)		0 (2)	0
Andy Cole	1						1	0
Nick Culkin	1						1	0
Jimmy Davis	15 (3)	6	4	1			19 (3)	7
Bojan Djordjic	16 (2)	1	4	1			20 (2)	2
Darren Fletcher	1				4		5	0
Diego Forlan	2	2	1				3	2
Quinton Fortune	13	4					13	4
David Fox	1 (6)		1		4		6 (6)	0
Colin Heath			1 (2)		4	6	5 (2)	6
Chris Humphreys			1		4	2	5	2
Denis Irwin	4		1				5	0
Ronny Johnsen	1						1	0
Eddie Johnson			(1)		0 (1)	1	0 (2)	1
James Jowsey					4		4	0
Lee Lawrence					4		4	0
Mark Lynch	3 (1)	1	1				4 (1)	1
Alan McDermott	(3)		2 (1)				2 (4)	0
David May	11	2					11	2
Kalam Mooniaruck			1		2 (2)		3 (2)	0
Ben Muirhead	3 (6)	2	3	1			6 (6)	3
Daniel Nardiello	12 (7)	2	2 (2)	1			14 (9)	3
Phil Neville	3						3	0
John O'Shea	10	1	3				13	1
David Poole			(1)		0 (1)		0 (2)	0
Danny Pugh	10 (2)	2	2				12 (2)	2
Paul Rachubka	4						4	0
John Rankin	5 (2)		3				8 (2)	0
Kieran Richardson	4 (1)	1	1 (1)		4	1	9 (2)	2
Lee Roche	16 (2)		2 (1)				18 (3)	0
Gary Sampson	(2)		2				2 (2)	0
Lee Sims	(1)				4		4 (1)	0
Ole Gunnar Solskjaer	2	1					2	1
Michael Stewart	18	2	4	1			22	3
Luke Steele	1		1				2	0
Alan Tate	3 (4)		2				5 (4)	0
Kris Taylor					3		3	0
Paul Tierney	18 (1)		2 (1)				20 (2)	0
Mads Timm	1 (1)	1			1 (1)	1	2 (2)	2
Raimond van der Gouw	7						7	0
Ronnie Wallwork	17	3	3				20	3
Danny Webber	13 (3)	8	3	2			16 (3)	10
Ben Williams	3		3				6	0
Matty Williams	2 (8)		1				3 (8)	0
Neil Wood	2 (3)	1					2 (3)	1
Dwight Yorke	8	3	1				9	3

YOUTH CUP GAMES 2001/02

Date	Opponents	Rnd	Venue	Res	Att	1	2	3	4	5	6	7	8	9	10	11	SUB	SUB	SUB
04-Dec	QPR	R 3	Away	3-1	2330	Jowsey	Sims	Lawrence	Fox	Cogger	Bardsley	Timm 1	Humphreys	Heath 2	Fletcher	Richardson	12 Mooniaruck (7)	14 Johnson (8)	15 Collett (11)
23-Jan	Birmingham	R 4	Away	3-2	1789	Jowsey	Sims	Lawrence	Fox	Bardsley	K.Taylor	Mooniaruck	Fletcher	Heath 1	Humphreys	Richardson	16 Timm (7)	15 Collett (3)	16 Poole (10)
06-Feb	Hartlepool United♦	R 5	Home	3-2	3732	Jowsey	Sims	Lawrence	Fox	Bardsley	K.Taylor	Mooniaruck	Fletcher	Heath 1	Humphreys 2	Richardson 1	12 Cogger (2)	14 Mooniaruck (7)	15 Johnson 1 (10)
01-Mar	Barnsley†	R 6	Home	3-3	3538	Jowsey	Sims	Lawrence	Fox	Bardsley	K.Taylor	Byrne	Fletcher	Heath 2	Humphreys	Richardson	12 Cogger (2)		

♦After extra time
†Lost 1-3 after penalties

Season 2002/03

MANCHESTER UNITED RESERVES 2002/03 (FA PREMIER RESERVE LEAGUE: NORTH) AND MANCHESTER SENIOR CUP

Date	Opponents	Comp	Venue	Res	Att	1	2	3	4	5	6	7	8	9	10	11	12	13	14	15	16
21-Aug	West Brom	League	Home	1-0		Steele	Roche	Hilton	Tate	May	Pugh	Chadwick	Fletcher	M Williams	Djordjic	Muirhead	Heaton	Rankin (8)	Lynch (3)	Bardsley (6)
04-Sep	Everton	League	Away	0-1		Ricardo	G Neville	Pugh	Roche	May	Rankin	Chadwick	Lynch	Nardiello	Richardson	Tate	B Williams	Eagles (11)	Muirhead (6)	Jones
19-Sep	Liverpool	League	Away	1-1	4,352	Carroll	G Neville	Tierney	Tate	May	Fletcher	Chadwick	Stewart	Nardiello 1	Pugh	M Williams (9)	B Williams	Lynch (11)	Richardson (2)	Roche
26-Sep	Bradford City	League	Home	2-0		Ricardo	Lynch	Tierney	May	Taylor	Fletcher	Chadwick	Stewart 1	Fortan	Pugh	Moonianuck (4)	B Williams	Collett (5)	Humphreys 1 (6)	
04-Oct	Manchester City	MSC	Home	1-0	1,246	Carroll	Roche	Tate	Roche	May	Tate	Chadwick	Stewart	Nardiello	Fortune	Lynch	B Williams	Heath (10)	Pugh (11)	Tierney
08-Oct	Blackburn Rovers	League	Away	5-0	2,420	Ricardo	Roche	Tierney	Tate	May	P Neville	Chadwick	Richardson 1	Muirhead 1	Fortune	Nardiello (5)	B Williams (1)	Heath (10)	Rankin (3)	
17-Oct	Birmingham City	League	Home	3-0		Ricardo	Lynch	Tate	May	Pugh	Moonianuck	Richardson	Richardson	Fortan 1	Pugh	Roche	Jowsey	B Williams	Fox (11)	Johnson (9)
22-Oct	Manchester City	League	Home	0-5	2,266	B Williams	Lynch	Copger	Tate	Taylor	Richardson	Rankin	Heath	Nardiello	Pugh	Eckersley (3)	Nevins	Port		
31-Oct	Sunderland	League	Home	1-3		Carroll	Roche	Tierney	May	Lynch	Wood 1	Chadwick 1	Rankin	Nardiello	Pugh	Richardson (8)	B Williams	Sims (7)	Taylor	Bardsley
21-Nov	Aston Villa	League	Home	6-2		Carroll	Lynch	Rankin	Roche	Taylor	Wood 1	Chadwick	Richardson	Nardiello 2	Davis 1	Heath (9)	M Williams (10)	Murihead	Fox (8)	Johnson
19-Dec	Newcastle United	League	Away	2-3		Ricardo	Lynch	Rankin	Pugh	Lynch	Keane	Chadwick	Butt	Nardiello	Davis	Fletcher	Jowsey	Wood (8)	Taylor	
14-Jan	Sheffield Wed	League	Away	2-0		Carroll	Rankin	Pugh	Roche	Stewart	Stewart	Richardson	Butt 1	Nardiello 1	Wood 1	Fletcher (6)	T Lee	Heath (5)	M Williams	
23-Jan	Everton	League	Home	1-4		Ricardo	Lynch	Pugh	Roche	Muirhead	Wood	Chadwick	Davis	Nardiello	Fox	Jowsey (1)	Lawrence (6)	Heath (7)	Muirhead	
27-Jan	Manchester City	MSC	Away	0-3	3,288	Carroll	Lynch	Pugh	Roche	May	Wood	Stewart	Nardiello 1	Davis	Muirhead	M Williams	Jowsey	Fletcher (8)	Heath	
03-Feb	West Brom	League	Away	3-1	3,177	Jowsey	Lynch	Rankin	Roche	Pugh	Fox	Chadwick	Humphreys	Nardiello 1	Davis	Chadwick	Heaton	Heath (10)	Jones (6)	
10-Feb	Liverpool	League	Home	0-2		Jowsey	Lynch	Rankin	Roche	Pugh	Fletcher	Davis	Fox	M Williams	Heath	Cogger	Steele	Muirhead	Hilton	
13-Feb	Oldham Athletic	MSC	Away	1-2		Steele	Rankin	Hilton	Roche	Pugh	Davis	Fletcher 1	Wood	Nardiello	M Williams	Muirhead (9)	T Lee	Webber (10)	Heath (5)	
27-Feb	Blackburn Rovers	League	Home	1-3		Ricardo	Lynch	Pugh	Roche	Pugh	Davis	Wood	Richardson	Webber	Nardiello	Chadwick	Steele	Fox (11)	Nardiello (7)	Humphreys
06-Mar	Birmingham City	League	Away	0-1		Carroll	Lynch	Hilton	Roche	Pugh	Roche	Davis	Stewart	Nardiello	Webber	Wood	Jowsey	Fox (6)	M Williams (10)	Humphreys
13-Mar	Manchester City	League	Home	1-0		Ricardo	Lynch	Wood	Roche	Pugh	Humphreys	Davis	Humphreys	Webber 1	Fox	Heath	Steele	Jones	Bardsley	
20-Mar	Oldham Athletic*	MSC	Home	2-2		Carroll	Lynch	Pugh*	Roche	May*	Stewart	Davis*	Stewart	M Williams	Webber 2	Richardson*	Nardiello* (9)	Heath (6)	Heath (10)	Cogger
24-Mar	Sunderland	League	Away	0-1		Carroll	Lynch	Pugh*	Roche	Fox	Wood*	Davis	Fletcher	Nardiello	M Williams	Fortune	Heath (10)	Fox (11)	Humphreys (6)	Ebanks-Blake
27-Mar	Bradford City	League	Away	3-1		Carroll	Lynch	Pugh	Roche	P Neville	Wood	Davis	Fletcher	Nardiello 3	Heath	Fortune	Hilton (6)	Steele	Fox (11)	
31-Mar	Bolton Wanderers	League	Away	1-1		Carroll	Lynch	Pugh	Roche	Fletcher	Fletcher	Davis	Wood	Nardiello 1	Heath	Fortune	Fox	Steele	M Williams	Humphreys
03-Apr	Bolton Wanderers	League	Home	1-2		Ricardo	Lynch	Pugh	M Williams	Fox	Fletcher	Davis	Humphreys	Nardiello 1	Heath	Wood 1	B Williams	Jones	Sims	Cogger
09-Apr	Aston Villa	League	Away	2-2		Carroll	Lynch	Pugh	May	Fox	Fletcher	Davis	Heath 1	M Williams	Fortune	Cogger (11)	B Williams	Roche	Moonianuck	
14-Apr	Bury**	MSC	Home	2-2		Carroll	Lynch	Pugh	Pugh	May	Fletcher	Nardiello**1	Fox**	Davis	M Williams 1	M Williams (5)	Jowsey	Picken	Nevins	Cogger
17-Apr	Leeds United	League	Home	2-0		B Williams	Lynch	Pugh	Howard	Roche	Fox 1	Fletcher	Pugh	Nardiello 1	Heath	Heath	Ebanks-Blake (9)	Jowsey	Byrne (7)	
24-Apr	Newcastle United	League	Away	2-1	604	Carroll	Lynch	Hilton	Roche	Fox	Moonianuck	Pugh	Fletcher	Moonianuck	Heath 2	Flanagan	Ebanks-Blake (11)	Nevins	Eckersley (7)	
28-Apr	Leeds United	League	Away	1-2	3,728	B Williams	Lynch	Hilton	Bardsley	Lynch	Davis	Richardson	Ebanks-Blake	M Williams 1	Moonianuck	Lawrence	Jowsey (1)	Picken	Eagles (11)	Collett
01-May	Middlesbrough	League	Away	1-1		Jowsey	Sims	Hilton	Bardsley	Lynch	Eagles	Davis	Richardson	Ebanks-Blake	M Williams 1	Moonianuck	Heaton	Richardson (8)	Howard	McShane
06-May	Sheffield Wed	League	Away	3-0		Jowsey	Jowsey	Lynch	Bardsley	Eagles	Eagles 1	Davis 1	Collett	M Williams	M Williams 2	Moonianuck	Steele	Ebanks-Blake (11)	Sims	Sims
08-May	Middlesbrough	League	Home	0-0		Steele	Roche	Hilton	Lynch	Pugh	Fletcher	Davis	Stewart	Ebanks-Blake	M Williams	Richardson	B Williams	Moonianuck	Fox (9)	Eagles (1)

*Lost 6-7 on penalties
**Won 2-0 on penalties

Season 2002/03

RESERVES APPEARANCES AND GOALS 2002/03

Name	League Apps	League Gls	MSC Apps	MSC Gls	Youth Cup Apps	Youth Cup Gls	Season Total Apps	Season Total Gls
Phil Bardsley	3 (1)				2		5 (1)	0
Nicky Butt	2	1					2	1
Danny Byrne	1 (1)						1 (1)	0
Ramon Calliste					3 (3)		3 (3)	0
Roy Carroll	9		3				12	0
Luke Chadwick	12	1	2				14	1
John Cogger	1 (1)						1 (1)	0
Ben Collett	1 (1)				7	2	8 (1)	2
Jimmy Davis	18	3	4				22	3
Bojan Djordjic	1						1	0
Chris Eagles	2 (3)				8	2	10 (3)	2
Sylvan Ebanks-Blake	3 (2)				1 (5)	1	4 (7)	1
Adam Eckersley	(2)						0 (2)	0
Callum Flanagan					0 (1)		0 (1)	0
Darren Fletcher	12 (2)	1	3	1			15 (2)	2
Diego Forlan	4	5					4	5
Quinton Fortune	7		1				8	0
David Fox	9 (6)	1	2 (1)				11 (7)	1
Colin Heath	10 (5)	3	1 (2)	1			11 (7)	4
Kirk Hilton	8 (2)		2				10 (2)	0
Mark Howard	1 (1)				6 (1)		7 (2)	0
Chris Humphreys	3 (2)	1	(1)				3 (3)	1
Eddie Johnson	(1)				7	3	7 (1)	3
David Jones	(1)				8		8 (1)	0
James Jowsey	4 (2)						4 (2)	0
Roy Keane	1						1	0
Lee Lawrence	1 (1)				8		9 (1)	0
Mark Lynch	25 (2)		3				28 (2)	0
David May	8		4				12	0
Paul McShane					8		8	0
Kalam Mooniaruck	5 (2)						5 (2)	0
Ben Muirhead	2 (1)		1 (1)	1			3 (2)	1
Daniel Nardiello	21 (2)	16	4 (1)	1			25 (3)	17
Gary Neville	2						2	0
Phil Neville	3						3	0
David Poole	(1)				1 (1)		1 (2)	0
Danny Pugh	25	1	4 (1)				29 (1)	1
John Rankin	9 (2)		2				11 (2)	0
Ricardo	10						10	0
Kieran Richardson	11 (3)	1	3		8	5	22 (3)	6
Lee Roche	20		5				25	0
Lee Sims	2 (1)				8		10 (1)	0
Luke Steele	2		1		8		11	0
Michael Stewart	8	1	3				11	1
Alan Tate	6		1				7	0
Kris Taylor	3						3	0
Paul Tierney	5						5	0
Mads Timm	(1)				5	1	5 (1)	1
Danny Webber	3	1	1 (1)	2			4 (1)	3
Ben Williams	3 (1)		1				4 (1)	0
Matty Williams	12 (3)	6	2 (2)				14 (5)	6
Neil Wood	10 (1)		3		2 (1)		12 (2)	3

YOUTH CUP GAMES 2002/03

Date	Opponents	Rnd	Venue	Res	Att	1	2	3	4	5	6	7	8	9	10	11	SUB	SUB	SUB
04-Dec	Newcastle United[g]	R 3	Away	3-1	847	Steele	Sims	Lawrence	Howard	McShane	D. Jones	Eagles 1	Calliste	Johnson	Richardson 1	Collett	15 Ebanks-Blake (8)	16 Flanagan (9)	15 Calliste (8)
21-Jan	Sheffield Wed	R 4	Home	2-0	428	Steele	Sims	Lawrence	Howard	McShane	D. Jones	Eagles	Timm	Johnson	Richardson 1	Collett 1	16 Calliste (8)		
05-Feb	Sheffield United*	R 5	Home	1-1	416	Steele	Sims	Lawrence	Howard	McShane	D. Jones	Eagles	Timm	Johnson 1	Richardson	Poole	16 Calliste (11)		
06-Mar	Tranmere Rov	R 6	Home	3-1	913	Steele	Sims	Lawrence	Howard	McShane	D. Jones	Eagles 1	Timm 1	Calliste	Richardson	Collett	14 Ebanks-Blake (9)		14 Poole (10)
29-Mar	Charlton Athletic	SF1	Away	1-1	9074	Steele	Sims	Lawrence	Howard	McShane	D. Jones	Eagles	Calliste	Johnson 1	Richardson 1	Collett	16 Ebanks-Blake (8)		
09-Apr	Charlton Athletic	SF2	Home	2-0	4427	Steele	Sims	Lawrence	Bardsley	McShane	D. Jones	Eagles	Timm	Johnson	Richardson 1	Collett 1	16 Ebanks-Blake (8)		
15-Apr	Middlesboro	F1	Away	2-0	8310	Steele	Sims	Lawrence	Bardsley	McShane	D. Jones	Eagles	Timm	Johnson 1	Richardson	Collett	16 Ebanks-Blake (8)		
25-Apr	Middlesboro	F2	Home	1-1	14849	Steele	Sims	Lawrence	Howard	McShane	D. Jones	Eagles	Ebanks-Blake	Johnson 1	Richardson	Collett	12 Howard (5)		

[g] Own goal: Taylor
*Won 4-3 after penalties

Season 2003/04

MANCHESTER UNITED RESERVES 2003/04: FA PREMIER RESERVE LEAGUE (NORTH) AND MANCHESTER SENIOR CUP

Date	Opponents	Comp	Venue	Res	Att	1	2	3	4	5	6	7	8	9	10	11	12	13	14	15	16
12-Aug	Aston Villa	League	Away	1-1		Carroll	Sims	Tierney	Bardsley	Tate	D Jones	Byrne	Wood	Johnson 1	M Williams	Eagles	Poole	B Williams	A Eckersley (7)	Timm (9)	Nardiello (10)
20-Aug	Blackburn Rovers	League	Home	0-2	982	Carroll	G Neville	Lynch	Pugh	Tate	D Jones	Kleberson	Wood	Johnson	Timm	Richardson	Bardsley (2)	B Williams	D Jones	Calliste (7)	
20-Sep	Oldham Athletic	MSC	Away	4-3		Carroll	Lynch	Tierney	Bardsley	Tate	D Jones	Byrne	Wood	Nardiello 3	Timm	A Eckersley	Johnson (6)	Jowsey	Poole (7)	Sims	
02-Sep	Sunderland	League	Home	2-2		B Williams	Lynch 1	Pugh	Tate	Wood	Fortune	Johnson	Nardiello 1	Timm	Richardson	Steele	Eagles (7)	Tate	D Jones (11)		
04-Sep	Leeds United	League	Away	2-2	2,005	B Williams	Lynch	Pugh	Tierney	Tate	D Jones	Eagles	Fortune 1	Johnson	Nardiello 1	Richardson	Bardsley	Heaton	Bardsley	Byrne (11)	
09-Sep	Middlesbrough	League	Home	2-3		Carroll	Lynch	Pugh	Tierney	Tate	D Jones	Bellion	Fletcher 1	Nardiello 1	Timm 1	Richardson	Eagles (8)	B Williams	M Williams (7)	Sims	
18-Sep	West Brom	League	Away	4-2		Steele	Lynch	Pugh	Tierney	Tate	D Jones 2	Eagles	Fletcher 1	Nardiello 1	Timm	Richardson	Ebanks-Blake (9)	Heaton	A Eckersley	M Williams (10)	
22-Sep	Bolton Wanderers*	League	Home	1-1		Carroll	Pugh*	Tierney	Tate*	D Jones 1	Eagles*	Fletcher 1	Nardiello	M Williams	Richardson	Eagles (8)	Steele	A Eckersley	Johnson (9)	Byrne	
25-Sep	Birmingham City	League	Home	3-1		Heaton	Lynch	Tierney	McShane	Tate	D Jones 1	Eagles	Pugh	Johnson	Nardiello 2	Poole (10)	Steele	M Williams (12)	Ebanks-Blake (10)		
02-Oct	Everton	League	Away	2-3		Heaton	Lynch	Tierney	Bardsley	D Jones	Eagles	Richardson	Nardiello 2	Cooper	Pugh	Picken (8)	Heaton	A Eckersley (6)	Howard		
07-Oct	Liverpool	League	Home	1-0	4,830	Carroll	Lynch	Pugh	Tate	D Jones 1	Eagles	Wood	Nardiello	Bellion	Richardson	Nardiello (11)	B Williams	Cooper (9)	M Williams		
16-Oct	Wolves	League	Home	2-0	540	Carroll	Lynch	Pugh	Tierney	D Jones	Eagles 1	Wood	Johnson	M Williams	Richardson	B Williams (8)	Heaton	Johnson (10)	Picken		
23-Oct	Newcastle United	League	Away	4-0	3,102	B Williams	Lynch	Pugh	Tiemey	D Jones	Bardsley	Wood 1	Cooper 2	Bellion	M Williams	Cooper (7)	B Williams	A Eckersley	Ebanks-Blake 1 (9)		
30-Oct	Bolton Wanderers	League	Away	2-1		Carroll	Pugh	Bardsley	D Jones	Eagles	Wood 1	Cooper 1	Bellion	Richardson	B Williams (9)	D Jones (11)	Sims				
10-Nov	Leeds United	League	Home	2-1		Carroll	Lynch	Pugh	Bardsley	Tiemey	D Jones	Eagles	Wood 1	Cooper 1	Johnson	M Williams 1	Spector (2)	B Williams	Poole (7)	Flanagan	
20-Nov	Sunderland	League	Away	3-5		B Williams	Sims	Pugh	A Eckersley	Wood	D Jones	Poole 2	Byrne	Nardiello	Johnson	Cooper	R Jones	B Williams	Poole (9)	Calliste	
27-Nov	West Brom	League	Home	2-0		Jowsey	Pugh	Bardsley	Spector	D Jones	Cooper	Nardiello	M Williams 1	Cooper (9)	Timm (8)	Picken (6)	Howard				
04-Dec	Middlesbrough*	League	Away	2-2	2,197	B Williams	Jowsey	A Eckersley	Howard	Wood	D Jones 1	Eagles	Wood	Nardiello	M Williams	Eagles 1 (10)	Jowsey	Heaton	Lawrence (2)	Howard	
15-Dec	Everton	MSC	Away	1-2		Jowsey	Pugh	Bardsley	Tate	Fox	Heath	Wood	Cooper 1	Nardiello (9)	Heaton	M Williams (6)	Martin	McShane (3)			
22-Jan	Manchester City	League	Home	1-2		Jowsey	Carroll	Pugh	McShane	Fox	Solskjaer	M Williams	Bellion	Timm	Eagles 1 (10)	T Lee	Cooper (7)	A Eckersley (8)			
05-Feb	Aston Villa*	League	Home	3-0		Jowsey	Carroll	Lynch	Pugh	Howard	D Jones	Kleberson	Wood	Nardiello (9)	T Lee	Heath	Lawrence				
12-Feb	Bury	MSC	Home	1-0		Carroll	Fox	Lawrence	Pugh	Lynch	Timm	Bellion 1	Heath	Cooper (7)	T Lee	Poole (5)	Cooper (7)				
19-Feb	Liverpool	League	Home	1-1		Jowsey	Lynch	Pugh	Howard	Djemba-Djemba	Brown	Solskjaer	D Jones	Heath	Bellion 1	Timm	Cooper (7)	T Lee	Hogg	Collett	
24-Feb	Wolves	League	Away	4-3	1,839	Heaton	Pugh	Lynch	Pugh	D Jones	Solskjaer	Cooper	M Williams 2	Heath 1	Timm	Cooper (7)	T Lee	Collett	M Williams		
04-Mar	Manchester City	League	Home	3-3	2,224	Jowsey	Pugh	Lawrence	Tierney	Fox	D Jones	Cooper	Richardson 1	Poole	Heaton	T Lee	Collett	A Eckersley			
17-Mar	Birmingham City	League	Away	2-1		Carroll	Lynch	Lawrence	Tierney	Spector	D Jones	Eagles	Richardson 1	Cooper	Heaton	Ebanks-Blake	Collett	Sims			
23-Mar	Manchester City*	League	Away	2-1		Heaton	Lynch	Lawrence	Tierney	Spector	D Jones	Fox	Heath	Richardson 1	Neumayr	T Lee	Ebanks-Blake	Tierney	Lawrence		
08-Apr	Bolton Wanderers	League	Home	2-0	741	Heaton	Lynch	Pugh	Howard	Spector	Fox	D Jones 1	Cooper	Richardson 1	Poole	Ebanks-Blake (10)	Picken (7)	Collett (11)	Howard		
14-Apr	Blackburn Rovers	League	Away	2-2		Heaton	Lynch	Pugh	Tierney	Spector	D Jones 1	Poole 1	Cooper	Jowsey	Picken (7)	Tierney	Picken (6)				
21-Apr	Newcastle United	League	Home	2-1		Heaton	Lynch	Pugh	Howard	Spector	R Jones	Eagles 2	Cooper	Poole	Ebanks-Blake (10)	Calliste (11)	Collett	Howard (6)			
11-May	Manchester City	MSC Fin	Home	3-1	3,484	Carroll	Lynch	Tierney	Spector	Howard	D Jones	Fox	Cooper 2	Collett	N'Galula	Heaton	N'Galula (7)	Ebanks-Blake 1 (9)	Picken		

*Own goals: Ehiogu v Middlesbrough (away), Bewers v Aston Villa (home), McCarthy v Manchester City (away)

*Won 5-3 on penalties

Season 2003/04

RESERVES APPEARANCES AND GOALS 2003/04

Name	League Apps	League Gls	MSC Apps	MSC Gls	Youth Cup Apps	Youth Cup Gls	Season Tot Apps	Season Tot Gls
Phil Bardsley	6 (1)	1	2				8 (1)	1
David Bellion	7	1	1	1			8	2
Wes Brown	1						1	0
Danny Byrne	5 (1)		2				7 (1)	0
Ramon Calliste	(3)				3 (1)	3	3 (4)	3
Roy Carroll	9		2				11	0
Ben Collett	1 (1)						1 (1)	0
Kenny Cooper	4 (4)	5	2 (1)	3			6 (5)	8
Eric Djemba-Djemba	1						1	0
Chris Eagles	15 (4)	5	2				17 (4)	5
Sylvan Ebanks-Blake	1 (6)	1	(1)	1	4		5 (7)	2
Adam Eckersley	2 (2)		1 (1)		4		7 (3)	0
Callum Flanagan					0 (1)	1	0 (1)	1
Darren Fletcher	2	2					2	2
David Fox	7		2				9	0
Colin Heath	6	1	2				8	1
Tom Heaton	8				1		9	0
Steven Hogg	1				3 (1)		4 (1)	0
Mark Howard	5 (1)		1		4	2	10 (1)	2
Eddie Johnson	7 (3)	1	1 (2)				8 (5)	1
David Jones	19 (3)	5	4				23 (3)	5
Richie Jones	1				3		4	0
James Jowsey	4 (2)		1				5 (2)	0
Kleberson	3						3	0
Lee Lawrence	3		1 (1)				4 (1)	0
Mark Lynch	21	1	4				25	1
Phil Marsh					0 (2)		0 (2)	0
Paul McShane	3 (1)	1			4	1	7 (1)	2
Floribert N'Galula	1		(2)		3	0	4 (2)	0
Daniel Nardiello	10 (3)	9	3	3			13 (3)	12
Marcus Neumayr	(1)				0 (1)		0 (2)	0
Gary Neville	1						1	0
Phil Picken	2 (8)				3		5 (8)	0
David Poole	4 (5)	3	(3)				4 (8)	3
Danny Pugh	22		4	1			26	1
Jami Puustinen					0 (1)		0 (1)	0
Kieran Richardson	19	4	3				22	4
Lee Sims	4		1				5	0
Ole Gunnar Solskjaer	3						3	0
Jonathan Spector	7 (1)		1		3 (1)		11 (2)	0
Luke Steele	1						1	0
Alan Tate	10		2				12	0
Paul Tierney	19		3				22	0
Mads Timm	6 (3)	4	3 (1)	1			9 (4)	5
Ben Williams	4		2				6	0
Matty Williams	6 (6)	4	3				9 (6)	4
Neil Wood	13	3	2				15	3

YOUTH CUP GAMES 2003/04

Date	Opponents	Rnd	Venue	Res	Att	1	2	3	4	5	6	7	8	9	10	11	SUB	SUB	SUB
25-Nov	Rushden & Dia	R 3	Away	2-1	5214	Heaton	Picken	A.Eckersley	Howard 1	McShane	Spector	N'Galula	Hogg	Ebanks-Blake	Eagles	Calliste 1	15 Marsh (6)		15 Flanagan 1 (10)
13-Jan	Manchester City	R 4	Home	2-0	5547	Heaton	Howard	Hogg	N'Galula	McShane	R. Jones	Picken	Martin	Ebanks-Blake	Calliste 1	A. Eckersley	12 Spector (6)	14 Marsh (8)	
17-Feb	Norwich City[a]	R 5	Home	4-2	2958	Heaton	Howard 1	Hogg	Spector	McShane 1	R. Jones	Picken	Martin	Ebanks-Blake	Eagles	A. Eckersley	12 Calliste 1 (7)	14 Neumayr (10)	
06-Mar	Blackburn Rovers	R 6	Away	0-2	3206	Heaton	Howard	A.Eckersley	Spector	McShane	R. Jones	Eagles	N'Galula	Ebanks-Blake	Calliste	Martin	15 Hogg (6)	16 Puustinen (10)	

[a] Own goal: Halliday

Season 2004/05

MANCHESTER UNITED RESERVES 2004/05: FA PREMIER RESERVE LEAGUE (NORTH) AND MANCHESTER SENIOR CUP

Date	Opponents	Comp	Venue	Res	Att	1	2	3	4	5	6	7	8	9	10	11	12	13	14	15	16	17
12-Aug	Nottingham Forest	League	Home	2-0	244	Carroll	Picken	A Eckersley	M Howard	McShane	Heath	D Jones 1	Cooper 1		Ebanks-Blake	Djordjic	Poole (7)	Heaton	Timm (10)	Collett (11)	R Jones	
24-Aug	Wolves	League	Away	1-0	872	Heaton	Picken	Lawrence	M Howard	McShane	Fox	Poole 1	Calliste		Djordjic	Djordjic	N'Galula (8)	T Lee	Neumayr	Collett (10)		
09-Sep	Aston Villa	League	Home	0-0	703	Steele	Picken	M Howard	McShane	Fox	Heath	Rossi		Djordjic	Crockett	Collett	Crockett	N'Galula	Calliste (11)			
13-Sep	Bolton Wanderers	League	Away	3-0		Heaton	Picken	Tierney	M Howard	McShane	Fox	Eagles 1	D Jones	Rossi 1	Collett	Djordjic	Crockett	R Jones	Poole (7)			
27-Sep	Middlesbrough	League	Home	3-3		Heaton	Spector	Tierney	M Howard	McShane 1	Fox	Eagles 1	D Jones	Bellion 1	Rossi	Richardson	Picken (3)	Crockett	Poole	Collett		
07-Oct	Birmingham City	League	Away	2-3		Ricardo	Spector	N'Galula	McShane	Djordjic	Eagles 1	D Jones 1	Saba	Richardson	Pique	Crockett (6)	Heath	Poole (10)	Rossi (10)			
12-Oct	Manchester City	League	Away	1-2	2,783	Ricardo	Brown	M Howard	McShane	Djordjic	Eagles	D Jones 1	Bellion	Rossi	Richardson	Heaton	Ebanks-Blake (6)	N'Galula	Picken			
21-Oct	Liverpool	League	Home	5-2		Heaton	Picken	Pique	M Howard	Spector	Fletcher	D Jones 1	Ebanks-Blake 1	Rossi	Richardson 2	Heath 1 (7)	Crockett	Poole (11)	M Howard			
27-Oct	Blackburn Rovers	League	Away	2-2	1,131	Heaton	Picken	Lawrence	Pique	Spector	Eagles 1	D Jones	N'Galula	Poole 2	Rossi	Heath	Crockett	Hogg	R Jones	M Howard		
01-Nov	West Brom	League	Away	1-1		Heaton	Picken	Lawrence	Spector	McShane	Eagles	D Jones	N'Galula	Poole	Rossi	Heath	Crockett	M Howard	Collett			
11-Nov	Sunderland	League	Home	4-1		Ricardo	Picken	Lawrence	Pique 1	McShane	Eagles	D Jones 1	Ebanks-Blake	Rossi	Richardson	Heath	Poole (9)	Crockett	Collett (11)	M Howard		
15-Nov	Newcastle United	League	Away	3-0		Heaton	Picken	Lawrence	Pique	McShane	Heath	D Jones 1	Ebanks-Blake 3	Rossi	Poole (6)	Crockett	Collett (11)	Hogg (11)				
25-Nov	Everton*	League	Home	3-1		Heaton	Picken	Lawrence	M Howard	Spector	Eagles 1	D Jones	Ebanks-Blake	Poole 1	Richardson	Collett (11)	Crockett	Hogg	Timm (6)	Calliste		
07-Dec	Nottingham Forest	League	Away	0-1		Heaton	Picken	Tierney	Spector	M Howard	Marsh	Fox	Calliste	Timm	Collett	A Eckersley (11)	Crockett	Hogg	Shawcross	Mullan (7)		
14-Dec	Oldham Athletic	MSC	Home	5-1		Heaton	Picken	Spector 1	M Howard	McShane	Neumayr	Marsh	Ebanks-Blake 2	Rossi	Richardson 1	M Howard	Hogg (5)	Poole (6)	Hogg (11)	Mullan (7)		
21-Dec	Bury	MSC	Away	2-0		Crockett	Picken	Tierney	Lawrence	McShane	Neumayr	Marsh	Ebanks-Blake 2	Calliste 1	Timm	M Howard	Simpson	Marsh	Lawrence	Hogg (11)		Calliste (10)
13-Jan	Aston Villa	League	Away	4-4	1,586	Ricardo	Picken	A Eckersley	Lawrence	N'Galula	R Jones	D Jones	Poole 1	Rossi 1	Richardson 2	Poole (11)	Crockett	Cooper (9)	Collett	Hogg (3)		
17-Jan	Bolton Wanderers	MSC	Away	3-0		Ricardo	Picken	A Eckersley	J Evans	Hogg	R Jones	Martin	Cooper	Timm 1	Collett	Neumayr (8)	Crockett	Marsh	Calliste (10)	Campbell (9)		
27-Jan	Leeds United	League	Away	4-0	1,696	Heaton	Picken	A Eckersley	Spector	Hogg	Fox	Poole 1	Bellion	Richardson	Martin (9)	Crockett	Collett	Calliste (10)				
03-Feb	Manchester City	MSC	Home	1-5	663	T Howard	Picken	A Eckersley	Pique	Hogg	Bellion	D Jones 1	Ebanks-Blake	Rossi 1	Poole	Collett	Heaton	Martin (11)	Campbell			
10-Feb	Middlesbrough	League	Home	2-0	435	Heaton	Picken	A Eckersley	Pique	Spector	Fox	N'Galula	Ebanks-Blake 1	Rossi 1	Poole	Gray (8)	Crockett	Martin (9)	Neumayr (11)	R Jones (7)		
14-Feb	Birmingham City	League	Away	3-0	7,822	Heaton	Picken	A Eckersley	Pique	Spector	Fox	N'Galula 1	Poole 1	Ebanks-Blake	Rossi	Martin	D Jones (8)	Crockett	M Howard	Timm (7)		
17-Feb	Leeds United	League	Home	3-0		Heaton	Picken	A Eckersley	Pique	Spector	Heath 1	N'Galula	Poole	Rossi 2	Martin	D Jones (8)	Crockett	M Howard	Calliste (10)	Timm (7)		
01-Mar	Liverpool	League	Away	1-0	2,438	Ricardo	Picken	A Eckersley	Pique	Spector	Bellion	Poole	Bellion	Rossi 2	Martin	Heath (7)	Heaton	Crockett	Neumayr (11)	McShane		
10-Mar	Blackburn Rovers	League	Home	2-1		Ricardo	Picken	A Eckersley	Pique	Spector	Miller 1	Bellion 1	Poole	Rossi 1	Martin	McShane	Heaton	Timm (9)	Calliste (10)	Timm (7)		
16-Mar	Sunderland	League	Away	4-0		Ricardo	Picken	A Eckersley	Pique	Spector	Miller	Bellion 1	Poole 1	Rossi 2	Martin	Heath (7)	McShane	Heaton	Poole (9)	Fox (6)		
24-Mar	West Brom	League	Home	2-0		Ricardo	Picken	A Eckersley	Pique	Spector	Miller	Bellion 1	Bellion	Rossi 1	Martin 1	McShane (3)	T Lee	Marsh 1 (11)	Marsh (7)			
31-Mar	Newcastle United	League	Home	1-1	593	Heaton	Carroll	A Eckersley	Pique	Spector	Fox	Kieberson 1	Bellion	Poole 1	Rossi 1	Martin	Kieberson	T Lee	Marsh 1 (11)	Picken		
04-Apr	Everton	League	Away	2-1		Carroll	McShane	A Eckersley	Pique	Fox	Miller	Bellion 1	Smith	Rossi 1	Martin 3	D Jones (2)	Picken (5)	Fox	R Jones (9)	Lawrence		
14-Apr	Bolton Wanderers	League	Home	5-0		Carroll	McShane	A Eckersley	Pique	Miller	Fox	Bellion 1	P Neville	Poole	Rossi 1	Martin	Rossi (11)	T Lee	Marsh (10)	Heath		
18-Apr	Wolves	League	Home	3-0		Heaton	Carroll	Pique	Spector	Fox	D Jones 1	Heath 1	Poole	Rossi 1	Martin	Picken (5)	T Lee	Fox	R Jones (9)	Bardsley (2)		
28-Apr	Manchester City	League	Away	2-3	379	Carroll	McShane	Pique	Spector	Fox	Bellion 2	Heath 1	Smith	Rossi 1	Martin	Fox (6)	T Lee	Marsh (7)	R Jones	Bardsley (4)		
08-May	Manchester City	MSC Fin	Home	3-1	4,783	Carroll	Picken	N'Galula	J Evans	Bardsley	Miller 1	Bellion 2	Heath	Fox (6)	Rossi 1	Bardsley (3)	Heaton	Eagles (11)	Marsh (7)	Neumayr		
12-May	Charlton Athletic	Play-off	Away	4-2	7,102	Heaton	Picken	Lawrence	Pique	McShane	Fox	Eagles	Bellion	D Jones	Rossi 3	Martin	Bardsley	Crockett	N'Galula	Campbell (9)		

*Own goal: Bosnar

Season 2004/05

RESERVES APPEARANCES AND GOALS 2004/05

Name	Prem Lge* Apps	Gls	MSC Apps	Gls	Pontins Lge Apps	Gls	Pontins Cup Apps	Gls	Youth Cup Apps	Gls	Total Apps	Gls
Phil Bardsley	1 (2)		(1)		5		2				8 (3)	0
David Bellion	11	6	2	1	4 (1)	4	2	1			19 (1)	12
Fabien Brandy					1						1	0
Ramon Calliste	3 (3)		1 (2)	1	10	3	3 (1)	1			17 (6)	5
Fraizer Campbell	(1)				3 (1)	1	1	1	0 (1)		4 (3)	2
Roy Carroll	3										3	0
Ben Collett	1 (5)		2		12	1	4				19 (5)	1
Kenny Cooper	1 (2)	1	1		2						4 (2)	1
Lee Crockett	(1)		1		2		1		1		5 (1)	0
Bojan Djordjic	6				1						7	0
Chris Eagles	11 (1)	4	1 (1)		3 (1)	1					15 (3)	5
Sylvan Ebanks-Blake	12 (1)	11	2	2	3 (1)	4					17 (2)	17
Adam Eckersley	12 (1)		3		6						21 (1)	0
Jonny Evans	1		1		4		1 (1)		1		8 (1)	0
Sean Evans					2 (3)		1	1	0 (1)		3 (4)	1
Darren Fletcher	1										1	0
David Fox	14 (3)	1	2		8 (1)	2	2	1			26 (4)	4
Darron Gibson					5 (1)		1	2	1		7 (1)	2
David Gray	(1)				2 (2)		(1)				2 (4)	0
Colin Heath	15 (3)	4	1		7 (2)	6	1	1			23 (5)	11
Tom Heaton	18		3		12		2				35	0
Steven Hogg	1 (2)		2 (2)		8 (1)	1	1				12 (5)	1
Mark Howard	9		1		8		1				19	0
Tim Howard			1		1						2	0
David Jones	24 (2)	7	3		3 (1)	1	1 (1)	2			31 (4)	10
Richie Jones	1 (4)		2		12	1	2 (1)	2	1		18 (5)	3
Kleberson	2	1			2						4	1
Lee Lawrence	11 (1)		1		8		3				23 (1)	0
Michael Lea					2 (1)						2 (1)	0
Tommy Lee					3 (1)		1				4 (1)	0
Paul McShane	15 (1)	1	3		7 (1)	1	3 (1)				28 (3)	2
Phil Marsh	1 (6)	1			7 (3)	3	1 (2)		1		10 (11)	4
Lee Martin	11 (2)	4	2		8 (3)	2	1		1		23 (5)	6
Kyle Moran					(4)						0 (4)	0
Liam Miller	6	2					2				8	2
Jamie Mullan	(1)				1 (1)		(1)		1		2 (3)	0
Floribert N'Galula	11 (1)	1	2		13	1	4				30 (1)	2
Marcus Neumayr	1 (1)		1 (1)		14 (3)	3	2				18 (5)	3
Phil Neville	1										1	0
Phil Picken	23 (3)		5		9		2				39 (3)	0
Gerard Pique	16	1	1		7 (1)	1	2		1		27 (1)	2
David Poole	11 (8)	6	3 (1)	2	4 (1)	2	2				20 (10)	10
Jami Puustinen					(3)	1			1		1 (3)	1
Ricardo	7				2		1				10	0
Kieran Richardson	8	4	1	1	3	1					12	6
Danny Rose					(1)		(1)				0 (2)	0
Giuseppe Rossi	20 (3)	16	2	2	3 (4)	5	1 (1)		1		27 (8)	23
John Ruddy					1						1	0
Louis Saha	2				1		1	1			4	1
Ryan Shawcross					3 (2)		1		1		5 (2)	0
Danny Simpson					7		1		0 (1)		8 (1)	0
Alan Smith	1										1	0
Jonathan Spector	18		2	1	1 (3)		(1)				21 (4)	1
Luke Steele	1										1	0
Paul Tierney	5		1								6	0
Mads Timm	2 (5)		2	2			1	1			5 (5)	3

*Play-off included under Premier League statistics

YOUTH CUP GAMES 2004/05

Date	Opponents	Rnd	Venue	Res	Att							
16-Dec	Stoke City	R 3	Home	0-1	307	Crockett	J.Evans	Shawcross	R.Jones	Pique	Gibson	Martin	Marsh	Puustinen	Rossi	Mullan	S.Evans	Simpson	Campbell

SUB 16 Campbell (8)
SUB 15 Simpson (5)
SUB 14 S.Evans (9)
11
10
9
8
7
6
5
4
3
2
1

Season 2005/06

MANCHESTER UNITED RESERVES 2005/06: FA PREMIER RESERVE LEAGUE (NORTH) AND MANCHESTER SENIOR CUP

Date	Opponents	Comp	Venue	Res	Att	1	2	3	4	5	6	7	8	9	10	11	12	13	14	15	16	17
15-Aug	Bolton Wanderers	League	Away	3-0	900	Heaton	Bardsley	Pique	J Evans	Brown	R Jones	Heath 2	Smith 1	Cooper	Rossi	N'Galula	T Lee	J Evans (5)	Campbell (9)	Gibson (11)		
22-Aug	Manchester City*	MSC	Away	0-0	1,222	Steele	Bardsley*	A Eckersley	Pique	J Evans	R Jones'	S Evans	Miller	Campbell	Rossi	Martin	Gibson* (8)	Cooper* (10)	Shawcross	Simpson (7)		
01-Sep	Sunderland	League	Home	1-2	492	T Howard	J Evans	Pique	R Jones	Campbell	Gibson	S Evans	Rossi 1	Martin	T Lee	Mullan	K Lee	Neumayr			
06-Sep	Leeds United	League	Away	2-0		Steele	Bardsley	J Evans 1	Pique	R Jones	Neumayr	Cooper	Rossi 1	Martin	Ebanks-Blake (9)	S Evans (11)	Shawcross (2)	Rose				
13-Sep	Oldham Athletic	LSC	Away	1-2		Steele	K Lee	R Jones	Gibson	Neumayr	Martin	Ebanks-Blake	Cooper 1	Campbell (5)	Marsh	Puustinen						
19-Sep	Stockport County	MSC	Home	4-1		Steele	Simpson	Shawcross	J Evans	Miller 2	Campbell	Ebanks-Blake 1	Rossi (1)	T Lee	Gibson	Pique (4)	Cooper 1 (9)					
22-Sep	Birmingham City	League	Home	1-0		T Howard	Simpson	R Jones	Neumayr	Cooper	Martin	Ebanks-Blake 1	Rose	Cathcart	Marsh	Rose (11)						
26-Sep	Newcastle United	League	Away	0-2		Steele	K Lee	Shawcross	J Evans	Cooper	Gibson	Campbell	Rose	Mullan (11)	Hewson (7)	Marsh (10)						
03-Oct	Bury*	MSC	Home	5-0	204	T Lee	N'Galula	A Eckersley	Simpson	Pique	Marsh	Fox	Ebanks-Blake 1	Rossi 3	Crockett	Mullan (11)	J Evans (7)	Shawcross (2)				
06-Oct	Everton	League	Home	3-1	550	T Lee	A Eckersley	Bardsley	A Eckersley	Fox	Neumayr	Ebanks-Blake 1	Rossi 1	Martin	Zieler (9)	Mullan	Marsh (7)	Shawcross (5)				
10-Oct	Wolves	League	Away	4-1	829	T Lee	Simpson	A Eckersley	Pique	Fox 1	Neumayr	Gibson	Ebanks-Blake 1	Rossi 1	Martin 1	Cooper (9)	Amos	Mullan (11)				
20-Oct	Middlesbrough	League	Home	2-1	612	Steele	Simpson	A Eckersley	Brown	Fox	Neumayr	R Jones	Ebanks-Blake	Rossi 1	Martin	Cooper (9)	Marsh	Gray (7)				
31-Oct	Oldham Athletic	League	Away	1-5		Cathcart	T Lee	A Eckersley	Shawcross	Gibson	Mullan	Gray	Campbell 1	S Evans	Simpson	Cooper 1 (10)	Marsh	Fagan (4)	C Evans (8)			
03-Nov	Wigan Athletic	League	Home	2-1	431	T Howard	Simpson	A Eckersley	J Evans	Pique	Fox	R Jones	Hewson	Gray	Campbell 1	Simpson	Zieler	Marsh (7)				
07-Nov	Blackburn Rovers	League	Away	4-2	819	Steele	Simpson	K Lee	J Evans 1	Bardsley	Fox	Neumayr	Gibson	Ebanks-Blake 1	Rossi 2	Cooper (9)	Steele	Gibson (9)	Campbell	Marsh		
17-Nov	Manchester City	League	Away	4-1		T Howard	G Neville	A Eckersley	Pique	Fox	J Evans	Neumayr 1	Richardson	Ebanks-Blake	Rossi 3	Martin 1	Simpson (2)	T Lee	Gibson (6)	R Jones (11)		
23-Nov	Manchester United	League	Away	4-2		T Howard	Simpson	A Eckersley	Pique	Bardsley	Neumayr	Hewson	Saha	Ebanks-Blake	Rossi 3	Barnes	Steele	Ebanks-Blake	R Jones (11)	Cooper 1 (8)		
05-Dec	Liverpool	League	Away	0-2	2,738	Steele	Simpson	A Eckersley	Cathcart	Fox	Neumayr	Richardson	Solskjaer	Martin	Rossi	Barnes	Marsh (3)	Ebanks-Blake	Moran			
15-Dec	Bolton Wanderers	League	Home	0-2		T Lee	K Lee	A Eckersley	J Evans 1	Pique	Fox	Neumayr	R Jones	Ebanks-Blake 3	Rossi	Cooper (10)	Fagan 1 (5)	Marsh (8)	Rose (9)	Puustinen		
12-Jan	Leeds United	League	Home	5-0	703	T Lee	Simpson	K Lee	Bardsley	Pique	Fox	Solskjaer 1	Pique	Cooper 1	Martin	Cooper (10)	K Lee (3)	Steele	Moran 1 (7)	Puustinen		
26-Jan	Sunderland	League	Away	3-2		Steele	Marsh	K Lee	M Howard	Vidic	Pique	Neumayr	Pique	Cooper 1	Rossi 2	Moran	Gibson (11)	Heaton	S Evans 1 (11)	Brandy (11)		
02-Feb	Newcastle United	League	Home	4-0		Steele	Marsh	K Lee	M Howard	Pique	Pique	Gibson	Campbell 1	Rossi 3	Martin	Barnes	Fortune	Zieler	Cathcart (5)	Brandy (9)		
09-Feb	Aston Villa	League	Home	0-3		T Howard	Marsh	Bardsley	Bardsley	R Jones	Neumayr	Barnes	Solskjaer	Rossi	Solskjaer	Marsh (5)	Gibson (8)	Cathcart (2)	Campbell (11)	Moran		
14-Feb	Birmingham City	League	Home	4-0		Steele	M Howard	K Lee	M Howard 1	Gibson 1	Barnes	Neumayr	R Jones	Campbell	Solskjaer	Marsh	K Lee (3)	Zieler	Rose (9)	Moran		
21-Feb	Everton	League	Away	4-1		Steele	Marsh	Bardsley	M Howard	Pique	R Jones	Neumayr	Fletcher	Solskjaer 1	Rossi 2	Fortune	Gibson (5)	Moran	Chester	Rose (11)		
02-Mar	Wolves	League	Home	1-1		Steele	Marsh	Bardsley	M Howard	Pique	Gibson	Fletcher	Barnes	Solskjaer	Rossi	Fortune	Campbell (9)	Moran	Rose (11)	Gray		
07-Mar	Middlesbrough	League	Away	1-1		Steele	Evra	Bardsley	M Howard	Vidic	Richardson	R Jones	Fletcher	Solskjaer	Rossi	K Lee (3)	Gibson (5)	Steele	Campbell 1 (9)	K Lee		
15-Mar	Wigan Athletic	League	Away	0-4		T Howard	Marsh	Evra	Pique	Vidic	Gibson	Pique	Barnes	Brandy	Rossi	Marsh (5)	Zieler	S Evans 1 (11)	Moran (4)	Mullan		
23-Mar	Blackburn Rovers'	League	Home	2-3		Steele	Marsh	Evra	Shawcross	Richardson	R Jones	Hewson	Barnes	Campbell 1	Rossi	Fortune	Amos	Rose	Burns	Lea		
27-Mar	West Brom	League	Away	2-0	683	Steele	Marsh	K Lee	Pique	Rose	Neumayr	Pique	Campbell	Rossi 2	Mullan 1	J Evans (4)	Zieler	Gray (9)	Barnes (8)	Moran		
04-Apr	West Brom*	League	Home	6-0	1,302	Steele	Marsh	Rose	Pique	R Jones	Neumayr 1	Campbell 4	Rossi 1	Mullan	Gray (2)	Zieler	Rose	K Lee	Shawcross (4)			
22-Apr	Aston Villa	League	Away	1-0	6-0	Steele	Marsh	Fortune	J Evans	R Jones	Neumayr	Campbell 1	Rossi 1	Richardson	J Evans (2)	Zieler	Shawcross (4)	Gibson (8)	Mullan (11)			
25-Apr	Oldham Athletic	MSC Fin	Away	3-2	2,118	Steele	Marsh	Fortune	Heinze	Pique	R Jones	Gibson	Campbell 2	Rossi 1	J Evans (2)	Richardson	Gibson (8)	Rose	Gibson (4)	Shawcross		Burns (9)
30-Apr	Liverpool	League	Away	0-1	1,179	Steele	Marsh	K Lee	Heinze	Pique	Rose	R Jones	Gibson	Campbell	Rossi 1	Mullan	Barnes (10)	Gibson (3)	Gray (4)	Shawcross		
04-May	Tottenham Hotspur	Play-off	Home	2-0	2,416	T Howard	Gray	K Lee	Pique 1	J Evans	Gibson	Fletcher	Solskjaer 1	Rose	Hewson	Mullan	Rose (10)	Steele	R Jones (8)	Cathcart		

Own goals: Manchester City v West Bromwich Albion (home), Jones v Blackburn Rovers (home), ? v Bury (MSC home)
Won 5-3 on penalties

246

Season 2005/06

RESERVES APPEARANCES AND GOALS 2005/06

Name	League Apps	League Gls	MSC Apps	MSC Gls	LSC Apps	LSC Gls	Youth Cup Apps	Youth Cup Gls	Season Tot Apps	Season Tot Gls
Phil Bardsley	13		2						15	0
Michael Barnes	3 (2)								3 (2)	0
Fabien Brandy	1 (2)						1 (2)	2	2 (4)	2
Wes Brown	2								2	0
Aaron Burns	(2)						0 (3)		0 (5)	0
Fraizer Campbell	11 (4)	9	4	3	(1)		3	1	18 (5)	13
Craig Cathcart	1 (3)		1				3		5 (3)	0
Kenny Cooper	7 (8)	3	(2)	1	1	1			8 (10)	5
Sylvan Ebanks-Blake	7 (2)	9	2	2	1				10 (2)	11
Adam Eckersley	8		2						10	0
Corry Evans			(1)				0 (1)		0 (2)	0
Jonny Evans	12 (2)	2	3 (1)		1		2		18 (3)	2
Sean Evans	(5)	1	2		1		2	2	5 (5)	3
Patrice Evra	2								2	0
Chris Fagan	(1)	1	(1)						0 (2)	1
Darren Fletcher	1								1	0
Quinton Fortune	4								4	0
David Fox	10	1	1						11	1
Darron Gibson	14 (5)	2	1 (2)		1		3		19 (7)	2
David Gray	1 (6)		1 (1)				2		4 (7)	0
Colin Heath	1	2							1	2
Tom Heaton	1								1	0
Gabriel Heinze	1		1						2	0
Sam Hewson	3 (1)		1				2	1	6 (1)	1
Mark Howard	6 (1)	1							6 (1)	1
Tim Howard	7								7	0
Richie Jones	20 (1)	1	3		1				24 (1)	1
Michael Lea							1		1	0
Kieran Lee	10 (2)		2		1		4		17 (2)	0
Tommy Lee	5		2						7	0
Phil Marsh	11 (6)		2						13 (6)	0
Lee Martin	13	1	3		1				17	1
Kyle Moran	3 (2)	1							3 (2)	1
Liam Miller			2	2					2	2
Jamie Mullan	4 (3)	1	2				3 (1)		9 (4)	1
Floribert N'Galula			1						1	0
Marcus Neumayr	25	2	3		1				29	2
Gary Neville	2								2	0
John O'Shea	1								1	0
Phil Picken	1								1	0
Gerard Pique	21		3 (1)						24 (1)	0
Kieran Richardson	3								3	0
Danny Rose	6 (3)		1		(1)		4		11 (4)	0
Giuseppe Rossi	25	26	3 (1)	4					28 (1)	30
Louis Saha	1								1	0
Ryan Shawcross	5 (5)		2						7 (5)	0
Danny Simpson	10 (2)		2 (1)		1				13 (3)	0
Alan Smith	1	1							1	1
Ole Gunnar Solskjaer	8	2							8	2
Luke Steele	15		3		1				19	0
Nemanja Vidic	2								2	0
Ron-Robert Zieler							4		4	0

YOUTH CUP GAMES 2005/06

Date	Opponents	Rnd	Venue	Res	Att	1	2	3	4	5	6	7	8	9	10	11	SUB	SUB	SUB
15-Dec	Birmingham City	R 3	Away	2-0	459	Zieler	Lee	Lea	Cathcart	J.Evans	Gibson	Gray	Hewson	Campbell	S.Evans	Rose	16 C.Evans (7)	14 Burns (9)	12 Mullan (8)
18-Jan	Sunderland♦	R 4	Away	2-1	390	Zieler	Cathcart	Lee	J.Evans	Shawcross	Rose	Gray	Hewson 1	Campbell	S.Evans	Mullan	15 Fagan	14 Brandy 1 (4)	12 Burns (8)
07-Feb	Charlton Athletic	R 5	Home	2-1	874	Zieler	Gray	Lee	Cathcart	Shawcross	Mullan	Mullan	Gibson	Brandy 1	Campbell 1	S. Evans		14 Hewson (9)	12 Burns (11)
23-Feb	Manchester City	R 6	Away	0-1	6492	Zieler	Gray	Lee	Cathcart	Shawcross	Rose	Mullan	Gibson	Campbell	Hewson	S. Evans			14 Brandy (10)

♦After extra time

Season 2006/07

MANCHESTER UNITED RESERVES 2006/07: FA PREMIER RESERVE LEAGUE (NORTH) AND MANCHESTER SENIOR CUP

Date	Opponents	Comp	Venue	Res	Att	1	2	3	4	5	6	7	8	9	10	11	12	13	14	15	16	17
1-Aug	Preston North End†	LSC	Away	7-2		Heaton	K Lee	Rose 1	Shawcross	Miller	Eagles 1	D Jones 1		Smith	Rossi 2	S Evans (9)	Mullan	Zieler	N'Galula	Marsh 2 (10)	Barnes (11)	Burns
1-Aug	Blackburn Rovers	League	Home	1-0		Kuszczak	K Lee	Rose	Shawcross	Gray	Mullan	D Jones		Marsh 1	Smith	S Evans	N'Galula	Heaton	Burns	Burns (7)	Cathcart (9)	
5-Sep	Stockport County*	MSC	Away	1-1	1,203	Heaton	K Lee	Rose	Shawcross	D Jones	Barnes	K Lee		Smith	Burns 1	Burns (8)	Marsh (10)	Zieler	Lea	Cathcart (8)		
4-Sep	Manchester City	League	Away	1-0	1,056	Heaton	Gray	Rose	Cathcart	R Jones	K Lee	D Jones		Marsh 1	Smith	S Evans	Lea	Zieler	Barnes (6)	Brandy (11)		
7-Sep	Bolton Wanderers	LSC	Away	0-1	296	Heaton	K Lee	Rose	Lea	R Jones	Barnes	R Jones		Burns	Marsh 1	Mullan	Zieler	Barnes (6)	Fagan (9)			
5-Oct	Middlesbrough	League	Away	1-2	858	Heaton	Gray	Cathcart	Shawcross 1	Rose	Barnes	Hewson		Marsh	Burns	Mullan	Lea	Amos	Brandy (10)			
7-Sep	Bolton Wanderers	League	Home	4-1	471	Kuszczak	K Lee	Gray	Cathcart	D Jones	Mullan	R Jones		Smith	Marsh 3	Barnes	Heaton	Amos	Fagan	Brandy 1 (11)		
2-Oct	Bolton Wanderers	MSC	Away	1-0	193	Heaton	Barnes	Rose	Shawcross	R Jones	K Lee	K Lee		Smith	Marsh	S Evans	Lea (2)	Heaton	Burns	Gray (11)		
3-Oct	Wigan Athletic*	League	Home	5-2	602	Heaton	Gray	Lea	Cathcart	R Jones	K Lee	Rose		Marsh	Burns 3	Barnes 1	Brandy 1 (11)	Amos	Drinkwater (6)	Fagan (12)		
2-Nov	Sheffield United	League	Away	1-2	2,611	Kuszczak	Gray 1	Cathcart	Shawcross	Rose	K Lee	D Jones		Smith	Burns	Barnes	Hewson (4)	Heaton	Amos	N'Galula		
3-Nov	Manchester City	MSC	Home	4-2	767	Heaton	Gray	Rose	Lea	Cathcart	R Jones	K Lee		Marsh	Burns 2	Barnes 1	Mullan (3)	Chester	Marsh (6)	Brandy (12)		
7-Dec	Manchester City	League	Home	2-0	425	Kuszczak	Gray	Rose	Cathcart	Shawcross	K Lee	Park		Richardson 1	Marsh	Chester	Mullan (7)	Heaton	Marsh	Ekrem (9)		
5-Jan	Bury†	MSC	Away	1-0		Heaton	Lea	S Evans	Lea 1	N'Galula	Eagles	Hewson		Dong	Burns	S Evans (11)	Fagan	R Eckersley	Brandy	N'Galula		
1-Feb	Liverpool	League	Home	0-0	535	Heaton	K Lee	Lea	Silvestre	Brown	Smith	Eagles		Smith 1	Dong	S Evans	Crockett (1)	Barnes (11)	Burns (4)	Chester		
3-Feb	Bolton Wanderers	League	Away	0-0	651	Crockett	R Eckersley	Chester	Chester	K Lee	Mullan	Hewson		Dong	Eagles	Barnes	Crockett	N'Galula	Burns (11)	Drinkwater		
2-Feb	Middlesbrough	League	Home	1-1	401	Heaton	K Lee	Barnes	Lea	Eagles	Mullan	Dong		Smith	N'Galula	S Evans 1	Burns (11)	Crockett				
1-Mar	Newcastle United	League	Home	3-0	454	Heaton	K Lee	S Evans	Chester	N'Galula	Mullan 2	Smith		Eagles	Richardson	Barnes 1	Burns (8)	Crockett	Hewson (6)	R Eckersley	Cleverley	
3-Mar	Wigan Athletic	League	Away	0-2	360	Heaton	K Lee	S Evans	Lea	K Lee	Mullan	Dong		Burns	Eagles	Barnes	Derbyshire	Crockett	Cathcart (11)	R Eckersley	Cleverley (6)	
3-Mar	Sheffield United	League	Away	0-3		Zieler	McCormack	S Evans	Lea	K Lee	Mullan	Burns		Brandy 1	Eagles	Barnes	Derbyshire (8)	Crockett	Bryan (8)	Ekrem		
3-Mar	Oldham Athletic	MSC	Home	2-0		Zieler	R Eckersley	Drinkwater	Chester	K Lee	Mullan	Fagan		Brandy	Eagles	Barnes	Bryan 1 (10)	Fagan 1 (11)	James	Norwood		
2-Mar	Everton	League	Home	1-0		Heaton	R Eckersley	Lea	Cathcart 1	Drinkwater	Hewson 1	S Evans		Brandy	Eagles	Burns	Drinkwater	Zieler	Derbyshire	Bryan		
7-Mar	Everton	League	Away	2-1	2,089	Zieler	R Eckersley	Lea	Cathcart	Hewson 1	Mullan	K Lee		Burns	S Evans	Barnes	Marsh (8)	Crockett	Fagan 1 (11)	C Evans	Barnes (11)	
1-Apr	Blackburn Rovers	League	Away	1-1		Zieler	K Lee	Chester	Cathcart	Drinkwater	Mullan	Hewson		Brandy	Burns 1	Barnes	Marsh (8)	Crockett	Fagan (6)	Bryan	Galbraith (11)	
1-Apr	Newcastle United	League	Away	0-2	749	Heaton	K Lee	Lea	Chester	Cathcart	Mullan	Burns		Dong	Brandy	Barnes	Marsh (8)	Crockett	Hewson	Brandy	Chester (5)	
3-Apr	Liverpool	League	Away	1-0	842	Heaton	K Lee	S Evans	Lea	Cathcart	Mullan	Dong		Burns	Eagles 1	Marsh	McCormack	Zieler	Fagan (9)	Fagan (10)		
3-May	Manchester City	MSC Fin	Home	1-3	841	Heaton	R Eckersley	S Evans	Chester	Lea	Lea	Hewson		Burns	Marsh	Barnes 1	Brandy (10)	Drinkwater	Brandy	Drinkwater		

Own goal: Webster
Lost 0-3 on penalties
†Line up not in number order: v Preston North End (LSC away) and Bury (MSC away)

248

Season 2006/07

RESERVES APPEARANCES AND GOALS 2006/07

Name	League Apps	League Gls	MSC Apps	MSC Gls	LSC Apps	LSC Gls	Youth Cup Apps	Youth Cup Gls	Season Tot Apps	Season Tot Gls
Ben Amos							6		6	0
Michael Barnes	14 (4)	2	5	2	1 (1)				20 (5)	4
Fabien Brandy	2 (5)	1	1 (3)	2			8	4	11 (8)	7
Wes Brown	1								1	0
Antonio Bryan	(2)		(1)	1			0 (6)	1	0 (9)	2
Aaron Burns	11 (4)	4	6	3	1				18 (4)	7
Craig Cathcart	9 (2)	1	2 (1)				7	1	11 (3)	2
James Chester	6 (1)		2				7		15 (1)	0
Tom Cleverley	1 (1)								1 (1)	0
Lee Crockett	1 (1)								1 (1)	0
James Derbyshire			(1)				1		1 (1)	0
Fangzhou Dong	8		1						9	0
Daniel Drinkwater	2 (1)		1				8	1	11 (1)	1
Chris Eagles	10	1	1		1	1			12	2
Richard Eckersley	3		2				8		13	0
Magnus Eikrem			(1)				0 (1)		0 (2)	0
Corry Evans							3 (3)		3 (3)	0
Sean Evans	11 (1)	1	4		(1)				15 (2)	1
Chris Fagan	(5)	1	1 (2)		(1)		8	1	9 (8)	2
Darren Fletcher	1								1	0
Danny Galbraith	(1)		(1)				7 (1)		7 (3)	0
David Gray	6	1	1 (1)						7 (1)	1
Tom Heaton	11		5		2				18	0
Sam Hewson	3 (2)	1	3		1		8	5	15 (2)	6
Matty James							0 (1)		0 (1)	0
David Jones	4		1		1	1			6	1
Richie Jones	5		2		2				9	0
Tomasz Kuszczak	4								4	0
Michael Lea	14 (1)		5	1	1				20 (1)	1
Kieran Lee	18		5	1	2				25	1
Conor McCormack	1						0 (1)		1 (1)	0
Phil Marsh	6 (3)	5	3 (1)		1 (1)	2			10 (5)	7
Liam Miller					1				1	0
Scott Moffatt							0 (1)		0 (1)	0
Jamie Mullan	14 (2)	2	4		2				20 (2)	2
Floribert N'Galula	6		4						10	0
Ji-Sung Park	1								1	0
Kieran Richardson	2	1							2	1
Danny Rose	7		2		2	1			11	1
Giuseppe Rossi					1	2			1	2
Ryan Shawcross	6	1	2		2				10	1
Mikael Silvestre	1								1	0
Danny Simpson			1						1	0
Alan Smith	7	1	1		1				9	1
Kenny Strickland							2		2	0
Danny Welbeck							7 (1)	1	7 (1)	1
Ron-Robert Zieler	2		1				2 (1)		7 (1)	0

YOUTH CUP GAMES 2006/07

Date	Opponents	Rnd	Venue	Res	Att	1	2	3	4	5	6	7	8	9	10	11	SUB	SUB	SUB
16-Dec	Scunthorpe United	R 3	Home	3-0	238	Amos	R.Eckersley	Cleverley	Chester	Cathcart 1	Drinkwater	Eikrem	Hewson	Brandy 2	Fagan	Welbeck	12 C. Evans (6)	14 Galbraith (11)	16 Bryan (10)
17-Jan	Southampton	R 4	Home	2-0	332	Amos	R.Eckersley	Cleverley	Chester	Cathcart	Drinkwater	Derbyshire	Hewson 1	Brandy	Fagan	Galbraith	12 C. Evans (11)	14 Welbeck (7)	15 McCormack (6)
30-Jan	Crystal Palace	R 5	Away	2-0	332	Amos	R.Eckersley	Cleverley	Chester	Cathcart	Drinkwater	Welbeck	Hewson 1	Brandy 1	Fagan	Galbraith	14 Bryan (10)		
21-Feb	Birmingham City	R 6	Home	2-0	834	Amos	R.Eckersley	Cleverley	Chester	Cathcart	Drinkwater	Welbeck	Hewson	Brandy 1	Fagan	Galbraith	12 C. Evans (10)	14 Bryan (7)	
14-Mar	Arsenal	SF1	Away	0-1	38,187	Amos	R.Eckersley	Cleverley	Chester	Cathcart	Drinkwater	Welbeck 1	Hewson	Brandy 1	Fagan 1	Galbraith	13 Zieler (1)	14 Bryan 1 (2)	
02-Apr	Arsenal♦	SF2	Home	4-2	8,058	Amos	C.Evans	R.Eckersley	Chester	Cathcart	Drinkwater	Welbeck 1	Hewson	Brandy	Fagan	Galbraith		14 Bryan (6)	15 James (9)
16-Apr	Liverpool[o]	F1	Away	2-1	19,518	Zieler	R.Eckersley	C.Evans	Strickland	Chester	Drinkwater	Welbeck	Hewson 1	Brandy	Fagan	Galbraith		14 Bryan (6)	15 Eikrem (7)
26-Apr	Liverpool*	F2	Home	0-1	24,347	Zieler	R.Eckersley	C.Evans	Strickland	Cathcart	Drinkwater	Welbeck	Hewson	Brandy	Fagan	Galbraith		14 Bryan (6)	16 Moffatt (3)

[o]Own goal: Threlfall
♦After extra time
*Won 3-4 after penalties

Season 2007/08

MANCHESTER UNITED RESERVES 2007/08: FA PREMIER RESERVE LEAGUE (NORTH) AND MANCHESTER SENIOR CUP

Date	Opponents	Comp	Venue	Res	Att	1	2	3	4	5	6	7	8	9	10	11	12	13	14	15	16
30-Aug	Everton	League	Home	1-0	1,323	Heaton	K Lee	A Eckersley	Chester	Pique	S Evans	Gibson	Dong	Campbell	Martin	Barnes (10)	Zieler	R Eckersley (5)	Brandy 1 (9)		
04-Sep	Manchester City	League	Away	1-3	789	Heaton	R Eckersley	A Eckersley	Bardsley	Chester	K Lee	Hewson	Campbell 1	Anderson	Martin	Dong (7)	Woods	S Evans	Barnes (11)		
27-Sep	Bolton Wanderers*	League	Home	1-1		Heaton	Gray	A Eckersley	Chester	Barnes	K Lee	Barnes	Brandy	Campbell	S Evans (11)	Fagan	R Eckersley (4)	Drinkwater (10)			
01-Oct	Blackburn Rovers	League	Away	0-1	493	Zieler	Gray	A Eckersley	Chester	R Eckersley	K Lee	Barnes	Dong	Brandy	Martin	Amos	Drinkwater (7)	Fagan (11)			
11-Oct	Liverpool	League	Home	1-1		Zieler	Gray	A Eckersley	Chester	R Eckersley	K Lee 1	Cleverley	Hewson	Fagan	Barnes	C Evans	Woods	Drinkwater (7)	Welbeck (10)		
01-Nov	Stockport County†	MSC	Home	6-1	828	Heaton	Gray	J Evans	G Neville	Simpson	Barnes	Eagles 1	Dong 2	Brandy 2	S Evans 1	R Eckersley (4)	Chester	Bryan			
06-Nov	Middlesbrough	League	Away	2-1	849	Heaton	Gray	S Evans	R Eckersley	Chester	James	Bryan	K Lee	Dong 1	C Evans (2)	Zieler	Welbeck (7)	Norwood			
14-Nov	Wigan Athletic*	League	Away	1-0		Amos	Gray	Simpson	R Eckersley	Chester	K Lee	Eagles	Hewson	Brandy 1	Barnes	S Evans	Woods (1)	Cleverley (8)	Fagan		
22-Nov	Bury	MSC	Home	5-0	269	Zieler	K Lee	Simpson	Cleverley	C Evans	Barnes	Eagles 1	Hewson	Fagan 2	S Evans 1	Brandy	Welbeck 1 (9)	Eikrem (6)	Welbeck (10)		
29-Nov	Sunderland	League	Home	2-0	446	Simpson	Simpson	R Eckersley	Chester	K Lee	Barnes	Gray	Hewson	Dong 1	Barnes	S Evans	Zieler	R Eckersley	Fagan		
09-Jan	Everton	League	Away	2-2	2,044	Zieler	G Neville 1	Simpson	Chester	R Jones	Gray	Hewson	Brandy	Dong	S Evans 1	Heaton	Fagan (2)	Cleverley (3)	Lea		
17-Jan	Oldham Athletic	LSC	Home	4-0		Zieler	Lea	R Eckersley	Chester	Cathcart	McCormack 1	Hewson 1	Fagan 1	Norwood	S Evans 1	Amos	Drinkwater (9)	Brandao	Curran		
23-Jan	Bolton Wanderers	League	Away	0-1	726	Zieler	R Eckersley	Lea	Chester	Cathcart	Bryan	Hewson	Fagan	C Evans	S Evans 1	Galbraith	James	Norwood			
31-Jan	Manchester City	MSC	Home	3-2		Heaton	Gray	Lea	R Eckersley	Chester	Hewson	Cleverley	Welbeck 1	Welbeck	Eagles 2	Possebon (7)	Chester	Bryan (9)			
07-Feb	Manchester City	MSC	Home	2-0	558	Heaton	Gray	Lea	R Eckersley	Chester	Hewson	Barnes	Possebon	Welbeck	Eagles	S Evans 1	Simpson (5)	Galbraith (11)	Barnes (15)		
14-Feb	Blackburn Rovers	League	Home	1-2	389	Zieler	Gray	Pique	Chester	Cathcart	Eagles	Cleverley	Welbeck 1	Hewson	Barnes	S Evans	R Eckersley (8)	Chester	Dong (10)	Bryan	Galbraith
21-Feb	Wigan Athletic*	League	Home	1-1	272	Simpson	Lea	R Eckersley	Pique	Chester	R Jones	Eagles	Possebon	Welbeck	Eagles	S Evans	Zieler	R Jones	Cleverley (6)	Bryan (3)	Machada
26-Feb	Liverpool	League	Away	0-2	10,546	Heaton	G Neville	Simpson	R Eckersley	Chester	Hewson	Cleverley	Possebon	Welbeck	Barnes	Chester (2)	Zieler	Gray (2)	C Evans (8)	Bryan (11)	James
06-Mar	Middlesbrough	League	Home	2-1	360	Foster	G Neville	Simpson	Chester	Pique	Eagles 1	Eagles 1	Possebon	Welbeck	Fagan	Cleverley	Zieler	Fagan	Gray (10)		Barnes (11)
12-Mar	Sunderland	League	Away	0-1	1,032	Kuszczak	G Neville	Simpson	R Eckersley	Chester	Hewson	Cleverley	Possebon	Welbeck 3	Hewson	Barnes	Zieler	R Eckersley (3)	Galbraith (11)		C Evans
20-Mar	Manchester City	League	Home	4-1	741	Heaton	G Neville	Silvestre	Simpson 1	Chester	Gray	Possebon	Welbeck 1	Eagles	S Evans 1	Lea	Zieler	Norwood	Fagan		Brady (6)
27-Mar	Newcastle United	League	Away	3-1	547	Foster	G Neville	Silvestre	R Eckersley	Chester	Cleverley	Possebon	Welbeck 1	Macheda 1	Cleverley	Barnes	Amos	James	Galbraith (8)	Eikrem	Brady
01-Apr	Newcastle United	League	Away	1-1		Zieler	R Eckersley	Silvestre	R Eckersley	Cathcart	R Jones	Possebon	Macheda	Cleverley	Eagles 1	S Evans 1	Zieler	C Evans	Galbraith (11)	Fagan	Bryan (9)
21-Apr	Oldham Athletic	League	Away	2-0	2,839	Zieler	G Neville	R Eckersley	Chester	Cathcart	Hewson 1	R Jones	Possebon	Welbeck	Eagles 1	S Evans	Woods	C Evans	Fagan	Eikrem	
24-Apr	Bolton Wanderers	MSC	Away	2-1		Amos	Gray	Chester	Chester	Cathcart	Hewson 1	R Jones	Possebon 1	Welbeck	Eagles 1	S Evans	Amos	Galbraith (10)	James	Bryan (9)	
12-May	Bolton Wanderers	MSC Fin	Home	2-0		Zieler	Gray	Cleverley	Chester	Cathcart	Hewson	Barnes	Drinkwater	Machada	Eagles 1	S Evans	Fagan	Amos	Machada	James	Drinkwater

* Own goals: Stokes v Bolton Wanderers (home), Granqvist v Wigan Athletic (home)
† Line up not in number order: v Stockport (MSC home)

Season 2007/08

RESERVES APPEARANCES AND GOALS 2007/08

Name	League Apps	League Gls	MSC Apps	MSC Gls	LSC Apps	LSC Gls	Youth Cup Apps	Youth Cup Gls	Season Total Apps	Season Total Gls
Ben Amos	1		1				2		4	0
Luis Anderson	1								1	0
Phil Bardsley	2								2	0
Michael Barnes	8 (3)		4						12 (3)	0
Robbie Brady	(1)								0 (1)	0
Fabien Brandy	6 (2)	4	1	2					7 (2)	6
Antonio Bryan	2 (3)		(2)				1 (1)	1	3 (6)	1
Fraizer Campbell	3	1							3	1
Craig Cathcart	4		2		1				7	1
James Chester	16 (1)		4		2				22 (1)	0
Tom Cleverley	10 (3)	2	5		2				17 (3)	2
Fangzhou Dong	7 (2)		1		3	3			10 (2)	4
Daniel Drinkwater	(5)					1	2		3 (5)	0
Joe Dudgeon							1		1	0
Chris Eagles	10	3	5	5	1	1			16	9
Adam Eckersley	5								5	0
Richard Eckersley	11 (5)		4 (1)		1				16 (6)	0
Magnus Eikrem			(1)		(1)		2		0 (2)	0
Corry Evans	2 (2)		1				2		5 (2)	0
Jonny Evans	1		1						2	0
Sean Evans	9 (1)	2	6	3	2	1			17 (1)	6
Chris Fagan	3 (1)		1 (1)		2	1			5 (2)	3
Ben Foster	2								2	0
Danny Galbraith	(2)		(1)		(1)		1 (1)		1 (5)	0
Darron Gibson	1								1	0
Oliver Gill							1		1	0
David Gray	9 (1)		5		2				16 (1)	0
Tom Heaton	8		3						11	0
Sam Hewson	14	1	5	1	2	1			21	3
Matty James	1						2		3	0
Richie Jones	4		1						5	0
Tomasz Kuszczak	1								1	0
Michael Lea	2		2		1				5	0
Kieran Lee	8	1	2						10	1
Conor McCormack					1	1			1	1
Federico Macheda	2 (1)	1			1	1	2	1	5 (1)	3
Lee Martin	3								3	0
Scott Moffatt							2		2	0
Gary Neville	5	1	1						6	1
Oliver Norwood	(1)				1		0 (1)		1 (2)	0
Gerard Pique	6								6	0
Rodrigo Possebon	8		2 (1)		1	1			11 (1)	1
Mikael Silvestre	2								2	0
Cameron Stewart							0 (1)		0 (1)	0
Danny Simpson	8 (1)	1	1						9 (1)	1
Kenny Strickland							1		1	0
Danny Welbeck	7 (4)	5	4 (2)	2			2	1	13 (6)	8
Gary Woods	(1)								0 (1)	0
Ron-Robert Zieler	6		2		2				10	0

YOUTH CUP GAMES 2007/08

Date	Opponents	Rnd	Venue	Res	Att	1	2	3	4	5	6	7	8	9	10	11	SUB	SUB
13-Dec	Brighton	R 3	Home	2-1	306	Amos	Moffatt	Dudgeon	James	Strickland	C.Evans	Eikrem	Drinkwater	Welbeck	Macheda	Galbraith	14 Bryan 1 (11)	15 Stewart (7)
16-Jan	Carlisle United	R 4	Home	1-2	330	Amos	Moffatt	Stewart	James	Gill	C.Evans	Eikrem	Drinkwater	Welbeck 1	Macheda 1	Bryan	14 Galbraith (3)	15 Norwood (7)

251

Season 2008/09

MANCHESTER UNITED RESERVES 2008/09: FA PREMIER RESERVE LEAGUE, MANCHESTER SENIOR CUP AND LANCASHIRE SENIOR CUP

Date	Opponents	Comp	Venue	Res	Att	1	2	3	4	5	6	7	8	9	10	11	12	13	14	15	16
30-Jul	Liverpool	LSC Fin	Leyland	3-2	660	Zieler	Gray 1	R Eckersley	Cathcart	Chester	Simpson	Possebon	Gibson	Campbell	Cleverley 1	Hewson	Derbyshire	Amos	Drinkwater 1 (7)	Eikrem	C Evans (11)
03-Sep	Bury	MSC	Away	2-0		Foster	R Da Silva	R Eckersley	Gray	Chester	Stewart	Eikrem 1	Drinkwater	Welbeck	Cleverley 1	Derbyshire	R Brown (2)	Amos	Curran (6)	Brandao (7)	Bryan
18-Sep	Blackburn Rovers	League	Home	0-0	390	Foster	R Da Silva	R Eckersley	Chester	Possebon	Drinkwater	Hewson	Welbeck	Cleverley	Stewart (7)	Zieler (1)	Eikrem	C Evans	Macheda (10)		
02-Oct	Wigan Athletic	League	Home	1-2	401	Woods	Gray 1	R Eckersley	C Evans	Chester	Eikrem	Drinkwater	Manucho	Macheda	Hewson	Cleverley	Stewart (7)	Devlin	Bryan (10)	Derbyshire (5)	Gill
08-Oct	Bolton Wanderers	League	Away	3-0	550	Kuszczak	R Da Silva	R Eckersley	Gray	Gibson	James	Stewart	Drinkwater	Macheda	Hewson 1	Derbyshire	Norwood (9)	Woods	Brandao (7)	Bryan (11)	
14-Oct	Oldham Athletic	MSC	Home	2-1		Foster	R Eckersley	Gill	Woolton	James 1	Stewart	Eikrem	Drinkwater	Macheda	Hewson 1	Bryan	Eikrem (11)	Norwood	Strickland		
22-Oct	Manchester City	League	Away	3-0	702	Foster	R Da Silva	Gray	C Evans	James	Possebon 1	Drinkwater	Macheda	Manucho	Hewson	Derbyshire	Derbyshire (6)	Zieler	James	Bryan (8)	
30-Oct	Bolton Wanderers*	League	Home	0-0		Amos	R Eckersley*	Chester*	C Evans*	Possebon	Gibson*	Drinkwater	Manucho*	Hewson*	Cleverley*	Derbyshire	Zieler	Eikrem (8)	Wootton	Bryan (6)	
18-Nov	Hull City	MSC	Home	1-2	1,381	Zieler	Stewart 1	Derbyshire	Wootton	Possebon	Eikrem	Hewson	Drinkwater	Cleverley	Hewson	Bryan	Strickland	Johnstone	Pettucci (11)	Brandao (6)	
18-Dec	Everton	League	Away	1-1	923	Woods	Gray	Derbyshire	Chester	Gibson*	Eikrem	Drinkwater	Macheda	Cleverley	Hewson	Cleverley	Derbyshire	James (7)	Brady	Stewart (10)	
22-Jan	Accrington Stanley	LSC	Home	3-0		Amos	R Eckersley	F Da Silva	De Laet	James	Brandy 1	Drinkwater	Manucho 1	Macheda	Pettucci 1	Bryan	F Da Silva (7)	Devlin	Norwood (3)	Pettucci (11)	
26-Jan	Blackburn Rovers	League	Away	1-2	579	Amos	R Eckersley	Derbyshire	C Evans	Chester	Eikrem	Drinkwater	Macheda	Macheda	Pettucci 1	Cleverley	Stewart (2)	Devlin	Dudgeon (3)	Norwood (6)	
29-Jan	Liverpool	League	Home	0-0	628	Kuszczak	C Evans	Derbyshire	De Laet	Chester	Possebon	Drinkwater	Macheda	Macheda	Pettucci	Tosic	Stewart (10)	Norwood	Pettucci (11)	Bryan (7)	Dudgeon (3)
09-Feb	Stockport County**	MSC	Home	0-0		Amos	F Da Silva	Dudgeon	R Eckersley**	Gill	Norwood**	Possebon**	Macheda**	Macheda**	Pettucci**	Tosic	Wootton	Devlin	Ajose**(2)	King	King
12-Feb	Bolton Wanderers	League	Home	2-0	255	Foster	R Eckersley	F Da Silva 1	Gill	James	Stewart	Possebon	Macheda 1	Martin	Brady	Dudgeon	Amos	Pettucci (7)	King (11)		
18-Feb	Wigan Athletic	League	Away	5-4	420	Amos	R Eckersley	Dudgeon	C Evans	James	Welbeck 2	Possebon	Macheda 2	Martin 1	Stewart	Derbyshire (5)	Eikrem (11)	Brady (3)	Norwood		
26-Feb	Manchester City	League	Home	2-1	546	Amos	R Eckersley	F Da Silva	De Laet	James 1	Drinkwater	Anderson	Macheda	Martin	Derbyshire (3)	Bryan	Devlin	Norwood (8)	Brady (7)	Bryan	
02-Mar	Sunderland	League	Away	0-1	862	13, Devlin	F Da Silva	C Evans	Chester	James	Drinkwater	Macheda	Martin	Tosic	Derbyshire	Devlin	Norwood	Brady (6)			
05-Mar	Middlesbrough	League	Home	1-0	241	Zieler	F Da Silva 1	C Evans	Gill	James	Possebon	Brady	Martin	Tosic	Derbyshire	1, Amos	Norwood (7)	Stewart (9)	Brady (11)		
09-Mar	Manchester City	MSC	Away	1-0	402	Zieler	Brady	De Laet	Gill	James	Drinkwater	Gibson	Martin 1	Tosic	Derbyshire	Devlin	Norwood (11)	Stewart	Galbraith		
12-Mar	Liverpool	League	Away	2-2	3,955	Kuszczak	F Da Silva 1	De Laet	C Evans	De Laet	Drinkwater	Welbeck 1	Martin	Brady	Derbyshire (11)	James	Woods	Drinkwater (6)	Bryan		
16-Mar	Rochdale	LSC	Away	4-1		Zieler	F Da Silva 3	C Evans	Gill	Possebon	Drinkwater	Bryan	Macheda	Welbeck 1	Derbyshire	James	Amos	Brady (3)	Stewart (8)	Galbraith	
19-Mar	Hull City	League	Home	8-2	365	Kuszczak	R Eckersley	F Da Silva	C Evans	James	Possebon	Drinkwater	Macheda	Macheda 1	Welbeck 1	Derbyshire	Gill (3)	Drinkwater	Brady (8)	Bryan (11)	
24-Mar	Middlesbrough	League	Away	1-0	1,074	Amos	R Eckersley	F Da Silva	De Laet	James	Possebon 1	Possebon	Macheda	Martin	Brady	Wootton (4)	Zieler	Norwood (10)	Stewart (7)		
30-Mar	Newcastle United	League	Away	3-3	1,277	Zieler	G Neville	Dudgeon	R Eckersley	De Laet	Possebon	Macheda	Macheda 3	Martin	Stewart	R Brown (2)	Eikrem (7)	Zieler	Norwood (11)	Galbraith	Wootton
16-Apr	Everton	League	Home	2-0	591	Amos	R Eckersley	Gill	C Evans	James	Drinkwater 1	Drinkwater	Macheda	Martin 1	Tosic	Derbyshire	Dudgeon	Devlin (1)	Norwood (11)	James (9)	Galbraith (7)
20-Apr	Preston North End	LSC	Away	4-0		Amos	R Eckersley	Gill	C Evans	De Laet	Drinkwater	Drinkwater 1	Welbeck	Macheda	Martin 1	Tosic	Derbyshire (4)	Amos	Stewart (10)	Dudgeon (6)	Galbraith (7)
23-Apr	Newcastle United	League	Away	1-1	553	Kuszczak	R Eckersley	Gill	C Evans 1	De Laet	James	James	Macheda	Martin 1	Tosic	Derbyshire	Dudgeon	Eikrem (9)	Brandao (7)	Stewart 1 (7)	
29-Apr	Sunderland	Home	2-0	462	Amos	R Brown	F Da Silva	C Evans	Gill	James 1	Drinkwater	Possebon	Possebon (3)	Martin	Tosic	Dudgeon (3)	Amos	Wootton	Brady	Ajose (7)	
12-May	Bolton Wanderers	MSC Fin	Away	1-0		Amos	James	C Evans	De Laet	Possebon	Welbeck	Drinkwater	Drinkwater	Martin	Tosic 1	Dudgeon	Dudgeon	Devlin	Stewart (11)	Gill (7)	

*Lost 8-9 on penalties
**Lost 7-8 on penalties

252

Season 2008/09

RESERVES APPEARANCES AND GOALS 2008/09

Name	League Apps	League Gls	MSC Apps	MSC Gls	LSC Apps	LSC Gls	Youth Cup Apps	Youth Cup Gls	Season Total Apps	Season Total Gls
Nicholas Ajose	(1)		(1)		(1)	1	0 (1)		0 (4)	1
Ben Amos	6		3		2				11	0
Luis Anderson	1								1	0
Robbie Brady	4 (3)		2		(1)		1		7 (4)	0
Evandro Brandao	(1)		(1)						0 (2)	0
Fabien Brandy	2	1			1	1			3	2
Reece Brown	1 (1)		(1)						1 (2)	0
Wes Brown	1				1				2	0
Antonio Bryan	1 (6)		(1)		2				3 (7)	0
Fraizer Campbell					1				1	0
Craig Cathcart					1				1	0
James Chester	7		2		1				10	0
Tom Cleverley	6	2	3	1	1	1			10	4
James Curran			(1)						0 (1)	0
James Derbyshire	4 (6)		2		1 (1)				7 (7)	0
Conor Devlin	1 (1)								1 (1)	0
Daniel Drinkwater	12	1	3		2 (2)	2			17 (2)	3
Joe Dudgeon	2 (2)		1 (1)		(2)		1		4 (5)	0
Richard Eckersley	14		5		4				23	0
Magnus Eikrem	9 (4)	1	1 (3)	1	1				11 (7)	2
Corry Evans	16	1	3		3 (1)				22 (1)	1
Ben Foster	3		2						5	0
Danny Galbraith	(1)								0 (1)	0
Darron Gibson	4	1	2		1				7	1
Oliver Gill	6 (1)		3 (1)		2		1		12 (2)	0
David Gray	5	1	3		1	1			9	2
Sam Hewson	6	1	3	1	1				10	2
Matty James	15 (2)	2	3	1	2	1	1		21 (2)	4
Josh King	(1)								0 (1)	0
Tomasz Kuszczak	5								5	0
Ritchie De Laet	10	1	2		2				14	1
Federico Macheda	12 (1)	9	3		2	1	1		18 (1)	10
Manucho	3	1	1						4	1
Lee Martin	13	3	3	1	1	1			17	5
Ravel Morrison							1	1	1	1
Gary Neville	1								1	0
Oliver Norwood	(7)		1 (1)		(1)		1		2 (9)	0
Davide Petrucci	1 (3)		1		1	1	0 (1)		3 (4)	1
Rodrigo Possebon	14	2	4		2				20	2
Fabio Da Silva	9 (1)	3	1		2	3			12 (1)	6
Rafael Da Silva	3		1						4	0
Danny Simpson					1				1	0
Cameron Stewart	4 (10)	1	2 (2)		(2)		0 (1)		6 (15)	1
Zoran Tosic	7		2	1	1				10	1
Danny Welbeck	5	4	2		1	1	1		9	5
Gary Woods	2						1		3	0
Scott Wootton	1 (2)		1				1		3 (2)	0
Ron-Robert Zieler	3 (1)		1		2				6 (1)	0

YOUTH CUP GAMES 2008/09

Date	Opponents	Rnd	Venue	Res	Att	1	2	3	4	5	6	7	8	9	10	11	SUB	SUB	SUB
27-Nov	Chelsea	R 3	Home	2-3	1246	Woods	Tunnicliffe	Dudgeon	Wootton	Gill	James	Morrison	Norwood	Macheda	Welbeck	Brady	14 Petrucci (8)	15 Stewart (11)	16 Ajose (9)

Season 2009/10

MANCHESTER UNITED RESERVES 2009/10: FA PREMIER RESERVE LEAGUE, MANCHESTER SENIOR CUP & LANCASHIRE SENIOR CUP

Date	Opponents	Comp	Venue	Res	Att	1	2	3	4	5	6	7	8	9	10	11	12	13	14	15	16
17-Aug	Bolton Wanderers	LSC Final	Leyland	1-0	483	Amos	Chester	Dudgeon	James	Cathcart	C Evans	Stewart	Eikrem	Macheda 1	Welbeck	Tosic	Gray (5)	Zieler	Norwood	Hewson (11)	King (9)
24-Aug	Bolton Wanderers	League	Away	3-1	400	Amos	W Brown	De Laet	James	Cathcart 1	Chester	Gray	King	Welbeck	Tosic 1	Moffatt 1 (2)	Dudgeon	Zieler	Eikrem (11)	Hewson 1 (8)	Stewart (2)
27-Aug	Bury	MSC	Home	5-0	302	Zieler	Gray	Dudgeon	De Laet	Chester	De Laet	Hewson 1	Eikrem	Macheda 2	Norwood	Moffatt (2)	Amos	Chester (5)	James (4)		
03-Sep	Wigan Athletic	League	Home	2-1	382	Amos	F Da Silva	Dudgeon	James	De Laet	G Neville	Stewart	Anderson 1	Brandy	Eikrem 1	Norwood		Devlin	Gill (9)	Norwood (10)	King (7)
17-Sep	Liverpool	League	Away	0-1	1,331	Zieler	Gray	Dudgeon	C Evans	Chester	De Laet	Welbeck	Macheda	King	Eikrem	Tosic	Hewson	Amos	Norwood	Tunnicliffe	Brady (11)
01-Oct	Sunderland	League	Away	4-0	420	Amos	F Da Silva	Dudgeon	C Evans	De Laet	Gill	Stewart	Macheda 1	King 2	Eikrem 2	Tosic		Devlin	Brandy (10)		Cofie
06-Oct	Everton	League	Home	1-0	1,276 Van Der Sar	Dudgeon	F Da Silva	Gill	C Evans	Norwood	Macheda 1	King	Brandy 1	Eikrem	Amos	Lloyd-Weston	Stewart (8)	R Brown (2)	Brady (10)	
12-Oct	Oldham Athletic	MSC	Away	3-0	416	Amos	R Da Silva	F Da Silva	James	Gill	Norwood	Brandy 1	Norwood	Brady	Amos	Norwood (10)	King 1 (7)		
22-Oct	Blackburn Rovers	League	Home	3-0	660	Amos	R Brown	Dudgeon	De Laet	Gill	James	Obertan	Hewson	King	Eikrem 1	Brandy	Zieler	Macheda'(2)	Brandy 1 (9)	Macheda (8)
29-Oct	Liverpool	LSC	Home	1-1	792	Zieler	Gray	Dudgeon	Gill	De Laet	James	King	Hewson	King	Norwood	Tosic 1	Zieler	Lloyd-Weston	Norwood (10)	Stewart
03-Nov	Manchester City	League	Away	0-1	360	Zieler	De Laet	Dudgeon	C Evans	Gill	James	Stewart	Norwood	Brandy'	Eikrem	Tosic 1 (8)		Macheda' (2)	James (10)	
24-Nov	Hull City	League	Away	2-1	747	Zieler	Tunnicliffe	Gill	De Laet	James	Stewart	Hewson	Norwood	Eikrem	Tosic 2	Wootton (5)	Devlin	W Keane (8)	Tunnicliffe (8)	Ajose	Brandy (3)
14-Dec	Bolton Wanderers**	MSC	Away	2-2		Amos	McGinty	Wootton	Gill	Pogba 1	Stewart	Norwood**	Ajose 1	Eikrem	Ajose	Zieler	Massacci	Petrucci	Cofie (11)
21-Jan	Sunderland	League	Away	4-0	729	Amos	Dudgeon	De Laet	Gill	James	Stewart	C Evans	Diouf	Obertan	Fornasier	Zieler	Stewart (9)	Norwood 1 (7)	Brandy 1 (9)	
28-Jan	Bolton Wanderers	League	Home	1-0	225	Gray	F Da Silva	De Laet	James	Gill	Possebon	Stewart 1	Anderson	Obertan	Diouf 1	Moffatt	Zieler	Dudgeon (16)	Wootton (7)	Brandy (8)
18-Feb	Everton	League	Home	2-0	484	Foster	Gill	Possebon	Wootton	Stewart	Diouf	Norwood	R Brown (3)	Moffatt	Wootton (8)	Brandy (9)	
24-Feb	Blackburn Rovers	League	Away	1-1	2,803	Amos	R Brown	Gill	De Laet 1	Possebon	Stewart	Diouf	Norwood	Obertan	Moffatt	Zieler	Moffatt	Ajose	Brandy (9)
08-Mar	Stockport County	MSC	Away	1-0	358	Zieler	Moffatt	Gill	Wootton	Stewart	Possebon	Brandy	Norwood	Obertan		Cole (9)	W Keane 1 (11)		
11-Mar	Manchester City	League	Home	2-2	2,039	Zieler	R Brown 1	Gill	C Evans 1	De Laet	Stewart	Possebon	Diouf	W Keane 1	Norwood	Obertan	Devlin	Ekrem (2)	Stewart (9)	W Keane (7)	Brandy (11)
18-Mar	Burnley	League	Home	2-0	947	Zieler	R Brown	Dudgeon	C Evans 1	Gill	Stewart	Possebon	Brandy 1	Norwood	Obertan	Hargreaves	Devlin	Eikrem (6)	Ajose (9)	Stewart (9)
06-Apr	Hull City	League	Home	6-1	429	Foster	Moffatt	Dudgeon 1	C Evans 1	Gill 1	Stewart	Possebon	Brandy 1	Diouf 3	Norwood**	Ajose 1	Devlin	Eikrem (11)	Moffatt (3)	Ajose (7)	Cofie
13-Apr	Liverpool	League	Home	1-0	960	Foster	Dudgeon	Wootton	De Laet 1	Gill	Stewart	Possebon	Brandy	Norwood	Eikrem 1	Obertan	Devlin	Zieler	Moffatt (2)	Pogba (10)	W Keane (9)
22-Apr	Manchester City	MSC	Home	0-2	864	Foster	Dudgeon	Gill	De Laet	James	Possebon	Stewart	Brandy 1	Diouf 1	Norwood	Obertan 1	Devlin	Pogba (10)	Thorpe	Pogba (7)	Hussain
26-Apr	Wigan Athletic	League	Away	0-1	235	Zieler	M Keane	Dudgeon	C Evans	De Laet	Gill	Stewart	Macheda	Brandy	Norwood	Obertan	Devlin	R Brown (11)	Lingard (11)	W Keane (9)	Cole (9)
29-Apr	Burnley	League	Home	1-0	662	Zieler	R Da Silva	M Keane	C Evans	Gill	Cole 1	Stewart	Possebon	Lingard	Norwood	Hussain	Ekangamene (2)	Johnstone	Brady (5)	Cole (9)	Brandy (5)
03-May	Aston Villa***	Play-off	Home	3-3	2,165	Foster***	Dudgeon	C Evans	C Evans	Gill		Possebon***	Macheda***	Diouf 2	Norwood	Wootton	Zieler	Johnstone	Obertan (7)	W Keane (15)	

*Lost 3-4 on penalties
**Lost 2-3 on penalties
***Won 3-2 on penalties

Season 2009/10

RESERVES APPEARANCES AND GOALS 2009/10

Name	Reserves Apps	Reserves Gls	Youth Cup Apps	Youth Cup Gls	Season Tot Apps	Season Tot Gls
Nicholas Ajose	3(1)	1	3	1	6(1)	2
Ben Amos	9				9	
Luis Anderson	2	1			2	1
Febian Brandy	11(7)	5			11(7)	5
Robbie Brady	2(3)				2(3)	
Reece Brown	6(3)	1	1		7(3)	1
Wes Brown	1				1	
Craig Cathcart	4	1			4	1
James Chester	5(1)				5(1)	
John Cofie	0(3)		0(2)		0(5)	
Larnell Cole	1	1	1		2	1
Conor Devlin			3		3	
Mame Biram Diouf	6	6			6	6
Joe Dudgeon	18(1)	1			18(1)	1
Magnus Eikrem	11(6)	5			11(6)	5
Charni Ekangamene	0(1)				0(1)	
Corry Evans	20(2)	2			20(2)	2
Michele Fornasier	0(1)		1(1)		2(2)	
Ben Foster	6				6	
Ezekiel Fryers			1		1	
Darron Gibson	1				1	
Oliver Gill	23(2)	1			23(2)	1
David Gray	5(1)	1			5(1)	1
Sam Hewson	12(3)	4			12(3)	4
Etzaz Hussain	2		0(1)		2(1)	
Owen Hargreaves	1				1	
Matty James	11(2)				11(2)	
Michael Keane	2(2)	1			2(2)	
Will Keane	1(9)	2	3	2	4(9)	4
Joshua King	8(3)	3	2	2	10(3)	5
Ritchie De Laet	18	2			18	2
Jesse Lingard	1(1)		0(1)		1(2)	
Federico Macheda	7(2)	5			7(2)	5
Alberto Massaci			1(1)		1(1)	
Sean McGinty	1(1)		3		4(1)	
Scott Moffatt	2(2)	1			2(2)	1
Ravel Morrison	0(1)		1(1)		1(1)	
Gary Neville	1				1	
Oliver Norwood	22(2)				22(2)	
Gabriel Obertan	10(1)	2			10(1)	2
Davide Petrucci	0(1)				0(1)	
Paul Pogba	1(4)	1	3	1	4(4)	2
Rodrigo Possebon	11				11	
Fabio Da Silva	7				7	
Rafael Da Silva	3	1			3	1
Cameron Stewart	18(5)	2			18(5)	2
Zoran Tosic	8(1)	5			8(1)	5
Tom Thorpe			1		1	
Ryan Tunnicliffe			3		3	
Edwin van der Sar	1				1	
Danny Welbeck	4				4	
Scott Wootton	9(5)		3		12(5)	
Ron-Robert Zieler	10(1)				10(1)	

YOUTH CUP GAMES 2009/10

Date	Opponents	Rnd	Venue	Res	Att	1	2	3	4	5	6	7	8	9	10	11	SUB	SUB	SUB
10-Dec	Birmingham City	R 3	Home	2-0	635	Devlin	Fornasier	McGinty	Thorpe	Wootton	Tunnicliffe	Morrison	Pogba 1	W. Keane	Petrucci	Ajose 1	16 Massacci (4)	14 Cofie (11)	16 Lingard (10)
13-Jan	Burnley	R 4	Away	5-1	1036	Devlin	Massacci	Ajose	Wootton	McGinty	Tunnicliffe	Cole	Pogba	W. Keane 2	Petrucci 1	King 2	12 Fornasier (2)	15 Hussain (10)	16 Cofie (3)
28-Jan	Blackburn Rovers	R 5	Away	0-3	874	Devlin	R.Brown	Fryers	Wootton	McGinty	Tunnicliffe	Ajose	Pogba	W. Keane	Petrucci	King	14 Morrison (2)		

Season 2010/11

MANCHESTER UNITED RESERVES 2010/11: FA PREMIER RESERVE LEAGUE, MANCHESTER SENIOR CUP & LANCASHIRE SENIOR CUP

Date	Opponents	Comp	Venue	Res	Att	1	2	3	4	5	6	7	8	9	10	11	12	13	14	15	16
24-Aug	Manchester City	MSC	Away	3-1	1,569	Amos	R Da Silva	W Brown	Neville	Smalling	Carrick	Gibson	Macheda 2	Anderson	Cleverley 1	Gill (6)	Devlin	Dudgeon (3)	W Keane (8)	Norwood	
01-Sep	Oldham Athletic	MSC	Away	2-1	1,101	Devlin	W Brown	Gill	Wootton	Ferdinand	De Laet	Gibson	Cofie	Eikrem	Ajose 1	R Brown (5)	Coll	Tunnicliffe (4)	Lingard (8)		
09-Sep	Stockport County	MSC	Home	2-0	535	Johnstone	R Brown	De Laet	C Evans	W Brown	De Laet	Morrison	Anderson	W Keane 1	Eikrem	Ajose	Devlin		Brady		
16-Sep	Aston Villa	League	Home	1-4	583	Johnstone	De Laet	C Evans	R Brown	Gill	Obertan	Morrison	W Keane	Eikrem	Bebe	Vermijl		Brady (9)			
20-Sep	Bury◊	LSC	Away	5-1		Johnstone	Vermijl	14, Fryers	C Evans	Wootton	R Brown	Stewart	Morrison	W Keane	Eikrem	Brady 2	Devlin	Ajose 1 (8)	Cofie 1 (8)		
23-Sep	Bolton Wanderers	League	Home	4-0	391	Devlin	R Brown	Fryers	C Evans	Wootton	Gill	Stewart	Ajose 3	Eikrem	Brady 1	M Keane (8)	Johnstone	Tunnicliffe (7)	Cofie 1 (10)		
27-Sep	Blackburn Rovers	League	Away	2-2	3,644	Devlin	R Brown	C Evans	Wootton	Gill	Vermijl	Obertan	Ajose	Eikrem	Brady 1	Hussain (9)	Johnstone	Tunnicliffe (11)	Cofie 1 (2)		
02-Nov	Bolton Wanderers	League	Away	3-1	312	Devlin	Fryers	C Evans	Wootton	Gill	Vermijl	Obertan	Ajose	Eikrem		Johnstone	Thorpe (2)	Cofie (7)			
11-Nov	West Brom	League	Away	2-2	306	Amos	Vermijl 1	De Laet	Thorpe 1	Tunnicliffe	M Keane	Stewart 1	Vermijl	Ekiem	Pogba	Brady	Coll	Ekangamene	Lingard		
18-Nov	Wigan Athletic	League	Home	3-1	386	Amos	Vermijl	Dudgeon	Wootton	R Brown	M Keane	Stewart	Tunnicliffe	W Keane	Morrison	Fornasier 1 (6)	Jacob	McGinty (3)	Cofie (10)		
23-Nov	Manchester City	League	Away	1-1	1,726	Johnstone	R Brown	Dudgeon	Wootton	R Brown	Stewart	Tunnicliffe	W Keane 1	Ekiem	Bebe 2	Thorpe (3)	Cofie	Norwood (11)	Lingard		
16-Dec	Newcastle United	League	Home	5-1	357	Amos	M Keane	Blackett	Vermijl	Popba	Norwood	Tunnicliffe 1	W Keane 2	Ekiem	Morrison 2	Brady (2)	McGinty (2)	Lingard	Cofie (6)		
13-Jan	Bolton Wanderers	League	Home	1-0	371	Devlin	O'Shea	F Da Silva	Scholes	W Brown	Wootton	King 1	Bebe	Obertan	Dudgeon	Vermijl (7)	Jacob	Norwood (4)	Fryers	Massacci	
17-Jan	Bury‡	MSC	Away	8-0	27	Lindegaard	Gill	C Evans	W Brown	Wootton	King 2	Gibson	Brady 1	Brady 1	Vermijl 1 (7)	Devlin	Norwood (4)	Fryers			
26-Jan	Wigan Athletic	League	Away	0-0	361	Devlin	R Brown	Gill	R Brown	King	Norwood	Bebe	Obertan	Brady 1	Jacob	W Keane (11)	Coll	Barnby (6)	Vermijl (8)		
03-Feb	Rochdale	MSC	Home	6-1	238	Devlin	R Brown	McGinty	Wootton	Ekangamene	King 3	Norwood	F Da Silva 1		Giverin (2)	Johnstone	Morrison 1 (3)	Pettucci (7)	McGinty (5)		
13-Feb	Oldham Athletic‡	LSC	Home	3-0	1,152	Devlin	R Brown	F Da Silva	R Brown	Gill	Norwood	Brady	King 2	Morrison	Obertan	Barnby (8)	Devlin	Ekangamene	Pettucci (7)		
03-Mar	Wolves	League	Away	3-3	674	Devlin	R Brown	Dudgeon	R Brown	Gill	Wootton	Bebe 1	Brady	King	Obertan 1	Vermijl	Pettucci (9)	Fettis	McGinty		
09-Mar	Blackpool◊	League	Away	1-2		Lindegaard	R Brown	Dudgeon	Norwood	Gill	Wootton	Bebe 1	Tunnicliffe	King 1	Morrison	Pogba (7)	Johnstone	Thorpe	Giverin	Massacci	
17-Mar	Sunderland	League	Home	2-2	381	Devlin	R Brown	Vermijl	Norwood	Gill	Wootton	Tunnicliffe	King	Obertan	Obertan 2	M Keane		Pettucci (2)	Ekangamene (10)		
21-Mar	Newcastle Utd‡‡	League	Away	2-1										Morrison	Dudgeon		Pettucci (10)		Pettucci (7)	Blackett (9)	
01-Apr	West Ham United	League	Away	1-0	1,106	Johnstone	R Brown	M Keane 1	Wootton	Thorpe	Norwood	Cole	Tunnicliffe	King	Obertan 1	Pettucci	Pettucci (10)	Fettis	Pettucci (7)	Rothwell	
07-Apr	Manchester City	League	Home	3-1	855	Amos	Vermijl	R Brown	Dudgeon	R Brown	Bebe	Norwood 2	King	Anderson	King	Pettucci	Anderson 2 (2)	Devlin (1)	Rudge (11)	Ekangamene	
13-Apr	Everton	League	Home	2-0	450	Amos	R Brown	R Brown	Dudgeon	R Brown	Bebe 1	Norwood	Brady	Anderson	Obertan 1	Brady	Brady (10)	Johnstone	Vermijl (2)	Wilkinson	
18-Apr	Chelsea	League	Home	4-1	503	Amos	W Brown	R Brown	Dudgeon	Wootton	Gill	Bebe 1	Brady	Fletcher	Brady	Pettucci	Pettucci (10)	Pettucci	Rudge (11)	Rowley	
28-Apr	Arsenal	League	Home	0-0		Amos	W Brown	R Brown	Dudgeon	Wootton	Gill	Bebe	Norwood	Obertan	Fletcher	Vermijl (7)		Devlin	Pettucci	Tunnicliffe (10)	W Keane (11)
04-May	Liverpool	League	Away	2-2	732	Amos	Vermijl	Brady	Norwood	Wootton	Gill	Ajose 1	James	King	Obertan	Obertan 1	Morrison (7)	Devlin	Ekangamene (9)	Lawrence	Blackett (8)
11-May	Blackburn Rovers	Play-off		1-2		Amos	R Da Silva	Vermijl	Brady	Wootton	Gill	Ajose 1	Norwood	Obertan	Brady	Johnstone (7)	Cofie (7)	Devlin	Ekangamene	Ajose (2)	
16-May	Bolton Wanderers	MSC Final	Home	3-1		Lindegaard	R Da Silva	Gill			James	Fletcher	Norwood	Ajose 1	Brady	King (6)	Devlin	Leao	Pettucci 1 (8)		
20-May	Blackburn Rovers‡	LSC Semi	Home	0-1	26	Devlin		Brady	Norwood	Wootton	Gill				Petrucci	King	Ekangamene		Vermijl (11)	Barnby	

◦ Own goal: Basham
◊ Oliver Gill was injured during warm up and was replaced by Zeki Fryers v Bury (LSC away). Fryers originally named as a substitute wore the number 14 shirt
‡ Played at Carrington behind closed doors
‡‡ Played behind closed doors

Season 2010/11

RESERVES APPEARANCES AND GOALS 2010/11

Name	Reserve Apps	Reserve Gls	Youth Cup Apps	Youth Cup Gls	Season Tot Apps	Season Tot Gls
Nicholas Ajose	7 (2)	7			7 (2)	7
Ben Amos	9				9	0
Luis Anderson	4 (1)	2			4 (1)	2
Jack Barmby	0 (1)				0 (1)	0
Bebe	13	6			13	6
Tyler Blackett	12		4 (2)		16 (2)	0
Robbie Brady	15 (3)	4			15 (3)	4
Reece Brown	21 (2)	1			21 (2)	1
Wes Brown	9				9	0
Michael Carrick	1				1	0
Tom Cleverley	1	1			1	1
John Cofie	1 (7)	3	2 (2)		3 (9)	3
Larnell Cole	1		6 (2)	1	7 (2)	1
Mats Daehli			0 (1)		0 (1)	0
Conor Devlin	11 (1)				11 (1)	0
Joe Dudgeon	13 (1)				13 (1)	0
Magnus Eikrem	10	1			10	1
Charni Ekangamene	0 (2)				0 (2)	0
Corry Evans	6				6	0
Rio Ferdinand	1				1	0
Darren Fletcher	2				2	0
Michele Fornasier	0 (1)	1	8		8 (1)	1
Ezekiel Fryers	3		0 (2)		3 (2)	0
Darron Gibson	2				2	0
Oliver Gill	20 (2)				20 (2)	0
Etzaz Hussain	0 (1)				0 (1)	0
Matty James	1				1	0
Sam Johnstone	6		8		14	0
Michael Keane	3 (2)	1	7		10 (2)	1
Will Keane	7 (3)	6	7	8	14 (3)	14
Joshua King	15 (1)	8			15 (1)	8
Ritchie De Laet	5				5	0
Tom Lawrence			0 (3)		0 (3)	0
Anders Lindegaard	3				3	0
Jesse Lingard	1 (3)		5 (2)	2	6 (5)	2
Federico Macheda	2	3			2	3
Alberto Massaci			0 (1)		0 (1)	0
Sean McGinty	0 (3)		4		4 (3)	0
Ravel Morrison	9 (2)		5	5	14 (2)	5
Gary Neville	1				1	0
Oliver Norwood	17 (2)	2			17 (2)	2
Gabriel Obertan	19	9			19	9
John O'Shea	2				2	0
Davide Petrucci	3 (10)	2			3 (10)	2
Paul Pogba	2 (1)		8	2	10 (1)	2
Jack Rudge	0 (2)				0 (2)	0
Paul Scholes	1				1	0
Fabio Da Silva	4	1			4	1
Rafael Da Silva	3				3	0
Chris Smalling	1				1	0
Cameron Stewart	6	1			6	1
Tom Thorpe	3 (2)	1	8		11 (2)	1
Ryan Tunnicliffe	8 (5)	2	8		16 (5)	2
Gyliano van Velzen	0 (1)		8		8 (1)	0
Marnick Vermijl	18 (6)	3			18 (6)	3
Scott Wootton	27				27	0

YOUTH CUP GAMES 2010/11

Date	Opponents	Rnd	Venue	Res	Att	1	2	3	4	5	6	7	8	9	10	11	SUB	SUB	SUB
10-Jan	Portsmouth[9]	R3	Home	3-2	414	Johnstone	M.Keane	Blackett	Thorpe	Fornasier	Tunnicliffe	Cole	Pogba	Cofie	W.Keane	van Velzen	12 Fryers (7)	14 Lingard (2)	15 Massaci (5)
19-Jan	West Ham United	R4	Away	1-0	1,405	Johnstone	M.Keane	Blackett	Thorpe	Fornasier	Tunnicliffe	Cole	Pogba	Cofie	W.Keane	van Velzen	12 Fryers (11)		
16-Feb	Newcastle United	R5	Home	3-2	657	Johnstone	M.Keane	Blackett	Thorpe	Fornasier	Tunnicliffe	Cole	Pogba	van Velzen	Morrison 1	Lingard		15 McGinty (9)	16 Blackett (11)
13-Mar	Liverpool	R6	Away	2-3	10,199	Johnstone	M.Keane	McGinty	Thorpe	Fornasier	Tunnicliffe	Cole 1	Pogba 1	W. Keane	Morrison 2	Lingard 1	14 Lawrence (10)	15 Daehli (9)	
10-Apr	Chelsea	SF1	Away	4-0	5,518	Johnstone	M.Keane	McGinty	Thorpe	Fornasier	Tunnicliffe	Cole	Pogba 1	W. Keane 3	Morrison 1	Lingard 1	14 Lawrence (10)	15 Lawrence (10)	
20-Apr	Chelsea	SF2	Home	2-2	9,124	Johnstone	M.Keane	McGinty	Thorpe	Fornasier	Tunnicliffe	Cole	Pogba	W. Keane 1	Morrison	van Velzen	14 Lingard (8)		
17-May	Sheffield United	F1	Away	2-2	29,977	Johnstone	M.Keane	McGinty	Thorpe	Fornasier	Tunnicliffe Lingard 1		Pogba	W. Keane 2	Morrison 2	van Velzen	14 Cofie (11)		
23-May	Sheffield United	F2	Home	4-1	24,916	Johnstone	Massacci	McGinty	Thorpe	Fornasier	Tunnicliffe	Lingard	Pogba	W. Keane 2			12 Blackett (11)	14 Cole (7)	15 Cofie (10)

[9] Own goal: Fry

Season 2011/12

MANCHESTER UNITED RESERVES 2011/12: FA PREMIER RESERVE LEAGUE, MANCHESTER SENIOR CUP & LANCASHIRE SENIOR CUP

Date	Opponents	Comp	Venue	Res	Att	1	2	3	4	5	6	7	8	9	10	11	12	13	14	15	16	17
15-Aug	Arsenal	League	Away	1-2	2,000	Kuszczak	Cole	M Keane	R Brown	Fryers	Pogba	Gibson	Pogba	Diouf 1	Drinkwater	Norwood	W Keane (9)	Johnstone	Petrucci (2)	Lingard (11)	McGinty	
25-Aug	Swansea City	League	Away	1-2	545	Amos	Vermijl	McGinty	Fletcher	M Keane	Pogba 1	Pogba	W Keane	Diouf 2	Pettucci	Cole	Lingard 1 (11)	Johnstone	Cofie (10)	W Keane 1 (8)	Fornasier	
08-Sep	Bury	MSC	Home	6-0	545	Amos	Vermijl	McGinty	M Keane 1	Thorpe	Fryers	Pogba 1	Vermijl	Cofie	W Keane	Giverin	Massacci (9)	Jacob	Leao	Lawrence	Blackett 1 (8)	
12-Sep	Fulham	MSC	Home	2-0	318	Amos	M Keane 1	Cole	Thorpe	Fryers	Fryers	Pogba	Lingard	W Keane	Pettucci	Cole	Pettucci (8)	Jacob	Thorpe	W Keane (11)	Cofie	
15-Sep	Rochdale	MSC	Away	2-1	378	Amos	Vermijl	McGinty	R Brown	M Keane	Pogba	James	Pettucci	Macheda	Diouf	Cole	Giverin (7)	Jacob	Cofie	Leao		
27-Sep	Norwich City*	League	Away	4-2	3,894	Amos	Massacci	Fornasier	Thorpe	Fryers	Pogba 1	James	Macheda 1	W Keane	Pettucci	Cole 1	Vermijl (6)	Coll	Morrison (7)	Thorpe (4)	Cofie	
13-Oct	Bolton Wanderers	MSC	Away	1-0	120	Kuszczak	R Brown	McGinty	Fornasier	M Keane	Pogba	W Keane	Diouf	Macheda	Pettucci	Vermijl (6)	McGinty (3)	Coll	Morrison 1 (7)	Cofie		
20-Oct	Blackburn Rovers	League	Home	0-0	542	Amos	Vermijl	McGinty	Fornasier	R Brown	Pogba	Cole	Diouf	Pettucci	Macheda	Jacob	Morrison (11)	Lingard (10)	Thorpe			
03-Nov	Everton	League	Home	2-0	636	Amos	Vermijl	M Keane	Fornasier	Cole	Pogba	W Keane 1	Diouf	Pettucci	Lingard 1	Thorpe (6)	Coll	Cofie (8)	McGinty (3)			
17-Nov	Wigan Athletic	League	Home	4-1	556	Amos	Vermijl 1	McGinty	Thorpe	Wootton	M Keane 1	Pogba	Pettucci 1	W Keane 2	Pettucci	Lingard	Morrison 2	Jacob	Cofie (7)	Leao (4)		
22-Nov	Bolton Wanderers	League	Away	2-1	571	Amos	R Da Silva	M Keane	Fornasier	M Keane	Fryers	Pogba	W Keane 1	Diouf 1	Lingard	Pettucci (5)	Cofie (9)	Jacob	Giverin	Leao (4)		
08-Dec	Sunderland	League	Away	3-6	646	Kuszczak	Vermijl 1	McGinty	Wootton	M Keane 1	Lingard	Fornasier	W Keane 1	Pettucci	Macheda	Blackett	Massacci (11)	Sutherland	Cofie (8)	Giverin		
15-Dec	Liverpool	League	Home	4-0	699	Amos	Cole	Wootton	Fryers	Pogba	Gibson	Pogba	Diouf 2	Pogba	Fornasier	Lingard	Fornasier (6)	Jacob	Pettucci (11)	Cofie (7)		
22-Dec	Blackburn Rovers	LSC	Away	4-0	1,195	Amos	R Da Silva	Vermijl	Gibson	M Keane	Fryers	Cole	Pogba	W Keane 1	Pettucci	Macheda	Fornasier (6)	Jacob	Pettucci (9)	Lingard 1 (11)	Thorpe	
13-Jan	Stockport County‡	MSC	Away	1-0	39	Amos	Vermijl	Fryers	Fornasier	Thorpe	R Brown	Norwood	Diouf 1	W Keane 1	Pettucci 2	Lingard	Massacci (6)	Coll	McGinty	M Keane (3)		
26-Jan	Newcastle United*	League	Home	6-0	567	Johnstone	Vermijl	Fryers	Norwood	Cole	Pogba	F Da Silva	W Keane 1	Pettucci 1	Lingard	Massacci 1 (7)	Coll	Leao (9)	Thorpe (8)	Giverin		
01-Feb	Oldham Athletic‡	MSC	Home	3-0	24	Kuszczak	Vermijl	Fornasier	Giverin	F Da Silva	F Da Silva	Pogba	R Brown	King	Pettucci	Lingard 1	Massacci (11)	Coll	R Brown (8)	McGinty (8)	Giverin	Van Velzen (3)
09-Feb	Manchester City‡	MSC	Home	2-4	360	Johnstone	Vermijl	Fornasier	M Keane	Thorpe	Fryers	Cole 1	Pogba 1	W Keane	Pettucci	Lingard 1	Thorpe (6)	Sutherland	Fornasier	Leao	Giverin (3)	
13-Feb	Bolton Wanderers	League	Home	2-1	357	Johnstone	De Laet	R Brown 1	Vermijl	Fryers	Fryers	Cole 1	King	W Keane	Pettucci	Lingard	Giverin	Coll	R Brown (8)	Leao	Vesseli	
21-Feb	Wigan Athletic	League	Away	0-0	600	Amos	De Laet	Fornasier	M Keane	Vermijl	Vermijl	Turnicliffe	W Keane	Pettucci	Lingard	Thorpe (6)	Johnstone	Giverin	Massacci	Vesseli		
06-Mar	West Brom	League	Away	0-1	2,443	Johnstone	Vermijl	Fornasier	M Keane	Veseli	Turnicliffe	Turnicliffe	W Keane	Pettucci	Lingard	Coll	James (7)	Daehli (3)	Wilson (6)			
12-Mar	Blackburn Rovers	League	Away	1-0	495	Johnstone	De Laet	Vermijl	Turnicliffe	Smalling 1	M Keane	Pogba	Pettucci 1	W Keane	Lingard	Fryers	M Keane (4)	Vesseli (11)	Turnicliffe (8)	Vermijl (11)	Massacci	
22-Mar	Aston Villa	League	Away	3-1	1	Amos	De Laet	F Da Silva	James	Jones	Cleverley	Pogba	Pettucci 2	W Keane	Lingard 1	Thorpe (9)	Turnicliffe	Thorpe (7)	Vermijl (2)			
27-Mar	Everton†	League	Away	4-1	597	Johnstone	Vermijl	De Laet 1	Turnicliffe	Fryers	Cole	Pogba	Pettucci 1	W Keane 4	Lingard	Fornasier (3)	Coll	Turnicliffe (4)	Giverin			
16-Apr	Newcastle United	League	Home	6-3		Johnstone	De Laet 1	Fryers	Fryers	De Laet	Pettucci 1	W Keane 1	Lingard	Blackett (11)	Coll	Thorpe (3)	Giverin (2)	Ekangamene				
23-Apr	Chelsea‡	League	Away	4-1		Johnstone	Vermijl	Fryers	Thorpe	Fryers	De Laet 1	Pettucci	W Keane 1	Lingard	Giverin (11)	Blackett	Coll	Fornasier (2)	Van Velzen (7)			
26-Apr	Wolverhampton	League	Home	2-0	294	Johnstone	Vermijl	De Laet	M Keane	Fryers	Turnicliffe	W Keane	Pettucci 1	Fornasier	Giverin (4)	Jacob	Sutherland (7)	Van Velzen (7)	Blackett (11)			
01-May	Blackpool*	LSC Semi	Away	0-0	267	Johnstone	Giverin*	R Brown*	M Keane	Wootton	Turnicliffe	Hendrie	King*	Ekangamene*	Brady	Wilkinson	Johnstone	Gorre (7)	A Fletcher			
04-May	Sunderland	League	Home	0-0								Rudge		Pettucci 1	James	Fornasier (4)	Johnstone	Giverin	Wootton (4)			
10-May	Aston Villa**	League	Away	0-0	259	Lindegaard	Vermijl	Thorpe	M Keane	M Keane	Cole	Pettucci	Brady	Wilkinson	Lingard*	Johnstone	Giverin	Brady (2)				
17-May	Manchester City	MSC Final	Away	2-0	5,157	Amos	Vermijl	Fryers	Turnicliffe	Wootton	M Keane	Pogba	W Keane**	Pettucci	Lingard	Thorpe (10)	Coll	King* (10)	Giverin			

*Own goals: Drury v Norwich City (away), Söderberg v Newcastle United (home)
‡Played at Carrington behind closed doors
‡‡Played behind closed doors
*Won 3-1 on penalties
**Won 5-4 on penalties

Season 2011/12

RESERVES APPEARANCES AND GOALS 2011/12

Name	Reserves Apps	Reserves Gls	Youth Cup Apps	Youth Cup Gls	Season Tot Apps	Season Tot Gls
Ben Amos	14				14	0
Jack Barmby			6	6	6	6
Tyler Blackett	1 (4)	1	6	1	7 (4)	2
Robbie Brady	3 (1)				3 (1)	0
Reece Brown	10 (1)	1			10 (1)	1
Sam Byrne			3 (3)	1	3 (3)	1
Tom Cleverley	2				2	0
John Cofie	1 (5)				1 (5)	0
Larnell Cole	20	4			20	4
Mats Daehli	0 (1)		6		6 (1)	0
Mame Biram Diouf	10	10			10	10
Danny Drinkwater	1				1	0
Charni Ekangamene	1		2 (2)		3 (2)	0
Darren Fletcher	2				2	0
Michele Fornasier	15 (8)				15 (8)	0
Ezekiel Fryers	27	1			27	1
Darron Gibson	4				4	0
Luke Giverin	3 (5)	1			3 (5)	1
Kenji Gorre	1 (1)		0 (2)		1 (3)	0
Liam Grimshaw			3		3	0
Josh Harrop			0 (1)		0 (1)	0
Luke Hendrie	1		3 (2)		4 (2)	0
Nicholas Ioannou			5		5	0
Liam Jacob			2		2	0
Matty James	6 (1)				6 (1)	0
Adnan Januzaj			2		2	0
Sam Johnstone	10				10	0
Phil Jones	1				1	0
Michael Keane	28 (2)	5			28 (2)	5
Will Keane	26 (3)	19			26 (3)	19
Joshua King	2 (1)				2 (1)	0
Tomasz Kuszczak	5				5	0
Ritchie De Laet	10	2			10	2
Tom Lawrence			1	1	1	1
Rafael Leao	0 (3)				0 (3)	0
Anders Lindegaard	2				2	0
Jesse Lingard	21 (5)	9			21 (5)	9
Donald Love			1 (1)		1 (1)	0
Luke McCullough			5		5	0
Sean McGinty	1 (3)				1 (3)	0
Federico Macheda	8	2			8	2
Alberto Massacci	1 (6)	1			1 (6)	1
Ravel Morrison	1 (3)	3			1 (3)	3
Oliver Norwood	3				3	0
Ben Pearson			2		2	0
Davide Petrucci	25 (4)	8			25 (4)	8
Paul Pogba	20	3			20	3
Joe Rothwell			1		1	0
Louis Rowley			0 (1)		0 (1)	0
Jack Rudge	0 (1)		4 (1)		4 (2)	0
Fabio Da Silva	4				4	0
Rafael Da Silva	2				2	0
Chris Smalling	1	1			1	1
Jonny Sutherland			4		4	0
Tom Thorpe	12 (7)				12 (7)	0
Ryan Tunnicliffe	10 (2)	1			10 (2)	1
Gyliano van Velzen	0 (3)		6	4	6 (3)	4
Marnick Vermijl	25 (4)	1			25 (4)	1
Frederic Veseli	1 (2)				1 (2)	0
James Weir			2		2	0
James Wilson	0 (1)		1 (4)	2	1 (5)	2
Scott Wootton	5 (1)				5 (1)	0

YOUTH CUP GAMES 2011/12

Date	Opponents	Rnd	Venue	Res	Att	1	2	3	4	5	6	7	8	9	10	11	12	13	14	15	16
02-Dec	Torquay United[e]	R 3	Home	4-0	503	Jacob	Weir	Ekangamene	Blackett	McCullough	Rudge	Daehli	Januzaj	Van Velzen 1	Lawrence 1	Barmby 1	Hendrie (6)	Coll	Byrne (10)	Dalley	Love (8)
18-Jan	Derby County	R 4	Home	2-1	993	Jacob	Love	Blackett	Ioannou	McCullough	Ekangamene	Daehli	Hendrie	Van Velzen	Daehli	Barmby 2	Byrne (9)	Sutherland	Wilson (11)	Rowley (5)	Weir
02-Feb	Swansea City	R 5	Away	4-0	4080	Sutherland	Weir	Ekangamene	Ioannou	Blackett 1	Rudge	Barmby 1	Hendrie	Byrne 1	Daehli	Van Velzen 2	Wilkinson	Jacob	Wilson (7)	Gorre (9)	Harrop (8)
29-Feb	Charlton Athletic	R 6	Home	3-2	4461	Sutherland	Grimshaw	Blackett	Ioannou	McCullough	Rudge	Barmby 1	Hendrie	Byrne	Daehli	Van Velzen 1	Ekangamene (6)	Jacob	Wilson 1 (8)	Rowley	Gorre (7)
16-Mar	Chelsea	SF1	Home	1-2	7802	Sutherland	Grimshaw	Blackett	Ioannou	McCullough	Rudge	Barmby	Pearson	Wilson 1	Daehli	Van Velzen	Ekangamene (7)	Jacob	Byrne (8)	Hendrie (6)	Dalley
13-Apr	Chelsea	SF2	Away	1-1	4193	Sutherland	Grimshaw	Blackett	Ioannou	McCullough	Pearson	Barmby 1	Rothwell	Byrne	Daehli	Van Velzen	Hendrie	Jacob	Wilson (9)	Ekangamene	Rudge (10)

[e]Own goal: Beattie

Season 20012/13

MANCHESTER UNITED RESERVES / UNDER 21's 2012/13: FA PREMIER UNDER 21s LEAGUE, MANCHESTER SENIOR CUP & LANCASHIRE SENIOR CUP

Date	Opponents	Comp	Venue	Res	Att	1	2	3	4	5	6	7	8	9	10	11	12	13	14	15	16
08-Aug	Accrington Stanley	LSC Fin	Leyland	4-0	660	Johnstone	Vermijl	Blackett	Fornasier	Thorpe	Givenn	Cole 2	Turnicliffe	King 1	Pettucci	Bebe	Vessel (16)	Sutherland	Januzaj (11)	Daehli	Lawrence 1 (6)
18-Aug	Stoke City	League	Away	1-0		Johnstone	M Keane	Blackett	Thorpe	Wootton 1	Cole	Turnicliffe	King	Macheda	Lingard	Vessel	Gollini	Fornasier (10)	Januzaj	Lawrence (9)
29-Aug	Tottenham Hotspur	League	Home	2-1		Lindegaard	Wootton	Blackett	Evans	M Keane	Powell	Powell	King 1	Macheda 2	Cole (11)	Sutherland	Lingard (7)	Thorpe (2)		
20-Sep	Bury	MSC	Home	4-1	283	Johnstone	Vermijl 1	Blackett	Wootton	Turnicliffe	Brady	King 1	Macheda 1	Lingard 1	Vessel	Henriques 1 (2)	Gollini	Fornasier	Thorpe (2)		
28-Sep	Newcastle United	League	Home	4-2		Johnstone	Cole	Thorpe	Fornasier	Turnicliffe	King	Macheda 2	Pettucci 1	Lingard	Brady	Blackett (11)	Gollini	Vessel (3)	McGinty (8)		
01-Oct	Sunderland	League	Away	0-0	821	Johnstone	Ekangamene	Vessel	Thorpe	Fornasier	Cole	King	Macheda	Pettucci	Pettucci	Pereira	Gollini	McGinty (3)	Hendrie		
08-Oct	Southampton	League	Away	3-3	408	Gollini	Heriques	Blackett	Thorpe	M Keane	Bebe	Cole 1	Turnicliffe	King	Lingard	Pereira	Vessel 1 (7)	James (9)	Hendrie		
18-Oct	Bolton Wanderers	MSC	Home	2-1	342	Johnstone	McGinty	Thorpe	M Keane	Fornasier	Cole	Turnicliffe	Macheda 1	Powell 1	Lingard	Sutherland	Blackett	James	Barnby		
24-Oct	Stockport County	MSC	Away	2-1		Sutherland	Vermijl	James	Ekangamene	Wootton	Blackett	Henriques 1	Macheda	Powell	Januzaj	McCullough (11)	O'Hara	Hendrie (10)	Vessel	Lawrence (9)	
27-Oct	Tottenham Hotspur	League	Away	2-4		Sutherland	Vermijl	McGinty	M Keane	King	Brady	Lingard 1	King	Lingard 1	Brady	Ekangamene	Sutherland (4)	James	Lawrence 1 (9)		
05-Nov	Stoke City	League	Home	1-1	387	Johnstone	Vermijl	McGinty	Wootton	Fornasier	Cole	Turnicliffe	Powell	Powell 1	Vessel	Sutherland	Lawrence	Ekangamene			
12-Nov	Newcastle United	League	Away	2-1	417	Sutherland	Vessel	Wootton	Wootton	Fornasier	Turnicliffe	Macheda	Powell 1	Januzaj	Lingard	Lawrence 1 (9)	Ekangamene (10)	Hendrie (7)			
19-Nov	Aston Villa	League	Home	0-1		Sutherland	Vessel	James	McCullough	Fornasier	Bebe	Turnicliffe	Macheda	Henriques	Januzaj	Cole	J Pereira	James	Hendrie (7)		
26-Nov	Sunderland	League	Home	2-2	353	Johnstone	Vermijl 1	Vessel	Fornasier	Cole	Turnicliffe 1	Bebe	Henriques	Lawrence	Ekangamene	Daehli (8)	Gollini	Grimshaw (11)	Barnby (4)		
03-Dec	Southampton	League	Home	3-0	1,724	Johnstone	Vermijl	McGinty	Thorpe	Fornasier	Cole	Turnicliffe	King	Lingard	Powell	James	Bebe (8)	J Pereira	James	Lawrence (9)	
10-Dec	Aston Villa	League	Away	2-0	744	Sutherland	Vermijl	Buttner	Thorpe	Wootton	Turnicliffe	Powell	Pettucci	Pettucci	Cole	Ekangamene	Gollini	Vessel (8)	Lawrence	Fornasier (7)	
18-Dec	Morecambe	LSC	Away	1-0	904	Lindegaard	Wootton	Vermijl	M Keane	Fornasier	Bebe 1	Turnicliffe	Powell	Macheda	Cole	Januzaj	McGinty	Gollini	Ekangamene	Lawrence (7)	
02-Feb	Southampton	League	Away	3-1		Johnstone	Vermijl 1	McGinty	Brown	Fornasier	Ekangamene	Cole	Turnicliffe	Macheda 1	Pettucci	Cole	Thorpe (5)	Sutherland	Ekangamene	Januzaj (4)	
06-Feb	Oldham Athletic	MSC	Home	7-0		Johnstone	Vermijl 1	Fornasier	Brown	Ekangamene	Cole 4	Turnicliffe	Cofie	Januzaj 1	Lawrence 1 (9)	Blackett	Van Velzen (9)	Pearson (6)			
11-Feb	Arsenal	League	Home	2-2	381	Johnstone	Vermijl	Thorpe	Fornasier	Brown	Cole	Turnicliffe	Powell 1	Lingard 1	McGinty (2)	Sutherland	Blackett	Weir			
15-Feb	Tottenham Hotspur	League	Away	1-3		Johnstone	Vermijl	McGinty	Brown	Thorpe 1	Cole	Turnicliffe	Januzaj	Lingard 1	Ekangamene	Blackett	Sutherland	Ekangamene (11)	Lawrence	Van Velzen	
25-Feb	Liverpool	League	Away	0-0	789	Amos	Veseli	Buttner	Thorpe	Fornasier	Cole	Lawrence	Schlupp	Powell	Lingard	Ekangamene (7)	Gollini	Blackett (8)	McGinty	James	
01-Mar	West Ham United	League	Away	0-0		Johnstone	Vermijl	Veseli	Thorpe	Fornasier 1	McGinty	Ekangamene	Januzaj	Lingard	Blackett	Sutherland	Lawrence	Van Velzen	James		
06-Mar	West Ham United	League	Home	2-0	265	Lindegaard	Vermijl	Blackett	Thorpe	Veseli	McGinty	Powell 2	Ekangamene	Januzaj	Lingard	James (11)	Sutherland	Van Velzen	Lawrence (9)	Daehli	
11-Mar	Wolverhampton	League	Home	0-0	198	Lindegaard	Buttner	Blackett	Cole	Smalling	Anderson	Powell	Ekangamene	Januzaj	Lingard	McGinty	Sutherland	Lawrence (9)	Ekangamene	Daehli	
17-Mar	West Brom	League	Away	2-0	435	Lindegaard	Vermijl	Fornasier	Thorpe	Veseli	McGinty 1	Cole	Vessel	Ekangamene	Lingard	McCullough (11)	Gollini	Cofie 1 (3)	Lawrence (9)		
20-Mar	West Brom	League	Away	1-2	740	Gollini	Vermijl	Buttner	McGinty	Fornasier	Cole	Turnicliffe	Januzaj	Lingard	Powell	Blackett	Sutherland	Cofie	Fornasier (3)	Daehli	
09-Apr	Arsenal	League	Away	1-0	224	Amos	Veseli	Vermijl	Buttner	Fornasier	Cole	Turnicliffe	Powell	Januzaj	Lingard 1	Vessel	Sutherland	James (2)	Blackett (8)		
15-Apr	Southampton	League	Home	1-0	2,183	Amos	Vermijl	James	Fornasier	Ekangamene	Cole	Turnicliffe	Lingard 1	Januzaj	Veseli	McCullough (11)	Sutherland	Cofie	Ekangamene (9)	Lawrence (9)	
26-Apr	Wolves	League	Away	0-1	504	Amos	Vermijl	James	Fornasier	Ekangamene	Cole	Veseli	Turnicliffe	January	Blackett	Lingard	Sutherland (15)	Lawrence (9)	Fornasier (3)	Lawrence (9)	
30-Apr	West Brom	League	Home	1-0		Amos	Veseli	Buttner	Fornasier	Ekangamene	Cole 1	Turnicliffe	Powell	Lingard 1	Januzaj	Lawrence 1	Blackett	Sutherland (2)	Blackett	Hendrie	
03-May	Oldham Athletic	LSC sf	Home	3-1		Johnstone	Hendrie	James	Grimshaw	McCullough	Blackett	Pearson	Turnicliffe 1	Daehli 1	Cleverley	Lingard	Lawrence (9)	J Pereira	A Pereira (9)	McCullough	
06-May	Liverpool°	League	Home	1-1		Amos	Vermijl	Hendrie	Fornasier	McCullough	Weir	Pearson	Turnicliffe	Lingard	Lawrence 1	Daehli 1	Sutherland (4)	Pearson (6)	A Pereira (8)	Rudge	
14-May	Liverpool	Home	3-0		Amos	Vermijl	James	James	M Keane	Cole 3	Turnicliffe	Lingard	Januzaj	Lawrence (11)	Grimshaw (10)	A Pereira (7)	Grimshaw	Wilson (10)		
20-May	Tottenham Hotspur	Final	Home	3-2		Amos	Vermijl 1	Thorpe	Thorpe	Cole 2	Turnicliffe	Turnicliffe	Lingard	Januzaj	Januzaj	Pearson	Sutherland (10)	Lawrence	A Pereira	Wilson	Pearson (11)

° Own goals: Flanagan

Season 2012/13

RESERVES APPEARANCES AND GOALS 2012/13

Name	Reserves Apps	Reserves Gls	Youth Cup Apps	Youth Cup Gls	Season Tot Apps	Season Tot Gls
Ben Amos	10				10	0
Luis Anderson	1				1	0
Bebe	8 (1)	3			8 (1)	3
Jack Barmby			1		1	0
Tyler Blackett	10 (8)				10 (8)	0
Robbie Brady	5				5	0
Reece Brown	8				8	0
Alexander Buttner	6				6	0
Sam Byrne			0 (1)		0 (1)	0
Tom Cleverley	1				1	0
John Cofie	2 (1)	1			2 (1)	1
Larnell Cole	31 (1)	13			31 (1)	13
Mats Daehli	1	1	1		2	1
Declan Dalley			0 (1)		0 (1)	0
Charni Ekangamene	16 (4)	1			16 (4)	1
Jonny Evans	1				1	0
Darren Fletcher	2				2	0
Michele Fornasier	25 (3)	1			25 (3)	1
Luke Giverin	1				1	0
Pierluigi Gollini	2		1		3	0
Kenji Gorre					0	0
Liam Grimshaw	1 (1)		1		1 (1)	0
Josh Harrop					0	0
Luke Hendrie	2 (2)				2 (2)	0
Angelo Henriquez	4 (2)	2			4 (2)	2
Nicholas Ioannou			1	1	1	1
Reece James	7 (6)				7 (6)	0
Adnan Januzaj	21 (3)	2	1		22 (3)	2
Sam Johnstone	16				16	0
Michael Keane	9				9	0
Joshua King	8	2			8	2
Tom Lawrence	8 (16)	5			8 (16)	5
Anders Lindegaard	4				4	0
Jesse Lingard	25 (1)	7			25 (1)	7
Donald Love	0 (1)		1	1	0 (1)	1
Luke McCullough	2 (2)				2 (2)	0
Sean McGinty	11 (5)	1			11 (5)	1
Federico Macheda	12	8			12	8
Ben Pearson	2 (3)		1		2 (3)	0
Andreas Pereira	0 (2)				0 (2)	0
Davide Petrucci	8	1			8	1
Nick Powell	14	6			14	6
Jeffrey Schlupp	2				2	0
Louis Rowley			1		1	0
Jack Rudge			0 (1)		0 (1)	0
Chris Smalling	1				1	0
Jonny Sutherland	4				4	0
Tom Thorpe	30 (3)	3			30 (3)	3
Ryan Tunnicliffe	28	2			28	2
Gyliano van Velzen	1 (1)	1			1 (1)	1
Marnick Vermijl	26	5			26	5
Frederic Veseli	18 (6)	1			18 (6)	1
James Weir	1		1	1	2	1
James Wilson	0 (2)		1		0 (2)	0
Scott Wootton	9	1			9	1

YOUTH CUP GAMES 2012/13

Date	Opponents	Rnd	Venue	Res	Att	1	2	3	4	5	6	7	8	9	10	11	12	13	14	15	16
07-Dec	Burnley	R 3	Home	3-4	3146	Gollini	Love 1	Rowley	Grimshaw	Ioannou 1	Pearson	Barmby	Weir 1	Wilson	Januzaj	Daehli	Rudge (7)	Sutherland	Byrne (6)	Dalley (5)	Gorre

Appendix 2

First Team Appearances by Fergie's Fledglings under Sir Alex Ferguson

Notes: The number in brackets in the season heading denotes the cumulative total number of Fledglings making first team appearances. The date given is the date of the respective Fledgling's first team debut. The number of appearances and goals is the total first team tally under Sir Alex Ferguson and includes, league, cup and European games. The European appearances and goals, in brackets, are included in the total appearances and goals.

Season 1986/87: 2

13 December, Gary Walsh: 63 appearances (6 European appearances).

3 January, Tony Gill: 14 appearances, 1 goal.

Season 1987/88: 2 (4)

7 October, Deiniol Graham: 4 appearances, 1 goal.

9 May, Lee Martin: 109 appearances, 2 goals (2 European appearances).

Season 1988/89: 6 (10)

24 September, Lee Sharpe: 263 appearances, 36 goals (17 European appearances, 3 European goals).

24 September, Russell Beardsmore: 73 appearances, 4 goals (5 European appearances).

12 October, Mark Robins: 70 appearances, 17 goals (6 European appearances, 1 goal).

23 November, David Wilson: 6 appearances.

14 January, Giuliano Maiorana: 8 appearances.

10 May, Derek Brazil: 2 appearances.

Season 1989/90: 1 (11)

30 April, Mark Bosnich: 38 appearances (7 European appearances).

Season 1990/91: 4 (15)

26 February, Darren Ferguson: 30 appearances.

2 March, Ryan Giggs: 943 appearances, 168 goals (151 European appearances, 29 goals).

13 March, Neil Whitworth: 1 appearance.

2 April, Paul Wratten: 2 appearances.

Season 1991/92: 1 (16)

9 October, Ian Wilkinson: 1 appearance.

Season 1992/93: 4 (20)

16 September, Gary Neville: 602 appearances, 7 goals (119 European appearances, 2 goals).

23 September, David Beckham: 394 appearances, 85 goals (84 European appearances, 15 goals).

21 November, Nicky Butt: 387 appearances, 26 goals (71 European appearances, 2 goals).

5 January, Keith Gillespie: 14 appearances 2 goals.

Season 1993/94: 2 (22)

26 February, Ben Thornley: 14 appearances.

8 May, Colin McKee: 1 appearance.

Season 1994/95: 7 (29)

21 September, Paul Scholes: 718 appearances, 155 goals (136 European appearances, 26 goals).

21 September, Simon Davies: 20 appearances, 1 goal (3 European appearances, 1 goal).

21 September, John O'Kane: 7 appearances (1 European appearance).

5 October, Chris Casper: 7 appearances (1 European appearance).

5 October, Graeme Tomlinson: 2 appearances.

19 November, Kevin Pilkington: 8 appearances.

28 January, Phil Neville: 386 appearances, 8 goals (66 European appearances, 2 goals)

Season 1995/96: 2 (31)

16 September, Terry Cooke: 8 appearances 1 goal (1 European appearance).

20 September, Pat McGibbon: 1 appearance.

Season 1996/97: 2 (33)

23 October, Michael Appleton: 2 appearances.

23 November, Michael Clegg: 24 appearances (3 European appearances).

Season 1997/98: 7 (40)

14 October, John Curtis: 19 appearances (1 European appearance).

14 October, Philip Mulryne: 5 appearances.

14 October, Erik Nevland: 6 appearances, 1 goal.

25 October, Ronnie Wallwork: 28 appearances (1 European appearance).

25 February, Michael Twiss: 2 appearances.

4 May, Wes Brown: 362 appearances, 5 goals (66 European appearances, 1 goal).

10 May, Danny Higginbotham: 7 appearances (1 European appearance).

Season 1998/99: 3 (43)

21 October, Mark Wilson: 10 appearances (4 European appearances).

28 October, Jonathan Greening: 27 appearances (1 European appearance).

2 December, Alex Notman: 1 appearance.

Season 1999/00: 6 (49)

22 August, Nick Culkin: 1 appearance.

13 October, John O'Shea: 393 appearances, 15 goals (77 European appearances, 2 goals).

13 October, Luke Chadwick: 39 appearances, 2 goals (6 European appearances).

13 October, David Healy: 3 appearances.

13 October, Richie Wellens: 1 appearance.

11 January, Paul Rachubka: 3 appearances.

Season 2000/01: 3 (52)

31 October, Michael Stewart: 14 appearances (2 European appearances).

28 November, Danny Webber: 3 appearances (1 European appearance).

19 May, Bojan Djordjic: 2 appearances.

Season 2001/02: 3 (55)

5 November, Lee Roche: 3 appearances (1 European appearance)

5 November, Jimmy Davis: 1 appearance.

5 November, Daniel Nardiello: 4 appearances (1 European appearance)

Season 2002/03: 5 (60)

18 September, Danny Pugh: 7 appearances (3 European appearances)

23 October, Kieran Richardson: 81 appearances, 11 goals (16 European appearances, 2 goals).

29 October, Mads Timm: 1 appearance (1 European appearance).

12 March, Darren Fletcher: 312 appearances, 24 goals (65 European appearances, 3 goals).

18 March, Mark Lynch: 1 appearance (1 European appearance).

Season 2003/04: 4 (64)

28 October, Chris Eagles: 17 appearances, 1 goal (3 European appearances).

28 October, Eddie Johnson: 1 appearance.

3 December, Phil Bardsley: 18 appearances (3 European appearances).

3 December, Paul Tierney: 1 appearance.

Season 2004/05: 5 (69)

8 August, Jonathan Spector: 8 appearances (2 European appearances).

26 October, Gerard Pique: 23 appearances, 2 goals (4 European appearances, 2 goals).

26 October, Sylvan Ebanks-Blake: 2 appearances, 1 goal.

10 November, Giuseppe Rossi: 14 appearances, 4 goals (2 European appearances).

1 December, David Jones: 4 appearances.

Season 2005/06: 4 (73)

26 October, Adam Eckersley: 1 appearance.

26 October, Lee Martin: 3 appearances.

26 October, Ritchie Jones: 5 appearances.

26 October, Darron Gibson: 60 appearances, 10 goals (9 European appearances, 2 goals).

Season 2006/07: 5 (78)

25 October, David Gray: 1 appearance.

25 October, Phil Marsh: 1 appearance.

25 October, Michael Barnes: 1 appearance.

25 October, Kieran Lee: 3 appearances, 1 goal.

25 October, Ryan Shawcross: 2 appearances.

Season 2007/08: 3 (81)

19 August, Frazier Campbell: 4 appearances.

26 September, Danny Simpson: 8 appearances (3 European appearances).

26 September, Jonny Evans: 156 appearances, 5 goals (28 European appearances, 1 goal).

Season 2008/09: 7 (89)

17 August, Rafael da Silva: 130 appearances, 5 goals (25 European appearances).

Rodrigo Possebon: 8 appearances.

23 September, Ben Amos: 7 appearances (1 European appearance).

23 September, Danny Welbeck: 103 appearances, 19 goals (14 European appearances, 3 goals).

20 January, James Chester: 1 appearance

24 January, Fabio Da Silva: 53 appearances, 2 goals (16 European appearances).

24 January, Richard Eckersley: 4 appearances

5 April, Federico Macheda: 36 appearances 5 goals (7 European appearances).

Season 2009/10: 1 (90)

23 September, Joshua King: 2 appearances (1 European appearance).

Season 2010/11: 1 (91)

26 October, Ravel Morrison: 3 appearances.

Season 2011/12: 6 (97)

7 August, Tom Cleverley: 49 appearances, 4 goals (8 European appearances).

20 September, Ezekiel Fryers: 6 appearances (1 European appearance).

20 September, Paul Pogba: 7 appearances (1 European).

20 September, Larnell Cole: 1 appearance.

25 October, Michael Keane: 3 appearances.

31 December, Will Keane: 1 appearance.

Season 2012/13: 3 (100)

26 September, Scott Wootton: 4 appearances (2 European appearances).

26 September, Ryan Tunnicliffe: 2 appearances.

26 September, Robbie Brady: 1 appearance.

Appendix 3

Trivia

100 Fledglings made the Manchester United team. That means on average, Sir Alex Ferguson gave a debut to a Fledgling every 15 games of his reign.

12% of all players to have played for Manchester United or Newton Heath are Fledglings.

The class of 1992 collectively made 2,395 appearances for the first team under Sir Alex, scoring 289 goals. With that goal tally, they scored 16% of all first team Manchester United goals under Sir Alex Ferguson. The class of 1992 also collectively made 429 European appearances for Manchester United, scoring 75 goals.

11 members of the class of 1992: Kevin Pilkington, John O'Kane, Gary Neville, Chris Casper, David Beckham, Keith Gillespie, Ben Thornley, Nicky Butt, Simon Davies, Colin McKee and Ryan Giggs, made first team appearances for Manchester United.

26% of all goals scored by Manchester United under Sir Alex Ferguson were scored by Fledglings.

There were 1,067 collective European appearances by Fledglings under Sir Alex, with 97 goals.

The first player to officially become a Fledgling was Gary Walsh, the fiftieth was Michael Stewart, and the last was Robbie Brady.

When Lee Martin scored the goal to win Sir Alex's first trophy in 1990, he became the first and only Fledgling through the manager's entire reign to score the decisive winning goal in a Cup Final for Manchester United in match play.

The highest number of Fledglings to make their debut in a single game was five, on 25th October 2006, against Crewe Alexandra.

14 of the Fledglings to make the first team made more than 100 appearances whilst 20 only made one appearance.

The appearances total made by Fledglings under Sir Alex Ferguson is 6,297.

The goals total by Fledglings under Sir Alex Ferguson is 728.

The European appearances total made by Fledglings under Sir Alex Ferguson is 1,067.

The European goals total scored by Fledglings under Sir Alex Ferguson is 97.

About the Author

Wayne Barton is the football columnist for international sports broadcaster Setanta Sports. Travelling around England and North America, he has interviewed some of the biggest names in Manchester United's rich history including Harry Gregg, Tommy Docherty, Mike Duxbury, Mikael Silvestre, Alex Stepney, Lou Macari and Sammy McIlroy. He also worked with the late Brian Greenhoff on his 2012 autobiography and ghost wrote the 2014 autobiographies of Gordon Hill and Danny Higginbotham.